ANTHROPOLOGY 96/97

Nineteenth Edition

Editor

Elvio Angeloni
Pasadena City College

Elvio Angeloni received his B.A. from UCLA in 1963, his
M.A. in anthropology from UCLA in 1965, and his M.A. in
communication arts from Loyola Marymount University in
1976. He has produced several films, including *Little Warrior,*
winner of the Cinemedia VI Best Bicentennial Theme, and
Broken Bottles, shown on PBS. He most recently served as
an academic adviser on the instructional television series,
Faces of Culture.

A Library of Information from the Public Press

Cover illustration by Mike Eagle

Dushkin Publishing Group/
Brown & Benchmark Publishers
Sluice Dock, Guilford, Connecticut 06437

PEOPLES DISCUSSED IN
ANNUAL EDITIONS: ANTHROPOLOGY 96/97

Map Location Number	People	Article Number
1.	Yanomamö	1, 13, 24
2.	Punjabi	2
3.	!Kung - Kalahari Desert	3, 18, 19, 24
4.	Nigerian	8
5.	Tiv	10
6.	Eskimo (Inupiaq)	11
	Koyukon Indians	11
7.	Eskimo (Inuit)	12, 24
8.	Masai	14, 29, 41
9.	Raikas	15
10.	Kaliai	16
11.	Simbu	17
12.	Semai - Central Malaysia	18
	Mehinacu - Brazil	18
	Siuai - Solomon Islands	18
	Kaoka - Solomon Islands	18
	Trobrianders - South Pacific	18
13.	Tibetans	20
14.	Hausa	21
15.	Dobe San - Kalahari Desert	24
	Hadza - Tanzania	24
	Tiwi - Northeast coast of Australia	24
16.	Laguna Pueblo	25
17.	Tamasheqs	27
18.	Mbuti Pygmies	32
19.	Mayoruna - Brazil	33
	Amahaura - Brazil	33
20.	Fore - Papua New Guinea	44

Scale: 1 to 125,000,000

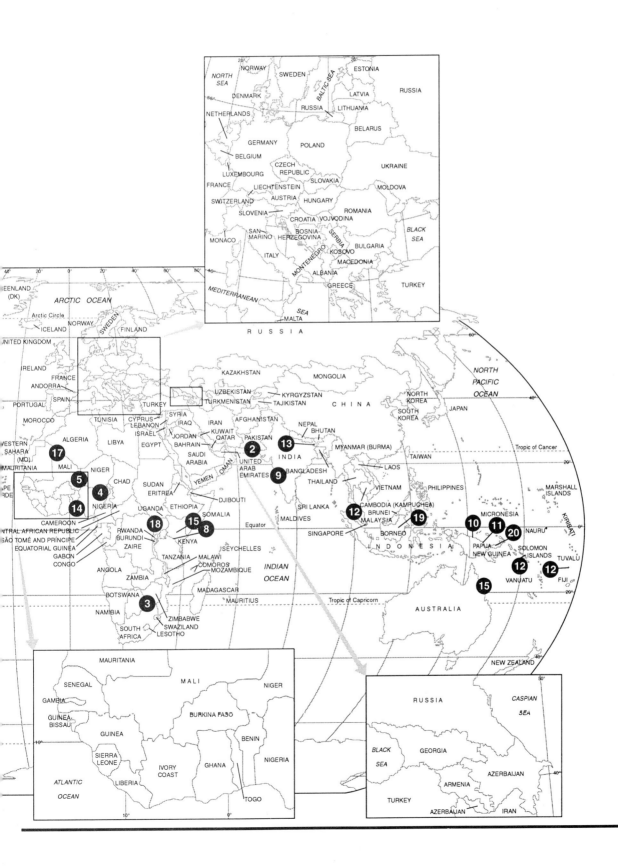

The Annual Editions Series

Annual Editions is a series of over 65 volumes designed to provide the reader with convenient, low-cost access to a wide range of current, carefully selected articles from some of the most important magazines, newspapers, and journals published today. Annual Editions are updated on an annual basis through a continuous monitoring of over 300 periodical sources. All Annual Editions have a number of features designed to make them particularly useful, including topic guides, annotated tables of contents, unit overviews, and indexes. For the teacher using Annual Editions in the classroom, an Instructor's Resource Guide with test questions is available for each volume.

VOLUMES AVAILABLE

Abnormal Psychology
Africa
Aging
American Foreign Policy
American Government
American History, Pre-Civil War
American History, Post-Civil War
American Public Policy
Anthropology
Archaeology
Biopsychology
Business Ethics
Child Growth and Development
China
Comparative Politics
Computers in Education
Computers in Society
Criminal Justice
Developing World
Deviant Behavior
Drugs, Society, and Behavior
Dying, Death, and Bereavement
Early Childhood Education
Economics
Educating Exceptional Children
Education
Educational Psychology
Environment
Geography
Global Issues
Health
Human Development
Human Resources
Human Sexuality

India and South Asia
International Business
Japan and the Pacific Rim
Latin America
Life Management
Macroeconomics
Management
Marketing
Marriage and Family
Mass Media
Microeconomics
Middle East and the Islamic World
Multicultural Education
Nutrition
Personal Growth and Behavior
Physical Anthropology
Psychology
Public Administration
Race and Ethnic Relations
Russia, the Eurasian Republics, and Central/Eastern Europe
Social Problems
Sociology
State and Local Government
Urban Society
Western Civilization, Pre-Reformation
Western Civilization, Post-Reformation
Western Europe
World History, Pre-Modern
World History, Modern
World Politics

Cataloging in Publication Data
Main entry under title: Annual Editions: Anthropology. 1996/97.
    1. Anthropology—Periodicals. I. Angeloni, Elvio, comp. II. Title: Anthropology.
301.2   74–84595   ISBN 0–697–31508–8

Nineteenth Edition

Printed in the United States of America

To the Reader

In publishing ANNUAL EDITIONS we recognize the enormous role played by the magazines, newspapers, and journals of the *public press* in providing current, first-rate educational information in a broad spectrum of interest areas. Within the articles, the best scientists, practitioners, researchers, and commentators draw issues into new perspective as accepted theories and viewpoints are called into account by new events, recent discoveries change old facts, and fresh debate breaks out over important controversies.

Many of the articles resulting from this enormous editorial effort are appropriate for students, researchers, and professionals seeking accurate, current material to help bridge the gap between principles and theories and the real world. These articles, however, become more useful for study when those of lasting value are carefully *collected, organized, indexed,* and *reproduced* in a *low-cost format,* which provides easy and permanent access when the material is needed. That is the role played by ANNUAL EDITIONS. Under the direction of each volume's *Editor,* who is an expert in the subject area, and with the guidance of an *Advisory Board,* we seek each year to provide in each ANNUAL EDITION a current, well-balanced, carefully selected collection of the best of the public press for your study and enjoyment. We think you'll find this volume useful, and we hope you'll take a moment to let us know what you think.

The nineteenth edition of *Annual Editions: Anthropology 96/97* contains a variety of articles on contemporary issues in social and cultural anthropology. In contrast to the broad range of topics and minimum depth typical of standard textbooks, this anthology provides an opportunity to read firsthand accounts by anthropologists of their own research. In allowing scholars to speak for themselves about the issues on which they are expert, we are better able to understand the kind of questions anthropologists ask, the ways in which they ask them, and how they go about searching for answers. Indeed, where there is disagreement among anthropologists, this format allows the readers to draw their own conclusions.

Given the very broad scope of anthropology—in time, space, and subject matter—the present collection of highly readable articles has been selected according to certain criteria. The articles have been chosen from both professional and nonprofessional publications for the purpose of supplementing the standard textbook in cultural anthropology that is used in introductory courses. Some of the articles are considered classics in the field, while others have been selected for their timely relevance. Included in this volume are a number of features designed to make it useful for students, researchers, and professionals in the field of anthropology. While the articles are arranged along the lines of broadly unifying themes, the *topic guide* can be used to establish specific reading assignments tailored to the needs of a particular course of study. Other useful features include the *table of contents* abstracts, which summarize each article and present key concepts in italics, and a comprehensive *index*. In addition, each unit is preceded by an overview that provides a background for informed reading of the articles, emphasizes critical issues, and presents *challenge questions*.

Annual Editions: Anthropology will continue to be updated annually. Those involved in producing the volume wish to make the next one as useful and effective as possible. Your criticism and advice is welcomed. Please fill out the article rating form on the last page of the book and let us know your opinions. Any anthology can be improved. This continues to be—annually.

Elvio Angeloni
Editor

Contents

Unit
1

Anthropological Perspectives

Five selections examine the role of anthropologists in studying different cultures. The innate problems in developing productive relationships between anthropologists and exotic cultures are considered by reviewing a number of fieldwork experiences.

The concepts in bold italics are developed in the article. For further expansion please refer to the Topic Guide and the Index.

Unit 2

Culture and Communication

Five selections discuss communication as an element of culture. Ingrained social and cultural values have a tremendous effect on an individual's perception or interpretation of both verbal and nonverbal communication.

Unit 3

The Organization of Society and Culture

Eight selections discuss the influence of the environment and culture on the organization of the social structure of groups.

The concepts in bold italics are developed in the article. For further expansion please refer to the Topic Guide and the Index.

Unit 4

Other Families, Other Ways

Five selections examine some of the influences on the family structure of different cultures. The strength of the family unit is affected by both economic and social pressures.

Unit 5

Gender and Status

Seven selections discuss some of the sex roles prescribed by the social, economic, and political forces of a culture.

The concepts in bold italics are developed in the article. For further expansion please refer to the Topic Guide and the Index.

Unit
6

Religion, Belief, and Ritual

Eight selections examine the role of ritual, religion, and belief in a culture. The need to develop a religion is universal among societies.

Unit

7

Sociocultural Change: The Impact of the West

Eight articles examine the influence that the developed world has had on primitive culture. Exposure to the industrial West often has disastrpis effects on the delicate balance of a primative society.

The concepts in bold italics are developed in the article. For further expansion please refer to the Topic Guide and the Index.

Topic Guide

This topic guide suggests how the selections in this book relate to topics of traditional concern to students and professionals involved with the study of anthropology. It is useful for locating articles that relate to each other for reading and research. The guide is arranged alphabetically according to topic. Articles may, of course, treat topics that do not appear in the topic guide. In turn, entries in the topic guide do not necessarily constitute a comprehensive listing of all the contents of each selection.

TOPIC AREA	TREATED IN	TOPIC AREA	TREATED IN
Acculturation	4. Cross-Cultural Experience 9. Gift of Tongues 15. Camels in the Land of Kings 17. From Shells to Money 25. Yellow Woman 34. Cargo Cults 41. Nomads at the Crossroads 42. Surviving the Revolution 43. Bicultural Conflict 44. Growing Up as a Fore 45. Last Chance for First Peoples	Cultural Identity	4. Cross-Cultural Experience 5. Cultural Relativism and Universal Rights 14. Mystique of the Masai 15. Camels in the Land of Kings 25. Yellow Woman 34. Cargo Cults 41. Nomads at the Crossroads 43. Bicultural Conflict 45. Last Change for First Peoples
Aggression and Violence	5. Cultural Relativism and Universal Rights 28. War against Women 36. Rituals of Death 39. Heart of Darkness 41. Nomads at the Crossroads 43. Bicultural Conflict 46. Easter's End	Cultural Relativity and Ethnocentrism	1. Doing Fieldwork among the Yąnomamö 3. Eating Christmas in the Kalahari 4. Cross-Cultural Experience 5. Cultural Relativism and Universal Rights 7. Why Don't You Say What You Mean? 8. Navigating Nigerian Bureaucracies 23. Arranging a Marriage in India 37. Body Ritual among the Nacirema 43. Bicultural Conflict
Children and Child Care	19. Memories of a !Kung Girlhood 21. Young Traders of Northern Nigeria 22. Death without Weeping 25. Yellow Woman 27. Female Circumcision 30. Little Emperors 32. Mbuti Pygmies 43. Bicultural Conflict	Culture Shock	1. Doing Fieldwork among the Yąnomamö 8. Navigating Nigerian Bureaucracies 34. Cargo Cults 43. Bicultural Conflict
Cooperation, Sharing, and Altruism	3. Eating Christmas in the Kalahari 12. Blood in Their Veins 16. Too Many Bananas 17. From Shells to Money 25. Yellow Woman	Ecology and Society	11. Understanding Eskimo Science 12. Blood in Their Veins 13. Yanomami Keep on Trekking 14. Mystique of the Masai 15. Camels in the Land of Kings 17. From Shells to Money 18. Life without Chiefs 20. When Brothers Share a Wife 24. Society and Sex Roles 33. No Pain, No Game 34. Cargo Cults 40. Why Can't People Feed Themselves? 41. Nomads at the Crossroads 45. Last Chance for First Peoples 46. Easter's End
Cross-Cultural Experience	1. Doing Fieldwork among the Yąnomamö 2. Doctor, Lawyer, Indian Chief 3. Eating Christmas in the Kalahari 4. Cross-Cultural Experience 5. Cultural Relativism and Universal Rights 7. Why Don't You Say What You Mean? 8. Navigating Nigerian Bureaucracies 9. Gift of Tongues 10. Shakespeare in the Bush 11. Understanding Eskimo Science 15. Camels in the Land of Kings 16. Too Many Bananas 22. Death without Weeping 23. Arranging a Marriage in India 34. Cargo Cults 39. Heart of Darkness 41. Nomads at the Crossroads 43. Bicultural Conflict 45. Last Chance for First Peoples	Economic and Political Systems	2. Doctor, Lawyer, Indian Chief 8. Navigating Nigerian Bureaucracies 9. Gift of Tongues 13. Yanomami Keep on Trekking 14. Mystique of the Masai 15. Camels in the Land of Kings 16. Too Many Bananas 17. From Shells to Money 18. Life without Chiefs 20. When Brothers Share a Wife 21. Young Traders of Northern Nigeria 22. Death without Weeping 24. Society and Sex Roles 25. Yellow Woman 26. Status, Property, and the Value of Virginity 30. Little Emperors 34. Cargo Cults 40. Why Can't People Feed Themselves? 41. Nomads at the Crossroads 42. Surviving the Revolution 45. Last Chance for First Peoples 46. Easter's End
Cultural Diversity	4. Cross-Cultural Experience 5. Cultural Relativism and Universal Rights 7. Why Don't You Say What You Mean? 8. Navigating Nigerian Bureaucracies 9. Gift of Tongues 23. Arranging a Marriage in India 25. Yellow Woman 26. Status, Property, and the Value of Virginity 41. Nomads at the Crossroads 43. Bicultural Conflict 45. Last Chance for First Peoples	Ethnographic Fieldwork	1. Doing Fieldwork among the Yąnomamö 2. Doctor, Lawyer, Indian Chief 3. Eating Christmas in the Kalahari 8. Navigating Nigerian Bureaucracies 16. Too Many Bananas

TOPIC AREA	TREATED IN	TOPIC AREA	TREATED IN
Gender/Sexuality	5. Cultural Relativism and Universal Rights 20. When Brothers Share a Wife 24. Society and Sex Roles 25. Yellow Woman 26. Status, Property, and the Value of Virginity 27. Female Circumcision 28. War against Women 30. Little Emperors 43. Bicultural Conflict	**Poverty**	22. Death without Weeping 34. Cargo Cults 40. Why Can't People Feed Themselves? 42. Surviving the Revolution
Health and Welfare	5. Cultural Relativism and Universal Rights 22. Death without Weeping 28. War against Women 30. Little Emperors 31. Psychotherapy in Africa 37. Body Ritual among the Nacirema 40. Why Can't People Feed Themselves? 45. Last Chance for First Peoples	**Rituals**	5. Cultural Relativism and Universal Rights 17. From Shells to Money 27. Female Circumcision 29. Initiation of a Maasai Warrior 31. Psychotherapy in Africa 32. Mbuti Pygmies 33. No Pain, No Game 34. Cargo Cults 35. Secrets of Haiti's Living Dead 36. Rituals of Death 37. Body Ritual among the Nacirema 38. Superstition and Ritual in American Baseball
Hunter-Collectors	11. Understanding Eskimo Science 12. Blood in Their Veins 18. Life without Chiefs 19. Memories of a !Kung Girlhood 32. Mbuti Pygmies 33. No Pain, No Game	**Social, Cultural, and Industrial Change**	9. Gift of Tongues 15. Camels in the Land of Kings 17. From Shells to Money 30. Little Emperors 31. Psychotherapy in Africa 34. Cargo Cults 39. Heart of Darkness 40. Why Can't People Feed Themselves? 41. Nomads at the Crossroads 42. Surviving the Revolution 43. Bicultural Conflict 44. Growing Up as a Fore 45. Last Chance for First Peoples 46. Easter's End
Language	4. Cross-Cultural Experience 6. Language, Appearance, and Reality 7. Why Don't You Say What You Mean? 8. Navigating Nigerian Bureaucracies 9. Gift of Tongues 10. Shakespeare in the Bush 43. Bicultural Conflict		
Marriage, Kinship, and Family Systems	4. Cross-Cultural Experience 17. From Shells to Money 19. Memories of a !Kung Girlhood 20. When Brothers Share a Wife 21. Young Traders of Northern Nigeria 22. Death without Weeping 23. Arranging a Marriage in India 24. Society and Sex Roles 25. Yellow Woman 26. Status, Property, and the Value of Virginity 28. War against Women 30. Little Emperors 43. Bicultural Conflict	**Social Equality**	7. Why Don't You Say What You Mean? 17. From Shells to Money 18. Life without Chiefs 25. Yellow Woman 26. Status, Property, and the Value of Virginity 28. War against Women 32. Mbuti Pygmies 34. Cargo Cults 41. Nomads at the Crossroads
Medicine and Healing	31. Psychotherapy in Africa 37. Body Ritual among the Nacirema 39. Heart of Darkness 45. Last Chance for First Peoples	**Social Relationships**	1. Doing Fieldwork among the Yąnomamö 2. Doctor, Lawyer, Indian Chief 3. Eating Christmas in the Kalahari 4. Cross-Cultural Experience 8. Navigating Nigerian Bureaucracies 16. Too Many Bananas 17. From Shells to Money 23. Arranging a Marriage in India 25. Yellow Woman 26. Status, Property, and the Value on Virginity 28. War against Women 30. Little Emperors 32. Mbuti Pygmies 34. Cargo Cults 35. Secrets of Haiti's Living Dead 39. Heart of Darkness
Patriarchy	24. Society and Sex Roles 26. Status, Property, and the Value of Virginity		

Anthropological Perspectives

For at least a century the goals of anthropology have been to describe societies and cultures throughout the world and to compare the differences and similarities among them. Anthropologists study in a variety of settings and situations, ranging from small hamlets and villages to neighborhoods and corporate offices of major urban centers throughout the world. They study hunters and gatherers, peasants, farmers, labor leaders, politicians, and bureaucrats. They examine religious life in Latin America as well as revolutionary movements.

Wherever practicable, anthropologists take on the role of the "participant observer," for it is through active involvement in the lifeways of people that they hope to gain an insider's perspective without sacrificing the objectivity of the trained scientist. Sometimes the conditions for achieving such a goal may seem to form an almost insurmountable barrier, but anthropologists' persistence, adaptability, and imagination may be called upon to overcome the odds against them.

The diversity of focus in anthropology means that it is earmarked less by its particular subject matter than by its perspective. Although the discipline relates to both the biological and social sciences, anthropologists know that the boundaries drawn between disciplines are highly artificial. For example, while it may be possible to examine only the social organization of a family unit or the organization of political power in a nation-state, in reality it is impossible to separate the biological from the social from the economic from the political. The explanatory perspective of anthropology, as the articles in this section exemplify, is to seek out interrelationships among all these factors.

The first four articles in this section illustrate varying degrees of difficulty an anthropologist may encounter in taking on the role of the participant observer. Napoleon Chagnon's "Doing Fieldwork among the Yąnomamö" shows, for instance, the hardships imposed by certain physical conditions, the unwillingness of the people to provide needed information, and the vast differences in values and attitudes to be bridged by the anthropologist just in order to get along.

Richard Kurin (in "Doctor, Lawyer, Indian Chief") and Richard Lee (in "Eating Christmas in the Kalahari") apparently had few problems with the physical conditions and the personalities of the people they were studying. However, they were not completely accepted by the communities until they modified their behavior to conform to the expectations of their hosts and found ways to participate as equals in the socioeconomic exchange systems.

Huang Shu-min (in "A Cross-Cultural Experience: A Chinese Anthropologist in the United States") shows how "culture shock" can work both ways, as he learns the importance of personal hygiene in the expression of American middle-class values.

The final article in this section ("Cultural Relativism and Universal Rights") goes to the heart of one of the key issues in anthropology: How does one maintain the objectivity of cultural relativism while not becoming a party to the violation of human rights? Taking the matter one step further, the author argues that anthropologists are in a unique position to actively promote human rights and are ethically bound to do so.

Much is at stake in these discussions, since the purpose of anthropology is not only to describe and explain, but to develop a special vision of the world in which cultural alternatives (past, present, and future) can be measured against one another and used as a guide for human action.

Looking Ahead: Challenge Questions

What is culture shock?

How can anthropologists who become personally involved with a community through participant observation maintain their objectivity as scientists?

In what ways do the results of fieldwork depend on the kinds of questions asked?

How does cross-cultural experience help us to understand ourselves?

In what sense is sharing intrinsic to egalitarianism?

How can we avoid the pitfalls of cultural relativity and ethnocentrism in dealing with what we think of as harmful practices in other cultures?

Doing Fieldwork among the Yąnomamö[1]

Napoleon A. Chagnon

VIGNETTE

The Yąnomamö are thinly scattered over a vast and verdant tropical forest, living in small villages that are separated by many miles of unoccupied land. They have no writing, but they have a rich and complex language. Their clothing is more decorative than protective. Well-dressed men sport nothing more than a few cotton strings around their wrists, ankles, and waists. They tie the foreskins of their penises to the waiststring. Women dress about the same. Much of their daily life revolves around gardening, hunting, collecting wild foods, collecting firewood, fetching water, visiting with each other, gossiping, and making the few material possessions they own: baskets, hammocks, bows, arrows, and colorful pigments with which they paint their bodies. Life is relatively easy in the sense that they can 'earn a living' with about three hours' work per day. Most of what they eat they cultivate in their gardens, and most of that is plantains—a kind of cooking banana that is usually eaten green, either roasted on the coals or boiled in pots. Their meat comes from a large variety of game animals, hunted daily by the men. It is usually roasted on

coals or smoked, and is always well done. Their villages are round and open—and very public. One can hear, see, and smell almost everything that goes on anywhere in the village. Privacy is rare, but sexual discreetness is possible in the garden or at night while others sleep. The villages can be as small as 40 to 50 people or as large as 300 people, but in all cases there are many more children and babies than there are adults. This is true of most primitive populations and of our own demographic past. Life expectancy is short.

The Yąnomamö fall into the category of Tropical Forest Indians called 'foot people'. They avoid large rivers and live in interfluvial plains of the major rivers. They have neighbors to the north, Carib-speaking Ye'kwana, who are true 'river people': They make elegant, large dugout canoes and travel extensively along the major waterways. For the Yąnomamö, a large stream is an obstacle and can be crossed only in the dry season. Thus, they have traditionally avoided larger rivers and, because of this, contact with outsiders who usually come by river.

They enjoy taking trips when the jungle abounds with seasonally ripe wild fruits and vegetables. Then, the large village—the *shabono*—is abandoned for a few weeks and everyone camps out for from one to several days

away from the village and garden. On these trips, they make temporary huts from poles, vines, and leaves, each family making a separate hut.

Two major seasons dominate their annual cycle: the wet season, which inundates the low-lying jungle, making travel difficult, and the dry season—the time of visiting other villages to feast, trade, and politic with allies. The dry season is also the time when raiders can travel and strike silently at their unsuspecting enemies. The Yąnomamö are still conducting intervillage warfare, a phenomenon that affects all aspects of their social organization, settlement pattern, and daily routines. It is not simply 'ritualistic' war: At least one-fourth of all adult males die violently in the area I lived in.

Social life is organized around those same principles utilized by all tribesmen: kinship relationships, descent from ancestors, marriage exchanges between kinship/descent groups, and the transient charisma of distinguished headmen who attempt to keep order in the village and whose responsibility it is to determine the village's relationships with those in other villages. Their positions are largely the result of kinship and marriage patterns; they come from the largest kinship groups within the village. They can, by their personal wit, wisdom, and charisma, become autocrats, but most of them are largely 'greaters' among equals. They, too, must clear gardens, plant crops, collect wild foods, and hunt. They are simultaneously peacemakers and valiant warriors. peacemaking often requires the threat or actual use of force, and most headmen have an acquired reputation for being *waiteri:* fierce.

The social dynamics within villages are involved with giving and receiving marriageable girls. Marriages are arranged by older kin, usually men, who are brothers, uncles, and the father. It is a political process, for girls are promised in marriage while they are young, and the men who do this attempt to create alliances with other men via marriage exchanges. There is a shortage of women due in part to a sex-ratio imbalance in the younger age categories, but also complicated by the fact that some men have multiple wives. Most fighting within the village stems from sexual affairs or failure to deliver a promised woman—or out-and-out seizure of a married woman by some other man. This can lead to internal fighting and conflict of such an intensity that villages split up and fission, each group then becoming a new village and, often, enemies to each other.

But their conflicts are not blind, uncontrolled violence. They have a series of graded forms of violence that ranges from chest-pounding and club-fighting duels to out-and-out shooting to kill. This gives them a good deal of flexibility in settling disputes without immediate resort to lethal violence. In addition, they have developed patterns of alliance and friendship that serve to limit violence—trading and feasting with others in order to become friends. These alliances can, and often do, result in intervillage exchanges of marriageable women, which leads to additional amity between villages. No good thing lasts forever, and most alliances crumble. Old friends become hostile and, occasionally, treacherous. Each village must therefore be keenly aware that its neighbors are fickle and must behave accordingly. The thin line between friendship and animosity must be traversed by the village leaders, whose political acumen and strategies are both admirable and complex.

Each village, then, is a replica of all others in a broad sense. But each village is part of a larger political, demographic, and ecological process, and it is difficult to attempt to understand the village without knowing something of the larger forces that affect it and it's particular history with all its neighbors.

COLLECTING THE DATA IN THE FIELD

I have now spent over 60 months with Yạnomamö, during which time I gradually learned their language and, up to a point, submerged myself in their culture and way of life.[2] As my research progressed, the thing that impressed me most was the importance that aggression played in shaping their culture. I had the opportunity to witness a good many incidents that expressed individual vindictiveness on the one hand and collective bellicosity on the other hand. These ranged in seriousness from the ordinary incidents of wife beating and chest pounding to dueling and organized raids by parties that set out with the intention of ambushing and killing men from enemy villages. One of the villages . . . was raided approximately twenty-five times during my first 15 months of fieldwork—six times by the group among whom I was living. And, the history of every village I investigated, from 1964 to 1991, was intimately bound up in patterns of warfare with neighbors that shaped its politics and determined where it was found at any point in time and how it dealt with it's current neighbors.

The fact that the Yạnomamö have lived in a chronic state of warfare is reflected in their mythology, ceremonies, settlement pattern, political behavior, and marriage practices. Accordingly, I have organized this case study in such a way that students can appreciate the effects of warfare on Yạnomamö culture in general and on their social organization and political relationships in particular.

I collected the data under somewhat trying circumstances, some of which I

will describe to give a rough idea of what is generally meant when anthropologists speak of 'culture shock' and 'fieldwork.' It should be borne in mind, however, that each field situation is in many respects unique, so that the problems I encountered do not necessarily exhaust the range of possible problems other anthropologists have confronted in other areas. There are a few problems, however, that seem to be nearly universal among anthropological fieldworkers, particularly those having to do with eating, bathing, sleeping, lack of privacy, loneliness, or discovering that the people you are living with have a lower opinion of you than you have of them—or you yourself are not as culturally or emotionally 'flexible' as you assumed.

The Yạnomamö can be difficult people to live with at times, but I have spoken to colleagues who have had difficulties living in the communities they studied. These things vary from society to society, and probably from one anthropologist to the next. I have also done limited fieldwork among the Yạnomamö's northern neighbors, the Carib-speaking Ye'kwana Indians. By contrast to many experiences I had among the Yanomamö, the Ye'kwana were very pleasant and charming, all of them anxious to help me and honor bound to show any visitor the numerous courtesies of their system of etiquette. In short, they approached the image of 'primitive man' that I had conjured up in my mind before doing fieldwork, a kind of 'Rousseauian' view, and it was sheer pleasure to work with them. Other anthropologists have also noted sharp contrasts in the people they study from one field situation to another. One of the most startling examples of this is in the work of Colin Turnbull, who first studied the Ituri Pygmies (1965, 1983) and found them delightful to live with, but then studied the Ik (1972) of the desolate outcroppings of the Kenya/Uganda/Sudan border region, a people he had difficulty coping with intellectually, emotionally, and physically. While it is possible that the anthropologist's reactions to a particular people are personal and idiosyncratic, it nevertheless remains true that there are enormous differences between whole peoples, differences that affect the anthropologist in often dramatic ways.

Hence, what I say about some of my experiences is probably equally true of the experiences of many other field-workers. I describe some of them here for the benefit of future anthropologists—because I think I could have profited by reading about the pitfalls and field problems of my own teachers. At the very least I might have been able to avoid some of my more stupid errors. In this regard there is a growing body of excellent descriptive work on field research. Students who plan to make a career in anthropology should consult these works, which cover a wide range of field situations in the ethnographic present.[3]

The Longest Day: The First One
My first day in the field illustrated to me what my teachers meant when they spoke of 'culture shock.' I had traveled in a small, aluminum rowboat propelled by a large outboard motor for two and a half days. This took me from the territorial capital, a small town on the Orinoco River, deep into Yąnomamö country. On the morning of the third day we reached a small mission settlement, the field 'headquarters' of a group of Americans who were working in two Yąnomamö villages. The missionaries had come out of these villages to hold their annual conference on the progress of their mission work and were conducting their meetings when I arrived. We picked up a passenger at the mission station, James P. Barker, the first non-Yąnomamö to make a sustained, permanent contact with the tribe (in 1950). He had just returned from a year's furlough in the United States, where I had earlier visited him before leaving for Venezuela. He agreed to accompany me to the village I had selected for my base of operations to introduce me to the Indians. This village was also his own home base, but he had not been there for over a year and did not plan to join me for another three months. Mr. Barker had been living with this particular group about five years.

We arrived at the village, Bisaasi-teri, about 2:00 P.M. and docked the boat along the muddy bank at the terminus of the path used by Yąnomamö to fetch their drinking water. It was hot and muggy, and my clothing was soaked with perspiration. It clung uncomfortably to my body, as it did thereafter for the remainder of the work. The small biting gnats, *bareto*, were out in astronomical numbers, for it was the beginning of the dry season. My face and hands were swollen from the venom of their numerous stings. In just a few moments I was to meet my first Yąnomamö, my first primitive man. What would he be like? I had visions of entering the village and seeing 125 social facts running about altruistically calling each other kinship terms and sharing food, each waiting and anxious to have me collect his genealogy. I would wear them out in turn. Would they like me? This was important to me; I wanted them to be so fond of me that they would adopt me into their kinship system and way of life. I had heard that successful anthropologists always get adopted by their people. I had learned during my seven years of anthropological training at the University of Michigan that kinship was equivalent to society in primitive tribes and that it was a moral way of life, 'moral' being something 'good' and 'desirable.' I was determined to work my way into their moral system of kinship and become a member of their society—to be 'accepted' by them.

How Did They Accept You?
My heart began to pound as we approached the village and heard the buzz of activity within the circular compound. Mr. Barker commented that he was anxious to see if any changes had taken place while he was away and wondered how many of them had died during his absence. I nervously felt my back pocket to make sure that my notebook was still there and felt personally more secure when I touched it.

The entrance to the village was covered over with brush and dry palm leaves. We pushed them aside to expose the low opening to the village. The excitement of meeting my first Yąnomamö was almost unbearable as I duck-waddled through the low passage into the village clearing.

I looked up and gasped when I saw a dozen burly, naked, sweaty, hideous men staring at us down the shafts of their drawn arrows! Immense wads of green tobacco were stuck between their lower teeth and lips making them look even more hideous, and strands of dark-green slime dripped or hung from their nostrils—strands so long that they clung to their pectoral muscles or drizzled down their chins. We arrived at the village while the men were blowing a hallucinogenic drug up their noses. One of the side effects of the drug is a runny nose. The mucus is always saturated with the green powder and they usually let it run freely from their nostrils. My next discovery was that there were a dozen or so vicious, underfed dogs snapping at my legs, circling me as if I were to be their next meal. I just stood there holding my notebook, helpless and pathetic. Then the stench of the decaying vegetation and filth hit me and I almost got sick. I was horrified. What kind of welcome was this for the person who came here to live with you and learn your way of life, to become friends with you? They put their weapons down when they recognized Barker and returned to their chanting, keeping a nervous eye on the village entrances.

We had arrived just after a serious fight. Seven women had been abducted the day before by a neighboring group, and the local men and their guests had just that morning recovered five of them in a brutal club fight that nearly ended in a shooting war. The abductors, angry because they had lost five of their seven new captives, vowed to raid the Bisaasi-teri. When we arrived and entered the village unexpectedly, the Indians feared that we were the raiders. On several occasions during the next two hours the men in the village jumped to their feet, armed themselves, nocked their arrows and waited nervously for the noise outside the village to be identified. My enthusiasm for collecting ethnographic facts diminished in proportion to the number of times such an alarm was raised. In fact, I was relieved when Barker suggested that we sleep across the river for the evening. It would be safer over there.

As we walked down the path to the boat, I pondered the wisdom of having decided to spend a year and a half with these people before I had even seen what they were like. I am not ashamed to admit that had there been a diplomatic way out, I would have ended my fieldwork then and there. I did not look forward to the next day—and months—when I would be left alone with the Yąnomanö; I did not speak a word of their language, and they were decidedly different from what I had imagined them to be. The whole situation was depressing, and I wondered why I ever decided to switch from physics and engineering in the first place. I had not eaten all day, I was soaking wet from perspiration, the *bareto* were biting me, and I was covered with red pigment, the result of a dozen or so complete examinations I had been given by as many very pushy Yąnomamö men. These examinations capped an otherwise grim day. The men would blow their noses into their hands, flick as much of the mucus off that would separate in a snap of the wrist, wipe the residue into their hair, and then carefully examine my face, arms, legs, hair, and the contents of my pockets. I asked Barker how to say, 'Your hands are dirty'; my comments were met by the Yąnomamö in the following way: They would 'clean' their hands by spitting a quantity of slimy tobacco juice into them, rub them together, grin, and then proceed with the examination.

Mr. Barker and I crossed the river and slung our hammocks. When he pulled his hammock out of a rubber bag, a heavy, disagreeable odor of mildewed cotton and stale wood smoke came with it. 'Even the missionaries are filthy,' I thought to myself. Within two weeks, everything I owned smelled the same way, and I lived with that odor for the remainder of the fieldwork. My own habits of personal cleanliness declined to such levels that I didn't even mind being examined by the Yąnomamö, as I was not much cleaner than they were after I had adjusted to the circumstances. it is difficult to blow your nose gracefully when you are stark naked and the invention of hankerchiefs is millenia away.

Life in the Jungle: Oatmeal, Peanut Butter, and Bugs

It isn't easy to plop down in the Amazon Basin for a year and get immediately into the anthropological swing of things. You have been told about horrible diseases, snakes, jaguars, electric eels, little spiny fish that will swim up your urine into your penis, quicksand, and getting lost. Some of the dangers are real, but your imagination makes them more real and threatening than many of them really are. What my teachers never bothered to advise me about, however, was the mundane, nonexciting, and trivial stuff—like eating, defecating, sleeping, or keeping clean. These turned out to be the bane of my existence during the first several months of field research. I set up my household in Barker's abandoned mud hut, a few yards from the village of Bisaasi-teri, and immediately set to work building my own mud/thatch hut with the help of the Yąnomamö. Meanwhile, I had to eat and try to do my 'field research.' I soon discovered that it was an enormously time-consuming task to maintain my own body in the manner to which it had grown accustomed in the relatively antiseptic environment of the northern United States. Either I could be relatively well fed and relatively comfortable in a fresh change of clothes and do very little fieldwork, or I could do considerably more fieldwork and be less well fed and less comfortable.

It is appalling how complicated it can be to make oatmeal in the jungle. First, I had to make two trips to the river to haul the water. Next, I had to prime my kerosene stove with alcohol to get it burning, a tricky procedure when you are trying to mix powdered milk and fill a coffee pot at the same time. The alcohol prime always burned out before I could turn the kerosene on, and I would have to start all over. Or, I would turn the kerosene on, optimistically hoping that the Coleman element was still hot enough to vaporize the fuel, and start a small fire in my palm-thatched hut as the liquid kerosene squirted all over the table and walls and then ignited. Many amused Yąnomanö onlookers quickly learned the English phrase 'Oh, Shit!', and, once they discovered that the phrase offended and irritated the missionaries, they used it as often as they could in their presence. I usually had to start over with the alcohol. Then I had to boil the oatmeal and pick the bugs out of it. All my supplies, of course, were carefully stored in rat-proof, moisture-proof, and insect-proof containers, not one of which ever served its purpose adequately. Just taking things out of the multiplicity of containers and repacking them afterward was a minor project in itself. By the time I had hauled the water to cook with, unpacked my food, prepared the oatmeal, milk, and coffee, heated water for dishes, washed and dried the dishes, repacked the food in the containers, stored the containers in locked trunks, and cleaned up my mess, the ceremony of preparing breakfast had brought me almost up to lunch time!

Eating three meals a day was simply out of the question. I solved the problem by eating a single meal that could be prepared in a single container, or, at most, in two containers, washed my dishes only when there were no clean ones left, using cold river water, and wore each change of clothing at least a week to cut down on my laundry problem—a courageous undertaking in the tropics. I reeked like a jockstrap that had been left to mildew in the bottom of some dark gym locker. I also became less concerned about sharing my provisions with the rats, insects, Yąnomamö, and the elements, thereby eliminating the need for my complicated storage process. I was able to last most of the day on *café con leche,* heavily sugared espresso coffee diluted about five to one with hot milk. I would prepare this in the evening and store it in a large thermos. Frequently, my single meal was no more complicated than a can of sardines and a package of soggy crackers. But at least two or three times a week I would do something 'special' and sophisticated, like make a batch of oatmeal or boil rice and add a can of tuna fish or tomato paste to it. I even saved time by devising a water system that obviated the trips to the river. I had a few sheets of tin roofing brought in and made a rain water trap; I caught the water on the tin surface, funneled it into an empty gasoline drum, and then ran a plastic hose from the drum to my hut. When the drum was exhausted in the dry season, I would get a few Yąnomamö boys to fill it with buckets of water from the river, 'paying' them with crackers, of which they grew all too fond all too soon.

I ate much less when I traveled with the Yąnomamö to visit other villages. Most of the time my travel diet consisted of roasted or boiled green plantains (cooking bananas) that I obtained from the Yąnomamö, but I always carried a few cans of sardines with me in case I got lost or stayed away longer than I had planned. I found peanut butter and crackers a very nourishing 'trail' meal, and a simple one to prepare. It was nutritious and portable, and only one tool was required to make the meal: a hunting knife that could be cleaned by wiping the blade on a convenient leaf. More importantly, it was one of the few foods the Yąnomamö would let me eat in relative peace. It looked suspiciously like animal feces to them, an impression I encouraged. I referred to the peanut butter as the feces of babies or 'cattle'. They found this disgusting and repugnant. They did not know what 'cattle' were, but were increasingly aware that I ate several canned products of such an animal. Tin cans were thought of as containers made of 'machete skins', but how the cows got inside was always a mystery to them. I went out of my way to describe my foods in such a way as to make them sound unpalatable to them, for it gave me some peace of mind while I ate: They wouldn't beg for a share of something that was too horrible to contem-

plate. Fieldworkers develop strange defense mechanisms and strategies, and this was one of my own forms of adaptation to the fieldwork. On another occasion I was eating a can of frankfurters and growing very weary of the demands from one of the onlookers for a share in my meal. When he finally asked what I was eating, I replied: 'Beef.' He then asked: 'Shąki![4] What part of the animal are you eating?' To which I replied, 'Guess.' He muttered a contemptuous epithet, but stopped asking for a share. He got back at me later, as we shall see.

Meals were a problem in a way that had nothing to do with the inconvenience of preparing them. Food sharing is important to the Yąnomamö in the context of displaying friendship. 'I am hungry!' is almost a form of greeting with them. I could not possibly have brought enough food with me to feed the entire village, yet they seemed to overlook this logistic fact as they begged for my food. What became fixed in their minds was the fact that I did not share my food with whomsoever was present—usually a small crowd—at each and every meal. Nor could I easily enter their system of reciprocity with respect to food. Every time one of them 'gave' me something 'freely', he would dog me for months to 'pay him back', not necessarily with food but with knives, fishhooks, axes, and so on. Thus, if I accepted a plantain from someone in a different village while I was on a visit, he would most likely visit me in the future and demand a machete as payment for the time that he 'fed' me. I usually reacted to these kinds of demands by giving a banana, the customary reciprocity in their culture—food for food—but this would be a disappointment for the individual who had nursed visions of that single plantain growing into a machete over time. Many years after beginning my fieldwork I was approached by one of the prominent men who demanded a machete for a piece of meat he claimed he had given me five or six years earlier.

Despite the fact that most of them knew I would not share my food with them at their request, some of them

always showed up at my hut during mealtime. I gradually resigned myself to this and learned to ignore their persistent demands while I ate. Some of them would get angry because I failed to give in, but most of them accepted it as just a peculiarity of the subhuman foreigner who had come to live among them. If or when I did accede to a request for a share of my food, my hut quickly filled with Yąnomamö, each demanding their share of the food that I had just given to one of them. Their begging for food was not provoked by hunger, but by a desire to try something new and to attempt to establish a coercive relationship in which I would accede to a demand. If one received something, all others would immediately have to test the system to see if they, too, could coerce me.

A few of them went out of their way to make my meals downright unpleasant—to spite me for not sharing, especially if it was a food that they had tried before and liked, or a food that was part of their own cuisine. For example, I was eating a cracker with peanut butter and honey one day. The Yąnomamö will do almost anything for honey, one of the most prized delicacies in their own diet. One of my cynical onlookers—the fellow who had earlier watched me eating frankfurters—immediately recognized the honey and knew that I would not share the tiny precious bottle. It would be futile to even ask. Instead, he glared at me and queried icily, 'Shąki! What kind of animal semen are you pouring onto your food and eating?' His question had the desired effect and my meal ended.

Finally, there was the problem of being lonely and separated from your own kind, especially your family. I tried to overcome this by seeking personal friendships among the Yąnomamö. This usually complicated the matter because all my 'friends' simply used my confidence to gain privileged access to my hut and my cache of steel tools and trade goods—and looted me when I wasn't looking. I would be bitterly disappointed that my erstwhile friend thought no more of me than to finesse our personal relationship exclusively with the intention of getting at my locked up possessions, and my depression would hit new lows every time I discovered this. The loss of the possessions bothered me much less than the shock that I was, as far as most of them were concerned, nothing more than a source of desirable items. No holds were barred in relieving me of these, since I was considered something subhuman, a non-Yąnomamö.

The hardest thing to learn to live with was the incessant, passioned, and often aggressive demands they would make. It would become so unbearable at times that I would have to lock myself in my hut periodically just to escape from it. Privacy is one of our culture's most satisfying achievements, one you never think about until you suddenly have none. It is like not appreciating how good your left thumb feels until someone hits it with a hammer. But I did not want privacy for its own sake; rather, I simply had to get away from the begging. Day and night for almost the entire time I lived with the Yąnomamö I was plagued by such demands as: 'Give me a knife, I am poor!'; 'If you don't take me with you on your next trip to Widokaiyateri, I'll chop a hole in your canoe!'; 'Take us hunting up the Mavaca River with your shotgun or we won't help you!'; 'Give me some matches so I can trade with the Reyaboböwei-teri, and be quick about it or I'll hit you!'; 'Share your food with me, or I'll burn your hut!'; 'Give me a flashlight so I can hunt at night!'; 'Give me all your medicine, I itch all over!'; 'Give me an ax or I'll break into your hut when you are away and steal all of them!' And so I was bombarded by such demands day after day, month after month, until I could not bear to see a Yąnomamö at times.

It was not as difficult to become calloused to the incessant begging as it was to ignore the sense of urgency, the impassioned tone of voice and whining, or the intimidation and aggression with which many of the demands were made. It was likewise difficult to adjust to the fact that the Yąnomamö refused to accept 'No' for an answer until or unless it seethed with passion and intimidation—which it did after a few

months. So persistent and characteristic is the begging that the early 'semi-official' maps made by the Venezuelan Malaria Control Service (*Malarialogía*) designated the site of their first permanent field station, next to the village of Bisaasi-teri, as *Yababuhii*: 'Gimme.' I had to become like the Yąnomamö to be able to get along with them on their terms: somewhat sly, aggressive, intimidating, and pushy.

It became indelibly clear to me shortly after I arrived there that had I failed to adjust in this fashion I would have lost six months of supplies to them in a single day or would have spent most of my time ferrying them around in my canoe or taking them on long hunting trips. As it was, I did spend a considerable amount of time doing these things and did succumb often to their outrageous demands for axes and machetes, at least at first, for things changed as I became more fluent in their language and learned how to defend myself socially as well as verbally. More importantly, had I failed to demonstrate that I could not be pushed around beyond a certain point, I would have been the subject of far more ridicule, theft, and practical jokes than was the actual case. In short, I had to acquire a certain proficiency in their style of interpersonal politics and to learn how to imply subtly that certain potentially undesirable, but unspecified, consequences might follow if they did such and such to me. They do this to each other incessantly in order to establish precisely the point at which they cannot goad or intimidate an individual any further without precipitating some kind of retaliation. As soon as I realized this and gradually acquired the self-confidence to adopt this strategy, it became clear that much of the intimidation was calculated to determine my flash point or my 'last ditch' position—and I got along much better with them. Indeed, I even regained some lost ground. It was sort of like a political, interpersonal game that everyone had to play, but one in which each individual sooner or later had to give evidence that his bluffs and implied threats could be backed up with a sanction. I suspect

that the frequency of wife beating is a component in this syndrome, since men can display their *waiteri* (ferocity) and 'show' others that they are capable of great violence. Beating a wife with a club is one way of displaying ferocity, one that does not expose the man to much danger—unless the wife has concerned, aggressive brothers in the village who will come to her aid. Apparently an important thing in wife beating is that the man has displayed his presumed potential for violence and the intended message is that other men ought to treat him with circumspection, caution, and even deference.

After six months, the level of Yąnomamö demand was tolerable in Bisaasi-teri, the village I used for my base of operations. We had adjusted somewhat to each other and knew what to expect with regard to demands for food, trade goods, and favors. Had I elected to remain in just one Yąnomamö village for the entire duration of my first 15 months of fieldwork, the experience would have been far more enjoyable than it actually was. However, as I began to understand the social and political dynamics of this village, it became patently obvious that I would have to travel to many other villages to determine the demographic bases and political histories that lay behind what I could understand in the village of Bisaasi-teri. I began making regular trips to some dozen neighboring Yąnomamö villages as my language fluency improved. I collected local genealogies there, or rechecked and cross-checked those I had collected elsewhere. Hence, the intensity of begging was relatively constant and relatively high for the duration of my fieldwork, for I had to establish my personal position in each village I visited and revisited.

For the most part, my own 'fierceness' took the form of shouting back at the Yąnomamö as loudly and as passionately as they shouted at me, especially at first, when I did not know much of the language. As I became more fluent and learned more about their political tactics, I became more sophisticated in the art of bluffing and brinksmanship. For example, I paid one young man a machete (then worth about $2.50) to cut a palm tree and help me make boards from the wood. I used these to fashion a flooring in the bottom of my dugout canoe to keep my possession out of the water that always seeped into the canoe and sloshed around. That afternoon I was working with one of my informants in the village. The long-awaited mission supply boat arrived and most of the Yąnomamö ran out of the village to see the supplies and try to beg items from the crew. I continued to work in the village for another hour or so and then went down to the river to visit with the men on the supply boat. When I reached the river I noticed, with anger and frustration, that the Yąnomamö had chopped up all my new floor boards to use as crude paddles to get their own canoes across the river to the supply boat.[5] I knew that if I ignored this abuse I would have invited the Yąnomamö to take even greater liberties with my possessions in the future. I got into my canoe, crossed the river, and docked amidst their flimsy, leaky craft. I shouted loudly to them, attracting their attention. They were somewhat sheepish, but all had mischievous grins on their impish faces. A few of them came down to the canoe, where I proceeded with a spirited lecture that revealed my anger at their audacity and license. I explained that I had just that morning paid one of them a machete for bringing me the palmwood, how hard I had worked to shape each board and place it in the canoe, how carefully and painstakingly I had tied each one in with vines, how much I had perspired, how many *bareto* bites I had suffered, and so on. Then, with exaggerated drama and finality, I withdrew my hunting knife as their grins disappeared and cut each one of their canoes loose and set it into the strong current of the Orinoco River where it was immediately swept up and carried downstream. I left without looking back and huffed over to the other side of the river to resume my work.

They managed to borrow another canoe and, after some effort, recovered their dugouts. Later, the headman of the village told me, with an approv-ing chuckle, that I had done the correct thing. Everyone in the village, except, of course, the culprits, supported and defended my actions—and my status increased as a consequence.

Whenever I defended myself in such ways I got along much better with the Yąnomamö and gradually acquired the respect of many of them. A good deal of their demeanor toward me was directed with the forethought of establishing the point at which I would draw the line and react defensively. Many of them, years later, reminisced about the early days of my fieldwork when I was timid and *mohode* ("stupid") and a little afraid of them, those golden days when it was easy to bully me into giving my goods away for almost nothing.

Theft was the most persistent situation that required some sort of defensive action. I simply could not keep everything I owned locked in trunks, and the Yąnomamö came into my hut and left at will. I eventually developed a very effective strategy for recovering almost all the stolen items: I would simply ask a child who took the item and then I would confiscate that person's hammock when he was not around, giving a spirited lecture to all who could hear on the antisociality of thievery as I stalked off in a faked rage with the thief's hammock slung over my shoulder. Nobody ever attempted to stop me from doing this, and almost all of them told me that my technique for recovering my possessions was ingenious. By nightfall the thief would appear at my hut with the stolen item or send it over with someone else to make an exchange to recover his hammock. He would be heckled by his covillagers for having got caught and for being embarrassed into returning my item for his hammock. The explanation was usually, 'I just borrowed your ax! I wouldn't think of stealing it!'

Collecting Yąnomamö Genealogies and Reproductive Histories

My purpose for living among Yąnomamö was to systematically collect certain kinds of information on genealogy, reproduction, marriage practices, kinship, settlement patterns, migrations, and politics. Much of the fundamental data was genealogical—who was the parent of whom, tracing these connections as far back in time as Yąnomamö knowledge and memory permitted. Since 'primitive' society is organized largely by kinship relationships, figuring out the social organization of the Yąnomamö essentially meant collecting extensive data on genealogies, marriage, and reproduction. This turned out to be a staggering and very frustrating problem. I could not have deliberately picked a more difficult people to work with in this regard. They have very stringent name taboos and eschew mentioning the names of prominent living people was well as all deceased friends and relatives. They attempt to name people in such a way that when the person dies and they can no longer use his or her name, the loss of the word in their language is not inconvenient. Hence, they name people for specific and minute parts of things, such as 'toenail of sloth,' 'whisker of howler monkey,' and so on, thereby being able to retain the words 'toenail' or 'whisker' but somewhat handicapped in referring to these anatomical parts of sloths and monkeys respectively. The taboo is maintained even for the living, for one mark of prestige is the courtesy others show you by not using your name publicly. This is particularly true for men, who are much more competitive for status than women in this culture, and it is fascinating to watch boys grow into young men, demanding to be called either by a kinship term in public, or by a teknonymous reference such as 'brother of Himotoma'. The more effective they are at getting others to avoid using their names, the more public acknowledgment there is that they are of high esteem and social standing. Helena Valero, a Brazilian woman who was captured as a child by a Yąnomamö raiding party, was married for many years to a Yąnomamö headman before she discovered what his name was (Biocca, 1970; Valero, 1984). The sanctions behind the taboo are more complex than just this, for they involve a combination of fear, respect, admiration, political deference, and honor.

At first I tried to use kinship terms alone to collect genealogies, but Yąnomamö kinship terms, like the kinship terms in all systems, are ambiguous at some point because they include so many possible relatives (as the term 'uncle' does in our own kinship system). Again, their system of kin classification merges many relatives that we 'separate' by using different terms: They call both their actual father and their father's brother by a single term, whereas we call one 'father' and the other 'uncle.' I was forced, therefore, to resort to personal names to collect unambiguous genealogies or 'pedigrees'. They quickly grasped what I was up to and that I was determined to learn everyone's 'true name', which amounted to an invasion of their system of prestige and etiquette, if not a flagrant violation of it. They reacted to this in a brilliant but devastating manner: They invented false names for everybody in the village and systematically learned them, freely revealing to me the 'true' identities of everyone. I smugly thought I had cracked the system and enthusiastically constructed elaborate genealogies over a period of some five months. They enjoyed watching me learn their names and kinship relationships. I naively assumed that I would get the 'truth' to each question and the best information by working in public. This set the stage for converting my serious project into an amusing hoax of the grandest proportions. Each 'informant' would try to outdo his peers by inventing a name even more preposterous or ridiculous than what I had been given by someone earlier, the explanations for discrepancies being 'Well, he has two names and this is the other one.' They even fabricated devilishly improbable genealogical relationships, such as someone being married to his grandmother, or worse yet, to his mother-in-law, a grotesque and horrifying prospect to the Yanomamö. I would collect the desired names and relationships by having my informant whisper the name of the person softly into my ear, noting that he or she was the parent of such and

such or the child of such and such, and so on. Everyone who was observing my work would then insist that I repeat the name aloud, roaring in hysterical laughter as I clumsily pronounced the name, sometimes laughing until tears streamed down their faces. The 'named' person would usually react with annoyance and hiss some untranslatable epithet at me, which served to reassure me that I had the 'true' name. I conscientiously checked and rechecked the names and relationships with multiple informants, pleased to see the inconsistencies disappear as my genealogy sheets filled with those desirable little triangles and circles, thousands of them.

My anthropological bubble was burst when I visited a village about 10 hours' walk to the southwest of Bisaasi-teri some five months after I had begun collecting genealogies on the Bisaasi-teri. I was chatting with the local headman of this village and happened to casually drop the name of the wife of the Bisaasi-teri headman. A stunned silence followed, and then a villagewide roar of uncontrollable laughter, choking, gasping, and howling followed. It seems that I thought the Bisaasi-teri headman was married to a woman named "hairy cunt." It also seems that the Bisaasi-teri headman was called 'long dong' and his brother 'eagle shit.' The Bisaasi-teri headman had a son called "asshole" and a daughter called 'fart breath.' And so on. Blood welled up my temples as I realized that I had nothing but nonsense to show for my five months' of dedicated genealogical effort, and I had to throw away almost all the information I had collected on this the most basic set of data I had come there to get. I understood at that point why the Bisaasi-teri laughed so hard when they made me repeat the names of their covillagers, and why the 'named' person would react with anger and annoyance as I pronounced his 'name' aloud.

I was forced to change research strategy—to make an understatement to describe this serious situation. The first thing I did was to begin working in private with my informants to eliminate the horseplay and distraction that

attended public sessions. Once I did this, my informants, who did not know what others were telling me, began to agree with each other and I managed to begin learning the 'real' names, starting first with children and gradually moving to adult women and then, cautiously, adult men, a sequence that reflected the relative degree of intransigence at revealing names of people. As I built up a core of accurate genealogies and relationships—a core that all independent informants had verified repetitiously—I could 'test' any new informant by soliciting his or her opinion and knowledge about these 'core' people whose names and relationships I was confident were accurate. I was, in this fashion, able to immediately weed out the mischievous informants who persisted in trying to deceive me. Still, I had great difficulty getting the names of dead kinsmen, the only accurate way to extend genealogies back in time. Even my best informants continued to falsify names of the deceased, especially closely related deceased. The falsifications at this point were not serious and turned out to be readily corrected as my interviewing methods improved (see below). Most of the deceptions were of the sort where the informant would give me the name of a living man as the father of some child whose actual father was dead, a response that enabled the informant to avoid using the name of a deceased kinsman or friend.

The quality of a genealogy depends in part on the number of generations it embraces, and the name taboo prevented me from making any substantial progress in learning about the deceased ancestors of the present population. Without this information, I could not, for example, document marriage patterns and interfamilial alliances through time. I had to rely on older informants for this information, but these were the most reluctant informants of all for this data. As I became more proficient in the language and more skilled at detecting fabrications, my informants became better at deception. One old man was particularly cunning and persuasive, following a sort of Mark Twain policy that the most effective lie is a sincere lie. He specialized in making a ceremony out of false names for dead ancestors. He would look around nervously to make sure nobody was listening outside my hut, enjoin me never to mention the name again, become very anxious and spooky, and grab me by the head to whisper a secret name into my ear. I was always elated after a session with him, because I managed to add several generations of ancestors for particular members of the village. Others steadfastly refused to give me such information. To show my gratitude, I paid him quadruple the rate that I had been paying the others. When word got around that I had increased the pay for genealogical and demographic information, volunteers began pouring into my hut to 'work' for me, assuring me of their changed ways and keen desire to divest themselves of the 'truth'.

Enter Rerebawä: Inmarried Tough Guy

I discovered that the old man was lying quite by accident. A club fight broke out in the village one day, the result of a dispute over the possession of a woman. She had been promised to a young man in the village, a man named Rerebawä, who was particularly aggressive. He had married into Bisaasi-teri and was doing his 'bride service'—a period of several years during which he had to provide game for his wife's father and mother, provide them with wild foods he might collect, and help them in certain gardening and other tasks. Rerebawä had already been given one of the daughters in marriage and was promised her younger sister as his second wife. He was enraged when the younger sister, then about 16 years old, began having an affair with another young man in the village, Bäkotawä, making no attempt to conceal it. Rerebawä challenged Bäkotawä to a club fight. He swaggered boisterously out to the duel with his 10-foot-long club, a roof-pole he had cut from the house on the spur of the moment, as is the usual procedure. He hurled insult after insult at both Bäkotawä and his father, trying to goad them into a fight.

His insults were bitter and nasty. They tolerated them for a few moments, but Rerebawä's biting insults provoked them to rage. Finally, they stormed angrily out of their hammocks and ripped out roof-poles, now returning the insults verbally, and rushed to the village clearing. Rerebawä continued to insult them, goading them into striking him on the head with their equally long clubs. Had either of them struck his head—which he held out conspicuously for them to swing at—he would then have the right to take his turn on their heads with his club. His opponents were intimidated by his fury, and simply backed down, refusing to strike him, and the argument ended. He had intimidated them into submission. All three retired pompously to their respective hammocks, exchanging nasty insults as they departed. But Rerebawä had won the showdown and thereafter swaggered around the village, insulting the two men behind their backs at every opportunity. He was genuinely angry with them, to the point of calling the older man by the name of his long-deceased father. I quickly seized on this incident as an opportunity to collect an accurate genealogy and confidentially asked Rerebawä about his adversary's ancestors. Rerebawä had been particularly 'pushy' with me up to this point, but we soon became warm friends and staunch allies: We were both 'outsiders' in Bisaasi-teri and, although he was a Yąnomamö, he nevertheless had to put up with some considerable amount of pointed teasing and scorn from the locals, as all inmarried 'sons-in-law' must. He gave me the information I requested of his adversary's deceased ancestors, almost with devilish glee. I asked about dead ancestors of other people in the village and got prompt, unequivocal answers: He was angry with everyone in the village. When I compared his answers to those of the old man, it was obvious that one of them was lying. I then challenged his answers. He explained, in a sort of 'you damned fool, don't you know better?' tone of voice that everyone in the village knew the old man was lying to me and gloating over it when I was out of earshot. The

names the old man had given to me were names of dead ancestors of the members of a village so far away that he thought I would never have occasion to check them out authoritatively. As it turned out, Rerebawä knew most of the people in that distant village and recognized the names given by the old man.

I then went over all my Bisaasi-teri genealogies with Rerebawä, genealogies I had presumed to be close to their final form. I had to revise them all because of the numerous lies and falsifications they contained, much of it provided by the sly old man. Once again, after months of work, I had to recheck everything with Rerebawä's aid. Only the living members of the nuclear families turned out to be accurate; the deceased ancestors were mostly fabrications.

Discouraging as it was to have to recheck everything all over again, it was a major turning point in my fieldwork. Thereafter, I began taking advantage of local arguments and animosities in selecting my informants, and used more extensively informants who had married into the village in the recent past. I also began traveling more regularly to other villages at this time to check on genealogies, seeking out villages whose members were on strained terms with the people about whom I wanted information. I would then return to my base in the village of Bisaasi-teri and check with local informants the accuracy of the new information. I had to be careful in this work and scrupulously select my local informants in such a way that I would not be inquiring about *their* closely related kin. Thus, for each of my local informants, I had to make lists of names of certain deceased people that I dared not mention in their presence. But despite this precaution, I would occasionally hit a new name that would put some informants into a rage, or into a surly mood, such as that of a dead 'brother' or 'sister'[6] whose existence had not been indicted to me by other informants. This usually terminated my day's work with that informant, for he or she would be too touchy or upset to continue any further, and I would be reluctant to take a chance on accidentally discovering another dead close kinsman soon after discovering the first.

These were unpleasant experiences, and occasionally dangerous as well, depending on the temperament of my informant. On one occasion I was planning to visit a village that had been raided recently by one of their enemies. A woman, whose name I had on my census list for that village, had been killed by the raiders. Killing women is considered to be bad form in Yąnomamö warfare, but this woman was deliberately killed for revenge. The raiders were unable to bushwhack some man who stepped out of the village at dawn to urinate, so they shot a volley of arrows over the roof into the village and beat a hasty retreat. Unfortunately, one of the arrows struck and killed a woman, an accident. For that reason, her village's raiders *deliberately* sought out and killed a woman in retaliation—whose name was on my list. My reason for going to the village was to update my census data on a name-by-name basis and estimate the ages of all the residents. I knew I had the name of the dead woman in my list, but nobody would dare to utter her name so I could remove it. I knew that I would be in very serious trouble if I got to the village and said her name aloud, and I desperately wanted to remove it from my list. I called on one of my regular and usually cooperative informants and asked him to tell me the woman's name. He refused adamantly, explaining that she was a close relative—and was angry that I even raised the topic with him. I then asked him if he would let me whisper the names of *all* the women of that village in his ear, and he would simply have to nod when I hit the right name. We had been 'friends' for some time, and I thought I was able to predict his reaction, and thought that our friendship was good enough to use this procedure. He agreed to the procedure, and I began whispering the names of the women, one by one. We were alone in my hut so that nobody would know what we were doing and nobody could hear us. I read the names softly, continuing to

the next when his response was a negative. When I ultimately hit the dead woman's name, he flew out of his chair, enraged and trembling violently, his arm raised to strike me: 'You son-of-a-bitch!' he screamed. 'If you say her name in my presence again, I'll kill you in an instant!' I sat there, bewildered, shocked, and confused. And frightened, as much because of his reaction, but also because I could imagine what might happen to me should I unknowingly visit a village to check genealogy accuracy without knowing that someone had just died there or had been shot by raiders since my last visit. I reflected on the several articles I had read as a graduate student that explained the 'genealogical method,' but could not recall anything about its being a potentially lethal undertaking. My furious informant left my hut, never again to be invited back to be an informant. I had other similar experiences in different villages, but I was always fortunate in that the dead person had been dead for some time, or was not very closely related to the individual into whose ear I whispered the forbidden name. I was usually cautioned by one of the men to desist from saying any more names lest I get people 'angry'.[7]

Kąobawä: The Bisaasi-teri Headman Volunteers to Help Me

I had been working on the genealogies for nearly a year when another individual came to my aid. It was Kąobawä, the headman of Upper Bisaasi-teri. The village of Bisaasi-teri was split into two components, each with its own garden and own circular house. Both were in sight of each other. However, the intensity and frequency of internal bickering and argumentation was so high that they decided to split into two separate groups but remain close to each other for protection in case they were raided. One group was downstream from the other; I refer to that group as the 'Lower' Bisaasi-teri and call Kąobawä's group 'Upper' (upstream) Bisaasi-teri, a convenience they themselves adopted after separating from each other. I spent most

of my time with the members of Kąobawä's group, some 200 people when I first arrived there. I did not have much contact with Kąobawä during the early months of my work. He was a somewhat retiring, quiet man, and among the Yąomamö, the outsider has little time to notice the rare quiet ones when most everyone else is in the front row, pushing and demanding attention. He showed up at my hut one day after all the others had left. He had come to volunteer to help me with the genealogies. He was 'poor,' he explained, and needed a machete. He would work only on the condition that I did not ask him about his own parents and other very close kinsmen who had died. He also added that he would not lie to me as the others had done in the past.

This was perhaps the single most important event in my first 15 months of field research, for out of this fortuitous circumstance evolved a very warm friendship, and among the many things following from it was a wealth of accurate information on the political history of Kąobawä's village and related villages, highly detailed genealogical information, sincere and useful advice to me, and hundreds of valuable insights into the Yąnomamö way of life. Kąobawä's familiarity with his group's history and his candidness were remarkable. His knowledge of details was almost encyclopedic, his memory almost photographic. More than that, he was enthusiastic about making sure I learned the truth, and he encouraged me, indeed, *demanded* that I learn all details I might otherwise have ignored. If there were subtle details he could not recite on the spot, he would advise me to wait until he could check things out with someone else in the village. He would often do this clandestinely, giving me a report the next day, telling me who revealed the new information and whether or not he thought they were in a position to know it. With the information provided by Kąobawä and Rerebawä, I made enormous gains in understanding village interrelationships based on common ancestors and political histories and became lifelong friends with both. And both men knew that I had to learn about his recently deceased kin from the other one. It was one of those quiet understandings we all had but none of us could mention.

Once again I went over the genealogies with Kąobawä to recheck them, a considerable task by this time. They included about two thousand names, representing several generations of individuals from four different villages. Rerebawä's information was very accurate, and Kąobawä's contribution enabled me to trace the genealogies further back in time. Thus, after nearly a year of intensive effort on genealogies, Yąnomamö demographic patterns and social organization began to make a good deal of sense to me. Only at this point did the patterns through time begin to emerge in the data, and I could begin to understand how kinship groups took form, exchanged women in marriage over several generations, and only then did the fissioning of larger villages into smaller ones emerge as a chronic and important feature of Yąomamö social, political, demographic, economic, and ecological adaptation. At this point I was able to begin formulating more sophisticated questions, for there was now a pattern to work from and one to flesh out. Without the help of Rerebawä and Kąobawä it would have taken much longer to make sense of the plethora of details I had collected from not only them, but dozens of other informants as well.

I spent a good deal of time with these two men and their families, and got to know them much better than I knew most Yąnomamö. They frequently gave their information in a way which related themselves to the topic under discussion. We became warm friends as time passed, and the formal 'informant/anthropologist' relationship faded into the background. Eventually, we simply stopped 'keeping track' of work and pay. They would both spend hours talking with me, leaving without asking for anything. When they wanted something, they would ask for it no matter what the relative balance of reciprocity between us might have been at that point. . . .

For many of the customary things that anthropologists try to communicate about another culture, these two men and their families might be considered to be 'exemplary' or 'typical'. For other things, they are exceptional in many regards, but the reader will, even knowing some of the exceptions, understand Yąnomamö culture more intimately by being familiar with a few examples.

Kąobawä was about 40 years old when I first came to his village in 1964. I say "about 40" because the Yąnomamö numeration system has only three numbers: one, two, and more-than-two. It is hard to give accurate ages or dates for events when the informants have no means in their language to reveal such detail. Kąobawä is the headman of his village, meaning that he has somewhat more responsibility in political dealings with other Yąnomamö groups, and very little control over those who live in his group except when the village is being raided by enemies. We will learn more about political leadership and warfare in a later chapter, but most of the time men like Kąobawä are like the North American Indian 'chief' whose authority was characterized in the following fashion: "One word from the chief, and each man does as he pleases." There are different 'styles' of political leadership among the Yąnomamö. Some leaders are mild, quiet, inconspicuous most of the time, but intensely competent. They act parsimoniously, but when they do, people listen and conform. Other men are more tyrannical, despotic, pushy, flamboyant, and unpleasant to all around them. They shout orders frequently, are prone to beat their wives, or pick on weaker men. Some are very violent. I have met headmen who run the entire spectrum between these polar types, for I have visited some 60 Yąnomamö villages. Kąobawä stands at the mild, quietly competent end of the spectrum. He has had six wives thus far—and temporary affairs with as many more, at least one of which resulted in a child that is publicly acknowledged as his child. When I first met him he had just two wives: Bahimi

and Koamashima. Bahimi had two living children when I first met her; many others had died. She was the older and enduring wife, as much a friend to him as a mate. Their relationship was as close to what we think of as 'love' in our culture as I have seen among the Yąnomamö. His second wife was a girl of about 20 years, Koamashima. She had a new baby boy when I first met her, her first child. There was speculation that Kąobawä was planning to give Koamashima to one of his younger brothers who had no wife; he occasionally allows his younger brother to have sex with Koamashima, but only if he asks in advance. Kąobawä gave another wife to one of his other brothers because she was *beshi* ("horny"). In fact, this earlier wife had been married to two other men, both of whom discarded her because of her infidelity. Kąobawä had one daughter by her. However, the girl is being raised by Kąobawä's brother, though acknowledged to be Kąobawä's child.

Bahimi, his oldest wife, is about five years younger than he. She is his cross-cousin—his mother's brother's daughter. Ideally, all Yąnomamö men should marry a cross-cousin. . . . Bahimi was pregnant when I began my fieldwork, but she destroyed the infant when it was born—a boy in this case—explaining tearfully that she had no choice. The new baby would have competed for milk with Ariwari, her youngest child, who was still nursing. Rather than expose Ariwari to the dangers and uncertainty of an early weaning, she chose to terminate the newborn instead. By Yąnomamö standards, this has been a very warm, enduring marriage. Kąobawä claims he beats Bahimi only 'once in a while, and only lightly' and she, for her part, never has affairs with other men.

Kąobawä is a quiet, intense, wise, and unobtrusive man. It came as something of a surprise to me when I learned that he was the headman of his village, for he stayed at the sidelines while others would surround me and press their demands on me. He leads more by example than by coercion. He can afford to be this way at his age, for he established his reputation for being forthright and as fierce as the situation required when he was younger, and the other men respect him. He also has five mature brothers or half-brothers in his village, men he can count on for support. He also has several other mature 'brothers' (parallel cousins, whom he must refer to as 'brothers' in his kinship system) in the village who frequently come to his aid, but not as often as his 'real' brothers do. Kąobawä has also given a number of his sisters to other men in the village and has promised his young (8-year-old) daughter in marriage to a young man who, for that reason, is obliged to help him. In short, his 'natural' or 'kinship' following is large, and partially because of this support, he does not have to display his aggressiveness to remind his peers of his position.

Rerebawä is a very different kind of person. He is much younger—perhaps in his early twenties. He has just one wife, but they have already had three children. He is from a village called Karohi-teri, located about five hours' walk up the Orinoco, slightly inland off to the east of the river itself. Kąobawä's village enjoys amicable relationships with Rerebawä's, and it is for this reason that marriage alliances of the kind represented by Rerebawä's marriage into Kąobawä's village occur between the two groups. Rerebawä told me that he came to Bisaasi-teri because there were no eligible women from him to marry in his own village, a fact that I later was able to document when I did a census of his village and a preliminary analysis of its social organization. Rerebawä is perhaps more typical than Kąobawä in the sense that he is chronically concerned about his personal reputation for aggressiveness and goes out of his way to be noticed, even if he has to act tough. He gave me a hard time during my early months of fieldwork, intimidating, teasing, and insulting me frequently. He is, however, much braver than the other men his age and is quite prepared to back up his threats with immediate action—as in the club fight incident just described above. Moreover, he is fascinated with political relationships and knows the details of intervillage relationships

over a large area of the tribe. In this respect he shows all the attributes of being a headman, although he has too many competent brothers in his own village to expect to move easily into the leadership position there.

He does not intend to stay in Kąobawä's group and refuses to make his own garden—a commitment that would reveal something of an intended long-term residence. He feels that he has adequately discharged his obligations to his wife's parents by providing them with fresh game, which he has done for several years. They should let him take his wife and return to his own village with her, but they refuse and try to entice him to remain permanently in Bisaasi-teri to continue to provide them with game when they are old. It is for this reason that they promised to give him their second daughter, their only other child, in marriage. Unfortunately, the girl was opposed to the marriage and ultimately married another man, a rare instance where the woman in the marriage had this much influence on the choice of her husband.

Although Rerebawä has displayed his ferocity in many ways, one incident in particular illustrates what his character can be like. Before he left his own village to take his new wife in Bisaasi-teri, he had an affair with the wife of an older brother. When it was discovered, his brother attacked him with a club. Rerebawä responded furiously: He grabbed an ax and drove his brother out of the village after soundly beating him with the blunt side of the single-bit ax. His brother was so intimidated by the thrashing and promise of more to come that he did not return to the village for several days. I visited this village with Koabawä shortly after this event had taken place; Rerebawä was with me as my guide. He made it a point to introduce me to this man. He approached his hammock, grabbed him by the wrist, and dragged him out on the ground: 'This is the brother whose wife I screwed when he wasn't around!' A deadly insult, one that would usually provoke a bloody club fight among more valiant Yąnomamö. The man did nothing. He slunk sheepishly back into his hammock, shamed,

but relieved to have Rerebawä release his grip.

Even though Rerebawä is fierce and capable of considerable nastiness, he has a charming, witty side as well. He has a biting sense of humor and can entertain the group for hours with jokes and clever manipulations of language. And, he is one of few Yąnomamö that I feel I can trust. I recall indelibly my return to Bisaasi-teri after being away a year—the occasion of my second field trip to the Yąnomamö. When I reached Bisaasi-teri, Rerebawä was in his own village visiting his kinsmen. Word reached him that I had returned, and he paddled downstream immediately to see me. He greeted me with an immense bear hug and exclaimed, with tears welling up in his eyes, 'Shaki! Why did you stay away so long? Did you not know that my will was so cold while you were gone that I could not at times eat for want of seeing you again?' I, too, felt the same way about him—then, and now.

Of all the Yąnomamö I know, he is the most genuine and the most devoted to his culture's ways and values. I admire him for that, although I cannot say that I subscribe to or endorse some of these values. By contrast, Kąobawä is older and wiser, a polished diplomat. He sees his own culture in a slightly different light and seems even to question aspects of it. Thus, while many of his peers enthusiastically accept the 'explanations' of things given in myths, he occasionally reflects on them—even laughing at some of the most preposterous of them. . . . Probably more of the Yąnomamö are like Rerebawä than like Kąobawä, or at least try to be. . . .

NOTES

1. The word Yąnomamö is nasalized through its entire length, indicated by the diacritical mark ',' When this mark appears on any Yąnomamö word, the whole word is nasalized. The vowel 'ö' represents a sound that does not occur in the English language. It is similar to the umlaut 'ö' in the German language or the 'oe' equivalent, as in the poet Goethe's name. Unfortunately, many presses and typesetters simply eliminate diacritical marks, and this has led to multiple spellings of the word Yąnomamö—and

1. ANTHROPOLOGICAL PERSPECTIVES

multiple mispronunciations. Some anthropologists have chosen to introduce a slightly different spelling of the word Yąnomamö since I began writing about them, such as Yąnomami, leading to additional misspellings as their diacritics are characteristically eliminated by presses, and to the *incorrect* pronunciation 'Yanomameee.' Vowels indicated as 'ä' are pronounced as the 'uh' sound in the word 'duck'. Thus, the name Kąobawä would be pronounced 'cow-ba-wuh,' but entirely nasalized.

2. I spent a total of 60 months among the Yąnomamö between 1964 and 1991. The first edition of this case study was based on the first 15 months I spent among them in Venezuela. I have, at the time of this writing, made 20 field trips to the Yąnomamö and this edition reflects the new information and understandings I have acquired over the years. I plan to return regularly to continue what has now turned into a life-long study.

3. See Spindler (1970) for a general discussion of field research by anthropologists who have worked in other cultures. Nancy Howell has recently written a very useful book (1990) on some of the medical, personal, and environmental hazards of doing field research, which includes a selected bibliography on other fieldwork problems.

4. They could not pronounce "Chagnon." It sounded to them like their name for a pesky bee, shaki, and that is what they called me: pesky, noisome bee.

5. The Yąnomamö in this region acquired canoes very recently. The missionaries would purchase them from the Ye'kwana Indians to the north for money, and then trade them to the Yąnomamö in exchange for labor, produce, or 'informant' work in translating. It should be emphasized that those Yąnomamö who lived on navigable portions of the Upper Orinoco River moved there recently from the deep forest in order to have contact with the missionaries and acquire the trade goods the missionaries (and their supply system) brought.

6. Rarely were there actual brothers or sisters. In Yąnomamö kinship classifications, certain kinds of cousins are classified as siblings. See Chapter 4.

7. Over time, as I became more and more 'accepted' by the Yąnomamö, they became less and less concerned about my genealogical inquiries and, now, provide me with this information quite willingly because I have been very discrete with it. Now, when I revisit familiar villages I am called aside by someone who whispers to me things like, "Don't ask about so-and-so's father."

Doctor, Lawyer, Indian Chief

*As Punjabi villagers say, "You never really know who a man is
until you know who his grandfather and his ancestors were"*

Richard Kurin

*Richard Kurin is the Deputy Director
of Folklife Programs at the Smithsonian Institution.*

I was full of confidence when—
equipped with a scholarly proposal,
blessings from my advisers, and
generous research grants—I set out
to study village social structure in the
Punjab province of Pakistan. But
after looking for an appropriate
fieldwork site for several weeks without success, I began to think that my
research project would never get off
the ground. Daily I would seek out
villages aboard my puttering motor
scooter, traversing the dusty dirt
roads, footpaths, and irrigation
ditches that crisscross the Punjab.
But I couldn't seem to find a village
amenable to study. The major problem was that the villagers I did approach were baffled by my presence.
They could not understand why anyone would travel ten thousand miles
from home to a foreign country in
order to live in a poor village, interview illiterate peasants, and then
write a book about it. Life, they were
sure, was to be lived, not written
about. Besides, they thought, what of
any importance could they possibly

tell me? Committed as I was to ethnographic research, I readily understood their viewpoint. I was a *babu
log*—literally, a noble; figuratively, a
clerk; and simply, a person of the city.
I rode a motor scooter, wore tight-
fitting clothing, and spoke Urdu, a
language associated with the urban
literary elite. Obviously, I did not
belong, and the villagers simply did
not see me fitting into their society.

The Punjab, a region about the size
of Colorado, straddles the northern
border of India and Pakistan. Parti-
tioned between the two countries in
1947, the Punjab now consists of a
western province, inhabited by Muslims, and an eastern one, populated in
the main by Sikhs and Hindus. As its
name implies—*punj* meaning "five"
and *ab* meaning "rivers"—the region
is endowed with plentiful resources to
support widespread agriculture and a
large rural population. The Punjab
has traditionally supplied grains,
produce, and dairy products to the
peoples of neighboring and considerably more arid states, earning it a
reputation as the breadbasket of
southern Asia.

Given this predilection for agriculture, Punjabis like to emphasize that
they are earthy people, having values
they see as consonant with rural life.
These values include an appreciation
of, and trust in, nature; simplicity and

directness of expression; an awareness of the basic drives and desires
that motivate men (namely, *zan, zar,
zamin*—"women, wealth, land"); a
concern with honor and shame as
abiding principles of social organization; and for Muslims, a deep faith in
Allah and the teachings of his prophet
Mohammad.

Besides being known for its fertile
soils, life-giving rivers, and superla-
tive agriculturists, the Punjab is also
perceived as a zone of transitional
culture, a region that has experienced
repeated invasions of peoples from
western and central Asia into the
Indian subcontinent. Over the last
four thousand years, numerous
groups, among them Scythians, Par-
thians, Huns, Greeks, Moguls, Per-
sians, Afghans, and Turks, have
entered the subcontinent through the
Punjab in search of bountiful land,
riches, or power. Although Punjabis—notably Rajputs, Sikhs, and
Jats—have a reputation for courage
and fortitude on the battlefield, their
primary, self-professed strength has
been their ability to incorporate new,
exogenous elements into their society
with a minimum of conflict. Punjabis
are proud that theirs is a multiethnic
society in which diverse groups have
been largely unified by a common
language and by common customs
and traditions.

1. ANTHROPOLOGICAL PERSPECTIVES

Given this background, I had not expected much difficulty in locating a village in which to settle and conduct my research. As an anthropologist, I viewed myself as an "earthy" social scientist who, being concerned with basics, would have a good deal in common with rural Punjabis. True, I might be looked on as an invader of a sort; but I was benevolent, and sensing this, villagers were sure to incorporate me into their society with even greater ease than was the case for the would-be conquering armies that had preceded me. Indeed, they would welcome me with open arms.

I was wrong. The villagers whom I approached attributed my desire to live with them either to neurotic delusions or nefarious ulterior motives. Perhaps, so the arguments went, I was really after women, land, or wealth.

On the day I had decided would be my last in search of a village, I was driving along a road when I saw a farmer running through a rice field and waving me down. I stopped and he climbed on the scooter. Figuring I had nothing to lose, I began to explain why I wanted to live in a village. To my surprise and delight, he was very receptive, and after sharing a pomegranate milkshake at a roadside shop, he invited me to his home. His name was Allah Ditta, which means "God given," and I took this as a sign that I had indeed found my village.

"My" village turned out to be a settlement of about fifteen hundred people, mostly of the Nunari *qaum*, or "tribe." The Nunaris engage primarily in agriculture (wheat, rice, sugar cane, and cotton), and most families own small plots of land. Members of the Bhatti tribe constitute the largest minority in the village. Although traditionally a warrior tribe, the Bhattis serve in the main as the village artisans and craftsmen.

On my first day in the village I tried explaining in great detail the purposes of my study to the village elders and clan leaders. Despite my efforts, most of the elders were perplexed about why I wanted to live in their village. As a guest, I was entitled to the hospitality traditionally bestowed by Muslim peoples of Asia, and during the first evening I was assigned a place to stay. But I was an enigma, for guests leave, and I wanted to remain. I was also perceived as being strange, for I was both a non-Muslim and a non-Punjabi, a type of person not heretofore encountered by most of the villagers. Although I tried to temper my behavior, there was little I could say or do to dissuade my hosts from the view that I embodied the antithesis of Punjabi values. While I was able to converse in their language, Jatki, a dialect of western Punjabi, I was only able to do so with the ability of a four-year-old. This achievement fell far short of speaking the *t'et'*, or "genuine form," of the villagers. Their idiom is rich with the terminology of agricultural operations and rural life. It is unpretentious, uninflected, and direct, and villagers hold high opinions of those who are good with words, who can speak to a point and be convincing. Needless to say, my infantile babble realized none of these characteristics and evoked no such respect.

Similarly, even though I wore indigenous dress, I was inept at tying my *lungi*, or pant cloth. The fact that my *lungi* occasionally fell off and revealed what was underneath gave my neighbors reason to believe that I indeed had no shame and could not control the passions of my *nafs*, or "libidinous nature."

This image of a doltish, shameless infidel barely capable of caring for himself lasted for the first week of my residence in the village. My inability to distinguish among the five varieties of rice and four varieties of lentil grown in the village illustrated that I knew or cared little about nature and agricultural enterprise. This display of ignorance only served to confirm the general consensus that the mysterious morsels I ate from tin cans labeled "Chef Boy-ar-Dee" were not really food at all. Additionally, I did not oil and henna my hair, shave my armpits, or perform ablutions, thereby convincing some commentators that I was a member of a species of subhuman beings, possessing little in the form of either common or moral sense. That the villagers did not quite grant me the status of a person was reflected by their not according me a proper name. In the Punjab, a person's name is equated with honor and respect and is symbolized by his turban. A man who does not have a name, or whose name is not recognized by his neighbors, is unworthy of respect. For such a man, his turban is said to be either nonexistent or to lie in the dust at the feet of others. To be given a name is to have one's head crowned by a turban, an acknowledgment that one leads a responsible and respectable life. Although I repeatedly introduced myself as "Rashid Karim," a fairly decent Pakistani rendering of Richard Kurin, just about all the villagers insisted on calling me *Angrez* ("Englishman"), thus denying me full personhood and implicitly refusing to grant me the right to wear a turban.

As I began to pick up the vernacular, to question villagers about their clan and kinship structure and trace out relationships between different families, my image began to change. My drawings of kinship diagrams and preliminary census mappings were looked upon not only with wonder but also suspicion. My neighbors now began to think there might be a method to my madness. And so there was. Now I had become a spy. Of course it took a week for people to figure out whom I was supposedly spying for. Located as they were at a cross-roads of Asia, at a nexus of conflicting geopolitical interests, they had many possibilities to consider. There was a good deal of disagreement on the issue, with the vast majority maintaining that I was either an American, Russian, or Indian spy. A small, but nonetheless vocal, minority held steadfastly to the belief that I was a Chinese spy. I thought it all rather humorous until one day a group confronted me in the main square in front of the nine-by-nine-foot mud hut that I had rented. The leader spoke up and accused me of spying. The remainder of the group grumbled *jahsus! jahsus!* ("spy! spy!"), and I realized that this ad hoc committee of inquiry had the potential of becoming a mob.

To be sure, the villagers had good reason to be suspicious. For one, the times were tense in Pakistan—a national political crisis gripped the country and the populace had been anxious for months over the uncertainty of elections and effective governmental functions. Second, keenly aware of their history, some of the villagers did not have to go too far to imagine that I was at the vanguard of some invading group that had designs upon their land. Such intrigues, with far greater sophistication, had been played out before by nations seeking to expand their power into the Punjab. That I possessed a gold seal letter (which no one save myself could read) from the University of Chicago to the effect that I was pursuing legitimate studies was not enough to convince the crowd that I was indeed an innocent scholar.

I repeatedly denied the charge, but to no avail. The shouts of *jahsus! jahsus!* prevailed. Confronted with this I had no choice.

"Okay," I said. "I admit it. I am a spy!"

The crowd quieted for my long-awaited confession.

"I am a spy and am here to study this village, so that when my country attacks you we will be prepared. You see, we will not bomb Lahore or Karachi or Islamabad. Why should we waste our bombs on millions of people, on factories, dams, airports, and harbors? No, it is far more advantageous to bomb this strategic small village replete with its mud huts, livestock, Persian wheels, and one light bulb. And when we bomb this village, it is imperative that we know how Allah Ditta is related to Abdullah, and who owns the land near the well, and what your marriage customs are."

Silence hung over the crowd, and then one by one the assemblage began to disperse. My sarcasm had worked. The spy charges were defused. But I was no hero in light of my performance, and so I was once again relegated to the status of a nonperson without an identity in the village.

I remained in limbo for the next week, and although I continued my attempts to collect information about village life, I had my doubts as to whether I would ever be accepted by the villagers. And then, through no effort of my own, there was a breakthrough, this time due to another Allah Ditta, a relative of the village headman and one of my leading accusers during my spying days.

I was sitting on my woven string bed on my porch when Allah Ditta approached, leading his son by the neck. "Oh, *Angrez!*" he yelled, "this worthless son of mine is doing poorly in school. He is supposed to be learning English, but he is failing. He has a good mind, but he's lazy. And his teacher is no help, being more intent upon drinking tea and singing film songs than upon teaching English. Oh son of an Englishman, do you know English?"

"Yes, I know English," I replied, "after all, I am an *Angrez.*"

"Teach him," Allah Ditta blurted out, without any sense of making a tactful request.

And so, I spent the next hour with the boy, reviewing his lessons and correcting his pronunciation and grammar. As I did so, villagers stopped to watch and listen, and by the end of the hour, nearly one hundred people had gathered around, engrossed by this tutoring session. They were stupefied. I was an effective teacher, and I actually seemed to know English. The boy responded well, and the crowd reached a new consensus. I had a brain. And in recognition of this achievement I was given a name—"Ustad Rashid," or Richard the Teacher.

Achieving the status of a teacher was only the beginning of my success. The next morning I awoke to find the village sugar vendor at my door. He had a headache and wanted to know if I could cure him.

"Why do you think I can help you?" I asked.

Bhai Khan answered, "Because you are a *ustad,* you have a great deal of knowledge."

The logic was certainly compelling. If I could teach English, I should be able to cure a headache. I gave him two aspirins.

An hour later, my fame had spread. Bhai Khan had been cured, and he did not hesitate to let others know that it was the *ustad* who had been responsible. By the next day, and in fact for the remainder of my stay, I was to see an average of twenty-five to thirty patients a day. I was asked to cure everything from coughs and colds to typhoid, elephantiasis, and impotency. Upon establishing a flourishing and free medical practice, I received another title, *hakim,* or "physician." I was not yet an anthropologist, but I was on my way.

A few days later I took on yet another role. One of my research interests involved tracing out patterns of land ownership and inheritance. While working on the problem of figuring out who owned what, I was approached by the village watchman. He claimed he had been swindled in a land deal and requested my help. As the accused was not another villager, I agreed to present the watchman's case to the local authorities.

Somehow, my efforts managed to achieve results. The plaintiff's grievance was redressed, and I was given yet another title in the village—*wakil,* or "lawyer." And in the weeks that followed, I was steadily called upon to read, translate, and advise upon various court orders that affected the lives of the villagers.

My roles as teacher, doctor, and lawyer not only provided me with an identity but also facilitated my integration into the economic structure of the community. As my imputed skills offered my neighbors services not readily available in the village, I was drawn into exchange relationships known as *seipi. Seipi* refers to the barter system of goods and services among village farmers, craftsmen, artisans, and other specialists. Every morning Roshan the milkman would deliver fresh milk to my hut. Every other day Hajam Ali the barber would stop by and give me a shave. My next-door neighbor, Nura the cobbler, would repair my sandals when required. Ghulam the horse-cart driver would transport me to town when my motor scooter was in disrepair. The parents of my students would send me sweets and sometimes delicious meals. In return, none of my neighbors asked for direct payment for the specific actions performed. Rather, as they told me, they would call upon me when they had need of my services. And they did. Nura needed cough syrup for his children, the milkman's brother needed a job contact in the city, students wanted to continue their lessons, and so on. Through *seipi* relations, various neighbors gave goods and services to me, and I to them.

Even so, I knew that by Punjabi standards I could never be truly accepted into village life because I was not a member of either the Nunari or Bhatti tribe. As the villagers would say, "You never really know who a man is until you know who his grandfather and his ancestors were." And to know a person's grandfather or ancestors properly, you had to be a member of the same or a closely allied tribe.

The Nunari tribe is composed of a number of groups. The nucleus consists of four clans—Naul, Vadel, Sadan, and More—each named for one of four brothers thought to have originally founded the tribe. Clan members are said to be related to blood ties, also called *pag da sak*, or "ties of the turban." In sharing the turban, members of each clan share the same name. Other clans, unrelated by ties of blood to these four, have become attached to this nucleus through a history of marital relations or of continuous political and economic interdependence. Marital relations, called *gag da sak*, or "ties of the skirt," are conceived of as relations in which alienable turbans (skirts) in the form of women are exchanged with other, non-turban-sharing groups. Similarly, ties of political and economic domination and subordination are thought of as relations in which the turban of the client is given to that of the patron. A major part of my research work was concerned with reconstructing how the four brothers formed the Nunari tribe, how additional clans became associated with it, and how clan and tribal identity were defined by nomenclature, codes of honor, and the symbols of sharing and exchanging turbans.

To approach these issues I set out to reconstruct the genealogical relationships within the tribe and between the various clans. I elicited genealogies from many of the villagers and questioned older informants about the history of the Nunari tribe. Most knew only bits and pieces of this history, and after several months of interviews and research, I was directed to the tribal genealogists. These people, usually not Nunaris themselves, perform the service of memorizing and then orally relating the history of the tribe and the relationships among its members. The genealogist in the village was an aged and arthritic man named Hedayat, who in his later years was engaged in teaching the Nunari genealogy to his son, who would then carry out the traditional and hereditary duties of his position.

The villagers claimed that Hedayat knew every generation of the Nunari from the present to the founding brothers and even beyond. So I invited Hedayat to my hut and explained my purpose.

"Do you know Allah Ditta son of Rohm?" I asked.

"Yes, of course," he replied.

"Who was Rohm's father?" I continued.

"Shahadat Mohammad," he answered.

"And his father?"

"Hamid."

"And his?"

"Chigatah," he snapped without hesitation.

I was now quite excited, for no one else in the village had been able to recall an ancestor of this generation. My estimate was that Chigatah had been born sometime between 1850 and 1870. But Hedayat went on.

"Chigatah's father was Kamal. And Kamal's father was Nanak. And Nanak's father was Sikhu. And before him was Dargai, and before him Maiy. And before him was Siddiq. And Siddiq's father was Nur. And Nur's Asmat. And Asmat was of Channa. And Channa of Nau. And Nau of Bhatta. And Bhatta was the son of Koduk."

Hedayat had now recounted sixteen generations of lineal ascendants related through the turban. Koduk was probably born in the sixteenth century. But still Hedayat continued.

"Sigun was the father of Koduk. And Man the father of Sigun. And before Man was his father Maneswar. And Maneswar's father was the founder of the clan, Naul."

This then was a line of the Naul clan of the Nunari tribe, ascending twenty-one generations from the present descendants (Allah Ditta's sons) to the founder, one of four brothers who lived perhaps in the fifteenth century. I asked Hedayat to recite genealogies of the other Nunari clans, and he did, with some blanks here and there, ending with Vadel, More, and Saddan, the other three brothers who formed the tribal nucleus. I then asked the obvious question, "Hedayat, who was the father of these four brothers? Who is the founding ancestor of the Nunari tribe?"

"The father of these brothers was not a Muslim. He was an Indian rajput [chief]. The tribe actually begins with the conversion of the four brothers," Hedayat explained.

"Well then," I replied, "who was this Indian chief?"

He was a famous and noble chief who fought against the Moguls. His name was Raja Kurin, who lived in a massive fort in Kurinnagar, about twenty-seven miles from Delhi."

"What!" I asked, both startled and unsure of what I had heard.

"Raja Kurin is the father of the brothers who make up—"

"But his name! It's the same as mine," I stammered. "Hedayat, my name is Richard Kurin. What a coincidence! Here I am living with your tribe thousands of miles from my home and it turns out that I have the same name as the founder of the tribe! Do you think I might be related to Raja Kurin and the Nunaris?"

Hedayat looked at me, but only for an instant. Redoing his turban, he tilted his head skyward, smiled, and asked, "What is the name of your father?"

I had come a long way. I now had a name that could be recognized and respected, and as I answered Hedayat, I knew that I had finally and irrevocably fit into "my" village. Whether by fortuitous circumstances or by careful manipulation, my neighbors had found a way to take an invading city person intent on studying their life and transform him into one of their own, a full person entitled to wear a turban for participating in, and being identified with, that life. As has gone on for centuries in the region, once again the new and exogenous had been recast into something Punjabi.

Epilogue: There is no positive evidence linking the Nunaris to a historical Raja Kurin, although there are several famous personages identified by that name (also transcribed as Karan and Kurran). Estimated from the genealogy recited by Hedayat, the founding of the tribe by the four brothers appears to have occurred sometime between 440 and 640 years ago, depending on the interval assumed for each generation. On that basis, the most likely candidate for Nunari progenitor (actual or imputed) is Raja Karan, ruler of Anhilvara (Gujerat), who was defeated by the Khilji Ala-ud-Din in 1297 and again in 1307. Although this is slightly earlier than suggested by the genealogical data, such genealogies are often telescoped or otherwise unreliable.

Nevertheless, several aspects of Hedayat's account make this association doubtful. Hedayat clearly identifies Raja Kurin's conquerors as Moguls, whereas the Gujerati Raja Karan was defeated by the Khiljis. Second, Hedayat places the Nunari ancestor's kingdom only twenty-seven miles from Delhi. The Gujerati Raja Karan ruled several kingdoms, none closer than several hundred miles to Delhi.

Other circumstances, however, offer support for this identification of the Nunari ancestor. According to Hedayat, Raja Kurin's father was named Kam Deo. Although the historical figure was the son of Serung Deo, the use of "Deo," a popular title for the rajas of the Vaghela and Solonki dynasties, does seem to place the Nunari founder in the context of medieval Gujerat. Furthermore, Hedayat clearly identifies the saint (pir) said to have initiated the conversion of the Nunaris to Islam. This saint, Mukhdum-i-Jehaniyan, was a contemporary of the historical Raja Karan.

Also of interest, but as yet unexplained, is that several other groups living in Nunari settlement areas specifically claim to be descended from Raja Karan of Gujerat, who is said to have migrated northward into the Punjab after his defeat. Controverting this theory, the available evidence indicates that Raja Karan fled, not toward the Punjab, but rather southward to the Deccan, and that his patriline ended with him. It is his daughter Deval Devi who is remembered: she is the celebrated heroine of "Ashiqa," a famous Urdu poem written by Amir Khusrau in 1316. She was married to Khizr Khan, the son of Karan's conqueror; nothing is known of her progeny.

Eating Christmas in the Kalahari

Richard Borshay Lee

Richard Borshay Lee is a full professor of anthropology at the University of Toronto. He has done extensive field-work in southern Africa, is coeditor of Man the Hunter *(1968) and* Kalahari Hunter-Gatherers *(1976), and author of* The !Kung San: Men, Women, and Work in a Foraging Society.

The !Kung Bushmen's knowledge of Christmas is thirdhand. The London Missionary Society brought the holiday to the southern Tswana tribes in the early nineteenth century. Later, native catechists spread the idea far and wide among the Bantu-speaking pastoralists, even in the remotest corners of the Kalahari Desert. The Bushmen's idea of the Christmas story, stripped to its essentials, is "praise the birth of white man's god-chief"; what keeps their interest in the holiday high is the Tswana-Herero custom of slaughtering an ox for his Bushmen neighbors as an annual goodwill gesture. Since the 1930's, part of the Bushmen's annual round of activities has included a December congregation at the cattle posts for trading, marriage brokering, and several days of trance-dance feasting at which the local Tswana headman is host.

As a social anthropologist working with !Kung Bushmen, I found that the Christmas ox custom suited my purposes. I had come to the Kalahari to study the hunting and gathering subsistence economy of the !Kung, and to accomplish this it was essential not to provide them with food, share my own food, or interfere in any way with their food-gathering activities. While liberal handouts of tobacco and medical supplies were appreciated, they were scarcely adequate to erase the glaring disparity in wealth between the anthropologist, who maintained a two-month inventory of canned goods, and the Bushmen, who rarely had a day's supply of food on hand. My approach, while paying off in terms of data, left me open to frequent accusations of stinginess and hard-heartedness. By their lights, I was a miser.

The Christmas ox was to be my way of saying thank you for the cooperation of the past year; and since it was to be our last Christmas in the field, I determined to slaughter the largest, meatiest ox that money could buy, insuring that the feast and trance-dance would be a success.

Through December I kept my eyes open at the wells as the cattle were brought down for watering. Several animals were offered, but none had quite the grossness that I had in mind. Then, ten days before the holiday, a Herero friend led an ox of astonishing size and mass up to our camp. It was solid black, stood five feet high at the shoulder, had a five-foot span of horns, and must have weighed 1,200 pounds on the hoof. Food consumption calculations are my specialty, and I quickly figured that bones and viscera aside, there was enough meat—at least four pounds—for every man, woman, and child of the 150 Bushmen in the vicinity of /ai/ai who were expected at the feast.

Having found the right animal at last, I paid the Herero £20 ($56) and asked him to keep the beast with his herd until Christmas day. The next morning word spread among the people that the big solid black one was the ox chosen by /ontah (my Bushman name; it means, roughly, "whitey") for the Christmas feast. That afternoon I received the first delegation. Ben!a, an outspoken sixty-year-old mother of five, came to the point slowly.

"Where were you planning to eat Christmas?"

"Right here at /ai/ai," I replied.

"Alone or with others?"

"I expect to invite all the people to eat Christmas with me."

"Eat what?"

"I have purchased Yehave's black ox, and I am going to slaughter and cook it."

"That's what we were told at the well but refused to believe it until we heard it from yourself."

"Well, it's the black one," I replied expansively, although wondering what she was driving at.

"Oh, no!" Ben!a groaned, turning to her group. "They were right." Turning back to me she asked, "Do you expect us to eat that bag of bones?"

"Bag of bones! It's the biggest ox at /ai/ai."

"Big, yes, but old. And thin. Everybody knows there's no meat on that old ox. What did you expect us to eat off it, the horns?"

Everybody chuckled at Ben!a's one-liner as they walked away, but all I could manage was a weak grin.

That evening it was the turn of the young men. They came to sit at our evening fire. /gaugo, about my age, spoke to me man-to-man.

"/ontah, you have always been square with us," he lied. "What has happened to change your heart? That sack of guts and bones of Yehave's will hardly feed one camp, let alone all the Bushmen around /ai/ai." And he proceeded to enumerate the seven camps in the /ai/ai vicinity, family by family. "Perhaps you have forgotten that we are not few, but many. Or are you too blind to tell the difference between a proper cow and an old wreck? That ox is thin to the point of death."

"Look, you guys," I retorted, "that is a beautiful animal, and I'm sure you will eat it with pleasure at Christmas."

"Of course we will eat it; it's food. But it won't fill us up to the point where we will have enough strength to dance. We will eat and go home to bed with stomachs rumbling."

That night as we turned in, I asked my wife, Nancy: "What did you think of the black ox?"

"It looked enormous to me. Why?"

"Well, about eight different people have told me I got gypped; that the ox is nothing but bones."

"What's the angle?" Nancy asked. "Did they have a better one to sell?"

"No, they just said that it was going to be a grim Christmas because there won't be enough meat to go around. Maybe I'll get an independent judge to look at the beast in the morning."

Bright and early, Halingisi, a Tswana cattle owner, appeared at our camp. But before I could ask him to give me his opinion on Yehave's black ox, he gave me the eye signal that indicated a confidential chat. We left the camp and sat down.

"/ontah, I'm surprised at you: you've lived here for three years and still haven't learned anything about cattle."

"But what else can a person do but choose the biggest, strongest animal one can find?" I retorted.

"Look, just because an animal is big doesn't mean that it has plenty of meat on it. The black one was a beauty when it was younger, but now it is thin to the point of death."

"Well I've already bought it. What can I do at this stage?"

"Bought it already? I thought you were just considering it. Well, you'll have to kill it and serve it, I suppose. But don't expect much of a dance to follow."

My spirits dropped rapidly. I could believe that Ben!a and /gaugo just might be putting me on about the black ox, but Halingisi seemed to be an impartial critic. I went around that day feeling as though I had bought a lemon of a used car.

In the afternoon it was Tomazo's turn. Tomazo is a fine hunter, a top trance performer . . . and one of my most reliable informants. He approached the subject of the Christmas cow as part of my continuing Bushman education.

"My friend, the way it is with us Bushmen," he began, "is that we love meat. And even more than that, we love fat. When we hunt we always search for the fat ones, the ones dripping with layers of white fat: fat that turns into a clear, thick oil in the cooking pot, fat that slides down your gullet, fills your stomach and gives you a roaring diarrhea," he rhapsodized.

"So, feeling as we do," he continued, "it gives us pain to be served such a scrawny thing as Yehave's black ox. It is big, yes, and no doubt its giant bones are good for soup, but fat is what we really crave and so we will eat Christmas this year with a heavy heart."

The prospect of a gloomy Christmas now had me worried, so I asked Tomazo what I could do about it.

"Look for a fat one, a young one . . . smaller, but fat. Fat enough to make us //gom ('evacuate the bowels'), then we will be happy."

My suspicions were aroused when Tomazo said that he happened to know of a young, fat, barren cow that the owner was willing to part with. Was Tomazo working on commission, I wondered? But I dispelled this unworthy thought when we approached the Herero owner of the cow in question and found that he had decided not to sell.

The scrawny wreck of a Christmas ox now became the talk of the /ai/ai water hole and was the first news told to the outlying groups as they began to come in from the bush for the feast. What finally convinced me that real trouble might be brewing was the visit from u!au, an old conservative with a reputation for fierceness. His nickname meant spear and referred to an incident thirty years ago in which he had speared a man to death. He had an intense manner; fixing me with his eyes, he said in clipped tones:

"I have only just heard about the black ox today, or else I would have come here earlier. /ontah, do you honestly think you can serve meat like that to people and avoid a fight?" He paused, letting the implications sink in. "I don't mean fight you, /ontah; you are a white man. I mean a fight between Bushmen. There are many fierce ones here, and with such a small quantity of meat to distribute, how can you give everybody a fair share? Someone is sure to accuse another of taking too much or hogging all the choice pieces. Then you will see what happens when some go hungry while others eat."

The possibility of at least a serious argument struck me as all too real. I had witnessed the tension that surrounds the distribution of meat from a kudu or gemsbok kill, and had documented many arguments that sprang up from a real or imagined slight in meat distribution. The owners of a kill may spend up to two hours arranging and rearranging the piles of meat under the gaze of a circle of recipients before handing them out. And I also knew that the Christmas feast at /ai/ai would be bringing together groups that had feuded in the past.

Convinced now of the gravity of the situation, I went in earnest to search for a second cow; but all my inquiries failed to turn one up.

The Christmas feast was evidently going to be a disaster, and the incessant complaints about the meagerness of the ox had already taken the fun out of it for me. Moreover, I was

27

getting bored with the wisecracks, and after losing my temper a few times, I resolved to serve the beast anyway. If the meat fell short, the hell with it. In the Bushmen idiom, I announced to all who would listen:

"I am a poor man and blind. If I have chosen one that is too old and too thin, we will eat it anyway and see if there is enough meat there to quiet the rumbling of our stomachs."

On hearing this speech, Ben!a offered me a rare word of comfort. "It's thin," she said philosophically, "but the bones will make a good soup."

At dawn Christmas morning, instinct told me to turn over the butchering and cooking to a friend and take off with Nancy to spend Christmas alone in the bush. But curiosity kept me from retreating. I wanted to see what such a scrawny ox looked like on butchering, and if there *was* going to be a fight, I wanted to catch every word of it. Anthropologists are incurable that way.

The great beast was driven up to our dancing ground, and a shot in the forehead dropped it in its tracks. Then, freshly cut branches were heaped around the fallen carcass to receive the meat. Ten men volunteered to help with the cutting. I asked /gaugo to make the breast bone cut. This cut, which begins the butchering process for most large game, offers easy access for removal of the viscera. But it also allows the hunter to spot-check the amount of fat on the animal. A fat game animal carries a white layer up to an inch thick on the chest, while in a thin one, the knife will quickly cut to bone. All eyes fixed on his hand as /gaugo, dwarfed by the great carcass, knelt to the breast. The first cut opened a pool of solid white in the black skin. The second and third cut widened and deepened the creamy white. Still no bone. It was pure fat; it must have been two inches thick.

"Hey /gau," I burst out, "that ox is loaded with fat. What's this about the ox being too thin to bother eating? Are you out of your mind?"

"Fat?" /gau shot back, "You call that fat? This wreck is thin, sick, dead!" And he broke out laughing. So did everyone else. They rolled on the ground, paralyzed with laughter. Everybody laughed except me; I was thinking.

I ran back to the tent and burst in just as Nancy was getting up. "Hey, the black ox. It's fat as hell! They were kidding about it being too thin to eat. It was a joke or something. A put-on. Everyone is really delighted with it!"

"Some joke," my wife replied. "It was so funny that you were ready to pack up and leave /ai/ai."

If it had indeed been a joke, it had been an extraordinarily convincing one, and tinged, I thought, with more than a touch of malice as many jokes are. Nevertheless, that it was a joke lifted my spirits considerably, and I returned to the butchering site where the shape of the ox was rapidly disappearing under the axes and knives of the butchers. The atmosphere had become festive. Grinning broadly, their arms covered with blood well past the elbow, men packed chunks of meat into the big cast-iron cooking pots, fifty pounds to the load, and muttered and chuckled all the while about the thinness and worthlessness of the animal and /ontah's poor judgment.

We danced and ate that ox two days and two nights; we cooked and distributed fourteen potfuls of meat and no one went home hungry and no fights broke out.

But the "joke" stayed in my mind. I had a growing feeling that something important had happened in my relationship with the Bushmen and that the clue lay in the meaning of the joke. Several days later, when most of the people had dispersed back to the bush camps, I raised the question with Hakekgose, a Tswana man who had grown up among the !Kung, married a !Kung girl, and who probably knew their culture better than any other non-Bushman.

"With us whites," I began, "Christmas is supposed to be the day of friendship and brotherly love. What I can't figure out is why the Bushmen went to such lengths to criticize and belittle the ox I had bought for the feast. The animal was perfectly good and their jokes and wisecracks practically ruined the holiday for me."

"So it really did bother you," said Hakekgose. "Well, that's the way they always talk. When I take my rifle and go hunting with them, if I miss, they laugh at me for the rest of the day. But even if I hit and bring one down, it's no better. To them, the kill is always too small or too old or too thin; and as we sit down on the kill site to cook and eat the liver, they keep grumbling, even with their mouths full of meat. They say things like, 'Oh this is awful! What a worthless animal! Whatever made me think that this Tswana rascal could hunt!'"

"Is this the way outsiders are treated?" I asked.

"No, it is their custom; they talk that way to each other too. Go and ask them."

/gaugo had been one of the most enthusiastic in making me feel bad about the merit of the Christmas ox. I sought him out first.

"Why did you tell me the black ox was worthless, when you could see that it was loaded with fat and meat?"

"It is our way," he said smiling. "We always like to fool people about that. Say there is a Bushman who has been hunting. He must not come home and announce like a braggard, 'I have killed a big one in the bush!' He must first sit down in silence until I or someone else comes up to his fire and asks, 'What did you see today?' He replies quietly, 'Ah, I'm no good for hunting. I saw nothing at all [pause] just a little tiny one.' Then I smile to myself," /gaugo continued, "because I know he has killed something big.

"In the morning we make up a party of four or five people to cut up and carry the meat back to the camp. When we arrive at the kill we examine it and cry out, 'You mean to say you have dragged us all the way out here in order to make us cart home your pile of bones? Oh, if I had known it was this thin I wouldn't have come.' Another one pipes up, 'People, to think I gave up a nice day in the shade for this. At home we may be hungry but at least we have nice cool water to drink.' If the horns are big, someone says, 'Did you think that somehow you were going to boil down the horns for soup?'

"To all this you must respond in kind. 'I agree,' you say, 'this one is not worth the effort; let's just cook the liver for strength and leave the rest for the hyenas. It is not too late to hunt today and even a duiker or a steenbok would be better than this mess.'

"Then you set to work nevertheless; butcher the animal, carry the meat back to the camp and everyone eats," /gaugo concluded.

Things were beginning to make sense. Next, I went to Tomazo. He corroborated /gaugo's story of the obligatory insults over a kill and added a few details of his own.

"But," I asked, "why insult a man after he has gone to all that trouble to track and kill an animal and when he is going to share the meat with you so that your children will have something to eat?"

"Arrogance," was his cryptic answer.

"Arrogance?"

"Yes, when a young man kills much meat he comes to think of himself as a chief or a big man, and he thinks of the rest of us as his servants or inferiors. We can't accept this. We refuse one who boasts, for someday his pride will make him kill somebody. So we always speak of his meat as worthless. This way we cool his heart and make him gentle."

"But why didn't you tell me this before?" I asked Tomazo with some heat.

"Because you never asked me," said Tomazo, echoing the refrain that has come to haunt every field ethnographer.

The pieces now fell into place. I had known for a long time that in situations of social conflict with Bushmen I held all the cards. I was the only source of tobacco in a thousand square miles, and I was not incapable of cutting an individual off for noncooperation. Though my boycott never lasted longer than a few days, it was an indication of my strength. People resented my presence at the water hole, yet simultaneously dreaded my leaving. In short I was a perfect target for the charge of arrogance and for the Bushmen tactic of enforcing humility.

I had been taught an object lesson by the Bushmen; it had come from an unexpected corner and had hurt me in a vulnerable area. For the big black ox was to be the one totally generous, unstinting act of my year at /ai/ai, and I was quite unprepared for the reaction I received.

As I read it, their message was this: There are no totally generous acts. All "acts" have an element of calculation. One black ox slaughtered at Christmas does not wipe out a year of careful manipulation of gifts given to serve your own ends. After all, to kill an animal and share the meat with people is really no more than Bushmen do for each other every day and with far less fanfare.

In the end, I had to admire how the Bushmen had played out the farce— collectively straight-faced to the end. Curiously, the episode reminded me of the *Good Soldier Schweik* and his marvelous encounters with authority. Like Schweik, the Bushmen had retained a thorough-going skepticism of good intentions. Was it this independence of spirit, I wondered, that had kept them culturally viable in the face of generations of contact with more powerful societies, both black and white? The thought that the Bushmen were alive and well in the Kalahari was strangely comforting. Perhaps, armed with that independence and with their superb knowledge of their environment, they might yet survive the future.

A Cross-Cultural Experience: A Chinese Anthropologist in the United States

Huang Shu-min

Huang Shu-min is a professor of Anthropology at Iowa State University, where he has been teaching since 1975. Born and raised in China and Taiwan, Huang spent much of his research periods in these two regions. He received his B.A. in Anthropology from National Taiwan University (1967) and his M.A. and Ph.D. in Anthropology from Michigan State University (1973, 1977).

Using a variety of interesting and sometimes humorous encounters with Americans, Professor Huang Shu-min describes how these experiences can lead to a better understanding of one's own culture. He emphasizes that although these experiences can lead to greater awareness, it is difficult even for anthropologists to free themselves of the assumptions about their own culture.

Born and raised in many areas of China, including the Mainland, Hong Kong, and Taiwan, I have developed a deep appreciation for the enormous cultural variations in China. Ever since I can remember, I seemed to have been surrounded by people—including my own family members—who speak many languages and entertain various tastes in food and clothing that characterize regional differences in China.

However, despite my exposure to such a diverse way of life, I was probably brought up as a normal, average Chinese, taught to believe in the traditional Chinese values, manners, and beliefs characteristic of Confucian literati. A reverence for age and custom, a high motivation toward scholarly achievement, and a strong sense of responsibility toward society had all been incorporated into my thinking throughout the process of growth.

Contact with anthropology in my college years in Taiwan, however, brought about basic changes in my life. Anthropology claims that much of our behavior, customs, and even ways of thinking are molded by our culture, which is essentially a set of artificially designed symbols accumulated throughout human history. Accepting such a premise, I began to question the validity and rationale of all the values, beliefs, and even ways of thinking that I once had stood for and cherished. As a consequence, I was, to borrow a phrase from Muriel Dimen-Schein (1977), "drawn to its (anthropology's) moral emphasis that our culture was not the best or only way to live, and alternatives existed." My soul-searching along this line has not led to a total rejection of my culture; rather, I began to develop a habit of looking at my own behavior from an objective point of view and to be critical of things that I had taken for granted.

My career in anthropology has eventually brought me to study and to teach in the United States. Situated in an entirely different culture, I have been able not only to look at my own culture from this objective point of view but also to make a constant comparison between my own cultural practices and those of Americans. To bring my professional training into everyday situations, which involves explaining ordinary events against both the Chinese and American frames of thought, I have tried to explore the extent to which human beings are influenced by their specific cultures. The following incidents have occurred during my residence in the United States and form the foundation for some of my reflections.

INTRODUCTION TO AMERICA

My initiation into American culture was through my older sister, who had lived in San Francisco for some time before I arrived in 1970. Apparently aghast at my appearance when we met at the airport, especially my dandruff-ridden hair and unshaved face, she warned me that Americans are extremely sensitive about physical appearances. I should from then on use dandruff-proof shampoo and shave my face every day—even though there is not much to work on.

I was puzzled by her notions, for I had heard about the counterculture movement in the United States, especially on campuses across the country. My limited knowledge about the counterculture seemed to indicate the development of an alternative way of life, which also implied, to some extent, the rejection of American middle-class values. If that was the case, why bother with this physical appearance–laden life-style? I kept this question to myself, for I thought my sister was just old-fashioned and conservative, and so there was no point in arguing with her.

I stayed in San Francisco for a month, and during that period I made many sightseeing tours around the city. My specific interest was in the hippie ghettoes. As a novice in anthropology, I believed that the counterculture movement presented a unique opportunity to study how culture can be changed in a well-intentioned manner. Based on my superficial observations, these people appeared to be sincere about developing an alternative way of life in direct opposition to that of middle-class values: long and uncombed hair, bare feet, patched blue jeans and free-floating along the sidewalks, for example.

I was very much impressed by what I saw. But then I suddenly noticed that I had not seen anyone with dandruff. I brought up this question to an acquaintance who was very much involved in this particular way of life. "Oh, yes," he replied in a typically nonchalant manner, "dandruff is indeed a problem to many of us. But we use dandruff-proof shampoo."

Disappointed? No. It only confirmed an idea that I had but could not prove with evidence: While we may claim to reject our culture's values and moral standards en masse, in the deeper layer of the heart and mind, our thinking and behavior may still operate, even though unconsciously, under the same set of beliefs.

CULTURE AND HAIR COLOR

My graduate years at Michigan State University were some of the most interesting experiences during my time at school. We had a large student body—thirty-odd in my first-year class. A great number of my classmates were from different nations, and many of the other American students also had had personal experiences in other parts of the world. We formed a very close group, often having parties, picnics, and other activities together.

One day after class, we stayed in the classroom chatting about recent events. Suddenly, someone in the group mentioned the long absence of a female classmate: "Strange, I have not seen the little redhead for the past few days!"

Little redhead? The notion did not ring a bell at all. How could he refer to someone in such a strange way? Did this person really have red hair? Why had I never noticed this? I took a hard look around the classroom and realized that there were indeed different hair styles and colors among my classmates, something that I had never paid attention to!

The discovery that Americans frequently divide their hair into categories and use this taxonomical difference as a point of reference was something entirely new to me. Chinese would never refer to another person by describing his or her hair, for every Chinese has dark, straight hair, except the aged and bald. Because hair is an insignificant difference, Chinese probably do not have an acute conceptual system to categorize people on the basis of hair traits and, as a consequence, tend to neglect this physical characteristic entirely.

PRIMARY AND SECONDARY LANGUAGES

One incident that happened before I came to the States puzzled me for some time. In 1969, I was working with Professor and Mrs. Gallin in Taipei, studying rural migrants in the city. One day my father came to see me and also had a chat with Professor Gallin. Because my father does not speak English and his Mandarin has an accent that Professor Gallin could not quite follow, I had to serve as translator in the conversation. When my father spoke to me for the translation, I noticed that he used Taiwanese (or Min-nan), the native language in Taiwan, instead of the Mandarin or Cantonese that we normally use. Even though my father and I speak flawless Taiwanese, we never use it in our direct, personal conversation.

So, I mildly reminded my father that because Professor Gallin is not a Taiwanese, and because he was talking to him through me, there was no need to use this particular language. My suggestion was to no avail, and my father kept speaking to me in Taiwanese. After a few more protests, I decided to ignore it, thinking that my father was probably too excited by speaking to a "foreign barbarian."

When studying in Michigan, a similar incident occurred, which rekindled my old puzzlement. One day I was in the Gallins' house when another professor came for a visit and brought with him an Austrian friend. It was late in the afternoon, and we all decided to stay for dinner at the Gallins' invitation. Over the dinner table, Professor Gallin talked to this Austrian visitor about some general things, and suddenly he spoke in Chinese to this Austrian. He said, *Ch'ing-lai, puke-ch'i,* which literally means, "Please help yourself; don't be polite." Unaware of this slip of the tongue, Professor Gallin continued the conversation in English.

These two incidents led me to theorize that cognition probably operates on several planes. The first and probably the most "instinctive" cognitive plane involves a person's primary language and the intimate way of life and cultural values in which one is brought up. Beyond this are the secondary and tertiary planes, which involve bodies of knowledge of foreign cultures. So when people encounter another person who does not belong to their primary cognitive community, they would probably immediately project their secondary or tertiary cognitive systems to this person, thinking that would fit the circumstance. If my hypothesis is correct, then there would be nothing unusual if we see a student majoring in Spanish who tries to communicate with a Japanese tourist in Spanish!

1. ANTHROPOLOGICAL PERSPECTIVES

WHAT NOT TO SAY

It is a custom for Chinese to say something auspicious when two newly met friends part. Phrases like "Wish you make a fortune," or "Wish you success in your business" (or study, voyage, and so on) are appropriate on such occasions. Because in traditional China marriage was often arranged by parents, it was quite common for one to greet a couple in love with a phrase like "Wish you marry soon"—meaning that this couple would convince their parents to accept their own choice. This kind of greeting is still commonly used in Taiwan, and I suspect it is also true in Hong Kong, although to a lesser extent. But, used in a different cultural context, this kind of expression may cause some problems.

Once I was invited to a party in which the American host and hostess entertained a couple of their friends and some Chinese students. We were introduced to the host's younger sister and her boyfriend—both were college students and had lived together for some time. They professed their emotional attachment toward each other and also indicated their suspicion concerning the meaning of a formal marriage: "We prefer our current arrangement," said the young man. "If two persons really love each other, there is no need to bind them together with some kind of socially sanctioned contract."

It was a pleasant evening, and about the time we were to leave, a Chinese student approached the young lovers and inadvertently said, "Wish to see you marry soon!"

He probably did not literally mean what he had said nor even realize what he had said. But the reaction from this young couple was obvious. The young man was stunned and stood there with a stiffened mouth. Blushing, the young woman protested, "But we don't believe in marriage!"

FOOD

One aspect of American culture that I have not been able to develop full appreciation of is food. Brought up in a culture whose menu contains a wide range of food varieties and flavors, I consider American food rather plain. And, worst of all, when I have American meals, I often feel full rather quickly, sometimes after just the salad. But then in a short while, I will feel hungry.

Originally, I thought that this was a phenomenon peculiar to me, mainly because I do not have a taste for American food and hence cannot eat too much of it. Believing that Chinese dishes have a better taste than anything else, I never had the slightest idea that Americans could have the same problem when eating Chinese food.

One day, my wife and I invited a few colleagues of mine over for supper. Our conversation somehow had focused on food preparation in different cultures. I jokingly remarked that even though I am an anthropologist by training, my appetite does not really match my intellectual capacity. I told them of the peculiar problem I had in eating American meals and indicated the possible reason as I saw it. On hearing that, one of our guests burst into laughter. "This is exactly the same problem I have when I come to your house for dinner," he said. "Even though I am quite full now, I will be very hungry by the time I arrive home. And I used to think this was so because of the strange taste of Chinese food!" I was surprised to find that the same opinion was shared by others.

I was puzzled by this cross-cultural eating problem. Perhaps the differences in taste are not the cause of the problem. Comparing dietary differences between American and Chinese food from another angle, I began to realize that food variety and content is the main difference between them. Chinese food contains many starchy items, such as rice, bean products, and vegetables, while American food has more meat tissue. When eating meals, the human digestive system probably has certain expectations on the quantity of specific items habitually established in the culture. People may feel full when the quota for certain food items has been met but still feel hungry for the unmet ones. For that reason, we may all have problems eating a cross-cultural meal.

A COMPLEX PHENOMENON

Human culture is a complex phenomenon: It provides a way of life, cues for actions, and logic for reasoning for the members of a cultural community. Because we frequently all too strongly adhere to our own culture, we fail to understand or appreciate the alternative ways of life. It is not an easy task to eliminate the cultural bias that hinders a mutual understanding across cultural boundaries. Even among anthropologists, who claim to study human cultures objectively, the same kind of prejudices persist, for we are products of our unique cultures as are any other human beings. Anthropologists may be credited for providing a large amount of literature describing the "other cultures." But perhaps more is needed. Other cultures may serve as a mirror for us to look at our own practices as culture-bound human beings. We need to be as critical of our own ways of thinking, value standards, and behavior patterns as we are of the cultures that we study. It is hoped that, by such a consistent practice of self-examination, we may come to understand the deeper meaning of culture on a first-hand basis.

ACKNOWLEDGEMENT

I am grateful to Professor and Mrs. Bernard Gallin, both at Michigan State University, for introducing me to anthropology and American culture. Appreciations are also due to my colleagues and associates at Iowa State University, especially those who were involved in the course, "Cross-Cultural Exploration: Introduction to the Third World." Most of my ideas and reflections were discussed and developed in that class.

REFERENCE

Dimen-Schein, Muriel. 1977. The Anthropological Imagination. New York: McGraw-Hill.

Cultural Relativism and Universal Rights

Carolyn Fluehr-Lobban

Carolyn Fluehr-Lobban is a professor of anthropology and director of the Study Abroad/International Studies program at Rhode Island College

Cultural relativism, long a key concept in anthropology, asserts that since each culture has its own values and practices, anthropologists should not make value judgments about cultural differences. As a result, Anthropological pedagogy has stressed that the study of customs and norms should be value-free, and that the appropriate role of the anthropologist is that of observer and recorder.

Today, however, this view is being challenged by critics inside and outside the discipline, especially those who want anthropologists to take a stand on key human-rights issues. I agree that the time has come for anthropologists to become more actively engaged in safeguarding the rights of people whose lives and cultures they study.

Historically, anthropology as a discipline has declined to participate in the dialogue that produced international conventions regarding human rights. For example, in 1947, when the executive board of the American Anthropological Association withdrew from discussions that led to the "Universal Declaration of Human Rights," it did so in the belief that no such declaration would be applicable to all human beings. But the world and anthropology have changed. Because their research involved extended interaction with people at the grassroots, anthropologists are in a unique position to lend knowledge and expertise to the international debate regarding human rights.

Doing so does not represent a complete break with the traditions of our field. After all, in the past, anthropologists did not hesitate to speak out against such reprehensible practices as Nazi genocide and South African apartheid. And they have testified in U.S. courts against government rules that impinge on the religious traditions or sacred lands of Native Americans, decrying government policies that treat groups of people unjustly.

> *"The exchange of ideas across cultures is already fostering a growing acceptance of the universal nature of some human rights, regardless of cultural differences."*

However, other practices that violate individual rights or oppress particular groups have not been denounced. Anthropologists generally have not spoken out, for example, against the practice in many cultures of female circumcision, which critics call a mutilation of women. They have been unwilling to pass judgment on such forms of culturally based homicide as the killing of infants or the aged. Some have withheld judgment on acts of communal violence, such as clashes between Hindus and Muslims in India or Tutsis and Hutus in Rwanda, perhaps because the animosities between those groups are of long standing.

Moreover, as a practical matter, organized anthropology's refusal to participate in drafting the 1947 human-rights declaration has meant that anthropologists have not had much of a role in drafting later human-rights statements, such as the United Nations' "Convention on the Elimination of All Forms of Discrimination Against Women," approved in 1979. In many international forums discussing women's rights, participants have specifically rejected using cultural relativism as a barrier to improving women's lives.

The issue of violence against women throws the perils of cultural relativism into stark relief. Following the lead of human-rights advocates, a growing number of anthropologists and others are coming to recognize that violence against women should be acknowledged as a violation of a basic human right to be free from harm. They believe that such violence cannot be excused or justified on cultural grounds.

Let me refer to my own experience. For nearly 25 years, I have conducted research in the Sudan, one of the African countries where the practice of female circumcision is widespread, affecting the vast majority of females in the northern Sudan. Chronic infections are a common result, and sexual intercourse and childbirth are rendered difficult and painful. However, cultural ideology in the Sudan holds that an uncircumcised woman is not respectable, and few families would risk their daughter's chances of marrying by not having her circumcised. British colonial officials outlawed the practice in 1946, but this served only to make it surreptitious and thus more dangerous. Women found it harder to get treatment for mistakes or for side effects of the illegal surgery.

"The issue of violence against women throws the perils of cultural relativism into stark relief."

For a long time I felt trapped between, on one side, my anthropologist's understanding of the custom and of the sensitivities about it among the people with whom I was working, and, on the other, the largely feminist campaign in the West to eradicate what critics see as a "barbaric" custom. To ally myself with Western feminists and condemn female circumcision seemed to me to be a betrayal of the value system and culture of the Sudan, which I had come to understand. But as I was asked over the years to comment on female circumcision because of my expertise in the Sudan, I came to realize how deeply I felt that the practice was harmful and wrong.

In 1993, female circumcision was one of the practices deemed harmful by delegates at the international Human Rights Conference in Vienna. During their discussions, they came to view circumcision as a violation of the rights of children as well as of the women who suffer its consequences throughout life. Those discussions made me realize that there was a moral agenda larger than myself, larger than Western culture or the culture of the northern Sudan or my discipline. I decided to join colleagues from other disciplines and cultures in speaking out against the practice.

Some cultures are beginning to change, although cause and effect are difficult to determine. Women's associations in the Ivory Coast are calling for an end to female circumcision. In Egypt, the Cairo Institute of Human Rights has reported the first publicly acknowledged marriage of an uncircumcised woman. In the United States, a Nigerian woman recently was granted asylum on the ground that her returning to her country would result in the forcible circumcision of her daughter, which was deemed a violation of the girl's human rights.

To be sure, it is not easy to achieve consensus concerning the point at which cultural practices cross the line and become violations of human rights. But it is important that scholars and human-rights activists discuss the issue. Some examples of when the line is crossed may be clearer than others. The action of a Japanese wife who feels honor-bound to commit suicide because of the shame of her husband's infidelity can be explained and perhaps justified by the traditional code of honor in Japanese society. However, when she decides to take the lives of her children as well, she is committing murder, which may be easier to condemn than suicide.

What about "honor" killings of sisters and daughters accused of sexual misconduct in some Middle Eastern and Mediterranean societies? Some anthropologists have explained this practice in culturally relativist terms, saying that severe disruptions of the moral order occur when sexual impropriety is alleged or takes place. To restore the social equilibrium and avoid feuds, the local culture required the shedding of blood to wash away the shame of sexual dishonor. The practice of honor killings, which victimizes mainly women, has been defended in some local courts as less serious than premeditated murder, because it stems from long-standing cultural traditions. While some judges have agreed, anthropologists should see a different picture: a pattern of cultural discrimination against women.

As the issue of domestic violence shows, we need to explore the ways that we balance individual and cultural rights. The "right" of a man to discipline, slap, hit, or beat his wife (and often, by extension, his children) is widely recognized across many cultures in which male dominance is an accepted fact of life. Indeed, the issue of domestic violence has only recently been added to the international human-rights agenda, with the addition of women's rights to the list of basic human rights at the Vienna conference.

The fact that domestic violence is being openly discussed and challenged in some societies (the United States is among the leaders) helps to encourage dialogue in societies in which domestic violence has been a taboo subject. This dialogue is relatively new, and no clear principles have emerged. But anthropologists could inform and enrich the discussion, using their knowledge of family and community life in different cultures.

Cases of genocide may allow the clearest insight into where the line between local culture and universal morality lies. Many anthropologists have urged the Brazilian and Venezuelan governments to stop gold miners from slaughtering the Yanomami people, who are battling the encroachment of miners on their rain forests. Other practices that harm individuals or categories of people (such as the elderly, women, and enslaved or formerly enslaved people) may not represent genocide *per se,* and thus may present somewhat harder questions about the morality of traditional practices. We need to focus on the harm done, however, and not on the scale of the abuse. We need to be sensitive to cultural differences but not allow them to override widely recognized human rights.

The exchange of ideas across cultures is already fostering a growing acceptance of the universal nature of some human rights, regardless of cultural differences. The right of individuals to be free from harm or the threat of harm, and the right of cultural minorities to exist freely within states, are just two examples of rights that are beginning to be universally recognized—although not universally applied.

Fortunately, organized anthropology is beginning to change its attitude toward cultural relativism and human rights. The theme of the 1994 convention of the American Anthropological Association was human rights. At the sessions organized around the topic, many anthropologists said they no longer were absolutely committed to cultural relativism. The association has responded to the changing attitude among its members by forming a Commission for Human Rights, charged with developing a specifically anthropological perspective on those rights, and with challenging violations and promoting education about them.

Nevertheless, many anthropologists continue to express strong support for cultural relativism. One of the most contentious issues arises from the fundamental question: What authority do we Westerners have to impose our own concept of universal rights on the rest of humanity? It is true that Western ideas of human rights have so far dominated international discourse. On the other hand, the cultural relativists' argument is often used by repressive governments to deflect international criticism of their abuse of their citizens. At the very least, anthropologists need to condemn such misuse of cultural relativism, even if it means that they may be denied permission to do research in the country in question.

Personally, I would go further: I believe that we should not let the concept of relativism stop us from using national and international forums to examine ways to protect the lives and dignity of people in every culture. Because of our involvement in local societies, anthropologists could provide early warnings of abuses—for example, by reporting data to international human-rights organizations, and by joining the dialogue at international conferences. When there is a choice between defending human rights and defending cultural relativism, anthropologists should choose to protect and promote human rights. We cannot just be bystanders.

Culture and Communication

Anthropologists are interested in all aspects of human behavior and how they interrelate with each other. Language is a form of such behavior (albeit primarily verbal behavior) and therefore worthy of study. It is patterned and passed down from one generation to the next through learning, not instinct. In keeping with the idea that language is integral to human social interaction, it has long been recognized that human communication through language is by its nature different from the kind of communication found among other animals. Central to this difference is the fact that humans communicate abstractly with symbols that have meaning independent of the immediate sensory experiences of either the sender or receiver of messages. Thus, for instance, humans are able to refer to the future and the past instead of just the here and now.

Recent experiments have shown that anthropoid apes can be taught a small portion of Ameslan (American Sign Language). It must be remembered, however, that their very rudimentary ability has to be tapped by painstaking human effort, and that the degree of difference between apes and humans serves only to emphasize the peculiarly human need for and development of language.

Just as the abstract quality of symbols lifts our thoughts beyond immediate sense perception, it also in-

hibits our ability to think about and convey the full meaning of our personal experience. No categorical term can do justice to its referents—the variety of forms to which the term refers. The degree to which this is an obstacle to clarity of thought and communication relates to the degree of abstraction in the symbols involved. The word "chair," for instance, would not present much difficulty since it has rather objective referents. Consider the trouble we have, however, in thinking and communicating with words whose referents are not quite so tied to immediate sense perception—words such as "freedom," "democracy," and "justice." At best, the likely result is symbolic confusion—an inability to think or communicate in objectively definable symbols. At its worst, language may be used to purposefully obfuscate, as is shown in the article "Language, Appearance, and Reality: Doublespeak in 1984."

A related issue has to do with the fact that languages differ as to what is relatively easy to express within the restrictions of their particular vocabularies. Thus, although a given language may not have enough words to cope with a new situation or a new field of activity, the typical solution is to invent words or to borrow them (see "The Gift of Tongues"). In this way, it may be said that any language can be used to teach anything. This

point is illustrated by Laura Bohannan's attempt to convey the "true" meaning of Shakespeare's *Hamlet* to the West African Tiv. Much of her task is devoted to finding the most appropriate words in the Tiv language to convey her Western thoughts. At least part of her failure is due to the fact that some of the words are just not there, and her inventions are, to the Tiv at least, unacceptable.

Taken collectively, the articles in this section show how symbolic confusion may occur between individuals or groups as well as demonstrate the tremendous potential of recent research to enhance effective communication among all of us.

Looking Ahead: Challenge Questions

What are the common strategies used throughout the world to overcome linguistic barriers?

Does language restrict our thought processes?

Under what circumstances may indirectness convey more security and power than directness?

In what ways is communication difficult in a cross-cultural situation?

What kinds of messages are transmitted through non-verbal communication?

How has this section enhanced your ability to communicate more effectively?

Language, Appearance, and Reality: Doublespeak in 1984

William D. Lutz

William D. Lutz, chair of the Department of English at Rutgers University, is also chair of the National Council of Teachers of English (NCTE) Committee on Public Doublespeak and editor of the Quarterly Review of Doublespeak.

There are at least four kinds of doublespeak. The first kind is the euphemism, a word or phrase that is designed to avoid a harsh or distasteful reality. When a euphemism is used out of sensitivity for the feelings of someone or out of concern for a social or cultural taboo, it is not doublespeak. For example, we express grief that someone has *passed away* because we do not want to say to a grieving person, "I'm sorry your father is dead." The euphemism *passed away* functions here not just to protect the feelings of another person but also to communicate our concern over that person's feelings during a period of mourning.

However, when a euphemism is used to mislead or deceive, it becomes doublespeak. For example, the U.S. State Department decided in 1984 that in its annual reports on the status of human rights in countries around the world it would no longer use the word *killing*. Instead, it uses the phrase *unlawful or arbitrary deprivation of life*. Thus the State Department avoids discussing the embarrassing situation of the government-sanctioned killings in countries that are supported by the United States. This use of language constitutes doublespeak because it is designed to mislead, to cover up the unpleasant. Its real intent is at variance with its apparent intent. It is language designed to alter our perception of reality.

A second kind of doublespeak is jargon, the specialized language of a trade, profession, or similar group. It is the specialized language of doctors, lawyers, engineers, educators, or car mechanics. Jargon can serve an important and useful function. Within a group, jargon allows members of the group to communicate with each other clearly, efficiently, and quickly. Indeed, it is a mark of membership in the group to be able to use and understand the group's jargon. For example, lawyers speak of an *involuntary conversion* of property when discussing the loss or destruction of property through theft, accident, or condemnation. When used by lawyers in a legal situation, such jargon is a legitimate use of language, since all members of the group can be expected to understand the term.

However, when a member of the group uses jargon to communicate with a person outside the group, and uses it knowing that the nonmember does not understand such language, then there is doublespeak. For example, a number of years ago a commercial airliner crashed on takeoff, killing three passengers, injuring twenty-one others, and destroying the airplane, a 727. The insured value of the airplane was greater than its book value, so the airline made a profit of three million dollars on the destroyed airplane. But the airline had two problems: it did not want to talk about one of its airplanes crashing and it had to account for the three million dollars when it issued its annual report to its stockholders. The airline solved these problems by inserting a footnote in its annual report explaining that this three million dollars was due to "the involuntary conversion of a 727." Note that airline officials could thus claim to have explained the crash of the airplane and the subsequent three million dollars in profit. However, since most stockholders in the company, and indeed most of the general public, are not familiar with legal jargon, the use of such jargon constitutes doublespeak.

A third kind of doublespeak is gobbledygook or bureaucratese. Basically, such doublespeak is simply a matter of piling on words, of overwhelming the audience with words, the bigger the better. For example, when Alan Greenspan was chairman of the President's Council of Economic Advisors, he made this statement when testifying before a Senate committee:

It is a tricky problem to find the particular calibration in timing that would be appropriate to stem the acceleration in risk premiums created by falling incomes without prematurely aborting the decline in the inflation-generated risk premiums.

Did Alan Greenspan's audience really understand what he was saying? Did he believe his statement really explained anything? Perhaps there is some meaning beneath all those words, but it would take some time to search it out. This seems to be language that pretends to communicate but does not.

The fourth kind of doublespeak is inflated language. Inflated language designed to make the ordinary seem extraordinary, the common, uncommon; to make everyday things seem impressive; to give an air of importance to people, situations, or things

From *ETC* (Et Cetera), Winter 1987, pp. 383-391. Excerpted from *The Legacy of Language: A Tribute to Charlton Laird,* edited by Philip C. Boardman. © 1987 by the University of Nevada Press. Reprinted by permission of the publisher.

that would not normally be considered important; to make the simple seem complex. With this kind of language, car mechanics become *automotive internists,* elevator operators become members of the *vertical transportation corps,* used cars become not just *pre-owned* but *experienced cars.* When the Pentagon uses the phrase *pre-emptive counterattack* to mean that American forces attacked first, or when it uses the phrase *engage the enemy on all sides* to describe an ambush of American troops, or when it uses the phrase *tactical redeployment* to describe a retreat by American troops, it is using doublespeak. The electronics company that sells the television set with *non-multicolor capability* is also using the doublespeak of inflated language.

Doublespeak is not a new use of language peculiar to the politics or economics of the twentieth century. Thucydides in *The Peloponnesian War* wrote that

revolution thus ran its course from city to city. . . . Words had to change their ordinary meanings and to take those which were now given them. Reckless audacity came to be considered the courage of a loyal ally; prudent hesitation, specious cowardice; moderation was held to be a cloak for unmanliness; ability to see all sides of a question, inaptness to act on any. Frantic violence become the attribute of manliness; cautious plotting, a justifiable means of self-defense. The advocate of extreme measures was always trustworthy; his opponent, a man to be suspected.[1]

Caesar in his account of the Gallic Wars described his brutal conquest as "pacifying" Gaul. Doublespeak has a long history.

Military doublespeak seems always to have been with us. In 1947 the name of the War Department was changed to the more pleasing if misleading *Defense Department.* During the Vietnam War the American public learned that it was an *incursion,* not an invasion; a *protective reaction strike* or a *limited duration protective reaction strike* or *air support,* not bombing; and *incontinent ordinance,* not bombs and artillery shells, fell on civilians. This use of language continued with the invasion of Grenada, which was conducted not by the United States Army, Navy, or Air Force, but by the Caribbean Peace Keeping Forces. Indeed, according to the Pentagon, it was not an invasion of Grenada, but a *predawn, vertical insertion.* And it wasn't that the armed forces lacked intelligence data on Grenada before the invasion, it was just that "we were not micromanaging Grenada intelligencewise until about that time frame." In today's army forces, it's not a shovel but a *combat emplacement evacuator,* not a toothpick but a *wood interdental stimulator,* not a pencil but a portable, handheld communications inscriber, not a bullet hole but a *ballistically induced aperture in the subcutaneous environment.*

Members of the military and politicians are not the only ones who use doublespeak. People in all parts of society use it. Take educators, for example. On some college campuses what was once the Department of Physical Education is now the *Department of Human Kinetics* or the *College of Applied Life Studies.* Home Economics is now the *School of Human Resources and Family Studies.* College campuses no longer have libraries but *learning resource centers.* Those are not desks in the classroom, they are *pupil stations.* Teachers—*classroom managers* who apply an *action plan* to a *knowledge base*—are concerned with the *basic fundamentals,* which are *inexorably linked* to the *education user's* (not student's) *time-on-task.* Students don't take tests; now it is *criterion referencing testing* which measures whether a student has achieved the *operational curricular objectives.* A school system in Pennsylvania uses the following grading system on report cards: "no effort, less than minimal effort, minimal effort, more than minimal effort, less than full effort, full effort, better than full effort, effort increasing, effort decreasing." Some college students in New York come from *economically nonaffluent* families, while the coach at a Southern university wasn't fired, "he just won't be asked to continue in that job." An article in a scholarly journal suggests teaching students three approaches to writing to help them become better writers: "concretization of goals, procedural facilitation, and modeling planning." An article on family relationships entitled "Familial Love and Intertemporal Optimality" observes that "an altruistic utility function promotes intertemporal efficiency. However, altruism creates an externality that implies that satisfying the condition for efficiency, does not insure intertemporal optimality." A research report issued by the U.S. Office of Education contains this sentence: "In other words, feediness is the shared information between toputness, where toputness is at a time just prior to the inputness." Educations contributes more than its share to current doublespeak.

The world of business has produced large amounts of doublespeak. If an airplane crash is one of the worst things that can happen to an airline company, a recall of automobiles because of a safety defect is one of the worst things that can happen to an automobile company. So a few years ago, when one of the three largest car companies in America had to recall two of its models to correct mechanical defects, the company sent a letter to all those who had bought those models. In its letter, the company said that the rear axle bearings of the cars "can deteriorate" and that "continued driving with a failed bearing could result in disengagement of the axle shaft and adversely affect vehicle control." This is the language of nonresponsibility. What are "mechanical deficiencies"—poor design, bad workmanship? If they do, what causes the deterioration? Note that "continued driving" is the subject of the sentence and suggests that it is not the company's poor manufacturing which is at fault but the driver who persists in driving. Note, too, "failed bearing," which implies that the bearing failed, not the company. Finally, "adversely affect vehicle control" means nothing more than that the driver could lose control of the car and get killed.

If we apply Hugh Rank's criteria for examining such language, we quickly discover the doublespeak here. What the car company should be saying to its customers is that the car the company sold them has a serious defect which should be corrected immediately—otherwise the customer runs the risk of being killed. But the reader of the letter must find this message beneath the doublespeak the company has used to disguise the harshness of its message. We will probably never know how many of the customers never brought their cars in for the necessary repairs because they did not think the problem serious enough to warrant the inconvenience involved.

When it come time to fire employees, business has produced more than enough doublespeak to deal with the unpleasant situation. Employees are, of course, never fired. They are *selected out, placed out, non-retained, released, dehired, non-renewed.* A corporation will *eliminate the redundancies in the human resources area,* assign *candidates for derecruitment* to a *mobility pool,* revitalize the department by placing executives on *special assignment, enhance the efficiency of operations, streamline the field sales organization,* or *further rationalize marketing efforts.* The reality behind all this doublespeak is that companies are firing employees, but no one wants the stockholders, public, or competition to know that times are tough and people have to go.

Recently the oil industry has been hard hit by declining sales and a surplus of oil. Because of *reduced demand for product,* which results in *spare refining capacity* and problems in *down-stream operations,* oil companies have been forced to *re-evaluate and consolidate their operations* and take *appropriate cost reduction actions,* in order to *enhance the efficiency of operations,* which has meant the *elimination of marginal outlets, accelerating the divestment program,* and the *disposition of low throughput marketing units.* What this doublespeak really means is that oil companies have fired employees, cut back on expenses, and closed gas stations and oil refineries because there's surplus of oil and people are not buying as much gas and oil as in the past.

One corporation faced with declining business sent a memorandum to its employees advising them that the company's "business plans are under revi-

sion and now reflect a more moderate approach toward our operating and capital programs." The result of this "more moderate approach" is a "surplus of professional/technical employees." To "assist in alleviating the surplus, selected professional and technical employees" have been "selected to participate" in a "Voluntary Program." Note that individuals were selected to "resign voluntarily." What this memorandum means, of course, is that expenses must be cut because of declining business, so employees will have to be fired.

It is rare to read that the stock market *fell.* Members of the financial community prefer to say that the stock market *retreated, eased, made a technical adjustment* or a *technical correction,* or perhaps that *prices were off due to profit taking,* or *off in light trading,* or *lost ground.* But the stock market never falls, not if stockbrokers have their say. As a side note, it is interesting to observe that the stock market never rises because of a *technical adjustment* or *correction,* nor does it ever *ease* upwards.

The business sections of newspapers, business magazines, corporate reports, and executive speeches are filled with words and phrases such as *marginal rates of substitution, equilibrium price, getting off margin, distribution coalition, non-performing assets,* and *encompassing organizations.* Much of this is jargon or inflated language designed to make the simple seem complex, but there are other examples of business doublespeak that mislead, that are designed to avoid a harsh reality. What should we make of such expressions as *negative deficit* or *revenue excesses* for profit, *invest in* for buy, *price enhancement* or *price adjustment* for price increase, *shortfall* for a mistake in planning or *period of accelerated negative growth* or *negative economic growth* for recession?

Business doublespeak often attempts to give substance to wind, to make ordinary actions seem complex. Executives *operate* in *timeframes* within the *context* of which a *task force* will serve as the proper *conduit* for all the necessary *input* to *program a scenario* that,

within acceptable *parameters,* and with the proper *throughput,* will *generate* the *maximum output* for a *print out* of *zero defect terminal objectives* that will *enhance the bottom line.*

There are instances, however, where doublespeak becomes more than amusing, more than a cause for a weary shake of the head. When the anesthetist turned the wrong knob during a Caesarean delivery and killed the mother and unborn child, the hospital called it a *therapeutic misadventure.* The Pentagon calls the neutron bomb "an efficient nuclear weapon that eliminates an enemy with a minimum degree of damage to friendly territory." The Pentagon also calls expected civilian casualties in a nuclear war *collateral damage.* And it was the Central Intelligence Agency which during the Vietnam War created the phrase *eliminate with extreme prejudice* to replace the more direct verb *kill.*

Identifying doublespeak can at times be difficult. For example, on July 27, 1981, President Ronald Reagan said in a speech televised to the American public: "I will not stand by and see those of you who are dependent on Social Security deprived of the benefits you've worked so hard to earn. You will continue to receive your checks in the full amount due you." This speech had been billed as President Reagan's position on Social Security, a subject of much debate at the time. After the speech, public opinion polls revealed that the great majority of the public believed that President Reagan had affirmed his support for Social Security and that he would not support cuts in benefits. However, five days after the speech, on July 31, 1981, an article in the *Philadelphia Inquirer* quoted White House spokesman David Gergen as saying that President Reagan's words had been "carefully chosen." What President Reagan did mean, according to Gergen, was that he was reserving the right to decide who was "dependent" on those benefits, who had "earned" them, and who, therefore, was "due" them.[2]

The subsequent remarks of David Gergen reveal the real intent of President Reagan as opposed to his apparent intent. Thus Hugh Rank's criteria for analyzing language to determine whether it is doublespeak, when applied in light of David Gergen's remarks, reveal the doublespeak of President Reagan. Here indeed is the insincerity of which Orwell wrote. Here, too, is the gap between the speaker's real and declared aim.

In 1982 the Republican National Committee sponsored a television advertisement which pictured an elderly, folksy postman delivering Social Security checks "with the 7.4% cost-of-living raise that President Reagan promised." The postman then added that "he promised that raise and he kept his promise, in spite of those sticks-in-the-mud who tried to keep him from doing what we elected him to do." The commercial was, in fact, deliberately misleading. The cost-of-living increases had been provided automatically by law since 1975, and President Reagan tried three times to roll them back or delay them but was overruled by congressional opposition. When these discrepancies were pointed out to an official of the Republican National Committee, he called the commercial "inoffensive" and added, "Since when is a commercial supposed to be accurate? Do women really smile when they clean their ovens?"

Again, applying Hugh Rank's criteria to this advertisement reveals the doublespeak in it once we know the facts of past actions by President Reagan. Moreover, the official for the Republican National Committee assumes that all advertisements, whether for political candidates or commercial products, are lies, or in his doublespeak term, *inaccurate*. Thus, the real intent of the advertisement was to mislead while the apparent purpose was to inform the public of President Reagan's position on possible cuts in Social Security benefits. Again there is insincerity, and again there is a gap between the speaker's real and declared aims.

In 1981 Secretary of State Alexander Haig testified before congressional committees about the murder of three American nuns and a Catholic lay worker in El Salvador. The four women had been raped and shot at close range, and there was clear evidence that the crime had been committed by soldiers of the Salvadoran government. Before the House Foreign Affairs Committee, Secretary Haig said,

I'd like to suggest to you that some of the investigations would lead one to believe that perhaps the vehicle the nuns were riding in may have tried to run a roadblock, or may accidentally have been perceived to have been doing so, and there'd been an exchange of fire and then perhaps those who inflicted the casualties sought to cover it up. And this could have been at a very low level of both competence and motivation in the context of the issue itself. But the facts on this are not clear enough for anyone to draw a definitive conclusion.

The next day, before the Senate Foreign Relations Committee, Secretary Haig claimed that press reports on his previous testimony were inaccurate. When Senator Claiborne Pell asked whether Secretary Haig was suggesting the possibility that "the nuns may have run through a roadblock." Secretary Haig replied, "You mean that they tried to violate . . .? Not at all, no, not at all. My heavens! The dear nuns who raised me in my parochial schooling would forever isolate me from their affections and respect." When Senator Pell asked Secretary Haig, "Did you mean that the nuns were firing at the people, or what did 'exchange of fire' mean?" Secretary Haig replied, "I haven't met any pistol-packing nuns in my day, Senator. What I meant was that if one fellow starts shooting, then the next thing you know they all panic." Thus did the secretary of state of the United States explain official government policy on the murder of four American citizens in a foreign land.

Secretary Haig's testimony implies that the women were in some way responsible for their own fate. By using such vague wording as "would lead one to believe" and "may accidentally have been perceived to have been," he avoids any direct assertion. The use of "inflicted the casualties" not only avoids using the word *kill* but also implies that at the worst the kill-ings were accidental or justifiable. The result of this testimony is that the secretary of state has become an apologist for murder. This is indeed language in defense of the indefensible; language designed to make lies sound truthful and murder respectable; language designed to give an appearance of solidity to pure wind.

These last three examples of doublespeak should make it clear that doublespeak is not the product of careless language or sloppy thinking. Indeed, most doublespeak is the product of clear thinking and is language carefully designed and constructed to appear to communicate when in fact it does not. It is language designed not to lead but to mislead. It is language designed to distort reality and corrupt the mind. It is not a tax increase but *revenue enhancement* or *tax base broadening*, so how can you complain about higher taxes? It is not acid rain, but *poorly buffered precipitation*, so don't worry about all those dead trees. That is not the Mafia in Atlantic City, New Jersey, those are *members of a career offender cartel*, so don't worry about the influence of organized crime in the city. The judge was not addicted to the pain-killing drug he was taking, it was just that the drug had "established an interrelationship with the body, such that if the drug is removed precipitously, there is a reaction," so don't worry that his decisions might have been influenced by his drug addiction. It's not a Titan II nuclear-armed, intercontinental ballistic missile with a warhead 630 times more powerful than the atomic bomb dropped on Hiroshima, it is just a *very large, potentially disruptive re-entry system*, so don't worry about the threat of nuclear destruction. It is not a neutron bomb but a *radiation enhancement device*, so don't worry about escalating the arms race. It is not an invasion but a *rescue mission*, or a *predawn vertical insertion*, so don't worry about any violations of United States or international law.

Doublespeak has become so common in our everyday lives that we fail to notice it. We do not protest when we are asked to check our packages at the desk "for our convenience" when it is not for our convenience at all but for someone else's convenience. We see advertisements for *genuine imitation leather, virgin vinyl,* or *real counterfeit diamonds* and do not question the language or the supposed quality of the product. We do not speak of slums or ghettos but of the *inner city* or *substandard housing where the disadvantaged* live and thus avoid talking about the poor who have to live in filthy, poorly heated, ramshackle apartments or houses. Patients do not die in the hospital; it is just *negative patient care outcome.*

Doublespeak which calls cab drivers *urban transportation specialists,* elevator operators *members of the vertical transportation corps,* and automobile mechanics *automotive internists* can be considered humorous and relatively harmless. However, doublespeak which calls a fire in a nuclear reactor building *rapid oxidation,* an explosion in a nuclear power plant an *energetic disassembly,* the illegal overthrow of a legitimate administration *destabilizing a government,* and lies *inoperative statements* is language which attempts to avoid responsibility, which attempts to make the bad seem good, the negative appear positive, something unpleasant appear attractive, and which seems to communicate but does not. It is language designed to alter our perception of reality and corrupt our minds. Such language does not provide us with the tools needed to develop and preserve civilization. Such language breeds suspicion, cynicism, distrust, and, ultimately, hostility.

Doublespeak is insidious because it can infect and ultimately destroy the function of language, which is communication between people and social groups. If this corrupting process does occur, it can have serious conse-

quences in a country that depends upon an informed electorate to make decisions in selecting candidates for office and deciding issues of public policy. After a while we may really believe that politicians don't lie but only *misspeak,* that illegal acts are merely *inappropriate actions,* that fraud and criminal conspiracy are just *miscertification.* And if we really believe that we understand such language, then the world of *Nineteen Eighty-four* with its control of reality through language is not far away.

The consistent use of doublespeak can have serious and far-reaching consequences beyond the obvious ones. The pervasive use of doublespeak can spread so that doublespeak becomes the coin of the political realm with speakers and listeners convinced that they really understand such language. President Jimmy Carter could call the aborted raid to free the hostages in Tehran in 1980 an "incomplete success" and really believe that he had made a statement that clearly communicated with the American public. So, too, President Ronald Reagan could say in 1985 that "ultimately our security and our hopes for success at the arms reduction talks hinge on the determination that we show here to continue our program to rebuild and refortify our defenses" and really believe that greatly increasing the amount of money spent building new weapons will lead to a reduction in the number of weapons in the world.

The task of English teachers is to teach not just the effective use of language but respect for language as well. Those who use language to conceal or prevent or corrupt thought must be called to account. Only by teaching respect for and love of language can teachers of English instill in students

the sense of outrage they should experience when they encounter doublespeak. But before students can experience that outrage, they must first learn to use language effectively, to understand its beauty and power. Only then will we begin to make headway in the fight against doublespeak, for only by using language well will we come to appreciate the perversion inherent in doublespeak.

In his book *The Miracle of Language,* Charlton Laird notes that

language is . . . the most important tool man ever devised. . . . Language is [man's] basic tool. It is the tool more than any other with which he makes his living, makes his home, makes his life. As man becomes more and more a social being, as the world becomes more and more a social community, communication grows ever more imperative. And language is the basis of communication. Language is also the instrument with which we think, and thinking is the rarest and most needed commodity in the world.[3]

In this opinion Laird echoes Orwell's comment that "if thought corrupts language, language can also corrupt thought."[4] Both men have given us a legacy of respect for language, a respect that should prompt us to cry "Enough!" when we encounter doublespeak. The greatest honor we can do Charlton Laird is to continue to have the greatest respect of language in all its manifestations, for, as Laird taught us, language is a miracle.

NOTES AND REFERENCES

1. Thucydides, *The Peloponnesian Way,* 3.82.
2. David Hess, "Reagan's Language on Benefits Confused, Angered Many," *Philadelphia Inquirer,* July 31, 1981, p. 6-A.
3. Charlton Laird, *The Miracle of Language* (New York: Fawcett, Premier Books, 1953), p. 224.
4. Orwell, *The Collected Essays,* 4:137.

Why Don't You Say What You Mean?

Directness is not necessarily logical or effective. Indirectness is not necessarily manipulative or insecure.

Deborah Tannen

Deborah Tannen is University Professor of Linguistics at Georgetown University.

A university president was expecting a visit from a member of the board of trustees. When her secretary buzzed to tell her that the board member had arrived, she left her office and entered the reception area to greet him. Before ushering him into her office, she handed her secretary a sheet of paper and said: "I've just finished drafting this letter. Do you think you could type it right away? I'd like to get it out before lunch. And would you please do me a favor and hold all calls while I'm meeting with Mr. Smith?"

When they say down behind the closed door of her office, Mr. Smith began by telling her that he thought she had spoken inappropriately to her secretary. "Don't forget," he said. "*You're* the president!"

Putting aside the question of the appropriateness of his admonishing the president on her way of speaking, it is revealing—and representative of many Americans' assumptions that the indirect way in which the university president told her secretary what to do struck him as self-deprecating. He took it as evidence that she didn't think she had the right to make demands of

her secretary. He probably thought he was giving her a needed pep talk, bolstering her self-confidence.

I challenge the assumption that talking in an indirect way necessarily reveals powerlessness, lack of self-confidence or anything else about the character of the speaker. Indirectness is a fundamental element in human communication. It is also one of the elements that varies most from one culture to another, and one that can cause confusion and misunderstanding when speakers have different habits with regard to using it. I also want to dispel the assumption that American women tend to be more indirect than American men. Women and men are both indirect, but in addition to differences associated with their backgrounds—regional, ethnic and class—they tend to be indirect in different situations and in different ways.

At work, we need to get others to do things, and we all have different ways of accomplishing this. Any individual's ways will vary depending on who is being addressed—a boss, a peer or a subordinate. At one extreme are bald commands. At the other are requests so indirect that they don't sound like requests at all, but are just a statement of need or a description of a situation. People with direct styles of asking others to do things perceive indirect requests—if they perceive them as requests at all—as manipulative. But this is often just a way of blaming others for our discomfort with their styles.

The indirect style is no more manipulative than making a telephone call, asking "Is Rachel there?" and expecting whoever answers the phone to put Rachel on. Only a child is likely to answer "Yes" and continue holding the phone—not out of orneriness but because of inexperience with the conventional meaning of the questions. (A mischievous adult might do it to tease.) Those who feel that indirect orders are illogical or manipulative do not recognize the conventional nature of indirect requests.

Issuing orders indirectly can be the prerogative of those in power. Imagine, for example, a master who says "It's cold in here" and expects a servant to make a move to close a window, while a servant who says the same thing is not likely to see his employer rise to correct the situation and make him more comfortable. Indeed, a Frenchman raised in Brittany tells me that his family never gave bald commands to their servants but always communicated orders in indirect and highly polite ways. This pattern renders less surprising the finding of David Bellinger and Jean Berko Gleason that fathers' speech to their young children had a higher incidence than mothers' of both direct imperatives like "Turn the bolt with the wrench" *and* indirect orders like "The wheel is going to fall off."

The use of indirectness can hardly be understood without the cross-cul-

From *The New York Times Magazine*, August 28, 1994, pp. 46-49. Adapted from *Talking 9 to 5: How Women's and Men's Conversational Styles Affect Who Gets Heard, Who Gets Credit, and What Gets Done at Work* by Deborah Tannen, Ph.D. © 1994 by Deborah Tannen, Ph.D. Reprinted by permission of William Morrow & Company, Inc.

tural perspective. Many Americans find it self-evident that directness is logical and aligned with power while indirectness is akin to dishonesty and reflects subservience. But for speakers raised in most of the world's cultures, varieties of indirectness are the norm in communication. This is the pattern found by a Japanese sociolinguist, Kunihiko Harada, in his analysis of a conversation he recorded between a Japanese boss and a subordinate.

The markers of superior status were clear. One speaker was a Japanese man in his late 40's who managed the local branch of a Japanese private school in the United States. His conversational partner was Japanese-American woman in her early 20's who worked at the school. By virtue of his job, his age and his native fluency in the language being taught, the man was in the superior position. Yet when he addressed the woman, he frequently used polite language and almost always used indirectness. For example, he had tried and failed to find a photography store that would make a black-and-white print from a color negative for a brochure they were producing. He let her know that he wanted her to take over the task by stating the situation and allowed her to volunteer to do it: (This is a translation of the Japanese conversation.)

On this matter, that, that, on the leaflet? This photo, I'm thinking of changing it to black-and-white and making it clearer. . . . I went to a photo shop and asked them. They said they didn't do black-and-white. I asked if they knew any place that did. They said they didn't know. They weren't very helpful, but anyway, a place must be found, the negative brought to it, the picture developed.

Harada observes, "Given the fact that there are some duties to be performed and that there are two parties present, the subordinate is supposed to assume that those are his or her obligation." It was precisely because of his higher status that the boss was free to choose whether to speak formally or informally, to assert his power or to play it down and build rapport—an option not available to the subordinate,

who would have seemed cheeky if she had chosen a style that enhanced friendliness and closeness.

The same pattern was found by a Chinese sociolinguist, Yuling Pan, in a meeting of officials involved in a neighborhood youth program. All spoke in ways that reflected their place in the hierarchy. A subordinate addressing a superior always spoke in a deferential way, but a superior addressing a subordinate could either be authoritarian, demonstrating his power, or friendly, establishing rapport. The ones in power had the option of choosing which style to use. In this spirit, I have been told by people who prefer their bosses to give orders indirectly that those who issue bald commands must be pretty insecure; otherwise why would they have to bolster their egos by throwing their weight around?

I am not inclined to accept that those who give orders directly are really insecure and powerless, any more than I want to accept that judgment of those who give indirect orders. The conclusion to be drawn is that ways of talking should not be taken as obvious evidence of inner psychological states like insecurity or lack of confidence. Considering the many influences on conversational style, individuals have a wide range of ways of getting things done and expressing their emotional states. Personality characteristics like insecurity cannot be linked to ways of speaking in an automatic, self-evident way.

Those who expect orders to be given indirectly are offended when they come unadorned. One woman said that when her boss gives her instructions, she feels she should click her heels, salute, and say "Yes, Boss!" His directions strike her as so imperious as to border on the militaristic. Yet I received a letter from a man telling me that indirect orders were a fundamental part of his military training: He wrote:

Many years ago, when I was in the Navy, I was training to be a radio technician. One class I was in was taught by a chief radioman, a regular Navy man who had been to sea, and who was then in his third hitch. The

students, about 20 of us, were fresh out of boot camp, with no sea duty and little knowledge of real Navy life. One day in class the chief said it was hot in the room. The students didn't react, except to nod in agreement. The chief repeated himself: "It's hot in this room." Again there was no reaction from the students.

Then the chief explained. He wasn't looking for agreement or discussion from us. When he said that the room was hot, he expected us to do something about it—like opening the window. He tried it one more time, and this time all of us left our workbenches and headed for the windows. We had learned. And we had many opportunities to apply what we had learned.

This letter especially intrigued me because "It's cold in here" is the standard sentence used by linguists to illustrate an indirect way of getting someone to do something—as I used it earlier. In this example, it is the very obviousness and rigidity of the military hierarchy that makes the statement of a problem sufficient to trigger corrective action on the part of subordinates.

A man who had worked at the Pentagon reinforced the view that the burden of interpretation is on subordinates in the military—and he noticed the difference when he moved to a position in the private sector. He was frustrated when he'd say to his new secretary, for example, "Do we have a list of invitees?" and be told, "I don't know; we probably do" rather than "I'll get it for you." Indeed, he explained, at the Pentagon, such a question would likely be heard as a reproach that the list was not already on his desk.

The suggestion that indirectness is associated with the military must come as a surprise to many. But everyone is indirect, meaning more than is put into words and deriving meaning from words that are never actually said. It's a matter of where, when and how we each tend to be indirect and look for hidden meanings. But indirectness has a built-in liability. There is a risk that the other will either miss or choose to ignore your meaning.

On Jan. 13, 1982, a freezing cold, snowy day in Washington, Air Florida Flight 90 took off from National Airport, but could not get the lift it needed to keep climbing. It crashed into a bridge linking Washington to the state of Virginia and plunged into the Potomac. Of the 79 people on board all but 5 perished, many floundering and drowning in the icy water while horror-stricken bystanders watched helplessly from the river's edge and millions more watched, aghast, on their television screens. Experts later concluded that the plane had waited too long after de-icing to take off. Fresh buildup of ice on the wings and engine brought the plane down. How could the pilot and co-pilot have made such a blunder? Didn't at least one of them realize it was dangerous to take off under these conditions?

Charlotte Linde, a linguist at the Institute for Research on Learning in Palo Alto, Calif., has studied the "black box" recordings of cockpit conversations that preceded crashes as well as tape recordings of conversations that took place among crews during flight simulations in which problems were presented. Among the black box conversations she studied was the one between the pilot and co-pilot just before the Air Florida crash. The pilot, it turned out, had little experience flying in icy weather. The co-pilot had a bit more, and it became heartbreakingly clear on analysis that he had tried to warn the pilot, but he did so indirectly.

The co-pilot repeatedly called attention to the bad weather and to ice building up on other planes:

Co-pilot: Look how the ice is just hanging on his, ah, back, back there, see that? . . .
Co-pilot: See all those icicles on the back there and everything?
Captain: Yeah.

He expressed concern early on about the long waiting time between de-icing:

Co-pilot: Boy, this is a, this is a losing battle here on trying to de-ice those things, it [gives] you a false feeling of security, that's all that does.

Shortly after they were given clearance to take off, he again expressed concern:

Co-pilot: Let's check these tops again since we been setting here awhile.
Captain: I think we get to go here in a minute.

When they were about to take off, the co-pilot called attention to the engine instrument readings, which were not normal:

Co-pilot: That don't seem right, does it? [three-second pause] Ah, that's not right. . . .
Captain: Yes, it is, there's 80.
Co-pilot: Naw, I don't think that's right. [seven-second pause] Ah, maybe it is.
Captain: Hundred and twenty.
Co-pilot: I don't know.

The takeoff proceeded, and 37 seconds later the pilot and co-pilot exchanged their last words.

The co-pilot repeatedly called attention to dangerous conditions, but the captain didn't get the message.

The co-pilot had repeatedly called the pilot's attention to dangerous conditions but did not directly suggest they abort the takeoff. In Linde's judgment, he was expressing his concern indirectly, and the captain didn't pick up on it—with tragic results.

That the co-pilot was trying to warn the captain indirectly is supported by evidence from another airline accident—a relatively minor one—investigated by Linde that also involved the unsuccessful use of indirectness.

On July 9, 1978, Allegheny Airlines Flight 453 was landing at Monroe County Airport in Rochester, when it overran the runway by 728 feet. Everyone survived. This meant that the captain and co-pilot could be interviewed. It turned out that the plane had

been flying too fast for a safe landing. The captain should have realized this and flown around a second time, decreasing his speed before trying to land. The captain said he simply had not been aware that he was going too fast. But the co-pilot told interviewers that he "tried to warn the captain in subtle ways, like mentioning the possibility of a tail wind and the flowness of flap extension." His exact words were recorded in the black box. The crosshatches indicate words deleted by the National Transportation Safety Board and were probably expletives:

Co-pilot: Yeah, it looks like you got a tail wind here.
Yeah.
[?]: Yeah [it] moves awfully # slow.
Co-pilot: Yeah the # flaps are slower than a #.
Captain: We'll make it, gonna have to add power.
Co-pilot: I know.

The co-pilot thought the captain would understand that if there was a tail wind, it would result in the plane going too fast, and if the flaps were slow, they would be inadequate to break the speed sufficiently for a safe landing. He thought the captain would then correct for the error by not trying to land. But the captain said he didn't interpret the co-pilot's remarks to mean they were going too fast.

Linde believes it is not a coincidence that the people being indirect in these conversations were the co-pilots. In her analyses of flight-crew conversations she found it was typical for the speech of subordinates to be more mitigated—polite, tentative or indirect. She also found that topics broached in a mitigated way were more likely to fail, and that captains were more likely to ignore hints from their crew members than the other way around. These findings are evidence that not only can indirectness and other forms of mitigation be misunderstood, but they are also easier to ignore.

In the Air Florida case, it is doubtful that the captain did not realize what the co-pilot was suggesting when he said, "Let's check these tops again since we been setting here awhile" (though it seems safe to assume he did not realize the gravity of the co-pilot's concern). But the indirectness of the co-pilot's phrasing certainly made it easier for the pilot to ignore it. In this sense, the captain's response, "I think we get to go here in a minute," was an indirect way of saying, "I'd rather not." In view of these patterns, the flight crews of some airlines are now given training to express their concerns, even to superiors, in more direct ways.

The conclusion that people should learn to express themselves more directly has a ring of truth to it—especially for Americans. But direct communication is not necessarily always preferable. If more direct expression is better communication, then the most direct-speaking crews should be the best ones. Linde was surprised to find in her research that crews that used the most mitigated speech were often judged the best crews. As part of the study of talk among cockpit crews in flight simulations, the trainers observed and rated the performances of the simulation crews. The crews they rated top in performance had a higher rate of mitigation than crews they judged to be poor.

This finding seems at odds with the role played by indirectness in the examples of crashes that we just saw. Linde concluded that since every utterance functions on two levels—the referential (what it says) and the relational (what it implies about the speaker's relationships), crews that attend to the relational level will be better crews. A similar explanation was suggested by Kunihiko Harada. He believes that the secret of successful communication lies not in teaching subordinates to be more direct, but in teaching higher-ups to be more sensitive to indirect meaning. In other words, the crashes resulted not only because the co-pilots tried to alert the captains to danger indirectly but also because the captains were not attuned to the co-pilots' hints. What made for successful performance among the best crews might have been the ability—or willingness—of listeners to pick up on hints, just as members of families or longstanding couples come to understand each other's meaning without anyone being particularly explicit.

It is not surprising that a Japanese sociolinguist came up with this explanation; what he described is the Japanese system, by which good communication is believed to take place when meaning is gleaned without being stated directly—or at all.

While Americans believe that "the squeaky wheel gets the grease" (so it's best to speak up), the Japanese say, "The nail that sticks out gets hammered back in" (so it's best to remain silent if you don't want to be hit on the head). Many Japanese scholars writing in English have tried to explain to bewildered Americans the ethics of a culture in which silence is often given greater value than speech, and ideas are believed to be best communicated without being explicitly stated. Key concepts in Japanese give a flavor of the attitudes toward language that they reveal—and set in relief the strategies that Americans encounter at work when talking to other Americans.

Takie Sugiyama Lebra, a Japanese-born anthropologist, explains that one of the most basic values in Japanese culture is *omoiyari,* which she translates as "empathy." Because of *omoiyari,* it should not be necessary to state one's meaning explicitly; people should be able to sense each other's meaning intuitively. Lebra explains that it is typical for a Japanese speaker to let sentences trail off rather than complete them because expressing ideas before knowing how they will be received seems intrusive. "Only an insensitive, uncouth person needs a direct, verbal, complete message," Lebra says.

Sasshi, the anticipation of another's message through insightful guesswork, is considered an indication of maturity.

Considering the value placed on direct communication by Americans in general, and especially by American business people, it is easy to imagine that many American readers may scoff at such conversational habits. But the success of Japanese businesses makes it impossible to continue to maintain that there is anything inherently inefficient about such conversational conventions. With indirectness, as with all aspects of conversational style, our own habitual style seems to make sense—seems polite, right and good. The light case by the habits and assumptions of another culture can help us see our way to the flexibility and respect for other styles that is the only best way of speaking.

Navigating Nigerian Bureaucracies; or, "Why Can't You Beg?" She Demanded[1]

Elizabeth A. Eames

Bates College

Americans have a saying: "It's not what you know it's who you know." This aphorism captures the—usually subtle—use of old-boy networks for personal advancement in this country. But what happens when this principle becomes the primary dynamic of an entire social system? The period of three years I spent pursuing anthropological field research in a small Nigerian city was one of continual adjustment and reordering of expectations. This essay discusses a single case—how I discovered the importance personal ties have for Nigerian bureaucrats—but also illustrates the general process by which any open-minded visitor to a foreign land might decipher the rules of proper behavior. I was already familiar with Max Weber's work on bureaucracy and patrimony, yet its tremendous significance and explanatory power became clear to me only following the incidents discussed below.

I heard the same comment from every expatriate I met during my three years in Nigeria—U.S. foreign service officers, U.N. "experts," and visiting business consultants alike: "If you survive a stint in Nigeria, you can survive anywhere." The negative implications of this statement stem from outsiders' futile attempts to apply, in a new social setting, homegrown notions of how bureaucratic organizations function. This is indeed a natural inclination and all the more tempting where organizational structure appears bureaucratic. Yet in Nigeria, the officeholders behaved according to different rules; their attitudes and sentiments reflected a different moral code. A bureaucratic organizational structure coexisted with an incompatible set of moral imperatives. The resulting unwieldy, inflexible structure may be singled out as one of British colonialism's most devastating legacies.

Please bear in mind the problem of understanding that another culture works both ways. Any Nigerian student reading for the first time the following passage by a prominent American sociologist would probably howl with laughter:

The chief merit of a bureaucracy is its technical efficiency, with a premium placed on precision, speed, expert control, continuity, discretion and optimal returns on input. The structure is one which approaches the complete elimination of personalized relationships and nonrational considerations (hostility, anxiety, affectual involvements, etc.). (Merton 1968:250)

Even those well-educated administrative Nigerian officers who had once been required to incorporate such notions into their papers and exams do not live by them.

To many foreigners who have spent time in Nigeria, "the system" remains a mystery. What motivating principles explain the behavior of Nigerian administrative officers? How do local people understand the behavior of their fellow workers? Why do some people successfully maneuver their way through the system while others founder?

Recently I attended a party. As often happens at a gathering of anthropologists, we started swapping fieldwork stories and meandered onto the topic of our most unpleasant sensation or unsettling experience. That night, I heard tales of surviving strange diseases, eating repulsive foods, losing one's way in the rain forest, being caught between hostile rebel factions or kidnapped by guerrilla fighters. As for me? All that came to mind were exasperating encounters with intransigent clerks and secretaries. I began to ponder why these interactions had proved so unsettling.

My discipline—social anthropology—hinges on the practice of "participant-observation." To a fledgling anthropologist, the "fieldwork" research experience takes on all of the connotations of initiation into full membership. For some, a vision-quest; for others, perhaps, a trial-by-ordeal: The goal is to experience another way of life from the inside and to internalize, as does a growing child, the accumulating lessons of daily life. But the anthropologist is not a child; therefore, she or he experiences not conversion but self-revelation.

I came to understand my Americanness during the period spent coming to terms with Nigerian-ness. I found that I believed in my right to fair treatment and justice simply because I was a

From *The Naked Anthropologist,* edited by Philip R. Devita, Wadsworth Publishing Company, 1992, pp. 184-190. © 1992 by Elizabeth A. Eames. Reprinted by permission of the author.

human being. I believed in equal protection under the law. But my Nigerian friends did not. What I found was a social system where status, relationships, and rights were fundamentally negotiable and justice was never impartial. In the United States, impersonalized bureaucracies are the norm: We do not question them, our behavior automatically adjusts to them. But imagine spending a year working in a corporation where none of these rules applied.

You see, a Nigerian immigration officer will sign your form only if doing so will perpetuate some mutually beneficial relationship or if she or he wishes to initiate a relationship by putting you in her or his debt. For those unlucky enough to be without connections (this must necessarily include most foreigners), the only other option is bribery—where the supplicant initiates a personal relationship of sorts and the ensuing favor evens matters up.

Hence, Nigeria becomes labeled "inefficient," "tribalistic," and "corrupt." And so it is. Yet this system exists and persists for a profound reason: Whereas in Europe and Asia power and authority always derived from ownership of landed property, in West Africa the key ingredient was a large number of loyal dependents. Because land was plentiful and agriculture was of the extensive slash-and-burn variety, discontented subordinates could simply move on. The trick was to maintain power over subordinates through ostentatious displays of generosity. This meant more than simply putting on a lavish feast: You must demonstrate a willingness to use your influence to support others in times of need. Even now, all Nigerians participate in such patron-client relationships. In fact, all legitimate authority derives from being in a position to grant favors and not the other way around.

Actually, only a miniscule portion of my time in the field was spent dealing with Nigeria's "formal sector." My research entailed living within an extended family household (approximately a dozen adults and two dozen children), chatting with friends, visiting women in their market stalls, even at

times conducting formal or informal interviews. And during the years spent researching women's economic resources and domestic responsibilities, I came to understand—indeed, to deeply admire—their sense of moral responsibility to a wide-ranging network of kin, colleagues, neighbors, friends, and acquaintances. Even now, I often take the time to recall someone's overwhelming hospitality, a friendly greeting, the sharing and eating together. Such warm interpersonal relations more than made up for the lack of amenities.

The longer I stayed, however, the clearer it became that what I loved most and what I found most distressing about life in Nigeria were two sides of the same coin, inextricably related.

The first few months in a new place can be instructive for those with an open mind:

LESSON ONE: THE STRENGTH OF WEAK TIES

My first exposure to Nigerian civil servants occurred when, after waiting several months prior to departure from the United States, I realized my visa application was stalled somewhere in the New York Consulate. Letter writing and telephoning proved futile, and as my departure date approached, panic made me plan a personal visit.

The waiting room was populated by sullen, miserable people—a roomful of hostile eyes fixed on the uniformed man guarding the office door. They had been waiting for hours on end. Any passing official was simultaneously accosted by half a dozen supplicants, much as a political celebrity is accosted by the news media. Everyone's immediate goal was to enter through that door to the inner sanctum; so far, they had failed. But I was lucky: I had the name of an acquaintance's wife's schoolmate currently employed at the consulate. After some discussion, the guard allowed me to telephone her.

Mrs. Ojo greeted me cordially, then—quickly, quietly—she coaxed my application forms through the maze of cubicles. It was a miracle!

"What a wonderful woman," I thought to myself. "She understands." I thought she had taken pity on me and acted out of disgust for her colleagues' mishandling of my application. I now realize that by helping me she was reinforcing a relationship with her schoolmate. Needless to say, my gratitude extended to her schoolmate's husband, my acquaintance. As I later came to understand it, this natural emotional reaction—gratitude for favors granted—is the currency fueling the system. Even we Americans have an appropriate saying: "What goes around comes around." But at this point, I had merely learned that, here as elsewhere, connections open doors.

LESSON TWO: NO IMPERSONAL TRANSACTIONS ALLOWED

Once on Nigerian soil I confronted the mayhem of Muritala Muhammad airport. Joining the crowd surrounding one officer's station, jostled slowly forward, I finally confronted her face-to-face. Apparently I was missing the requisite currency form. No, sorry, there were none available that day. "Stand back' she declared. "You can't pass here today." I waited squeamishly. If I could only catch her eye once more! But then what? After some time, a fellow passenger asked me what the problem was. At this point, the officer, stealing a glance at me while processing someone else, inquired: "Why can't you beg?" The person being processed proclaimed: "She doesn't know how to beg! Please, O! Let her go." And I was waved on.

A young post office clerk soon reinforced my conclusion that being employed in a given capacity did not in and of itself mean one performed it. Additional incentive was required. Again, I was confronted with a mass of people crowded round a window. Everyone was trying to catch the clerk's attention, but the young man was adept at avoiding eye contact. Clients were calling him by name, invoking the name of mutual friends, and so on. After some time, he noticed me, and I grabbed the opportunity to ask for stamps. In a voice full of recrimination, yet tinged with regret, he announced more to the crowd than to me: "Why can't you greet?" and proceeded to ignore me. This proved my tip-off to the elaborate and complex cultural code of greetings so central to Nigerian social life. In other words, a personal relationship is like a "jump start" for business transactions.

LESSON THREE: EVERY CASE IS UNIQUE

Mrs. Ojo had succeeded in obtaining for me a three-month visa, but I planned to stay for over two years. Prerequisite for a "regularized" visa was university affiliation. This sounded deceptively simple. The following two months spent registering as an "occasional postgraduate student" took a terrible toll on my nervous stomach. The worst feeling was of an ever-receding target, an ever-thickening tangle of convoluted mazeways. No one could tell me what it took to register, for in fact, no one could possibly predict what I would confront farther down the road. Nothing was routinized, everything was personalized, and no two cases could possibly be alike.

This very unpredictability of the process forms a cybernetic system with the strength of personal ties, however initiated. "Dash" and "Long-leg" are the locally recognized means for cutting through red tape or confronting noncooperative personnel. "Dash" is local parlance for gift or bribe. "Long-leg" (sometimes called "L-L" or "L-squared") refers to petitioning a powerful person to help hack your way through the tangled overgrowth. To me, it evokes the image of something swooping down from on high to stomp on the petty bureaucrat causing the problem.

During my drawn-out tussle with the registrar's office, I recounted my problem to anyone who would listen. A friend's grown son, upon hearing of my difficulties, wrote a note on his business card to a Mr. Ade in the

Exams Section. Amused by his attempt to act important, I thanked Ayo politely. When I next saw him at his mother's home, he took the offensive and accused me of shunning him. It came out that I had not seen Mr. Ade. But, I protested, I did not know the man. Moreover, he worked in exams, not the registry. That, I learned, was not the point. I was supposed to assume that Mr. Ade would have known someone in the registry. Not only had I denied Ayo the chance to further his link to Mr. Ade, but ignoring his help was tantamount to denying any connection to him or—more important for me—his mother.

This revelation was reinforced when I ran into a colleague. He accused me of not greeting him very well. I had greeted him adequately but apologized nonetheless. As the conversation progressed, he told me that he had heard I had had "some difficulty." He lamented the fact that I had not called on him, since as Assistant Dean of Social Science he could have helped me. His feelings were truly hurt, provoking his accusation of a lackluster greeting. Indeed, things were never the same between us again, for I had betrayed—or denied—our relationship.

LESSON FOUR: YOUR FRIENDS HAVE ENEMIES

Well, I did eventually obtain a regularized visa, and it came through "long-leg." But the problems inherent in its use derive from the highly politicized and factionalized nature of Nigerian organizations, where personal loyalty is everything.

Early on, I became friendly with a certain social scientist and his family. Thereby, I had unwittingly become his ally in a long drawn-out war between himself and his female colleagues. The disagreement had its origins ten years before in accusations of sex discrimination but had long since spilled over into every aspect of departmental functioning. Even the office workers had chosen sides. More significant, though, was the fact that my friend's chief

antagonist and I had similar theoretical interests. Though in retrospect I regret the missed opportunity, I realize that I was in the thick of things before I could have known what was happening. Given the original complaint, my sympathies could have been with the other camp. But ambiguous loyalty is equivalent to none.

Once I had learned my lessons well, life became more pleasant. True, every case was unique and personal relationships were everything. But, as my friends and allies multiplied, I could more easily make "the system" work for me.

Most Nigerians develop finely honed interpersonal skills, which stand them in good stead when they arrive in the United States. They easily make friends with whomever they run across, and naturally, friends will grant them the benefit of the doubt if there is room to maneuver. The psychological need remains, even in our seemingly formalized, structured world, for a friendly, personable encounter.

On the other hand, as I was soon to learn for myself, anyone adept at working this way suffers tremendous pain and anxiety from the impersonal enforcement of seemingly arbitrary rules. For instance, a friend took it as a personal affront when his insurance agent refused to pay a claim because a renewal was past due.

As a result of my Nigerian experience, I am very sensitive to inflexible and impersonal treatment, the flip side of efficiency:

Leaving Nigeria to return to Boston after two and a half years, I stopped for a week in London. I arrived only to find that my old college friend, with whom I intended to stay, had recently moved. Playing detective, I tried neighbors, the superintendent, directory assistance. Tired and bedraggled, I thought of inquiring whether a forwarding address had been left with the post office. Acknowledging me from inside his cage, the small, graying man reached for his large, gray ledger, peered in, slapped it shut, and answered:

"Yes."

"But . . . what is it?" I asked, caught off guard.

He peered down at me and replied: "I cannot tell you. We are not allowed. We must protect him from creditors."

I was aghast. In no way did I resemble a creditor.

Noticing my reaction, he conceded: "But, if you send him a letter, I will forward it."

Bursting into tears of frustration, in my thickest American accent, displaying my luggage and my air ticket, I begged and cajoled him, to no avail. I spent my entire London week in a bed 'n breakfast, cursing petty bureaucrats as my bill piled up. *"That,"* I thought, *"could never happen in Nigeria!"*

NOTE

1. The theoretical analysis from a lengthier essay has been deleted from this presentation. In the original version, great pains were taken to avoid any possible evolutionary interpretation of the relationship between patrimonial and bureaucratic authority. Over the millenia, bureaucracies have been invented and reinvented in Africa, Asia, and Europe. Moreover, patrimonial relationships exist everywhere bureaucracies exist.

The suggested readings (below) provide the bases for most of my original analysis of aspects of interactional and bureaucratic organization discovered in my Nigerian fieldwork. For those interested, a more thorough analysis can be found in my original essay of the same title in L. Perman (ed.), *Work in Modern Society* (Dubuque, IA: Kendall/Hunt Publishing Company, 1986).

I am grateful to Oladele Akinla, Paul Brodwin, Anne Hornsby, Dorinne Kondo, Anne Sweetser, and Jeong-Ro Yoon for helpful comments on an earlier version of this essay.

REFERENCE

MERTON, ROBERT K.
1968 Social Theory and Social Structure. New York: Free Press. Chapter VIII: Bureaucratic Structure and Personality.

SUGGESTED READING

BENDIX, REINHARD
1977 Max Weber: An Intellectual Portrait. Berkeley and Los Angeles: University of California Press (first publ. 1960).

The Gift of Tongues

The world's peoples have devised ingenious strategies for communicating across linguistic and cultural boundaries

Stephen Wurm

Stephen Wurm, of Australia, is Professor of Linguistics in the Research School of Pacific Studies of the Australian National University in Canberra. Among his 300 publications are Papuan Languages of Oceania *(1982),* Language Atlas of the Pacific Area *(1981–1983) and* Language Atlas of China *(1987–1990).*

More than 5,000 different languages are currently spoken in the world, with a very much larger number of dialects. Many of them are mutually unintelligible or virtually so, and are spoken by small groups of people.

The need for communication across linguistic and cultural boundaries—which has become even more pressing and widespread in recent decades as a result of dramatic increases in the movements of people in many parts of the world—can be met in a number of different ways. One common method is for speakers of two different languages that are used adjacently to each other to learn to speak, at least to some extent, the language of their neighbours. This is called active two-way bilingualism. If only one of two groups that speak different languages learns the language of its neighbours, this is called active one-way bilingualism. For instance, if two neighbouring groups live near the seashore but only one of them has access to the sea and possesses a commodity such as salt or fish that the other group is eager to acquire, the

sellers of such commodities are in an economically more powerful position than the potential buyers, and their language takes precedence over that of the inland tribe when contact occurs.

AMBASSADORS AND NEGOTIATORS

One interesting case of bilingualism has been observed among certain traditionally hostile tribes in Papua New Guinea who speak different languages but need to communicate with each other in order to settle disputes. These tribes customarily exchange children who then learn the language of the tribe that has adopted them, in addition to their own. Afterwards, they act as ambassadors and interpreters, helping to negotiate settlements or other matters arising from tribal disputes. Their safety is ensured by strict laws on both sides.

Members of very small language communities which are surrounded by larger linguistic groups usually learn to speak several of their neighbours' languages. Such people may play an important cultural role as interpreters, negotiators and intermediaries.

Another solution to the intercommunication problem occurs when the speakers of two or several closely related neighbouring languages learn to understand, but not to speak, their neighbours' languages. Participants in such situations speak their own language and are understood by all their

communication partners, and vice versa. This is called passive bilingualism or passive multilingualism. It is especially common between speakers of different Turkic or Mongolian languages in Central Asia, but is also found in parts of Africa and New Guinea.

LINGUA FRANCAS

The cases mentioned so far involve languages that are native to at least one of the communicating groups. However, there are many situations in which languages not native to any of the speakers are used as a means of intercommunication. They occur frequently between speakers of European and non-European metropolitan languages, such as when a Frenchman, a Norwegian, a Hungarian and a Japanese communicate with each other in English. Such a contact language used for wider communication is called a lingua franca.

There are many of these languages in the world, and they achieve their status for a variety of reasons, one of which may be that their speakers possess some appealing cultural features or achieve cultural or political supremacy, which makes their language prestigious in the eyes of speakers of other languages. Many of them emerge as a result of trading relations in which the speakers of a given language take their wares far and wide for sale, and use only their own language, which their customers have to learn, at least rudimentarily, in order to trade with them. Examples of such traders' lingua francas are Kiswahili in East Africa, Bazaar Malay in the East Indies (though it is now receding before Indonesian), and several trade languages in the New Guinea area. In centuries past, Iranian languages such as Sogdian and Middle Persian, and later Modern Persian, were used as trade lingua francas on the silk route across Asia.

PIDGIN LANGUAGES

The majority of such trade lingua francas become simplified when used as such, but they continue in their original full form within the communities that use them as their native tongues. Some trade languages have become pidgin languages, that is languages that are sharply reduced in their grammatical complexity and vocabulary. Examples include a Russian-Chinese pidgin used in the Chinese-Russian border areas in Siberia from the eighteenth to the twentieth centuries, a number of pidgins developed from local indigenous languages in parts of New Guinea before the time of European contacts, and an Inuit pidgin used between Inuit and Alaskan Indians in northern Alaska during the nineteenth century.

A more common way for a pidgin language to emerge is as a means of communication when representatives of a metropolitan culture establish a colonial-type rule over indigenous populations. Quite often, however, such tongues become lingua francas that permit wider intercommunication between speakers of different local languages. This is especially true in areas in which many different tongues are spoken, as is the case in Papua New Guinea, and parts of Africa, northern

Siberia and South America. The grammars and sound structures of these pidgins reflect, in varying degrees, features of the language or languages of the local indigenous population, while their vocabularies are usually, but not always, based on the metropolitan language with an admixture of indigenous elements. Most such pidgins, where they are still spoken, have become the first language of communities, replacing their original native languages. Such languages are called creoles.

There are, however, some parts of the world in which very prominent and widely-used pidgin languages have not, or have only to a very limited extent, replaced local languages. These areas include New Guinea and regions adjacent to it, where several large pidgin languages play very important roles because of the enormous multiplicity and diversity of the local tongues. Nevertheless, the indigenous populations adhere tenaciously to their native languages, which are their most cherished symbols of cultural and ethnic identity.

Many pidgin languages that are in close contact with the metropolitan languages on which much of their vocabulary is based tend to gradually approximate to that language in both vocabulary and grammar and to move towards that language via what is called the post-pidgin (or post-creole) stage. Eventually they become substandard forms of the metropolitan language concerned.

MESSAGES OF RELIGION AND POWER

The so-called mission languages, also known as church languages, constitute another type of language of wider intercommunication. These are local languages originally adopted by European mission organizations as the vehi-

cle of their activities. When the missions extended their work beyond the boundaries of the indigenous language they had adopted, they usually continued to use the adopted local tongue in the new areas, making it thereby an artificially-introduced lingua franca. With the reduction of missionary work in many parts of the world and the nativization of religious activities introduced by Westerners, such languages have in some cases turned into secular lingua francas.

A somewhat similar situation is that in which a local language is adopted as the language of administration by a colonial or conquering power. The language chosen for this purpose is usually fairly widely spoken in the area in question and enjoys some prestige. The Dutch introduced Standard Malay as the official administrative language and general lingua franca in what is now Indonesia. In the same way, the post-colonial rulers of Indonesia adopted Indonesian as the official language even before the country became officially independent. (Indonesian is based on Standard Malay, which made its introduction fairly easy.)

An example of the introduction of a conqueror's language as the general language in the invaded area was the compulsory introduction of the Quechua language of the Incas in what is today Peru in South America. This took place a comparatively short time before the arrival of the Spaniards.

The metropolitan languages of present or past colonial or similar rulers constitute another type of lingua franca in certain areas. Even after most colonies become independent, the languages remain lingua francas, usually among members of elite groups. Their use is beginning to spread in former colonial areas, especially among members of the young generation, at the expense of other lingua francas, in particular of pidgin languages.

Shakespeare in the Bush

Laura Bohannan

Laura Bohannan is a former professor of anthropology at the University of Illinois, at Chicago.

Just before I left Oxford for the Tiv in West Africa, conversation turned to the season at Stratford. "You Americans," said a friend, "often have difficulty with Shakespeare. He was, after all, a very English poet, and one can easily misinterpret the universal by misunderstanding the particular."

I protested that human nature is pretty much the same the whole world over; at least the general plot and motivation of the greater tragedies would always be clear—everywhere—although some details of custom might have to be explained and difficulties of translation might produce other slight changes. To end an argument we could not conclude, my friend gave me a copy of *Hamlet* to study in the African bush: it would, he hoped, lift my mind above its primitive surroundings, and possibly I might, by prolonged meditation, achieve the grace of correct interpretation.

It was my second field trip to that African tribe, and I thought myself ready to live in one of its remote sections—an area difficult to cross even on foot. I eventually settled on the hillock of a very knowledgeable old man, the head of a homestead of some hundred and forty people, all of whom were either his close relatives or their wives and children. Like the other elders of the vicinity, the old man spent most of his time performing ceremonies seldom seen these days in the more accessible parts of the tribe. I was delighted. Soon there would be three months of enforced isolation and leisure, between the harvest that takes place just before the rising of the swamps and the clearing of new farms when the water goes down. Then, I thought, they would have even more time to perform ceremonies and explain them to me.

I was quite mistaken. Most of the ceremonies demanded the presence of elders from several homesteads. As the swamps rose, the old men found it too difficult to walk from one homestead to the next, and the ceremonies gradually ceased. As the swamps rose even higher, all activities but one came to an end. The women brewed beer from maize and millet. Men, women, and children sat on their hillocks and drank it.

People began to drink at dawn. By midmorning the whole homestead was singing, dancing, and drumming. When it rained, people had to sit inside their huts: there they drank and sang or they drank and told stories. In any case, by noon or before, I either had to join the party or retire to my own hut and my books. "One does not discuss serious matters when there is beer. Come, drink with us." Since I lacked their capacity for the thick native beer, I spent more and more time with *Hamlet*. Before the end of the second month, grace descended on me. I was quite sure that *Hamlet* had only one possible interpretation, and that one universally obvious.

Early every morning, in the hope of having some serious talk before the beer party, I used to call on the old man at his reception hut—a circle of posts supporting a thatched roof above a low mud wall to keep out wind and rain. One day I crawled through the low doorway and found most of the men of the homestead sitting huddled in their ragged cloths on stools, low plank beds, and reclining chairs, warming themselves against the chill of the rain around a smoky fire. In the center were three pots of beer. The party had started.

The old man greeted me cordially. "Sit down and drink." I accepted a large calabash full of beer, poured some into a small drinking gourd, and tossed it down. Then I poured some more into the same gourd for the man second in seniority to my host before I handed my calabash over to a young man for further distribution. Important people shouldn't ladle beer themselves.

2. CULTURE AND COMMUNICATION

"It is better like this," the old man said, looking at me approvingly and plucking at the thatch that had caught in my hair. "You should sit and drink with us more often. Your servants tell me that when you are not with us, you sit inside your hut looking at a paper."

The old man was acquainted with four kinds of "papers": tax receipts, bride price receipts, court fee receipts, and letters. The messenger who brought him letters from the chief used them mainly as a badge of office, for he always knew what was in them and told the old man. Personal letters for the few who had relatives in the government or mission stations were kept until someone went to a large market where there was a letter writer and reader. Since my arrival, letters were brought to me to be read. A few men also brought me bride price receipts, privately, with requests to change the figures to a higher sum. I found moral arguments were of no avail, since in-laws are fair game, and the technical hazards of forgery difficult to explain to an illiterate people. I did not wish them to think me silly enough to look at any such papers for days on end, and I hastily explained that my "paper" was one of the "things of long ago" of my country.

"Ah," said the old man. "Tell us."

I protested that I was not a story-teller. Story telling is a skilled art among them; their standards are high, and the audiences critical—and vocal in their criticism. I protested in vain. This morning they wanted to hear a story while they drank. They threatened to tell me no more stories until I told them one of mine. Finally, the old man promised that no one would criticize my style "for we know you are struggling with our language." "But," put in one of the elders, "you must explain what we do not understand, as we do when we tell you our stories." Realizing that here was my chance to prove *Hamlet* universally intelligible, I agreed.

The old man handed me some more beer to help me on with my story-telling. Men filled their long wooden pipes and knocked coals from the fire to place in the pipe bowls; then, puffing contentedly, they sat back to listen. I began in the proper style, "Not yesterday, not yesterday, but long ago, a thing occurred. One night three men were keeping watch outside the homestead of the great chief, when suddenly they saw the former chief approach them."

"Why was he no longer their chief?"

"He was dead," I explained. "That is why they were troubled and afraid when they saw him."

"Impossible," began one of the elders, handing his pipe on to his neighbor, who interrupted, "Of course it wasn't the dead chief. It was an omen sent by a witch. Go on."

Slightly shaken, I continued. "One of these three was a man who knew things"—the closest translation for scholar, but unfortunately it also meant witch. The second elder looked triumphantly at the first. "So he spoke to the dead chief saying, 'Tell us what we must do so you may rest in your grave,' but the dead chief did not answer. He vanished, and they could see him no more. Then the man who knew things—his name was Horatio—said this event was the affair of the dead chief's son, Hamlet."

There was a general shaking of heads round the circle. "Had the dead chief no living brothers? Or was this son the chief?"

"No," I replied. "That is, he had one living brother who became the chief when the elder brother died."

The old men muttered: such omens were matters for chiefs and elders, not for youngsters; no good could come of going behind a chief's back; clearly Horatio was not a man who knew things.

"Yes, he was," I insisted, shooing a chicken away from my beer. "In our country the son is next to the father. The dead chief's younger brother had become the great chief. He had also married his elder brother's widow only about a month after the funeral."

"He did well," the old man beamed and announced to the others, "I told you that if we knew more about Europeans, we would find they really were very like us. In our country also," he added to me, "the younger brother marries the elder brother's widow and becomes the father of his children. Now, if your uncle, who married your widowed mother, is your father's full brother, then he will be a real father to you. Did Hamlet's father and uncle have one mother?"

His question barely penetrated my mind; I was too upset and thrown too far off balance by having one of the most important elements of *Hamlet* knocked straight out of the picture. Rather uncertainly I said that I thought they had the same mother, but I wasn't sure—the story didn't say. The old man told me severely that these genealogical details made all the difference and that when I got home I must ask the elders about it. He shouted out the door to one of his younger wives to bring his goatskin bag.

Determined to save what I could of the mother motif, I took a deep breath and began again. "The son Hamlet was very sad because his mother had married again so quickly. There was no need for her to do so, and it is our custom for a widow not to go to her next husband until she has mourned for two years."

"Two years is too long," objected the wife, who had appeared with the old man's battered goatskin bag. "Who will hoe your farms for you while you have no husband?"

"Hamlet," I retorted without thinking, "was old enough to hoe his mother's farms himself. There was no need for her to remarry." No one looked convinced. I gave up. "His mother and the great chief told Hamlet not to be sad, for the great chief himself would be a father to Hamlet. Furthermore, Hamlet would be the next chief: therefore he must stay to learn the things of a chief. Hamlet agreed to remain, and all the rest went off to drink beer."

While I paused, perplexed at how to render Hamlet's disgusted solilo-quy to an audience convinced that Claudius and Gertrude had behaved in the best possible manner, one of the younger men asked me who had married the other wives of the dead chief.

"He had no other wives," I told him.

"But a chief must have many wives! How else can he brew beer and prepare food for all his guests?"

I said firmly that in our country even chiefs had only one wife, that they had servants to do their work, and that they paid them from tax money.

It was better, they returned, for a chief to have many wives and sons who would help him hoe his farms and feed his people; then everyone loved the chief who gave much and took nothing—taxes were a bad thing.

I agreed with the last comment, but for the rest fell back on their favorite way of fobbing off my questions: "That is the way it is done, so that is how we do it."

I decided to skip the soliloquy. Even if Claudius was here thought quite right to marry his brother's widow, there remained the poison motif, and I knew they would disapprove of fratricide. More hopefully I resumed, "That night Hamlet kept watch with the three who had seen his dead father. The dead chief again appeared, and although the others were afraid, Hamlet followed his dead father off to one side. When they were alone, Hamlet's dead father spoke."

"Omens can't talk!" The old man was emphatic.

"Hamlet's dead father wasn't an omen. Seeing him might have been an omen, but he was not." My audience looked as confused as I sounded. "It *was* Hamlet's dead father. It was a thing we call a 'ghost.'" I had to use the English word, for unlike many of the neighboring tribes, these people didn't believe in the survival after death of any individuating part of the personality.

"What is a 'ghost'? An omen?"

"No, a 'ghost' is someone who is dead but who walks around and can talk, and people can hear him and see him but not touch him."

They objected. "One can touch zombis."

"No, no! It was not a dead body the witches had animated to sacrifice and eat. No one else made Hamlet's dead father walk. He did it himself."

"Dead men can't walk," protested my audience as one man.

I was quite willing to compromise. "A 'ghost' is the dead man's shadow."

But again they objected. "Dead men cast no shadows."

"They do in my country," I snapped.

The old man quelled the babble of disbelief that arose immediately and told me with that insincere, but courteous, agreement one extends to the fancies of the young, ignorant, and superstitious, "No doubt in your country the dead can also walk without being zombis." From the depths of his bag he produced a withered fragment of kola nut, bit off one end to show it wasn't poisoned, and handed me the rest as a peace offering.

"Anyhow," I resumed, "Hamlet's dead father said that his own brother, the one who became chief, had poisoned him. He wanted Hamlet to avenge him. Hamlet believed this in his heart, for he did not like his father's brother." I took another swallow of beer. "In the country of the great chief, living in the same homestead, for it was a very large one, was an important elder who was often with the chief to advise and help him. His name was Polonius. Hamlet was courting his daughter, but her father and her brother . . .[I cast hastily about for some tribal analogy] warned her not to let Hamlet visit her when she was alone on her farm, for he would be a great chief and so could not marry her."

"Why not?" asked the wife, who had settled down on the edge of the old man's chair. He frowned at her for asking stupid questions and growled, "They lived in the same homestead."

"That was not the reason," I informed them. "Polonius was a stranger who lived in the homestead because he helped the chief, not because he was a relative."

"Then why couldn't Hamlet marry her?"

"He could have," I explained, "but Polonius didn't think he would. After all, Hamlet was a man of great importance who ought to marry a chief's daughter, for in his country a man could have only one wife. Polonius was afraid that if Hamlet made love to his daughter, then no one else would give a high price for her."

"That might be true," remarked one of the shrewder elders, "but a chief's son would give his mistress's father enough presents and patronage to more than make up the difference. Polonius sounds like a fool to me."

"Many people think he was," I agreed. "Meanwhile Polonius sent his son Laertes off to Paris to learn the things of that country, for it was the homestead of a very great chief indeed. Because he was afraid that Laertes might waste a lot of money on beer and women and gambling, or get into trouble by fighting, he sent one of his servants to Paris secretly, to spy out what Laertes was doing. One day Hamlet came upon Polonius's daughter Ophelia. He behaved so oddly he frightened her. Indeed"—I was fumbling for words to express the dubious quality of Hamlet's madness—"the chief and many others had also noticed that when Hamlet talked one could understand the words but not what they meant. Many people thought that he had become mad." My audience suddenly became much more attentive. "The great chief wanted to know what was wrong with Hamlet, so he sent for two of Hamlet's age mates [school friends would have taken long explanation] to talk to Hamlet and find out what troubled his heart. Hamlet, seeing that they had been bribed by the chief to betray him, told them nothing. Polonius, however, insisted that Hamlet was mad because he had been forbidden to see Ophelia, whom he loved."

"Why," inquired a bewildered voice, "should anyone bewitch Hamlet on that account?"

"Bewitch him?"

"Yes, only witchcraft can make anyone mad, unless, of course, one sees the beings that lurk in the forest."

2. CULTURE AND COMMUNICATION

I stopped being a storyteller, took out my notebook and demanded to be told more about these two causes of madness. Even while they spoke and I jotted notes, I tried to calculate the effect of this new factor on the plot. Hamlet had not been exposed to the beings that lurk in the forests. Only his relatives in the male line could bewitch him. Barring relatives not mentioned by Shakespeare, it had to be Claudius who was attempting to harm him. And, of course, it was.

For the moment I staved off questions by saying that the great chief also refused to believe that Hamlet was mad for the love of Ophelia and nothing else. "He was sure that something much more important was troubling Hamlet's heart."

"Now Hamlet's age mates," I continued, "had brought with them a famous storyteller. Hamlet decided to have this man tell the chief and all his homestead a story about a man who had poisoned his brother because he desired his brother's wife and wished to be chief himself. Hamlet was sure the great chief could not hear the story without making a sign if he was indeed guilty, and then he would discover whether his dead father had told him the truth."

The old man interrupted, with deep cunning, "Why should a father lie to his son?" he asked.

I hedged: "Hamlet wasn't sure that it really was his dead father." It was impossible to say anything, in that language, about devil-inspired visions.

"You mean," he said, "it actually was an omen, and he knew witches sometimes send false ones. Hamlet was a fool not to go to one skilled in reading omens and divining the truth in the first place. A man-who-sees-the-truth could have told him how his father died, if he really had been poisoned, and if there was witchcraft in it; then Hamlet could have called the elders to settle the matter."

The shrewd elder ventured to disagree. "Because his father's brother was a great chief, one-who-sees-the-truth might therefore have been afraid to tell it. I think it was for that reason that a friend of Hamlet's father—a witch and an elder—sent an omen so his friend's son would know. Was the omen true?"

"Yes," I said, abandoning ghosts and the devil; a witch-sent omen it would have to be. "It was true, for when the storyteller was telling his tale before all the homestead, the great chief rose in fear. Afraid that Hamlet knew his secret he planned to have him killed."

The stage set of the next bit presented some difficulties of translation. I began cautiously. "The great chief told Hamlet's mother to find out from her son what he knew. But because a woman's children are always first in her heart, he had the important elder Polonius hide behind a cloth that hung against the wall of Hamlet's mother's sleeping hut. Hamlet started to scold his mother for what she had done."

There was a shocked murmur from everyone. A man should never scold his mother.

"She called out in fear, and Polonius moved behind the cloth. Shouting, 'A rat!' Hamlet took his machete and slashed through the cloth." I paused for dramatic effect. "He had killed Polonius!"

The old men looked at each other in supreme disgust. "That Polonius truly was a fool and a man who knew nothing! What child would not know enough to shout, 'It's me!'" With a pang, I remembered that these people are ardent hunters, always armed with bow, arrow, and machete; at the first rustle in the grass an arrow is aimed and ready, and the hunter shouts "Game!" If no human voice answers immediately, the arrow speeds on its way. Like a good hunter Hamlet had shouted, "A rat!"

I rushed in to save Polonius's reputation. "Polonius did speak. Hamlet heard him. But he thought it was the chief and wished to kill him earlier that evening. . . ." I broke down, unable to describe to these pagans, who had no belief in individual afterlife, the difference between dying at one's prayers and dying "unhousel'd, disappointed, unaneled."

This time I had shocked my audience seriously. "For a man to raise his hand against his father's brother and and the one who has become his father—that is a terrible thing. The elders ought to let such a man be bewitched."

I nibbled at my kola nut in some perplexity, then pointed out that after all the man had killed Hamlet's father.

"No," pronounced the old man, speaking less to me than to the young men sitting behind the elders. "If your father's brother has killed your father, you must appeal to your father's age mates; *they* may avenge him. No man may use violence against his senior relatives." Another thought struck him. "But if his father's brother had indeed been wicked enough to bewitch Hamlet and make him mad that would be a good story indeed, for it would be his fault that Hamlet, being mad, no longer had any sense and thus was ready to kill his father's brother."

There was a murmur of applause. *Hamlet* was again a good story to them, but it no longer seemed quite the same story to me. As I thought over the coming complications of plot and motive, I lost courage and decided to skim over dangerous ground quickly.

"The great chief," I went on, "was not sorry that Hamlet had killed Polonius. It gave him a reason to send Hamlet away, with his two treacherous mates, with letters to a chief of a far country, saying that Hamlet should be killed. But Hamlet changed the writing on their papers, so that the chief killed his age mates instead." I encountered a reproachful glare from one of the men whom I had told undetectable forgery was not merely immoral but beyond human skill. I looked the other way.

"Before Hamlet could return, Laertes came back for his father's funeral. The great chief told him Hamlet had killed Polonius. Laertes swore to kill Hamlet because of this, and because his sister Ophelia, hearing her father had been killed by the man she loved, went mad and drowned in the river."

"Have you already forgotten what we told you?" The old man was reproachful. "One cannot take vengeance on a madman; Hamlet killed Polonius in his madness. As for the girl, she not only went mad, she was drowned. Only witches can make people drown. Water itself can't hurt anything. It is merely something one drinks and bathes in."

I began to get cross. "If you don't like the story, I'll stop."

The old man made soothing noises and himself poured me some more beer. "You tell the story well, and we are listening. But it is clear that the elders of your country have never told you what the story really means. No, don't interrupt! We believe you when you say your marriage customs are different, or your clothes and weapons. But people are the same everywhere; therefore, there are always witches and it is we, the elders, who know how witches work. We told you it was the great chief who wished to kill Hamlet, and now your own words have proved us right. Who were Ophelia's male relatives?"

"There were only her father and her brother." *Hamlet* was clearly out of my hands.

"There must have been many more; this also you must ask of your elders when you get back to your country. From what you tell us, since Polonius was dead, it must have been Laertes who killed Ophelia, although I do not see the reason for it."

We had emptied one pot of beer, and the old men argued the point with slightly tipsy interest. Finally one of them demanded of me, "What did the servant of Polonius say on his return?"

With difficulty I recollected Reynaldo and his mission. "I don't think he did return before Polonius was killed."

"Listen," said the elder, "and I will tell you how it was and how your story will go, then you may tell me if I am right. Polonius knew his son would get into trouble, and so he did. He had many fines to pay for fighting, and debts from gambling. But he had only two ways of getting money quickly. One was to marry off his sister at once, but it is difficult to find a man who will marry a woman desired by the son of a chief. For if the chief's heir commits adultery with your wife, what can you do? Only a fool calls a case against a man who will someday be his judge. Therefore Laertes had to take the second way: he killed his sister by witchcraft, drowning her so he could secretly sell her body to the witches."

I raised an objection. "They found her body and buried it. Indeed Laertes jumped into the grave to see his sister once more—so, you see, the body was truly there. Hamlet, who had just come back, jumped in after him."

"What did I tell you?" The elder appealed to the others. "Laertes was up to no good with his sister's body. Hamlet prevented him, because the chief's heir, like a chief, does not wish any other man to grow rich and powerful. Laertes would be angry, because he would have killed his sister without benefit to himself. In our country he would try to kill Hamlet for that reason. Is this not what happened?"

"More or less," I admitted. "When the great chief found Hamlet was still alive, he encouraged Laertes to try to kill Hamlet and arranged a fight with machetes between them. In the fight both the young men were wounded to death. Hamlet's mother drank the poisoned beer that the chief meant for Hamlet in case he won the fight. When he saw his mother die of poison, Hamlet, dying, managed to kill his father's brother with his machete."

"You see, I was right!" exclaimed the elder.

"That was a very good story," added the old man, "and you told it with very few mistakes. There was just one more error, at the very end. The poison Hamlet's mother drank was obviously meant for the survivor of the fight, whichever it was. If Laertes had won, the great chief would have poisoned him, for no one would know that he arranged Hamlet's death. Then, too, he need not fear Laertes' witchcraft; it takes a strong heart to kill one's only sister by witchcraft.

"Sometime," concluded the old man, gathering his ragged toga about him, "you must tell us some more stories of your country. We, who are elders, will instruct you in their true meaning, so that when you return to your own land your elders will see that you have not been sitting in the bush, but among those who know things and who have taught you wisdom."

The Organization of Society and Culture

Human beings do not interact with one another or think about their world in random fashion. Instead, they engage in both structured and recurrent physical and mental activities. In this section, such patterns of behavior and thought—referred to here as the organization of society and culture— may be seen in a number of different contexts, from the cattle-herding Masai of East Africa (in "Mystique of the Masai") to the Yanomami of Amazonia (in "The Yanomami Keep on Trekking").

Of special importance are the ways in which people make a living—in other words, the production, distribution, and consumption of goods and services. It is only by knowing the basic subsistence systems that we can hope to gain insight into the other levels of social and cultural phenomena, for, as anthropologists have found, they are all inextricably bound together, as related in "Camels in the Land of Kings."

Noting the various aspects of a sociocultural system in harmonious balance, however, does not imply an anthropological seal of approval. To understand infanticide (killing of the newborn) in the manner that it is practiced among some peoples is neither to condone nor condemn it. The adaptive patterns that have been in existence for a great length of time, such as many of the patterns of hunters and gatherers, probably owe their existence to their contributions to long-term human survival.

The articles in this section demonstrate that anthropologists are far more interested in problems than they are in place. The article "The Blood in Their Veins" conveys the hardships of living in the Arctic in such personal terms that the reader cannot help but understand the actions of Inuit (Eskimos) from their viewpoint. In fact, if it were not for the firsthand descriptions, such as that provided by Richard Nelson in "Understanding Eskimo Science," the very notion that such people could have such a profound understanding of their environment would have been beyond belief.

Anthropologists, however, are not content with the data derived from individual experience. On the contrary, personal descriptions must become the basis for sound anthropological theory. Otherwise, they remain meaningless, isolated relics of culture in the manner of museum pieces. Thus, in "Too Many Bananas, Not Enough Pineapples, and No Watermelon at All: Three Object Lessons in Living with Reciprocity," David Counts provides us with

ground rules for reciprocity, derived from his own particular field experience and yet cross-culturally applicable. Karl Rambo, in "From Shells to Money," then shows that the adoption of money as a medium of exchange does not in itself usher in a market mentality, especially if a people's basic subsistence system remains intact. Finally, "Life without Chiefs" expresses that constant striving in anthropology to develop a general perspective from particular events by showing how shifts in technology may result in centralization of political power and marked changes in lifestyle.

While the articles in this section are to some extent descriptive, they also serve to challenge both academic and commonsense notions about why people behave and think as they do. They remind us that assumptions are never really safe. Any time anthropologists can be kept on their toes, the field as a whole is the better for it.

Looking Ahead: Challenge Questions

What traditional Inuit (Eskimo) practices do you find contrary to values professed in your society, but important to Eskimo survival under certain circumstances?

What can contemporary hunter-collector societies tell us about the quality of life in the prehistoric past?

In what ways can the Masai be seen as ecological conservationists?

Why do the Simbu value money as a medium of ceremonial exchange rather than as a means to accumulate personal wealth?

Under what circumstances do social stratification and centralization of power appear in human societies?

What are the rules of reciprocity?

Understanding Eskimo Science

Traditional hunters' insights into the natural world are worth rediscovering.

Richard Nelson

Just below the Arctic Circle in the boreal forest of interior Alaska; an amber afternoon in mid-November; the temperature -20°; the air adrift with frost crystals, presaging the onset of deeper cold.

Five men—Koyukon Indians—lean over the carcass of an exceptionally large black bear. For two days they've traversed the Koyukuk River valley, searching for bears that have recently entered hibernation dens. The animals are in prime condition at this season but extremely hard to find. Den entrances, hidden beneath 18 inches of powdery snow, are betrayed only by the subtlest of clues—patches where no grass protrudes from the surface because it's been clawed away for insulation, faint concavities hinting of footprint depressions in the moss below.

Earlier this morning the hunters took a yearling bear. In accordance with Koyukon tradition, they followed elaborate rules for the proper treatment of killed animals. For example, the bear's feet were removed first, to keep its spirit from wandering. Also, certain parts were to be eaten away from the village, at a kind of funeral feast. All the rest would be eaten either at home or at community events, as people here have done for countless generations.

Koyukon hunters know that an animal's life ebbs slowly, that it remains aware and sensitive to how people treat its body. This is especially true for the potent and demanding spirit of the bear.

The leader of the hunting group is Moses Sam, a man in his 60s who has trapped in this territory since childhood. He is known for his detailed knowledge of the land and for his extraordinary success as a bear hunter. "No one else has that kind of luck with bears," I've been told. "Some people are born with it. He always takes good care of his animals—respects them. That's how he keeps his luck."

Moses pulls a small knife from his pocket, kneels beside the bear's head, and carefully slits the clear domes of its eyes. "Now," he explains softly, "the bear won't see if one of us makes a mistake or does something wrong."

Contemporary Americans are likely to find this story exotic, but over the course of time episodes like this have been utterly commonplace, the essence of people's relationship to the natural world. After all, for 99 percent of human history we lived exclusively as hunter-gatherers; by comparison, agriculture has existed only for a moment and urban societies scarcely more than a blink.

From this perspective, much of human experience over the past several million years lies beyond our grasp. Probably no society has been so deeply alienated as ours from the community of nature, has viewed the natural world from a greater distance of mind, has lapsed into a murkier comprehension of its connections with the sustaining environment. Because of this, we have great difficulty understanding our rootedness to earth, our affinities with non-human life.

I believe it's essential that we learn from traditional societies, especially those whose livelihood depends on the harvest of a wild environment—hunters, fishers, trappers, and gatherers. These people have accumulated bodies of knowledge much like our own sciences. And they can give us vital insights about responsible membership in the community of life, insights founded on a wisdom we'd long forgotten and now are beginning to rediscover.

Since the mid-1960s I have worked as an ethnographer in Alaska, living intermittently in remote northern communities and recording native traditions centered around the natural world. I spent about two years in Koyukon Indian villages and just over a year with Inupiaq Eskimos on the Arctic coast—traveling by dog team and snowmobile, recording traditional knowledge, and learning the hunter's way.

Eskimos have long inhabited some of the harshest environments on earth, and they are among the most exquisitely adapted of all human groups. Because plant life is so scarce in their northern terrain, Eskimos depend more than any other people on hunting.

Eskimos are famous for the cleverness of their technology—kayaks, harpoons, skin clothing, snow houses, dog teams. But I believe their greatest genius, and the basis of their success, lies in the less tangible realm of the intellect—the nexus of mind and nature. For what repeatedly struck me above all else was their profound knowledge of the environment.

Several times, when my Inupiaq hunting companion did something especially clever, he'd point to his head

This article first appeared in *Audubon*, September/October 1993, pp. 102-109. Adapted from *Biophilia* by Richard Nelson, Island Press, 1993. © 1993 by Richard Nelson. Reprinted by permission of Susan Bergholz Literary Services, New York.

and declare: "You see—Eskimo scientist!" At first I took it as hyperbole, but as time went by I realized he was speaking the truth. Scientists had often come to his village, and he saw in them a familiar commitment to the empirical method.

Traditional Inupiaq hunters spend a lifetime acquiring knowledge—from others in the community and from their own observations. If they are to survive, they must have absolutely reliable information. When I first went to live with Inupiaq people, I doubted many things they told me. But the longer I stayed, the more I trusted their teachings.

The Inupiaq hunter possesses as much knowledge as a highly trained scientist in our own society.

For example, hunters say that ringed seals surfacing in open leads—wide cracks in the sea ice—can reliably forecast the weather. Because an unexpected gale might set people adrift on the pack ice, accurate prediction is a matter of life and death. When seals rise chest-high in the water, snout pointed skyward, not going anywhere in particular, it indicates stable weather, the Inupiaq say. But if they surface briefly, head low, snout parallel to the water, and show themselves only once or twice, watch for a sudden storm. And take special heed if you've also noticed the sled dogs howling incessantly, stars twinkling erratically, or the current running strong from the south. As time passed, my own experiences with seals and winter storms affirmed what the Eskimos said.

Like a young Inupiaq in training, I gradually grew less skeptical and started to apply what I was told. For example, had I ever been rushed by a polar bear, I would have jumped away to the animal's *right* side. Inupiaq elders say polar bears are left-handed, so you have a slightly better chance to

avoid their right paw, which is slower and less accurate. I'm pleased to say I never had the chance for a field test. But in judging assertions like this, remember that Eskimos have had close contact with polar bears for several thousand years.

During winter, ringed and bearded seals maintain tunnel-like breathing holes in ice that is many feet thick. These holes are often capped with an igloo-shaped dome created by water sloshing onto the surface when the animal enters from below. Inupiaq elders told me that polar bears are clever enough to excavate around the base of this dome, leaving it perfectly intact but weak enough that a hard swat will shatter the ice and smash the seal's skull. I couldn't help wondering if this were really true; but then a younger man told me he'd recently followed the tracks of a bear that had excavated one seal hole after another, exactly as the elders had described.

In the village where I lived, the most respected hunter was Igruk, a man in his 70s. He had an extraordinary sense of animals—a gift for understanding and predicting their behavior. Although he was no longer quick and strong, he joined a crew hunting bowhead whales during the spring migration, his main role being that of adviser. Each time Igruk spotted a whale coming from the south, he counted the number of blows, timed how long it stayed down, and noted the distance it traveled along the open lead, until it vanished toward the north. This way he learned to predict, with uncanny accuracy, where hunters could expect the whale to resurface.

I believe the expert Inupiaq hunter possesses as much knowledge as a highly trained scientist in our own society, although the information may be of a different sort. Volumes could be written on the behavior, ecology, and utilization of Arctic animals—polar bear, walrus, bowhead whale, beluga, bearded seal, ringed seal, caribou, musk ox, and others—based entirely on Eskimo knowledge.

Comparable bodies of knowledge existed in every Native American cul-

ture before the time of Columbus. Since then, even in the far north, Western education and cultural change have steadily eroded these traditions. Reflecting on a time before Europeans arrived, we can imagine the whole array of North American animal species—deer, elk, black bear, wolf, mountain lion, beaver, coyote, Canada goose, ruffed grouse, passenger pigeon, northern pike—each known in hundreds of different ways by tribal communities; the entire continent, sheathed in intricate webs of knowledge. Taken as a whole, this composed a vast intellectual legacy, born of intimacy with the natural world. Sadly, not more than a hint of it has ever been recorded.

Like other Native Americans, the Inupiaq acquired their knowledge through gradual accretion of naturalistic observations—year after year, lifetime after lifetime, generation after generation, century after century. Modern science often relies on other techniques—specialized full-time observation, controlled experiments, captive-animal studies, technological devises like radio collars—which can provide similar information much more quickly.

Yet Eskimo people have learned not only *about* animals but also *from* them. Polar bears hunt seals not only by waiting at their winter breathing holes, but also by stalking seals that crawl up on the ice to bask in the spring warmth. Both methods depend on being silent, staying downwind, keeping out of sight, and moving only when the seal is asleep or distracted. According to the elders, a stalking bear will even use one paw to cover its conspicuous black nose.

Inupiaq methods for hunting seals, both at breathing holes and atop the spring ice, are nearly identical to those of the polar bear. Is this a case of independent invention? Or did ancestral Eskimos learn the techniques by watching polar bears, who had perfected an adaptation to the sea-ice environment long before humans arrived in the Arctic?

The hunter's genius centers on knowing an animal's behavior so well he can turn it to his advantage. For instance, Igruk once saw a polar bear far off across flat ice, where he couldn't stalk it without being seen. But he knew an old technique of mimicking a seal. He lay down in plain sight, conspicuous in his dark parka and pants, then lifted and dropped his head like a seal, scratched the ice, and imitated flippers with his hands. The bear mistook his pursuer for prey. Each time Igruk lifted his head the animal kept still; whenever Igruk "slept" the bear crept closer. When it came near enough, a gunshot pierced the snowy silence. That night, polar bear meat was shared among the villagers.

"Each animal knows way more than you do," a Koyukon Indian elder was fond of telling me.

A traditional hunter like Igruk plumbs the depths of his intellect—his capacity to manipulate complex knowledge. But he also delves into his animal nature, drawing from intuitions of sense and body and heart: feeling the wind's touch, listening for the tick of moving ice, peering from crannies, hiding as if he himself were the hunted. He moves in a world of eyes, where everything watches—the bear, the seal, the wind, the moon and stars, the drifting ice, the silent waters below. He is beholden to powers we have long forgotten or ignored.

In Western society we rest comfortably on our own accepted truths about the nature of nature. We treat the environment as if it were numb to our presence and blind to our behavior. Yet despite our certainty on this matter, accounts of traditional people throughout the world reveal that most of humankind has concluded otherwise. Perhaps our scientific method really does follow the path to a single, absolute truth. But there may be wisdom in accepting other possibilities and opening ourselves to different views of the world.

I remember asking a Koyukon man about the behavior and temperament of the Canada goose. He described it as a gentle and good-natured animal, then added: "Even if [a goose] had the power to knock you over, I don't think it would do it."

For me, his words carried a deep metaphorical wisdom. They exemplified the Koyukon people's own restraint toward the world around them. And they offered a contrast to our culture, in which possessing the power to overwhelm the environment has long been sufficient justification for its use.

We often think of this continent as having been a pristine wilderness when the first Europeans arrived. Yet for at least 12,000 years, and possibly twice that long, Native American people had inhabited and intensively utilized the land; had gathered, hunted, fished, settled, and cultivated; had learned the terrain in all its details, infusing it with meaning and memory; and had shaped every aspect of their life around it. That humans could sustain membership in a natural community for such an enormous span of time without profoundly degrading it fairly staggers the imagination. And it gives strong testimony to the adaptation of mind—the braiding together of knowledge and ideology—that linked North America's indigenous people with their environment.

A Koyukon elder, who took it upon himself to be my teacher, was fond of telling me: "Each animal knows way more than you do." He spoke as if it summarized all that he understood and believed.

This statement epitomizes relationships to the natural world among many Native American people. And it goes far in explaining the diversity and fecundity of life on our continent when the first sailing ship approached these shores.

There's been much discussion in recent years about what biologist E. O. Wilson has termed "biophilia"—a deep, pervasive, ubiquitous, all-embracing affinity for nonhuman life. Evidence for this "instinct" may be elusive in Western cultures, but not among tradi-

tional societies. People like the Koyukon manifest biophilia in virtually all dimensions of their existence. Connectedness with nonhuman life infuses the whole spectrum of their thought, behavior, and belief.

It's often said that a fish might have no concept of water, never having left it. In the same way, traditional peoples might never stand far enough outside themselves to imagine a generalized concept of biophilia. Perhaps it would be impossible for people so intimately bound with the natural world, people who recognize that all nature is our own embracing community. Perhaps, to bring a word like *biophilia* into their language, they would first need to separate themselves from nature.

In April 1971 I was in a whaling camp several miles off the Arctic coast with a group of Inupiaq hunters, including Igruk, who understood animals so well he almost seemed to enter their minds.

Onshore winds had closed the lead that migrating whales usually follow, but one large opening remained, and here the Inupiaq men placed their camp. For a couple of days there had been no whales, so everyone stayed inside the warm tent, talking and relaxing. The old man rested on a soft bed of caribou skins with his eyes closed. Then, suddenly, he interrupted the conversation: "I think a whale is coming, and perhaps it will surface very close. . . ."

To my amazement everyone jumped into action, although none had seen or heard anything except Igruk's words. Only he stayed behind, while the others rushed for the water's edge. I was last to leave the tent. Seconds after I stepped outside, a broad, shining back cleaved the still water near the opposite side of the opening, accompanied by the burst of a whale's blow.

Later, when I asked how he'd known, Igruk said, "There was a ringing inside my ears." I have no explanation other than his; I can only report what I saw. None of the Inupiaq crew members even commented afterward, as if nothing out of the ordinary had happened.

The Blood in Their Veins

Farley Mowat

Barely visible from Gene Lushman's rickety dock at the mouth of Big River, Anoteelik stroked his kayak to seaward on the heaving brown waters of Hudson Bay. Vanishing, then reappearing on the long, slick swells, the kayak was so distant it might have been nothing more than an idle gull drifting aimlessly on the undulating waters.

I had helped Anoteelik prepare for that journey. Together we had carried the skin-wrapped packages of dress goods, food and tobacco down from Lushman's trading shack. Then the squat, heavy-bodied Eskimo, with his dreadfully scarred face, lashed the cargo to the afterdeck and departed. I watched him until the bright flashing of his double-bladed paddle was only a white flicker against the humped outlines of a group of rocky reefs lying three miles offshore.

This was the third time I had seen Anoteelik make his way out of the estuary to the farthest islet on the sombre rim of the sea but it was the first time I understood the real reason behind his yearly solitary voyage.

Gene Lushman, barrenland trapper and trader, had first drawn my attention to him three years earlier.

"See that old Husky there? Old Ano . . . tough old bugger . . . one of the inland people and queer like all of them. Twenty years now, every spring soon as the ice clears, Ano, he heads off out to the farthest rock, and every year he takes a hundred dollars of my best trade goods along. For why? Well, me son, that crazy old bastard is taking the stuff out there to his dead wife! That's

true, so help me God! He buried her there . . . far out to sea as there was a rock sticking up high enough to hold a grave!

"Father Debrie, he's tried maybe a half dozen times to make the old fellow quit his nonsense. It has a bad influence on the rest of the Huskies—they're supposed to be Christians, you know—but Ano, he just smiles and says: 'Yes, Father,' and every spring he turns in his fox skins to me and I sell him the same bill of goods, and he takes it and dumps it on that rock in the Bay."

It was the waste that bothered and puzzled Gene. Himself the product of a Newfoundland outport, he could not abide the waste . . . a hundred dollars every spring as good as dumped into the sea.

"Crazy old bastard!" he said, shaking his head in bewilderment.

Although he had traded with the Big River people for a good many years, Gene had never really bridged the gap between them and himself. He had learned only enough of their language for trade purposes and while he admired their ability to survive in their harsh land he had little interest in their inner lives, perhaps because he had never been able to stop thinking of them as a "lesser breed." Consequently, he never discovered the reason for Anoteelik's strange behaviour.

During my second year in the country, I became friendly with Itkut, old Anoteelik's son—indeed his only offspring. Itkut was a big, stocky man still in the full vigour of young manhood; a man who laughed a lot and liked making jokes. It was he who gave me my Eskimo name, *Kipmetna,* which translates as "noisy little dog." Itkut and I spent a lot of time together

that summer, including making a long boat trip north to Marble Island after walrus. A few days after our return, old Ano happened into Itkut's tent to find me struggling to learn the language under his son's somewhat less-than-patient guidance. For a while Ano listened to the garbled sounds I was making, then he chuckled. Until that moment the old man, with his hideously disfigured face, had seemed aloof and unapproachable, but now the warmth that lay hidden behind the mass of scar tissue was revealed.

"Itkut gave you a good name," he said smiling. "Indeed, the dog-spirit must live in your tongue. *Ayorama—* it doesn't matter. Let us see if we can drive it out."

With that he took over the task of instructing me, and by the time summer was over we had become friends.

One August night when the ice fog over the Bay was burning coldly in the long light of the late-setting sun, I went to a drum dance at Ano's tent. This was forbidden by the priest at Eskimo Point, who would send the R.C.M.P. constable down to Big River to smash the drums if he heard a dance was being held. The priest was a great believer in an ever-present Devil, and he was convinced the drums were the work of that Devil. In truth, these gatherings were song-feasts at which each man, woman or child took the drum in turn and sang a song. Sometimes it was an ancient song from far out of time, a voice from the shadowy distances of Innuit history; or perhaps it might be a comic song in which the singer made fun of himself. Often it was the story of a spectacular hunting incident; or it

From *The Snow Walker* by Farley Mowat, pp. 96-114. © 1975 by McClelland and Steward, Ltd. Reprinted by permission of Little, Brown and Company.

might be a song of tragic happenings and of the spirits of the land.

That night Itkut sang a song of the Hunting of Omingmuk, the muskox. As the story unwound, Ano's face came alight with pride—and with love.

Toward dawn people began to drift away and Ano suggested we walk to the shore and have a smoke. Flocks of plover, grey and ephemeral in the half light, fled shrilling before us, and out on the dim wastes of the sea spectral loons yapped at one another.

Ano's face was turned to the sea.

"I know you wonder at me, Kipmetna, yet you look at this torn face of mine and your questions are never heard. You watch as I make my spring journey out to the rock in the sea and your questions remain silent. That is the way also with my People. Tonight, perhaps because Itkut sang well and brought many memories to me from a long time ago, I would tell you a story."

Once there was a woman, and it was she who was my belly and my blood. Now she waits for me in that distant place where the deer are as many as the stars.

She was Kala, and she was of the Sea People, and not of my People who lived far from the sea on the great plains where no trees grow. But I loved her beyond all things in the sea or on the land. Some said I loved her too much, since I could never find the strength to share her, even with my song-cousin, Tanugeak. Most men respected my love and the angeokok, Mahuk, said that the sea-mother, Takanaluk Arnaluk, was pleased by the love I had for my wife.

My mother was Kunee and my father was Sagalik. I was born by the shore of Tulemaliguak, Lake of the Great Bones, far west of here, in the years when the camps of the inland people were almost emptied of life by the burning breath of the white man's sickness. My father died of it soon after my birth.

I was born in the late summer months, and Kunee, my mother, was dead before autumn. Then I was taken into the childless tent of Ungyala and his wife Aputna. They were not young people. Once they had lived very far to the south but their camps too had been stricken by the sickness and they had fled north. They too had been burned by the flame in the lungs, and their sons and daughters had died.

Soon after they took me into their tent, Ungyala and Aputna made ready to flee again, for there were not enough people left in our camps even to bury the dead. So we three went west . . . far off to the west into a land where the Innuit had never lived for fear of the Indians who sometimes came out of the forests into the plains. The deer were plentiful in that place and we lived very well while I grew toward the age of a man and learned to hunt by myself and to drive the long sled over the hard-packed snow.

All the same, it was a lonely land we had come to. There were not even any Indians—perhaps they too, had been burned by the plague. We saw no inukok, little stone men set on the hills to tell us that other men of our race had travelled those long, rolling slopes. It was a good land but empty, and we hungered to hear other voices.

In the winter of the year when I became angeutnak, almost a man, the blizzards beat upon us for a very long time. Ungyala and I had made good kills of deer in the autumn so we three did not suffer; yet we longed for the coming of spring, the return of the deer and the birds. We yearned for the voices of life, for the voices we heard were of wind and, sometimes I thought, of those spirits who hide in the ground.

In the month when the wolves begin to make love there came a break in the storms. Then I, in the pride of my youth and filled with a hunger I could not yet name, decided to make a journey to the northwest. I said I hoped to kill muskox and bring fresh meat to the camp. Ungyala agreed to my going, though he was not very willing for he was afraid of the lands to the northwest. I took seven dogs and drove the komatik over the snow-hidden hills for three days, and saw no living thing. That land was dead, and my heart was chilled, and only

because I was stubborn and young did I go on.

On the fourth day I came to the lip of a valley, and as I began to descend my lead dog threw up her head. In a moment the dogs were plunging into soft snow, the traces all tangled, and all of them yelling like fiends. I stopped them and walked cautiously forward until I could look down into the flat run of a gulley that lay sheltered by walls of grey stone. There was movement down there. It was kakwik, the wolverine, digging with his slashing front claws into the top of what looked like a drift. I ran back to my team and tried to unleash a few of the dogs so they could chase him, but now they were fighting each other; and before I could free them, kakwik was gone, lumbering up the long slope and over the rocks.

I kicked at the dogs, jumped on the sled, and drove headlong into the gulley; but when I slowed past the place where kakwik had dug, my heart went out of the chase.

He had been digging into the top of a buried snowhouse.

Ungyala believed that no men lived to the west and north of our land, yet here was a house. The door tunnel was snowed in and drifts had almost buried the place. I took my snow probe and slid it into a crack between blocks in the roof. It went in so easily I could tell the inside was empty of snow.

I grew cautious and more than a little afraid. The thought came that this might be the home of an Ino, a dwarf with knives where his hands should be. Yet the thought that this might instead be the home of true men gave me courage.

With my snowknife I cut a hole in the dome . . . squeezed through it and dropped to the floor. As my eyes grew used to the gloom, I saw that this had been a shelter for men . . . only now it was a tomb for the dead.

There were many bones lying about and even in that dim light I could see that not all had belonged to deer or muskox. One was a skull with black hair hanging down over gleaming white bone where the flesh of the cheeks had been cut away with a knife.

I was about to leap up to the hole in the roof and drag myself out of that terrible place when I saw a shudder of movement under a pile of muskox robes at the back of the sleeping ledge. I was sure something terrible crouched there in the darkness and I raised my snowknife to strike, and fear was a sliver of ice in my belly.

But it was no devil that crawled painfully out from under that pile of rotting hides.

Once, I remember, I found the corpse of a fawn wedged in a deep crevice among some great rocks. It had been missed by the ravens, foxes and wolves and, because it was autumn, the maggots had not eaten the meat. It had dried into a bundle of bones bound around the skin.

The girl who lay helpless before me on the ledge of the snowhouse looked like that fawn. Only her eyes were alive.

Although I was young, and greatly afraid, I knew what I must do. There was a soapstone pot on the floor. I slid the blade of my knife into the flesh of my left arm and let the hot blood flow into the bowl.

Through the space of one day and night I fed the thing I had found with the blood from my veins. Drop by drop was she fed. In between feedings I held her close in my arms under a thick new robe I had fetched from my sled, and slowly the warmth from my body drove the chill from her bones.

Life came back to her but it was nearly three days before she could sit up at my side without aid. Yet she must have had hidden strength somewhere within her for later that day when I came back into the snowhouse after feeding my dogs, all the human bones on the floor, to the last fragment, had vanished. She had found strength, even though death still had his hands on her throat, to bury those things under the hard snow of the floor.

On the fifth day she was able to travel so I brought her back to Ungyala's camp and my parents-by-right took her in and were glad she had come. Neither one made any comment when I told how I had found her and what else I had found in the snowhouse. But later, when Ungyala and I were on a journey away from the camp picking up meat from an autumn cache, he spoke to me thus:

"Anoteelik, my son, this person has eaten the flesh of the dead . . . so much you know. Yet until you too have faced death in the way that he came to this girl, do not judge of her act. She has suffered enough. The spirits of those she has eaten will forgive her . . . the living must forgive her as well."

The girl quickly recovered her youth—she who had seemed beyond age—and as she grew fat she grew comely and often my heart speeded its beat when she was near. She spoke almost no words except to tell us her name was Kala and that her family, who were Sea People, had come inland from the north coast in the fall to hunt muskox.

It was not until the ravens returned that one day when we men were far from camp, she broke into speech to my mother-by-right. Then she told how the family dogs had died of the madness which is carried by foxes and wolves, and how, marooned in the heart of the dark frozen plains, her parents and brother had followed the Snow Walker. She told how she also had waited for death until hunger brought its own madness . . . and she began to eat the flesh of the dead. When she finished her tale she turned from my mother-by-right and cried, "I am unworthy to live!" She would have gone into the night and sought her own end had my mother not caught her and bound her and held her until we returned.

She was calmer by the next day, but she asked that we build her a snowhouse set apart from the camp, and we followed her wish. She lived alone there for many days. Aputna took food to her and talked to her, but we two men never saw her at all.

It was good that spring came so soon after, for spring is the time for forgetting the past. The deer streamed back into our land. The ptarmigan mated and called from the hills, and the male lemmings sought out the females deep in the moss.

The snowhouses softened under the sun and then Kala came back and lived with us in the big skin tent that we built. She seemed to have put out of mind the dark happenings of the winter, and she willingly helped with the work . . . but it was seldom she laughed.

My desire for the girl had become heavy and big during the days she had kept out of sight. It was more than the thrust of my loins; for I had known pity for her, and pity breeds passion in men.

One evening after the snow was all gone, I came and sat by her side on a ridge overlooking our camp where she had gone to watch the deer streaming by. I spoke awkwardly of my love. Kala turned her face from me, but one hand crept to my arm and touched the place where I had thrust the knife into my vein. That night, as we all lay together inside the big tent, she came into my arms and we became husband and wife.

Such was my finding of Kala—a finding that brought me the happiest days of my life, for she was a woman of women. Her sewing was gifted by spirits, and her cooking made even Ungyala grow fat. She could hunt nearly as well as a man. And she was avid for love, as one who has once nearly drowned is avid for air. We four lived a good life all that summer and it seemed as if Kala had brought many good things to our land. The deer were never so fat, the muskox never so many, the trout in the rivers never so large. Even our two bitch dogs, which had been fruitless for over two years, gave birth to big litters and raised eleven fine pups that became the best sled dogs I ever owned. So we believed the girl was forgiven . . . that the spirits wished her to suffer no more.

On a day of the following winter, Ungyala and I were sent out of the snowhouse and we sat and shivered in the lee of some rocks until we heard the voice of my mother-by-right singing birth songs to the Whispering Ones who flame in the sky.

3. THE ORGANIZATION OF SOCIETY AND CULTURE

After the birth of Itkut, our son, a restlessness seemed to come over us all. Kala yearned to return to the sea. Aputna was feeling her years, and longed once again to hear the voices and see the faces of people she had known long ago. As for me, I was anxious to visit some trader and buy the things Ungyala had told me about; especially guns, for I thought that hunting with spears, bows and arrows did not let me show what a fine hunter I had become. Only Ungyala thought that perhaps we should stay where we were. He remembered too well that he and Aputna had twice had to flee for their lives when the people in the camps where they were living were struck down by the new kind of dying that came from beyond the borders of the Innuit lands. Yet in his heart he too wished to see people again, so we decided to go.

We had two good teams and two sleds. We drove north and then east, making a broad detour around the now empty camps where I had been born. We saw no sign of living men until we finally came to Big River. There we met two families who spent their summers near Eskimo Point and their winters inland on the edge of the plains. We stayed with them for the rest of that winter, hearing much about the world Ungyala and Aputna had almost forgotten and that Kala and I had never known. In the spring, before the ice softened, we followed Big River down to the coast.

So we took up a new way of life. Every autumn we journeyed in a big canoe, with our dogs running free on the shore, up Big River to a lake near its head where the southbound deer crossed a narrows. Here Ungyala and I speared fat bucks in the water and shot more of them out on the bare, rocky plains with the rifles we had traded for at the coast. By the time the first snows drove the deer out of the land, we would have more than enough meat for the winter, plenty of fat for our lamps, and the best of hides for our clothing and robes.

In the late days of autumn, after the deer had passed and before we began trapping white foxes, there was little to do. Sometimes then I would sit and

think and weigh up the worth of my life. It was good, but I understood that its goodness dwelt mainly in Kala. I loved her for the son she had borne, for the clothes that she made me, for the help that she gave me . . . but it went beyond that. I do not know how to explain it, but Kala held me in her soul. The love she gave me passed far beyond respect for a husband and entered that country of pleasure which we of the People do not often know. Such was our life as the child, Itkut, grew with the years.

Now I must tell how it was when we came to the coast. There we met the first white man we had ever seen. It was he who built the wood house at the mouth of Big River. He seemed a good man in some ways, but he was crazy for women. Before he had lived in the country a year, there were few women who had not spent a night in his house, for it was still our law then that a man might not refuse any gift that lay in his giving if another man asked. Kala never went to the house of the white man, though he asked me for her many times. He put shame upon me, for I was forced to refuse.

In the autumn of our fourth year in the new land, we had gone up the river as usual and made our camp at the lake of the Deer Crossing. Ours was the farthest camp from the sea, for we had come from the inland plains and they held no terrors for us. The coast dwellers did not care to go as far as we went. Our tent was pitched within sight of the ford and from the door we could look to see if the deer had arrived.

The time came when the forerunners of the big herd should have appeared, but the crossing remained empty of life. The darkening lichens on the bank were unmarked by the feet of the deer. The dwarf shrubs began to burn red in the first frosts. Ungyala and I walked many miles over the land, climbing the hills and staring out to the north. We saw none of the usual harbingers of the great herds—no ravens floating black in the pale sky, no wolves drifting white on the dark land.

Although we were worried, nothing was said. Kala and Aputna became

very busy fishing for trout, suckers and char in the river. They caught little, for the autumn run was nearly over, yet they fished night and day. The dogs began to grow hungry and their howling became so loud we had to move them some miles from the camp in case they frightened the deer. Thinking back to those days I wonder if it was hunger alone that made them so distressed. Maybe they already knew what we would not believe could be true.

The morning came when snow blew in the air . . . only a thin mist of fine snow but enough to tell us that winter had come and it had not brought the deer.

But a few days afterwards the deer came. Ungyala and I went out with light hearts but only a few deer had come to the river. These few were so poor and lacking in fat that we knew they were not the forerunners of the great herds but stragglers that lagged behind, being either too weak or too sick to keep up. We knew then that the deer spirit had led the herds southward by some different path.

The next day there were no deer at the crossing and none to be seen anywhere upon the sweep of the plains and we had killed barely enough meat to feed ourselves and the dogs for two months.

The real snows came and we began the winter with hearts that were shaken by misgivings. We thought of abandoning our camp and trying to make our way to the coast but we could not do this until enough snow had fallen to make sled travel possible. So we stayed where we were, hoping we would find some of the solitary winter deer that sometimes remain in the land. Ungyala and I roamed with pack dogs over the country for many long miles. A few hares and ptarmigan fell to our guns, but these were no more than food for our hopes.

Before long we ran out of fat, then there was neither light nor heat in the snowhouse. One day Ungyala and I resolved to travel southeast on a journey to some distant islands of little trees where in times past deer used to winter. We took only one small team of dogs, but even these we could not feed and they soon weakened until after a few days they could go no farther. That night we camped in the lee of some cliffs and it was too cold to sleep so we sat and the old man talked of the days of his youth. He was very weak and his voice almost too low to hear. At last he dozed and I covered him with both our robes; but before the dawn he had ceased to breathe, and so I buried my father-by-right in the snow in a grave I cut with my snowknife.

I turned back, but before I reached the snowhouse I heard women's voices singing the song of the dead. Aputna had seen the death of Ungyala in the eye of her mind, and the two women were mourning.

A little time after the death of Ungyala, I wakened one night to the muted whispering of the women. I lay with my face turned to the wall and listened to what Kala was saying to my mother-by-right.

"My mother, the time is not yet come for you to take your old bones to sleep in the snow. Your rest will come after. Now comes a time when I have need of your help."

I knew then that Aputna had decided to take the way of release, and had been held from it by Kala. I did not understand why my wife had restrained her, for it is the right of the old ones that they be the first to die when starvation comes to a camp. But I had small time to wonder, for Kala moved over beside me and spoke softly in my ear, and she told me what I dreaded to hear—that now I must take the few dogs that were left and make my way eastward, down river, until I found a camp that had meat to spare.

I refused, and I called her a fool, for she knew the other camps could be no better off then we were. Kala had always been a woman of sense yet I could not make her see that such a trip would be useless. I knew, and she knew, I could not hope to find help until I reached the coast camps where people depended more on seal meat than on deer, and such a trip, there

and back with weak dogs, could not take less than a month. It would be better, I told her, if we killed and ate all the dogs, let my mother-by-right go to her rest, and wait where we were, eking out our lives by fishing for what little could be caught through holes in the ice. Then, if it came to the worst, we three, Kala and Itkut and I, would at least lie down for the last time together.

She would not heed what I said and I heard for the first time the hard edge of anger in her voice.

"You *will* go!" she whispered fiercely. "If you do not, I shall myself put the noose of release on your son when you are gone out of the snow-house and so save him from the torments that were mine in a time you remember."

And . . . oh, Kipmetan . . . though I knew she was wrong, I could no longer refuse. No, and I did not, although I should have guessed at that which was hidden deep in her thoughts.

At parting next day only the old woman wept. There were no tears from Kala who knew what she knew, and none from young Itkut who was still too young to know what was afoot.

That was a journey! I walked eight days to the nearest camps of the people, for the dogs were too weak to do more than haul the empty sled along at a crawl. In that first camp I found it was as I had feared. Famine had got there before me. Things were nearly as bad all the way down the river. One by one I killed my dogs to keep me and their remaining brothers and sisters alive, and sometimes I shared a little of that lean, bitter meat with people in the camps that I passed.

I was almost in sight of the sea when I came to the camp of my song-cousin, Tanugeak. He and those with him were in good health for they had been living on the meat and the fat of seals Tanugeak had speared far out on the sea ice. They had none too much, though, for they had been helping feed many people who had already fled east from the inland camps. All the same, Tanugeak

proved his friendship. He gave me four seals and loaned me five of his own strong dogs, together with fish enough to feed them on the long journey home.

My strength was not much, but I began the up-river journey at once and I sang to the dogs as they ran strongly to the west. I had been away from my camp only two weeks, and now I hoped to return there in eight days at the most. So I sang as the sled ran smoothly over the hard river ice.

Two days up river and a few miles north of my track was a lake and by it two camps where I had stopped overnight on my way to the sea. In those camps I had been given soup made of old bones by people who were almost old bones themselves. Now, with much food on my sled, I did not turn off to give them at least a little of my meat and fat. I told myself I could spare neither the time nor the food if I was to save my own family from death . . . but I knew I did wrong. As my sled slipped into the darkening west I felt a foreboding and I almost turned back. If only I had . . . but such thoughts are useless, and they are a weakness in man; for he does what he does, and he must pay what he pays.

I decided to drive all that night, but when darkness came on it brought a blizzard that rose, full blown, right in my face. The thundering wind from the northwest lashed me with piercing arrows of snow until I could not tell where I was, and the dogs would face it no more. At last I made camp, turning the sled on its side and making a hole in a snowbank nearby for myself. I did not unharness the dogs but picketed them in their traces some way from the sled. Then I crawled into my robes, intending only to doze until the wind dropped. But I was more weary than I knew and I was soon so sound asleep that even the roar of the blizzard faded out of my mind.

All unknowing because of the storm, I had made my camp less than a mile upwind from another camp of the people. The surviving dogs of that camp were roaming about, a famished and half-mad pack. As I slept, they winded my load of seal meat.

I heard nothing until the damage was done. Only when the marauders attacked my own dogs did I awake. In my anguish and rage I flung myself on those beasts with only my small knife as a weapon. The dogs turned upon me and, though I killed some, the smell of fresh blood drove the remainder to fury. They tore the deerskin clothes from my body, savaged one arm until I dropped the knife, and slashed my face until the flesh hung down over my chin. They would have killed me if the fight with my own dogs had not drawn them off, leaving me to crawl back to my hole in the snow.

The morning broke clear and calm, as if no wind had ever blown. I could only manage to stand and shuffle about, and I went to the sled, but the meat was all gone. Nothing was left but some shreds of skin and some bones. Two of my own dogs had been killed and the remainder were hurt.

There was nothing to do. I began to look for my rifle in the debris near the sled but before I could find it I heard dogs howl in the distance and when I looked to the west I saw the domes of three snowhouses below the bank of the river. I turned and shuffled toward them.

I remember but little of the days I spent in that camp because my wounds festered and I was often unconscious. Those people were kind and they fed me with food they could ill spare—though in truth it was partly my food, for it was the meat of the dogs who had eaten the seals. Before I could travel again, the sun had begun to grow warm and to rise higher up in the sky. Yet the warmth of the oncoming spring could not thaw the chill in my heart.

I made a light sled for the two dogs I had left and prepared to depart. Those in the camps tried to keep me with them for they said that by now there would be no life in my snowhouse that stood by the lake of the deer crossing, and I would only die there myself if I returned before spring brought the deer herds back to the land.

But I did not fear death anymore so I set out. Weak as we were, the dogs and I made the journey home in ten days. We had luck, for we found a deer cache that must have been lost by some hunter in the spring of the previous year. It was a foul mess of hair, bones, and long-rotted meat, but it gave us the strength to continue.

When we came in sight of the lake my belly grew sick and my legs weakened and I could hardly go on; yet when I neared the camp life pounded back through my veins . . . for the snowhouse still stood and snow had recently been dug away from the door!

I shouted until my lungs crackled in the bright, cold air and when none answered, I began to run. I reached the passage and scrambled inside.

Abruptly Anoteelik ceased speaking. He sat staring out over the lightening waters of the Bay . . . out toward the islands that were still no more than grey wraiths on the shifting horizon. Tears were running down his disfigured cheeks . . . running like rain. Then with his head bowed forward over his knees, very quietly he finished the tale.

I was greeted by Aputna, my mother-by-right, and by Itkut. The old woman had shrunk to a miserable rag of a thing that should have been gone long ago; but Itkut seemed strong and his body was firm to the touch when I took him up in my arms.

I looked over his shoulder, and asked, "Where is Kala?" though I knew what the answer would be.

Aputna's reply was no louder than the whisper of wind on the hills.

"What was done . . . was done as she wished. As for me, I will not go away from this place, yet I only did what she said must be done . . . and Itkut still lives . . . Where is Kala? Hold your son close in your arms, love him well for the blood in his veins. Hold him close, oh, my son, for you hold your wife too in your arms."

When the ice left the river, Itkut and I came back down to the coast. Kala was of the Sea People, so I took her bones out to that island which lies far from the shore. While I live I shall take gifts to her spirit each spring . . . in the spring, when the birds make love on the slopes and the does come back to our land, their bellies heavy with fawn.

The Yanomami Keep on Trekking

In Amazonia, a break from gardening makes for a balanced diet

Kenneth Good

Kenneth Good went to Venezuela with plans to study the Yanomami of Hasupiweteri for fifteen months and ended up staying with them for twelve years. His personal odyssey is detailed in his book, coauthored with David Chanoff, Into the Heart: One Man's Pursuit of Love and Knowledge Among the Yanomama *(New York: Simon and Schuster, 1991). Good is now an assistant professor of anthropology at Jersey City State College.*

Bë kuami! "They are not home!" I remember my disappointment as I arrived at empty village after empty village on my month-long expedition. I had started out from the Yanomami community of Hasupiwëteri, on the upper Orinoco River in the Venezuelan Amazon, with the goal of reaching the banks of the Parakeet River, thirty-five miles to the south. It was 1976, the second of twelve consecutive years that I would live with the Hasupiwëteri at their changing locales. I and five of their strongest young men had set off with food, gear, and gifts to contact the scattered inland villages. No nonindigenous outsider had ever made this trip overland, through the hilly terrain covered with dense forest, although one group in the area had been visited once by helicopter. None of the Yanomami from my community had pene-

trated that far either, although some had reached the closest villages and knew by word of mouth of the others.

We had spent three days pushing along little-used trails barely visible to the inexperienced eye. One day out, we had visited the first village, but after that we had encountered no one. The third day had been especially difficult, as we chopped and hacked our way through an old, abandoned garden during a torrential downpour. I realized then why the Yanomami are "pioneering horticulturists," always planting their gardens in virgin forest. Who would want to reclear this snake-infested tangle of thorny brush? Beyond the garden we began the last of numerous ascents in the rolling hills to the community of Ashitowëteri. As we neared our destination, my excitement peaked. My guides told me we had reached the last stream before we would arrive, and as is the Yanomami custom when visiting another village, we stopped to bathe.

After a brief, refreshing dip we hurried down the trail until we arrived at the village gardens. Bananas and plantains in various stages of growth made up about nine-tenths of the well-tended vegetation. Off to one side we saw a few *ohina* root and manioc plants. Some cotton bushes and a couple of avocado trees were the only other visible crops. After several hundred yards, we were out of the gardens and stand-

ing before one of the largest and best-constructed communal shelters I had seen. But it was empty.

The Yanomami are what anthropologists call horticulturists, or gardeners. Although a large and important part of their diet consists of foods from hunting and gathering, they also grow plantains and bananas, using simple tools and a clearing technique known as slash-and-burn. Their crops enable them to live a more sedentary life than full-time hunter-gatherers, who have to follow their food as it becomes available in the forest. Their communities are larger and their homes and personal possessions are more elaborate. So where were the horticultural Yanomami of Ashitowëteri when I arrived to pay my respects?

I realized that there was only one thing they could be doing: they were on a *wayumi*, a trek in which the entire community packs up its possessions, abandons the communal shelter, and takes to the forest in one or several groups to hunt and gather wild foods. I already knew about the treks. It takes at most a few months' residence with the Yanomami to become familiar with them. But I could not contain my frustration at finding no one at home, and my feelings were shared by my Hasupiwëteri friends. While I wailed, "Why do they have to go trekking now?" my guides heaped scorn on our absent hosts, calling them peccaries for

Ripe plantains, the Yanomami's main cultivated crop, are peeled for a feast.

spending their days foraging in the forest.

Another frustration of arriving at an empty village is missing out on a good meal. When one travels long distances across the forest, the intermittent stops are critical for keeping up energy levels. Now we were forced to take what we could from the garden and pay for it another day. While the other men checked the trails to determine when the residents had left and in which direction, Karisi and I collected food from the Ashitowëteri gardens. Fortunately, on our way back after visiting several other empty villages, we came across the Ashitowëteri at one of their temporary camps. We showered them with our gifts—machetes, knives, and other desirable items—more than reciprocating for the food we had taken. It was the first of my several stays with this previously uncontacted community over the next ten years.

Not long after we returned to Hasupiwëteri, that community also determined to go trekking. While we had been away, the able-bodied men had gone on a hunt. They were planning to invite another village to a funeral ceremony, and meat was a major requirement for the event. The hunt had failed, as many of them do, and after our return they made a second attempt.

They returned with white-lipped peccaries and some small game. The hunters were happy to bring back such a quantity of smoked meat, even though out of a herd of more than fifty peccaries, a force of thirty-two hunters succeeded in bringing down only three.

When I awakened the morning after the feast was over, preparations for the trek were already under way. While the last few mature plantains from the garden roasted on the family hearth, men and women were packing all their possessions in bundles. Using a tumpline, the women bear the burden of portage, sometimes carrying loads of more than 100 pounds—plantains, aluminum pots, axes, hammocks, and even a child. Quickly I got out of my hammock and began organizing my own equipment and necessities (many supplies could be left behind, stashed in locked trunks). Fortunately, I could arrange for four young men to help carry my possessions.

While the women were still packing, the men marched out of the village, anxious to start down the trails before the animals were scared off by the larger group. Most carried little more than their bows and arrows, so they would be unencumbered for any hunting opportunity. Burdened as they are, the women and children move very slowly and rarely cover more than a

mile in a day. The men periodically stop and wait for them to catch up.

After only a few hours, still before noon, the men began to make camp for the night. Each cleared a small area, and in no more than half an hour erected a simple frame for the family shelter. Most then disappeared into the forest to hunt. When the women arrived, they cut *platanillo* leaves and covered the roof frames prepared by their husbands. After setting up house by hanging their hammocks, gourds, and other belongings, they took to the streams to crab or to the forest to gather wild foods.

Our trek lasted five weeks. If there was a large stand of food near a campsite or if hunting proved productive, the community would spend several nights there. Otherwise, they would pack up their belongings at daybreak, bundle the leaves from the roofs, and move on to another site. Men, women, and children, the old and the infirm moved through the forest, exploiting Amazonia's varied wild foods. In addition to the skill with which the Yanomami hunted and gathered, the ease with which they trekked reinforced my view that this was an ancient pattern of livelihood.

As I accompanied this trek and many more over the years, I kept detailed records of the Yanomami's activities, especially those related to food and nutrition, the subject of my research. The same thought was always on my mind: "Why do they trek?" Probably underlying my question was the ethnocentric notion that social progress consists of having a settled life, and that trekking is a kind of enforced hardship to acquire food in lean times. The Yanomami see it differently, however. For them the trek is a welcome event, one that raises the spirits. Trekking takes the community to fresh, cool forest areas that have not been exploited for a long period, perhaps not within living memory. Nevertheless, the question remains: Do the Yanomami really need to go trekking?

At first glance, the reason the Yanomami trek seems to be that they run out of mature plantains from their gardens. Plantains and bananas were most likely introduced into the New World by the conquistadors. Scientists generally believe that in pre-Columbian times, the Yanomami were hunters and gatherers and that they continue to trek because their forager culture has failed to make maximum use of agriculture. So why don't they just grow more plantains?

Decades ago, anthropologist Robert Carneiro, of the American Museum of Natural History, demonstrated that there is no environmental limitation in Amazonia on growing sufficient crops for a village to remain sedentary. My own studies of forest areas around the Yanomami communities confirm that there is almost always land suitable for expansion of cultivation. The men, who do all of the garden work, spend an average of less than two hours per day preparing the gardens. They could easily double that time without significantly changing their other activities. But they don't.

Instead, the Yanomami apparently take into consideration that they will trek and, therefore, plant no more than necessary for several months' supply. In fact they spend an average of 40 percent of the time in the forest trekking, and in some cases as much as 60 percent. The underlying practical reason seems to be that plantains (or manioc, in the case of other Amazonian tribes, such as the Kayapó) are rich in vitamins and minerals but have very little protein. Lacking a more balanced range of crops and domesticated food animals, the Yanomami must get their meat and fat as they have always done, from the wild animals of the forest.

Amazonian game species are relatively small and elusive, and hunters often fail in their quests. Even with this poor hunting record, when a village stays in one place for a long period of time, the local animals are quickly depleted. One way to compensate for this is for the men to leave their families and gardens and go out on long-distance hunts. Camping in the forest, with minimal food, they hunt from dawn to dusk for up to a week. Trekking, however, offers an alternative that keeps family members together and allows long-term exploitation of other forest areas. My studies show that on treks, hunting yields are double those near the garden location. Consumption of wild foods increases from 10 percent to almost 70 percent. (The diet still includes some crops, retrieved from the gardens during the early and late stages of the trek.)

While the group is out trekking for weeks or months, the young plantains in the gardens are maturing. When the wild foods become harder to obtain, the trekkers begin their return. They may even say that they get tired of wild foods and that their minds turn again to plantains. The truth is that they must go back. They cannot subsist year-round as hunter-gatherers because the domesticated crops have allowed their average village populations to grow to sixty or seventy. Wild foods are too dispersed to feed so large a group, even for one or two nights. But neither can the Yanomami be full-time farmers, because adequate protein is not provided at the garden sites.

Apart from fulfilling nutritional needs, there are other advantages to trekking. As a village grows larger, quarrels are more likely to erupt in the community. For example, even a large game animal does not yield enough meat for all the families. Meat is the only item in Yanomami culture that is shared village wide. To be slighted in the distribution causes very intense feelings. When such tensions reach a peak, the village can split, with each faction going on its own trek in a different direction. This separation allows for a cooling off of emotions.

Splitting up also makes for a better return on foraging. While today fifty or sixty Yanomami may trek together, most likely in the past, when they were full-time hunters and gatherers, they would have had to restrict their group size to a maximum of twenty or twenty-five. In a smaller group, the killing of a large animal will provide each family with a larger and more choice piece than would be possible if the entire community were living together. The increased supply is especially welcome because the Yanomami normally get to eat meat only twice a week and usually in very small portions.

When a large village splits up on the trek because of internal friction or because the group is simply too large to travel together, one group of families may begin new gardens at a distant campsite. On subsequent treks, the gardens will be expanded, and when they begin to produce crops, the families move there, eventually construct-

This woman sets out on a trek with all her household possessions.

A Reputation for War

R. Brian Ferguson

Kenneth Good

An adulterous affair caused two men to fight each other with clubs.

Ever since they were dubbed "the fierce people" by anthropologist Napoleon Chagnon in the 1960s, the Yanomami have typified primitive belligerence for hundreds of thousands of college students. The groups Chagnon lived with on the upper Orinoco River seemed endlessly embroiled in fights, duels, and treacherous raids, as the men competed over women and status or sought to avenge previous killings. The vivid descriptions of Yanomami character and warfare helped fuel a debate over whether humans were inevitably propelled toward violence. The debate was largely precipitated by Robert Ardrey's popular book *African Genesis* (1961), which argued that humans had a genetic heritage as "killer apes." Many academics countered that, far from being instinctive, warfare would have played a minor role throughout most of the human evolutionary career. They tied the advent of warfare to the agricultural revolution, with its sedentary communities and stores of food, and the subsequent rise of centralized states. Human nature, they declared, was almost by definition plastic, shaped by culture, and humans could be educated to solve their conflicts in other ways. Against the background of the Vietnam War, this was a more optimistic message.

Enter the Yanomami, a people apparently isolated from outside influences until recent times. They were proclaimed by some to be the living em-

bodiment of a violent evolutionary heritage. Others, rejecting this grim interpretation, sought an adaptive explanation for Yanomami behavior. They proposed that in the tropical Amazonian forest, which lacked rich concentrations of resources, warfare and hostility served to break up groups into sustainable size and then space them suitably across the landscape. In this view, although warfare had its costs, it contributed to the Yanomami's ability to survive within the limitations of their ecosystem.

Both of these interpretations took for granted that the Yanomami way of

life was pristine. But my historical studies, comparing the experiences of many different Yanomami groups, have led me to reject that view. I have found that these Amazonians have been affected by the presence of European Americans for up to 350 years, and that Yanomami warfare can only be understood in this light.

Outside influences began in the 1630s, when Portuguese, Spanish, and Dutch colonists, or their indigenous allies, came raiding for slaves. The ensuing violence wiped out the more complex societies that had existed in

ing a new communal shelter. In this way a village splits permanently, dealing peacefully with problems of disharmony and an inadequate supply of food, especially meat. Otherwise these problems can lead to a violent fission.

Trekking can also have a downside. When a community returns to its gardens after an extended stay in the forest, it sometimes finds that other Yanomami, also on trek, have made their way to the untended gardens and eaten the newly matured crops. This

results in a severe food crisis for the returnees, and on occasion, hostilities develop between villages. These may take the form of a chest-pounding match (opponents take turns slugging each other in the chest), a club fight, or even a raid. In the case of a raid, trekking also has a role to play. When raiders return home after attacking another village, they and the rest of their community often leave on a trek to avoid becoming sitting ducks in a revenge raid.

More than 95 percent of the Yanomami still live in their traditional deep-woods environment. But a few communities that have settled along rivers have adopted new ways of making a living, made possible by access to manufactured goods from traders or from a Western settlement. These Yanomami spend less effort on inland hunting. Instead, fishing takes on greater importance, the men taking to the rivers in canoes. They use manufactured hooks and lines, often fishing at night the Yanomami region—densely settled chiefdoms of river traders—and restricted the Yanomami to highland sanctuaries. Both peaceable and violent contacts between Yanomami and outsiders occurred from the mid-eighteenth century until 1950, when the first Protestant mission settled in alongside a Yanomami village, initiating extensive interactions that still continue.

When the political history of Yanomami living in various parts of their territory is reconstructed, a connection emerges between their wars (with one another or with neighboring peoples) and significant changes in the European American presence. The common thread in their fighting appears to be access to, and control over, sources of Western trade goods. Like other Amazonian groups, the Yanomami have rapidly come to regard steel tools, aluminum pots, cloth, and other manufactured items as necessities. Yanomami able to obtain these goods close to the source want them not only for their own use but also to trade with groups farther away. In exchange, other Yanomami provide local products, labor, wives, and political support. Friction arises because the interests involved in these exchange relationships are so vital and the inequalities are so pronounced. This friction can lead to raiding, directed at protecting or improving positions within the radiating trade networks.

In the first decade of this century, for example, the frenzied rubber-tapping boom in Amazonia led to a surge in Western trade goods passing along the Uraricoera and other rivers near Brazilian Yanomami territory. In a series of raids, ambushes, and at least one pitched battle, some local Yanomami groups carved out a niche in the trade system. They then gave up raiding, but soon were pressed from behind by the "wild" Yanomami in the mountains.

For some Yanomami, including those living around the mission posts of the upper Orinoco River, contact with resident outsiders has led to a much more sedentary way of life. Over time, hunting depleted local game supplies and was replaced by fishing, more intensive cultivation, and consumption of mission foods. Having lost their mobile way of life, these groups are unable to follow the traditional option of moving away when frictions arise. And with little hunting, they lose the custom of sharing meat, which as Kenneth Good has observed, is a source of solidarity. Worst of all, their exposure to outsiders brings them new diseases. with epidemics tearing great holes in the social fabric. For some Yanomami, such as those encountered by Chagnon, long and strong contact with the outside world created so much disruption that, for a time, violence became almost normal in interpersonal relations.

The Yanomami case shows the extraordinary reach and transforming effects a centrally governed society, or state, may have, extending way beyond its last outpost. The impact of disease, trade goods, migrations, and political restructurings can spread far in advance of face-to-face contact, and when the state's advance agents do arrive, they commonly bring even more destruction with them. Because they may possess firearms or dispense coveted trade goods, even contemporary missionaries and anthropologists can become important players in these conflicts and the focus of violent competition. That is what happened on the upper Orinoco.

The changing economic and political conditions in a remote "tribal zone" can lead to bloodshed, sometimes creating warfare in regions where little or none existed in the past. For centuries, Westerners have looked upon such carnage and used it to justify the obliteration of indigenous cultures in the name of civilization. What has not been acknowledged is that the "savage" behavior is itself often a result of foreign intrusion; that local conflicts are firmly connected to global processes. The Yanomami have taught us to proceed with extreme caution before assuming warfare in indigenous groups is pristine and isolated. Anthropologists can lead the way in applying this important lesson to so-called ethnic or tribal warfare in Africa and Europe.

R. Brian Ferguson, an associate professor of anthropology at the Newark campus of Rutgers University, is the author of Yanomami Warfare: A Political History *(Santa Fe: SAR Press, 1995).*

with lights acquired through trade or labor. Once they acquire or learn to make dugout canoes, they can fish over a greater range without moving the communal shelter or trekking. Watercraft are also used to add to the number of areas where gardens can be cleared, maintained, and harvested. They often use areas across the river from the settlement for gardening and hunting.

Yanomami river settlers grow larger gardens, aided in part by the greater availability of steel axes and machetes for forest clearing. They also learn from outsiders how to grow and process other foods besides plantains. Most common are cassava bread and manioc meal, both of which can be stored for use when plantains are not abundant. As a result, these communities engage in fewer treks; some have discontinued the practice altogether.

While the river settlements may have benefited from manufactured goods, Yanomami communities along the Venezuelan-Brazilian border have been devastated by outside contacts. A Brazilian policy of opening this area to settlers, cattle ranchers, loggers, and gold miners has resulted in the poisoning of rivers and streams with by-products of gold processing and the stripping of thousands of acres of forest for logging and pastures. An international outcry has provoked some government effort to halt this activity, but control of these very remote areas has been spotty at best. As a result, the Yanomami who live there have been deprived of the forest they use to feed themselves.

In 1993, the conflict of interests resulted in tragedy. With their large stores of steel tools, clothing, medicines, shotguns, and shells, Brazilian gold-mining camps in Yanomami territory had become a major attraction to nearby villagers, particularly the young men. The miners found the Yanomami's persistent requests for goods a great irritant and even threatened to respond with violence. The friction came to a head when a group of miners, annoyed by the requests, as well as by a demand that they return a confiscated shotgun, decided to kill the young men. Encountering them on the trail, they shot several of them execution-style. After a series of retaliatory raids by the Yanomami, the miners raided the village, killing about twelve. Those shot included men, women, and children, some of whom were hacked, dismembered, and decapitated with machetes after being gravely wounded.

Perhaps it is unrealistic to hope the Yanomami will be allowed to continue living by their traditional culture. But more is at stake than whether they will be absorbed culturally by the surrounding societies. Their very physical survival is in jeopardy. As national governments open up the tropical forests to development, the Yanomami will be pushed off the land. Already their rivers and streams are being polluted, while the animals they hunt for critical protein are being driven away by machinery used in lumbering and mining. Intensified by outside contact, malaria and respiratory diseases are also taking a toll. If these trends continue without restrictions, the Yanomami will die out. Their destiny is ultimately in the hands of those who have come to control the lands where the Yanomami have trekked for so many generations.

Mystique of the Masai

Pastoral as well as warlike, they have persisted in maintaining their unique way of life

Ettagale Blauer

Ettagale Blauer is a New York-based writer who has studied the Masai culture extensively in numerous trips to Africa and who specializes in writing about Africa and jewelry.

The noble bearing, self-assurance, and great beauty of the Masai of East Africa have been remarked upon from the time the first Europeans encountered them on the plains of what are now Kenya and Tanzania. (The word 'Masai' derives from their spoken language, Maa.) Historically, the Masai have lived among the wild animals on the rolling plains of the Rift Valley, one of the most beautiful parts of Africa. Here, the last great herds still roam freely across the plains in their semiannual migrations.

Although the appearance of people usually marks the decline of the game, it is precisely the presence of the Masai that has guaranteed the existence of these vast herds. Elsewhere in Kenya and Tanzania, and certainly throughout the rest of Africa, the herds that once roamed the lands have been decimated. But the Masai are not hunters, whom they call *iltorrobo*—poor men—because they don't have cattle. The Masai do not crave animal trophies, they do not value rhinoceros horns for aphrodisiacs, meat is not part of their usual diet, and they don't farm the land, believing it to be a sacrilege to break the earth. Traditionally, where Masai live, the game is unmolested.

In contrast to their peaceful and harmonious relationship to the wildlife, however, the Masai are warlike in relationship to the neighboring tribes, conducting cattle raids where they take women as well as cattle for their prizes, and they have been fiercely independent in resisting the attempts of colonial governments to change or subdue them. Although less numerous than the neighboring Kikuyu, the Masai have a strong feeling of being "chosen" people, and have been stubborn in maintaining their tribal identity.

However, that traditional tribal way of life is threatened by the exploding populations of Kenya and Tanzania (41 million people), who covet the vast open spaces of Masai Mara, Masai Amboseli, and the Serengeti Plain. Today, more than half of the Masai live in Kenya, with a style of life that requires extensive territory for cattle herds to roam in search of water and pastureland, and the freedom to hold ceremonies that mark the passage from one stage of life to the next. The Masai's need for land for their huge herds of cattle is not appreciated by people who value the land more for agriculture than for pasturage and for herds of wild animals.

3. THE ORGANIZATION OF SOCIETY AND CULTURE

The Masai live in countries that are attractive to tourists and whose leaders have embraced the values and life-style of the Western world. These two facts make it increasingly difficult for the Masai to live according to traditional patterns. The pressure to change in Kenya comes in part from their proximity to urban centers, especially the capital city of Nairobi, whose name is a Masai word meaning cool water.

Still, many Masai live in traditional homes and dress in wraps of bright cloth or leather, decorated with beaded jewelry, their cattle nearby. But the essence of the Masai culture—the creation of age-sets whose roles in life are clearly delineated—is under constant attack. In both Kenya and Tanzania, the governments continually try to "civilize" the Masai, to stop cattle raiding, and especially to put an end to the *morani*—the warriors—who are seen as the most disruptive of the age-sets.

TRADITIONAL LIFE

Masai legends trace the culture back some 300 years, and are recited according to age-groups, allowing fifteen years for each group. But anthropologists believe they arrived in the region some 1,000 years ago, having migrated from southern Ethiopia. As a racial group, they are considered a Nilo-Hamitic mix. Although deep brown in color, their features are not negroid. (Their extensive use of ochre may give their skin the look of American Indians but that is purely cosmetic.)

Traditional Masai people are governed by one guiding principle: that all the cattle on earth are theirs, that they were put there for them by *Ngai,* who is the god of both heaven and earth, existing also in the rains which bring the precious grass to feed the cattle. Any cattle they do not presently own are only temporarily out of their care, and must be recaptured. The Masai do not steal material objects; theft for them is a separate matter from raiding cattle, which is seen as the *return* of cattle to their rightful owners. From this basic belief, an entire culture has grown. The

grass that feeds the cattle and the ground on which it grows are sacred; to the Masai, it is sacrilege to break the ground for any reason, whether to grow food or to dig for water, or even to bury the dead.

Cattle provide their sole sustenance: milk and blood to drink, and the meat feast when permitted. Meat eating is restricted to ceremonial occasions, or when it is needed for gaining strength, such as when a woman gives birth or someone is recovering from an illness. When they do eat meat at a ceremony they consume their own oxen, which are sacrificed for a particular reason and in the approved way. Hunting and killing for meat are not Masai activities. It is this total dependence on their cattle, and their disdain for the meat of game

animals, that permits them to coexist with the game, and which, in turn, has kept intact the great herds of the Masai Mara and the Serengeti Plain. Their extraordinary diet of milk, blood, and occasionally, meat, keeps them sleek and fit, and Westerners have often noted their physical condition with admiration.

In 1925 Norman Leys wrote, "Physically they are among the handsomest of mankind, with slender bones, narrow hips and shoulders and most beautifully rounded muscles and limbs." That same description holds today. The Masai live on about 1,300 calories a day, as opposed to our consumption of nearly 3,000. They are invariably lean.

Traditional nomadic life of the Masai, however, was ferocious and warlike in relation to other tribes. The warriors

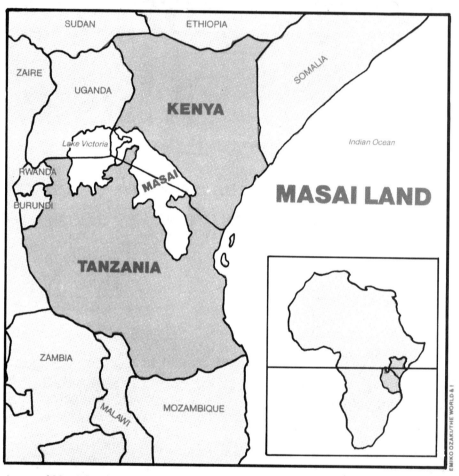

A map of Masai Land. The Masai's traditional territory exists within the two countries of Kenya and Tanzania.

(*morani*) built *manyattas,* a type of shelter, throughout the lands and used each for a few months at a time, then moved to another area when the grazing was used up. As the seasons changed, they would return to those manyattas. They often went out raiding cattle from neighboring tribes whom they terrorized with their great ferocity.

A large part of that aggressiveness is now attributed to drugs; the morani worked themselves into a frenzy as they prepared for a raid, using the leaves and barks of certain trees known to create such moods. A soup was made of fat, water, and the bark of two trees, *il kitosloswa* and *il kiluretti.* From the description, these seem to act as hallucinogens. As early as the 1840s, Europeans understood that the morani's extremely aggressive behavior derived from drug use. Drugs were used for endurance and for strength throughout warriorhood. During a meat feast, which could last a month, they took stimulants throughout, raising them to a virtual frenzy. This, combined with the natural excitement attendant to crowd behavior, made them formidable foes.

Having gained this supernatural energy and courage, they were ready to go cattle raiding among other tribes. To capture the cattle, the men of the other tribe had to be killed. Women were never touched in battle, but were taken to Masailand to become Masai wives. The rate of intermarriage was great during these years. Today, intermarriage is less frequent and the result mostly of chance meetings with other people. It is likely that intermarriage has actually prolonged the life of the Masai as a people; many observers from the early 1900s remarked upon the high rate of syphilis among the Masai, attributable to their habit of taking multiple sexual partners. Their birthrate is notably lower than the explosive population growth of the other peoples of Kenya and Tanzania. Still, they have increased from about 25,000 people at the turn of the century to the estimated 300,000-400,000 they are said to number today.

While the ceaseless cycle of their nomadic life has been sharply curtailed,

many still cross the border between the two countries as they have for hundreds of years, leading their cattle to water and grazing lands according to the demands of the wet and dry seasons. They are in tune with the animals that migrate from the Serengeti Plain in Tanzania to Masai Mara in Kenya, and back again.

MALE AGE-SETS

The life of a traditional Masai male follows a well-ordered progression through a series of life stages.

Masai children enjoy their early years as coddled and adored love objects. They are raised communally, with great affection. Children are a great blessing in Africa. Among the Masai, with the lack of emphasis on paternity, and with a woman's prestige tied to her children, natural love for children is enhanced by their desirability in the society. Children are also desired because they bring additional cattle to a family, either as bride-price in the case of girls or by raiding in the case of boys.

During their early years, children play and imitate the actions of the elders, a natural school in which they learn the rituals and daily life practices of their people. Learning how to be a Masai is the lifework of every one in the community. Infant mortality in Africa remains high; catastrophic diseases introduced by Europeans, such as smallpox, nearly wiped them out. That memory is alive in their oral traditions; having children is a protection against the loss of the entire culture, which they know from experience could easily happen. Africans believe that you must live to see your face reflected in that of a child; given the high infant mortality rate, the only way to protect that human chain is by having as many children as possible.

For boys, each stage of life embraces an age-group created at an elaborate ceremony, the highlight of their lives being the elevation to moran. Once initiated, they learn their age-group's specific duties and privileges. Males pass through four stages: childhood, boyhood, warriorhood, and elderhood.

Warriors, divided into junior and senior, form one generation, or age-set.

Four major ceremonies mark the passage from one group to another: boys who are going to be circumcised participate in the *Alamal Lenkapaata* ceremony, preparation for circumcision; *Emorata* is followed by initiation into warriorhood—status of moran; the passage from warrior to elderhood is marked by the *Eunoto* ceremony; and total elderhood is confirmed by the *Olngesherr.* All ceremonies have in common ritual head shaving, continual blessings, slaughter of an animal, ceremonial painting of face or body, singing, dancing, and feasting. *Laibons*—spiritual advisers—must be present at all ceremonies, and the entire tribe devotes itself to these preparations.

Circumcision is a rite of passage and more for teenage boys. It determines the role the boy will play throughout his life, as leader or follower. How he conducts himself during circumcision is keenly observed by all; a boy who cries out during the painful operation is branded a coward and shunned for a long time; his mother is disgraced. A boy who is brave, and who had led an exemplary life, becomes the leader of his age-group.

It takes months of work to prepare for these ceremonies so the exact date of such an event is rarely known until the last minute. Westerners, with contacts into the Masai community, often stay ready for weeks, hoping to be on hand when such a ceremony is about to take place. Each such ceremony may well be the last, it is thought.

Before they can be circumcised, boys must prove themselves ready. They tend the cattle—the Masai's only wealth—and guard them from predators whose tracks they learn to recognize. They know their cattle individually, the way we know people. Each animal has a name and is treated as a personality. When they feel they are ready, the boys approach the junior elders and ask them to open a new circumcision period. If this is approved, they begin a series of rituals, among them the Alamal Lenkapaata, the last step before the formal

Masai ceremony of the Alamal Lenkapaata which is part of the Morani (warrior) coming of age for young Masai men.

Young Masai Morani (warriors) dancing traditionally with their hair caked with red ochre mud and their legs in an abstract pattern in a traditional Masai Manyatta with long mud huts in the Rift Valley, Kenya.

Under a tree, elders from many areas gathered together and their discussion was very intense. John Galaty, professor of anthropology from McGill University in Montreal, who has studied the Masai extensively, flew in specifically to attend this ceremony. He is fluent in Masai and translated the elders' talk. "We are lucky," they said, "to be able to have this ceremony. The government does not want us to have it. We have to be very careful. The young men have to be warned that there should be no cattle raiding." And there wasn't any.

An ox was slaughtered, for meat eating is a vital element of this ceremony. The boys who were taking part cut off hunks of meat which they cooked over an open fire. Though there was a hut set aside for them, the boys spent little time sleeping. The next day, all the elders gathered to receive gifts of sugar and salt from John Keen, a member of Kenya's parliament, and himself a Masai. (Kenya has many Masai in government, including the Minister of Finance, George Saitoti.) The dancing, the meat eating, all the elements of the ceremony continued for several days. If this had been a wealthy group, they might have kept up the celebration for as long as a month.

Once this ceremony is concluded, the boys are allowed to hold councils and to discuss important matters. They choose one from their own group to be their representative. The Alamal Lenkapaata ceremony includes every boy of suitable age, preparing him for circumcision and then warriorhood. The circumcisions will take place over the next few years, beginning with the older boys in this group. The age difference may be considerable in any age-group since these ceremonies are held infrequently; once a circumcision period ends, though, it may not be opened again for many years.

initiation. The boys must have a laibon, a leader with the power to predict the future, to guide them in their decisions. He creates a name for this new generation. The boys decorate themselves with chalky paint, and spend the night out in the open. The elders sing and celebrate and dance through the night to honor the boys.

An Alamal Lenkapaata held in 1983 was probably the most recent to mark the opening of a new age-set. Ceremonies were held in Ewaso Ngiro, in the Rift Valley. As boys joined into groups and danced, they raised a cloud of dust around themselves. All day long, groups would form and dance, then break apart and later start again.

THE MORAN

The Masai who exemplifies his tribe is the moran. This is the time of life that expresses the essence of the Masai—bravery, willingness to defend their people and their cattle against all threats, confidence to go out on cattle raids to increase their own herds, and ability to stand up to threats even from Europeans, whose superior weapons subdued the Masai but never subjugated them. The Masai moran is the essence of that almost mythical being, the noble savage, a description invented by Europeans but here actually lived out. With his spear, his elaborately braided and reddened hair, his bountiful beaded jewelry, his beautiful body and proud bearing, the moran is the symbol of everything that is attractive about the Masai. When a young man becomes a moran, his entire culture looks upon him with reverence.

The life a moran enjoys as his birthright is centered on cattle raiding, enhancing his appearance, and sex. The need to perform actual work, such as building fences, rescuing a cow that has gone astray, and standing ready to defend their homeland—Masailand—is only occasionally required. Much of his time is devoted to the glorification of his appearance. His body is a living showcase of Masai art.

From the moment a boy undergoes the circumcision ceremony, he looks ahead to the time when he will be a moran. He grows his hair long so it can be braided into myriad tiny plaits, thickened with ochre and fat. The age-mates spend hours at this, the whole outdoors being their salon. As they work, they chat, always building the bonds between them. Their beaded jewelry is made by their girlfriends. Their bare legs are ever-changing canvases on which they trace patterns, using white chalk and ochre. Though nearly naked, they are a medley of patterns and colors.

After being circumcised, the young men "float" in society for up to two years, traveling in loose groups and living in temporary shelters called *inkangitie*. After that time they can build a manyatta. Before fully becoming a moran, however, they must enter a "holy house" at a special ceremony. Only a young man who has not slept with a circumcised woman can enter the holy house. The fear of violating this taboo is very strong, and young men who do not enter the house are beaten by their parents and carry the disrespect of the tribe all their lives.

The dancing of the morani celebrates everything that they consider beautiful and strong: morani dance competitively by jumping straight into the air, knees straight, over and over again, each leap trying to go higher than the last, as they sing and chant and encourage each other. The morani also dance with their young girlfriends. Each couple performs sinuous motions repeatedly, then breaks off and another couple takes their place. A hypnotic rhythm develops as they follow the chanting and hand clapping of their mates.

Although they are now forbidden by the governments of Kenya and Tanzania to kill a lion—a traditional test of manhood—or to go cattle raiding, they retain all the trappings of a warrior, without the possibility of practicing their skill. They occasionally manage a cattle raid, but even without it, they still live with pride and dignity. Masai remain morani for about fifteen years, building up unusually strong relationships among their age-mates with whom they live during that time. Hundreds of boys may become morani at one time.

Traditionally, every fifteen years saw the advent of a new generation of warriors. Now, both colonial governments and independent black-ruled governments have tampered with this social process, and have been successful in reducing the time men spend as warriors. By forcing this change, the governments hope to mold the Masai male into a more tractable citizen, especially by forbidding such disruptive activities as lion killing and cattle raiding. But tinkering with the Masai system can have unforeseen and undesirable consequences. It takes a certain number of years before a moran is ready to take on the duties of that age-group. They need time to build up herds of cattle to be used for bride-price and to learn to perform the decision-making tasks expected. This change also leaves the younger boys without warriors to keep them in check, and to guide them through the years leading up to the circumcision ceremony.

More significantly, since 1978 it has been illegal to build a manyatta, and warriors from that time have been left with no place to live. Their mothers cannot live with them, they cannot tend their cattle or increase their herds, they have no wives or jobs. Since, once they become warriors, they are not allowed to enter another person's house to eat, they are forced to steal other peoples' cattle and live off the land.

Circumcision exists for women as well as for men. From the age of nine until puberty, young girls live with the morani as sexual partners; it is an accepted part of Masai life that girls do not reach puberty as virgins. It is because of this practice that syphilis causes the most serious problems for the Masai. The girls, unfamiliar with their bodies, contract the disease and leave it untreated until sterility results. This sexual activity changes dramatically when a girl reaches puberty. At that time, she is circumcised and forbidden to stay with the warriors. This is to prevent her from becoming pregnant before she is married. As soon as she recovers from the circumcision, or clitoridectomy, an operation that destroys her ability to experience orgasm, she is considered ready for marriage. Circumcision is seen as a means of equalizing men and women. By removing any vestige of the appearance of the organs of the opposite sex, it purifies the gender. Although female circumcision has long been banned by the Kenyan government, few girls manage to escape the operation.

While the entire tribe devotes itself to the rituals that perpetuate the male age-set system, girls travel individually through life in their roles as lovers, wives, and child bearers, in all instances subservient to the boys and men. They have no comparable age-set system and hence do not develop the intensely felt friendships of the men who move through life together in groups, and who, during the period of senior warriorhood live together, away from their families.

It is during this period that the mothers move away from their homes. They build manyattas in which they live with their sons who have achieved the status of senior morani, along with their sons' girlfriends, and away from their own small children. The husbands, other wives, and the other women of the tribe, take care of these children.

The male-female relationship is dictated according to the male age-sets. When a newly circumcised girl marries, she joins the household of her husband's family, and likely will be one among several of his wives. Her role is to milk the cows, to build the house, and to bear children, especially male children. Only through childbirth can she achieve high status; all men, on the other hand, achieve status simply by graduating from one age-set to the next.

A childless Masai woman is virtually without a role in her society. One of the rarest ceremonies among the Masai is a blessing for women who have not given birth and for women who want more children. While the women play a peripheral role in the men's ceremonies, the men are vital to the women's, for it is a man who blesses the women. To prepare for the ritual, the women brew great quantities of beer and offer beer and lambs to the men who are to bless them.

In their preparation for this ceremony, and in conducting matters that pertain to their lives, the women talk things out democratically, as do the men. They gather in the fields and each woman presents her views. Not until all who want to speak have done so does the group move toward a consensus. As with the men, a good speaker is highly valued and her views are listened to attentively. But these sessions are restricted to women's issues; the men have the final say over all matters relating to the tribe. Boys may gather in councils as soon as they have completed the Alamal Lenkapaata; girls don't have similar opportunities. They follow their lovers, the morani, devotedly, yet as soon as they reach the age when they can marry, they are wrenched out of this love relationship and given in marriage to much older men, men who have cattle for bride-price.

Because morani do not marry until they are elevated to elderhood, girls must accept husbands who are easily twice their age. But just as the husband has more than one wife, she will have lovers, who are permitted as long as they are members of her husband's circumcision group, not the age group for whom she was a girlfriend. This is often the cause of tension among the Masai. All the children she bears are considered to be her husband's even though they may not be his biologically. While incest taboos are clearly observed and various other taboos also pertain, multiple partners are expected. Polygamy in Masailand (and anywhere it prevails) dictates that some men will not marry at all. These men are likely to be those without cattle, men who cannot bring bride-price. For the less traditional, the payment of bride-price is sometimes made in cash, rather than in cattle, and to earn money, men go to the cities to seek work. Masai tend to find jobs that permit them to be outside and free; for this reason, many of the night watchmen in the capital city of Nairobi are Masai. They sit around fires at night, chatting, in an urban version of their life in the countryside. . . .

RAIDING, THEFT, AND THE LAW

Though now subject to national laws, the Masai do not turn to official bodies or courts for redress. They settle their own disputes democratically, each man giving his opinion until the matter at hand is settled. Men decide all matters for the tribe (women do not take part in these discussions), and they operate virtually without chiefs. The overriding concern is to be fair in the resolution of problems because kinship ties the Masai together in every aspect of their lives. Once a decision is made, punishment is always levied in the form of a fine. The Masai have no jails, nor do they inflict physical punishment. For a people who value cattle as much as they do, there is no greater sacrifice than to give up some of their animals.

The introduction of schools is another encroachment upon traditional life which was opposed by the Masai. While most African societies resisted sending their children to school, the Masai reacted with particular intensity. They compared school to death or enslavement; if children did go to school, they would be lost to the Masai community. They would forget how to survive on the land, how to identify animals by their tracks, and how to protect the cattle. All of these things are learned by example and by experience.

David Read is a white Kenyan, fluent in Masai who said that, as a boy: "I may not have been able to read or write, but I knew how to live in the bush. I could hunt my dinner if I had to."

The first school in their territory was opened in 1919 at Narok but few children attended. The Masai scorned the other tribes, such as the Kikuyu, who later embraced Western culture and soon filled the offices of the government's bureaucracies. The distance between the Masai and the other tribes became even greater. The Masai were seen as a painful reminder of the primitivism that Europeans as well as Africans had worked so hard to erase. Today, however, many Masai families will keep one son at home to maintain traditional life, and send another one to school. In this way, they experience the benefits of literacy, opportunities for employment, money, connections to the government, and new knowledge, especially veterinary practices, while keeping their traditions intact. Masai who go to school tend to succeed, many of them graduating from college with science degrees. Some take up the study of animal diseases, and bring this knowledge back to help their communities improve the health of their cattle. The entire Masai herd was once nearly wiped out during the rinderpest epidemic in the late nineteenth century. Today, the cattle are threatened by tsetse flies. But where the Masai were able to rebuild their herds in the past, today, they would face tremendous pressure to give up cattle raising entirely.

LIVING CONDITIONS

While the Masai are admired for their great beauty, their living conditions are breeding grounds for disease. Since they keep their small livestock (sheep and goats) in the huts where they live, they are continually exposed to the animals' excrement.The cattle are just outside, in an open enclosure, and their excrement is added to the mix. Flies abound wherever cattle are kept, but with the animals living right next to the huts, they are ever-present. Like many tribal groups living in relative isolation, the Masai are highly vulnerable to diseases brought in by others. In the 1890s, when the rinderpest hit their cattle, the Masai were attacked by smallpox which, coupled with drought, reduced their numbers almost to the vanishing point.

For the most part, the Masai rely on the remedies of their traditional medicine and are renowned for their extensive knowledge and use of natural plants to treat illnesses and diseases of both people and cattle. Since they live in an area that had hardly any permanent sources of water, the Masai have learned to live without washing. They are said to have one bath at birth, another at marriage. Flies are pervasive; there is scarcely a picture of a Masai taken in their home environment that does not show flies alit on them.

Their rounded huts, looking like mushrooms growing from the ground, are built by the women. On a frame of wooden twigs, they begin to plaster mud and cow dung. Layers and layers of this are added until the roof reaches the desired thickness. Each day, cracks and holes are repaired, especially after the rains, using the readily available dung. Within the homes, they use animal hides. Everything they need can be made from the materials at hand. There are a few items such as sugar, tea, and cloth that they buy from the *dukas,* or Indian shops, in Narok, Kajiado, and other nearby towns, but money is readily obtained by selling beaded jewelry, or simply one's own image. Long ago, the Masai discovered their photogenic qualities. If they cannot survive as war-

riors by raiding, they will survive as icons of warriors, permitting tourists to take their pictures for a fee, and that fee is determined by hard bargaining. One does not simply take a picture of a Masai without payment; that is theft.

Their nomadic patterns have been greatly reduced; now they move only the cattle as the seasons change. During the dry season, the Masai stay on the higher parts of the escarpment and use the pastures there which they call *osukupo.* This offers a richer savannah with more trees. When the rains come, they move down to the pastures of the Rift Valley to the plains called *okpurkel.*

Their kraals are built a few miles from the water supply. The cattle drink on one day only, then are grazed the next, so they can conserve the grazing by using a larger area than they would be able to if they watered the cattle every day. But their great love of cattle has inevitably brought them to the point of overstocking. As the cattle trample their way to and from the waterhole, they destroy all vegetation near it, and the soil washes away. Scientists studying Masai land use have concluded that with the change from a totally nomadic way of life, the natural environmental resistance of this system was destroyed; there is no self-regulating mechanism left. Some Masai have permitted wheat farming on their land for the exploding Kenyan population, taking away the marginal lands that traditionally provided further grazing for their cattle.

PRESSURE TO CHANGE

In June 1901, Sir Charles Eliot, colonial governor of Kenya, said, "I regard the Masai as the most important and dangerous of the tribes with whom we have to deal in East Africa and I think it will be long necessary to maintain an adequate military force in the districts which they inhabit."

The traditional Masai way of life has been under attack ever since. The colonial British governments of Kenya and Tanzania (then Tanganyika) outlawed Masai cattle raiding and tried to stifle the initiation ceremony; the black

governments that took over upon independence in the 1960s continued the process. The Masai resisted these edicts, ignored them, and did their best to circumvent them throughout the century. In some areas, they gave in entirely—cattle raiding, the principal activity of the morani—rarely occurs, but their ceremonies, the vital processes by which a boy becomes a moran and a moran becomes an elder, remain intact, although they have been banned over and over again. Stopping these ceremonies is more difficult than just proclaiming them to be over, as the Kenyan government did in 1985.

Some laws restrict the very essence of a Masai's readiness to assume the position of moran. Hunting was banned entirely in Kenya and nearly so in Tanzania (except for expensive permits issued to tourists, and restricted to designated hunting blocks), making it illegal for a moran to kill a lion to demonstrate his bravery and hunting skills. Although the Masai ignore the government whenever possible, at times such as this, conflict is unavoidable. Lions are killed occasionally, but stealthily; some modern Masai boys say, "Who needs to kill a lion? It doesn't prove anything."

The Kenyan governments requirement that Masai children go to school has also affected the traditional roles of girls and women, who traditionally married at age twelve or thirteen and left school. Now the government will send fathers and husbands to jail for taking these girls out of school. There was a case in Kenya in 1986 of a girl who wrote to the government protesting the fact that her father had removed her from school to prepare for marriage. Her mother carried the letter to the appropriate government officials, the father was tried, and the girl was allowed to return to school.

Sometimes there is cooperation between governmental policy and traditional life-style. Ceremonies are scheduled to take place in school holidays, and while government policies continue to erode traditional customs, the educated and traditional groups within the

Masai community try to support each other.

TRADITION IN THE FACE OF CHANGE

Although the Masai in both countries are descended from the same people, national policies have pushed the Kenyan Masai further away from their traditions. The Tanzanian Masai, for example, still dress occasionally in animal skins, decorated with beading. The Kenyan Masai dress almost entirely in cloth, reserving skins for ceremonial occasions.

In 1977, Kenya and Tanzania closed their common border, greatly isolating the Tanzanian Masai from Western contact. Though the border has been reopened, the impact on the Masai is clear. The Kenyan Masai became one of the sights of the tourist route while the Tanzanian Masai were kept from such interaction. This has further accelerated change among the Kenyan Masai. Tepilit Ole Saitoti sees a real difference in character between the Masai of Kenya and Tanzania. "Tem-peramentally," he says, "the Tanzanian Masai tend to be calmer and slower than those in Kenya."

Tribal people throughout Africa are in a constant state of change, some totally urbanized, their traditions nearly forgotten; others are caught in the middle, part of the tribe living traditionally, some moving to the city and adopting Western ways. The Masai have retained their culture, their unique and distinctive way of life, longer than virtually all the other tribes of East Africa, and they have done so while living in the very middle of the tourist traffic. Rather than disappear into the bush, the Masai use their attractiveness and mystique to their own benefit. Masai Mara and Amboseli, two reserves set aside for them, are run by them for their own profit.

Few tribes in Africa still put such a clear cultural stamp on an area; few have so successfully resisted enormous efforts to change them, to modernize and "civilize" them, to make them fit into the larger society. We leave it to Tepilit Ole Saitoti to predict the future of his own people: "Through their long and difficult history, the Masai have fought to maintain their traditional way of life. Today, however, they can no longer resist the pressures of the modern world. The survival of Masai culture has ceased to be a question; in truth, it is rapidly disappearing."

BIBLIOGRAPHY

Bleeker, Sonia, *The Masai, Herders of East Africa*, 1963.

Fedders, Andrew, *Peoples and Cultures of Kenya*, TransAfrica Books, Nairobi, 1979.

Fisher, Angela, *Africa Adorned*, Harry N. Abrams Inc., New York, 1984.

Kinde, S.H., *Last of the Masai*, London, 1901.

Kipkorir, B., *Kenya's People, People of the Rift Valley*, Evans Bros. Ltd., London, 1978.

Lamb, David, *The Africans*, Vintage Books, New York, 1984.

Moravia, Alberto, *Which Tribe Do You Belong To?*, Farrar, Straus & Giroux, Inc., New York, 1974.

Ole Saitoti, Tepilit, *Masai*, Harry N. Abrams, Inc., New York, 1980.

Ricciardi, Mirella, *Vanishing Africa*, Holt, Rinehard & Winston, 1971.

Sankan, S. S. *The Masai*, Kenya Literature Bureau, Nairobi, 1971.

Thomson, Joseph, *Through Masai Land*, Sampson Low, Marston & Co., London, 1885.

Tignor, Robert, *The Colonial Transformation of Kenya, The Kamba, Kikuyu and Masai from 1900 to 1939*, Princeton, NJ, 1976.

Camels in the Land of Kings

*The Raikas of India, traditional suppliers of camels,
find their herds are dwindling*

Ilse Köhler-Rollefson

Ilse Köhler-Rollefson had her first close encounters with camels in 1979, while doing archeological fieldwork in Jordan. Soon thereafter she received a degree of doctor of veterinary medicine from the Veterinary College of Hanover, Germany, and in 1990 began researching camel pastoralism, first in the Sudan and then among the Raikas in India. She is the founder and president of the League for Pastoral Peoples, an advocacy and support organization for pastoralists worldwide.

In February, against a backdrop of several hundred camels spread out to graze, five turbaned men huddle beside an impromptu campfire. Passing around a clay pipe, they discuss the outcome of the previous fair in Pushkar, the west Indian town where each November they sell their annual crop of young male camels. Even the batch of fluffy baby camels playfully darting around does not distract the men from their gloomy thoughts. One, a younger man named Gautamji, finally summarizes their predicament for me:

> Look at us. Only fifty years ago we had 10,000 camels—so many that we never even cared when we lost one in the jungle. Twenty years ago, there were 5,000. Now, only about 1,000 camels belong to our village. Ten years from now, or even sooner, we will have no more camels.

The men are Raikas, members of a Hindu caste that specializes in breeding livestock. While they also keep sheep, goats, and cattle, the Raikas are renowned as experts in camel breeding. Inhabitants of the state of Rajasthan, "the land of kings," many of them take pride in their centuries-old heritage as caretakers of the camel breeding herds that the local maharajahs once maintained to insure a supply of the animals for warfare.

Rajasthan's bleak landscape is dotted with forts and palaces that testify to past glory and heroism. Before independence, the region, which includes the harsh Thar Desert in the west, comprised several kingdoms. The rulers, who belonged to the Rajput warrior caste, were known for their courage, preferring death to defeat. Perpetually involved in internecine battles between their desert kingdoms or in repelling invading Muslim forces, the maharajahs used camel corps and relied on batteries of pack camels to provide logistical support in their arid territories.

The Raikas were one of many castes that provided specialized services to the Rajputs in exchange for their protection. When India gained independence in 1947, the feudal system was dissolved, and most of the royal camels became the property of the Raikas. The military uses for camels have dwindled over the years, but India's security forces still use them to patrol the boundary with Pakistan. Fortunately for the Raikas, however, a new purpose for camels developed: they came to play a crucial economic role as draft power.

In the past forty years, the camel cart has quietly revolutionized transportation in many parts of western India, notably in the states of Rajasthan and Gujarat. Modeled on the oxcart, the camel cart is considerably larger and equipped with used airplane tires that enable it to go anywhere, regardless of the condition, or even the presence, of roads. Ownership of a camel and cart for hauling loads provides a decent livelihood for thousands of people. In India's arid west, camels represent an indispensable source of energy that saves the cost of imported fuel.

The market for camels is still going strong, but the Raikas, who are the main suppliers of camels to farmers and small-scale transport entrepreneurs, are pessimistic about the future. The reason is simple. As traditionally practiced, camel breeding relies on access to large expanses of open, often communally owned land—once amply available for grazing under the formal control of village councils. Within the span of this century, however, Rajasthan has witnessed phenomenal population growth, with the Thar Desert now deemed the most densely populated desert in the world. The consequent expansion and intensification of crop cultivation is one of the factors responsible for eliminating pastureland. Furthermore, some of the Raikas' traditional summer pastures in the Aravalli Hills, east of the desert, have been listed as nature reserves, and access to them has been drastically curbed. Although partly denuded of its dense vegetation, this ancient range still harbors considerable wildlife, including wolves, jackals, and a few tigers.

3. THE ORGANIZATION OF SOCIETY AND CULTURE

*India's Border Security Force, below, uses camels to patrol the Thar Desert,
which overlaps the boundary with Pakistan.
Raikas camp with their camels and goats, bottom right.*

Doranne Jacobson

With grazing land scarce, the majority of the Raika camels are now teetering on the brink of starvation, and their chronic hunger has resulted in a drop in their fertility. Under optimal circumstances, camels are slow reproducers, a female giving birth to one calf every two years. The Raikas traditionally sell off only the male calves, keeping the female calves to replenish the breeding stock, which they regard as an ancestral legacy. At best, therefore, they can hope to have one male calf to sell per year for every four breeding females. But now the situation is far worse, for many of the females experience a delay in sexual maturity, suffer abortions, or die. Reluctantly departing from custom, the Raikas are now also selling off some of the females. These factors, combined with the loss of animals due to disease, have led to a drastic drop in camel holdings.

In addition to their economic woes, the Raikas complain that while they were once respected members of the larger community, they are now harassed whenever they show up with their herds. They are bullied by forest officials and even driven away by landowners, who once welcomed them with gifts of food and tea for the fertilizing manure the camels left on the fields.

Having studied camel pastoralists in other countries, I have always been struck by the limited way in which the Raikas use their camels. These self-imposed restrictions make it difficult for them to see a way of solving their current dilemma. To begin with, they follow an absolute taboo against the slaughtering of camels and the consumption of their meat, something that, to my knowledge, does not exist among any other camel pastoralists.

When, at a recent conference that dealt with their problems, the Raikas learned that camels are a popular source of meat in parts of the Arab world, they sought, unsuccessfully, an immediate ban on the export of camels to those countries.

This uncompromising attitude may have rubbed off from the taboo regarding cows in the Raikas' Hindu religion. The local Muslim groups take the same stance, however, although they may be less adamant about it "The camel is our best friend—why should we kill it?" one Muslim commented. Since most of India's Muslims converted to Islam only in recent centuries, this attitude may be a holdover from their Hindu heritage.

In addition, the Raikas are nowhere near exploiting their herds' potentials for milk production. For African camel pastoralists, camel milk is often a staple. But the Raikas milk their camels only sporadically. This has to do partly with the social organization of herding. Unlike other camel pastoralists, who travel as a group, following a nomadic lifestyle and living in tents or other mobile dwellings, the Raikas reside in colonies at the outskirts of villages. Women, children, and older men stay year-round in permanent houses. Only some of the able-bodied men accompany the herds on

Ilse Köhler-Rollefson

migration, when they need to search for pasture.

Often traveling more than 100 miles, the herdsmen take no cooking equipment with them—their entire gear consists of a blanket, a rope, and a clay container used as a mincing vessel. Often they subsist almost exclusively on camel milk for weeks. But because a herd of 100 animals can be managed by about four men, only a few of the camels need to be milked.

While it is common practice among other camel-oriented cultures to sour camel milk, the Raikas maintain that milk must he drunk fresh without heating, and they refer to various gods and saints who prohibited the manufacture of curd from camel milk. Thus they take no advantage of the possibilities for processing camel milk into longer-lasting products such as cheese or ghee (clarified butter). Occasionally, however, they make kir (rice pudding) or condense the milk of newly lactating camels into an invigorating tonic.

Milking, other than for immediate consumption, is also discouraged by a Raika caste rule that the milk of their animals should not be sold. The feeling is that one should not profit from milk, and that excess milk should be given to the needy. "Selling milk is like selling your children," I was once told by a Raika elder.

Utilization of the products of the dead animal, such as leather and bones, is also taboo for the Raikas and left to members of lower castes. The Raikas do shear their camels for wool on the occasion of the annual festival that marks the transition from the cold to the hot season. The wool is spun by the men and then handed over to a caste of weavers and leatherworkers, who weave it into blankets.

The restrictions the Raikas place on their use of camels should not be regarded as inherently irrational. The taboos once served the Raikas well, given that the herders' express purpose was producing the maximum number of transport animals. Exploiting camels for milk would probably have resulted in longer birth intervals and a higher mortality rate in the young camels. But the traditional taboos may now prevent

the Raikas from adapting to changing circumstances.

Shedding old views will be difficult, however. For the Raikas, camels represent more than utilitarian objects. The group's association with this animal is an essential part of Raika identity. According to their mythology, Lord Shiva, one of the three principal manifestations of God in the Hindu pantheon, created the Raikas expressly to look after camels. I have many times listened to renderings of the touching story in which Parvati, Lord Shiva's wife, playfully shaped the first camel from a lump of clay. She then beseeched Shiva to breathe life into her toy, but the living camel proceeded to cause a lot of trouble. Implored by Parvati to stop the nuisance, Shiva then created the first Raika from a piece of his own skin and his sweat.

The camel is also an essential component of a Raika wedding. The bride's dowry includes a number of female camels given to the groom's family. And the bridegroom sits on a camel during critical parts of the marriage ceremony and, from the animal's back, touches the wooden arch erected for the occasion.

The strong emotional attachment of the Raikas to their camels is matched by the depth of their traditional knowledge about all aspects of camel breeding and management. As is the prerequisite for all pastoralists, the Raikas are intimately familiar with the terrain, the seasonal availability of pasture, and the properties of forage plants. Although the herdsmen are illiterate, they keep careful mental notes of their camels' pedigrees and can recite the ancestry and life history of each individual animal they own. They conceptualize their breeding stock as representatives of certain female bloodlines known for particular qualities. Stud camels are carefully selected for desired traits, including the performance of their female relatives. To avoid inbreeding, the stud camels are changed every four years.

For observers from a Western culture, in which farm animals are often regarded as unpredictable and are restrained accordingly, the way the

Raikas supervise and control the movements of hundreds of camels without any visible effort is particularly impressive. Much is done by voice, and a simple command can suffice to separate mothers and young into two different groups. The Raikas distinguish their female animals less in terms of milk yield and more in terms of easy milking. In the case of some camels, anybody can just walk up and milk them, while others have a close relationship to a particular herder and can be easily milked only by him. Many will not yield their milk unless their young are nearby, but some will comply when talked to in a sweet voice.

Another important component of the Raikas' indigenous knowledge is animal health maintenance. The Raikas distinguish a long list of diseases for which they have an array of treatments. The scourge of camel breeding is trypanosomiasis, a parasitic blood disease that resembles human malaria. Transmitted by biting flies, it is prevalent especially in years with above-average rainfall. The Raikas can diagnose it from the smell of the camel's urine—a method that has been deemed equivalent in accuracy to examining a blood smear under the microscope. Unfortunately, while the Raikas have several treatments for this disease, none of them cure it, and modern therapeutics are beyond their financial means.

For camel pox, which afflicts mainly young animals, the Raikas have developed a simple, effective vaccination. They take a sample of the blistered skin from an infected animal, mix it with water, and then rub it into shallow incisions in the nose of the animal to be protected. For chronic diseases, Raika animal healers resort to "firing"—they apply a heated iron to prescribed or affected areas. Firing is an accepted practice in Western veterinary medicine, especially with horses, because it is thought to increase blood circulation and thus promote healing.

The Raikas' large body of traditional knowledge and their aptitude in handling and managing camels are invaluable assets, yet these will be doomed to oblivion if camel breeding becomes

3. THE ORGANIZATION OF SOCIETY AND CULTURE

an obsolete occupation. How can the Raikas adapt to the decrease in pastureland? With more investment, particularly in terms of better veterinary care and provision of fodder, the productivity of the herds could be increased. But such inputs are expensive and seem beyond the relatively meager incomes that can be made from selling male camels.

Because the Raikas have placed so many cultural restrictions on camel utilization, I was not particularly optimistic that they would find a solution to their quandary. I could not expect them to break with their traditions and slaughter unproductive animals or commercialize milk production. Yet sometimes—and especially in India—extraordinary things happen. Not long ago, my field assistant, Ruparam Raika, heard rumors about camel milk being sold in some remote areas of southern Rajasthan and the adjoining state of Madhya Pradesh. Soon after, Ruparam and I, along with my longtime interpreter and adopted brother, Hanwant Singh, made a trip to the area in question and discovered a thriving camel milk market.

The market had its beginnings about twenty years ago when some Rebaris—members of a caste closely related to the Raikas—started selling milk from a few of their camels to the owners of tea stalls. Their desperate attempt to break out of poverty paid off. They established extensive customer networks and expanded their herds accordingly and still could not supply enough milk to fulfill the demand.

In India, milk is an essential ingredient of tea, but also in the Rebaris' favor were the advantages of their product over the competition. The numerous tea shops generally have no

Ilse Köhler-Rollefson

A camel cart with rubber tires is used to transport goods. The need for draft animals currently creates the main demand for camels in northwest India.

refrigeration, and because camel milk can be kept longer without going sour, it wins out over cow and buffalo milk. It is also cheaper. Fear for their market share even induced some cow and buffalo milk sellers to stage a protest and strike against camel milk, charging that it was a human health hazard. In line with scientific findings, however, a number of local authorities supported camel milk as being of good nutritional value.

As news filtered back to the Raikas of the handsome profits being made from camel milk sales, they did not take long to reconsider their staunch resistance to such ventures. They have already submitted a list of camel breeders willing to break with tradition and have requested support in making the economic transition. Two nongovernmental organizations with which I

am involved have taken up their proposal and have launched the Camel Husbandry Improvement Project, or CHIP, to investigate how camel breeding can once again become economically rewarding.

Whether camel milk can now do for the Raikas what the camel cart did earlier remains to be seen. A prerequisite for milk production is a better fodder supply. The options that need to be explored are purchasing supplementary feed, rehabilitating communal grazing grounds, and reopening some of the forest areas in the Aravalli Hills to grazing. For the sake of the economic health of the Raikas, the survival of their camels, and the perpetuation of their traditional knowledge, I hope solutions can be found.

Too Many Bananas, Not Enough Pineapples, and No Watermelon at All: Three Object Lessons in Living with Reciprocity

David Counts

McMaster University

NO WATERMELON AT ALL

The woman came all the way through the village, walking between the two rows of houses facing each other between the beach and the bush, to the very last house standing on a little spit of land at the mouth of the Kaini River. She was carrying a watermelon on her head, and the house she came to was the government "rest house," maintained by the villagers for the occasional use of visiting officials. Though my wife and I were graduate students, not officials, and had asked for permission to stay in the village for the coming year, we were living in the rest house while the debate went on about where a house would be built for us. When the woman offered to sell us the watermelon for two shillings, we happily agreed, and the kids were delighted at the prospect of watermelon after yet another meal of rice and bully beef. The money changed hands and the

seller left to return to her village, a couple of miles along the coast to the east.

It seemed only seconds later that the woman was back, reluctantly accompanying Kolia, the man who had already made it clear to us that he was the leader of the village. Kolia had no English, and at that time, three or four days into our first stay in Kandoka Village on the island of New Britain in Papua New Guinea, we had very little Tok Pisin. Language difficulties notwithstanding, Kolia managed to make his message clear: The woman had been outrageously wrong to sell us the watermelon for two shillings and we were to return it to her and reclaim our money immediately. When we tried to explain that we thought the price to be fair and were happy with the bargain, Kolia explained again and finally made it clear that we had missed the point. The problem wasn't that we had paid too much; it was that we had paid at all. Here he was, a leader, responsible for us while we were living in his village, and we had shamed him. How would it look if he let guests in his village *buy* food? If we wanted watermelons, or bananas, or anything else,

all that was necessary was to let him know. He told us that it would be all right for us to give little gifts to people who brought food to us (and they surely would), but *no one* was to sell food to us. If anyone were to try—like this woman from Lauvore—then we should refuse. There would be plenty of watermelons without us buying them.

The woman left with her watermelon, disgruntled, and we were left with our two shillings. But we had learned the first lesson of many about living in Kandoka. We didn't pay money for food again that whole year, and we did get lots of food brought to us . . . but we never got another watermelon. That one was the last of the season.

LESSON 1: *In a society where food is shared or gifted as part of social life, you may not buy it with money.*

TOO MANY BANANAS

In the couple of months that followed the watermelon incident, we managed to become at least marginally competent in Tok Pisin, to negotiate the con-

From *The Humbled Anthropologist: Tales from the Pacific* by David Counts, Wadsworth Publishing Company, 1990, pp. 18-24.

struction of a house on what we hoped was neutral ground, and to settle into the routine of our fieldwork. As our village leader had predicted, plenty of food was brought to us. Indeed, seldom did a day pass without something coming in—some sweet potatoes, a few taro, a papaya, the occasional pineapple, or some bananas—lots of bananas.

We had learned our lesson about the money, though, so we never even offered to buy the things that were brought, but instead made gifts, usually of tobacco to the adults or chewing gum to the children. Nor were we so gauche as to haggle with a giver over how much of a return gift was appropriate, though the two of us sometimes conferred as to whether what had been brought was a "two-stick" or a "three-stick" stalk, bundle, or whatever. A "stick" of tobacco was a single large leaf, soaked in rum and then twisted into a ropelike form. This, wrapped in half a sheet of newsprint (torn for use as cigarette paper), sold in the local trade stores for a shilling. Nearly all of the adults in the village smoked a great deal, and they seldom had much cash, so our stocks of twist tobacco and stacks of the Sydney *Morning Herald* (all, unfortunately, the same day's issue) were seen as a real boon to those who preferred "stick" to the locally grown product.

We had established a pattern with respect to the gifts of food. When a donor appeared at our veranda we would offer our thanks and talk with them for a few minutes (usually about our children, who seemed to hold a real fascination for the villagers and for whom most of the gifts were intended) and then we would inquire whether they could use some tobacco. It was almost never refused, though occasionally a small bottle of kerosene, a box of matches, some laundry soap, a cup of rice, or a tin of meat would be requested instead of (or even in addition to) the tobacco. Everyone, even Kolia, seemed to think this arrangement had worked out well.

Now, what must be kept in mind is that while we were following their rules—or seemed to be—we were *re-*

ally still buying food. In fact we kept a running account of what came in and what we "paid" for it. Tobacco as currency got a little complicated, but since the exchange rate was one stick to one shilling, it was not too much trouble as long as everyone was happy, and meanwhile we could account for the expenditure of "informant fees" and "household expenses." Another thing to keep in mind is that not only did we continue to think in terms of our buying the food that was brought, we thought of them as *selling it.* While it was true they never quoted us a price, they also never asked us if we needed or wanted whatever they had brought. It seemed clear to us that when an adult needed a stick of tobacco, or a child wanted some chewing gum (we had enormous quantities of small packets of Wrigley's for just such eventualities) they would find something surplus to their own needs and bring it along to our "store" and get what they wanted.

By late November 1966, just before the rainy reason set in, the bananas were coming into flush, and whereas earlier we had received banana gifts by the "hand" (six or eight bananas in a cluster cut from the stalk), donors now began to bring bananas, "for the children," by the *stalk!* The Kaliai among whom we were living are not exactly specialists in banana cultivation—they only recognize about thirty varieties, while some of their neighbors have more than twice that many—but the kinds they produce differ considerably from each other in size, shape, and taste, so we were not dismayed when we had more than one stalk hanging on our veranda. The stalks ripen a bit at the time, and having some variety was nice. Still, by the time our accumulation had reached *four* complete stalks, the delights of variety had begun to pale a bit. The fruits were ripening progressively and it was clear that even if we and the kids ate nothing but bananas for the next week, some would still fall from the stalk onto the floor in a state of gross overripeness. This was the situation as, late one afternoon, a woman came bringing yet another stalk of bananas up the steps of the house.

Several factors determined our reaction to her approach: one was that there was literally no way we could possibly use the bananas. We hadn't quite reached the point of being crowded off our veranda by the stalks of fruit, but it was close. Another factor was that we were tired of playing the gift game. We had acquiesced in playing it—no one was permitted to sell us anything, and in turn we only gave things away, refusing under any circumstances to sell tobacco (or anything else) for money. But there had to be a limit. From our perspective what was at issue was that the woman wanted something and she had come to trade for it. Further, what she had brought to trade was something we neither wanted nor could use, and it should have been obvious to her. So we decided to bite the bullet.

The woman, Rogi, climbed the stairs to the veranda, took the stalk from where it was balanced on top of her head, and laid it on the floor with the word, "Here are some bananas for the children." Dorothy and I sat near her on the floor and thanked her for her thought but explained, "You know, we really have too many bananas—we can't use these; maybe you ought to give them to someone else. . . ." The woman looked mystified, then brightened and explained that she didn't want anything for them, she wasn't short of tobacco or anything. They were just a gift for the kids. Then she just sat there, and we sat there, and the bananas sat there, and we tried again. "Look," I said, pointing up to them and counting, "we've got four stalks already hanging here on the veranda— there are too many for us to eat now. Some are rotting already. Even if we eat only bananas, we can't keep up with what's here!"

Rogi's only response was to insist that these were a gift, and that she didn't want anything for them, so we tried yet another tack: "Don't *your* children like bananas?" When she admitted that they did, and that she had none at her house, we suggested that she should take them there. Finally, still puzzled, but convinced we weren't going to keep the bananas, she replaced them on her head, went down the stairs, and made her way back through the village toward her house.

As before, it seemed only moments before Kolia was making his way up the stairs, but this time he hadn't brought the woman in tow. "What was wrong with those bananas? Were they no good?" he demanded. We explained that there was nothing wrong with the bananas at all, but that we simply couldn't use them and it seemed foolish to take them when we had so many and Rogi's own children had none. We obviously didn't make ourselves clear because Kolia then took up the same refrain that Rogi had—he insisted that we shouldn't be worried about taking the bananas, because they were a gift for the children and Rogi hadn't wanted anything for them. There was no reason, he added, to send her away with them—she would be ashamed. I'm afraid we must have seemed as if we were hard of hearing or thought he was, for our only response was to repeat our reasons. We went through it again—there they hung, one, two, three, *four* stalks of bananas, rapidly ripening and already far beyond our capacity to eat—we just weren't ready to accept any more and let them rot (and, we added to ourselves, pay for them with tobacco, to boot).

Kolia finally realized that we were neither hard of hearing nor intentionally offensive, but merely ignorant. He stared at us for a few minutes, thinking, and then asked: "Don't you frequently have visitors during the day and evening?" We nodded. Then he asked, "Don't you usually offer them cigarettes and coffee or milo?" Again, we nodded. "Did it ever occur to you to suppose," he said, "that your visitors might be hungry?" It was at this point in the conversation, as we recall, that we began to see the depth of the pit we had dug for ourselves. We nodded, hesitantly. His last words to us before he went down the stairs and stalked away were just what we were by that time afraid they might be. "When your guests are hungry, *feed them bananas!*"

LESSON 2: *Never refuse a gift, and never fail to return a gift. If you cannot*

use it, you can always give it away to someone else—there is no such thing as too much—there are never too many bananas.

NOT ENOUGH PINEAPPLES

During the fifteen years between that first visit in 1966 and our residence there in 1981 we had returned to live in Kandoka village twice during the 1970s, and though there were a great many changes in the village, and indeed for all of Papua New Guinea during that time, we continued to live according to the lessons of reciprocity learned during those first months in the field. We bought no food for money and refused no gifts, but shared our surplus. As our family grew, we continued to be accompanied by our younger children. Our place in the village came to be something like that of educated Kaliai who worked far away in New Guinea. Our friends expected us to come "home" when we had leave, but knew that our work kept us away for long periods of time. They also credited us with knowing much more about the rules of their way of life than was our due. And we sometimes shared the delusion that we understood life in the village, but even fifteen years was not long enough to relieve the need for lessons in learning to live within the rules of gift exchange.

In the last paragraph I used the word *friends* to describe the villagers intentionally, but of course they were not all our friends. Over the years some really had become friends, others were acquaintances, others remained consultants or informants to whom we turned when we needed information. Still others, unfortunately, we did not like at all. We tried never to make an issue of these distinctions, of course, and to be evenhanded and generous to all, as they were to us. Although we almost never actually refused requests that were made of us, over the long term our reciprocity in the village was balanced. More was given to those who helped us the most, while we gave assistance or donations of small items even to those who were not close or helpful.

One elderly woman in particular was a trial for us. Sara was the eldest of a group of siblings and her younger brother and sister were both generous, informative, and delightful persons. Her younger sister, Makila, was a particularly close friend and consultant, and in deference to that friendship we felt awkward in dealing with the elder sister.

Sara was neither a friend nor an informant, but she had been, since she returned to live in the village at the time of our second trip in 1971, a constant (if minor) drain on our resources. She never asked for much at a time. A bar of soap, a box of matches, a bottle of kerosene, a cup of rice, some onions, a stick or two of tobacco, or some other small item was usually all that was at issue, but whenever she came around it was always to ask for something—or to let us know that when we left, we should give her some of the furnishings from the house. Too, unlike almost everyone else in the village, when she came, she was always empty-handed. We ate no taro from her gardens, and the kids chewed none of her sugarcane. In short, she was, as far as we could tell, a really grasping, selfish old woman—and we were not the only victims of her greed.

Having long before learned the lesson of the bananas, one day we had a stalk that was ripening so fast we couldn't keep up with it, so I pulled a few for our own use (we only had one stalk at the time) and walked down through the village to Ben's house, where his five children were playing. I sat down on his steps to talk, telling him that I intended to give the fruit to his kids. They never got them. Sara saw us from across the open plaza of the village and came rushing over, shouting, "My bananas!" Then she grabbed the stalk and went off gorging herself with them. Ben and I just looked at each other.

Finally it got to the point where it seemed to us that we had to do something. Ten years of being used was long enough. So there came the afternoon when Sara showed up to get some tobacco—again. But this time, when we gave her the two sticks she had demanded, we confronted her.

First, we noted the many times she had come to get things. We didn't mind sharing things, we explained. After all, we had plenty of tobacco and soap and rice and such, and most of it was there so that we could help our friends as they helped us, with folktales, information, or even gifts of food. The problem was that she kept coming to get things, but never came to talk, or to tell stories, or to bring some little something that the kids might like. Sara didn't argue—she agreed. "Look," we suggested, "it doesn't have to be much, and we don't mind giving you things—but you can help us. The kids like pineapples, and we don't have any—the next time you need something, bring something—like maybe a pineapple." Obviously somewhat embarrassed, she took her tobacco and left, saying that she would bring something soon. We were really pleased with ourselves. It had been a very difficult thing to do, but it was done, and we were convinced that either she would start bringing things or not come. It was as if a burden had lifted from our shoulders.

It worked. Only a couple of days passed before Sara was back, bringing her bottle to get it filled with kerosene. But this time, she came carrying the biggest, most beautiful pineapple we had seen the entire time we had been there. We had a friendly talk, filled her kerosene container, and hung the pineapple up on the veranda to ripen just a little further. A few days later we cut and ate it, and whether the satisfaction it gave came from the fruit or from its source would be hard to say, but it was delicious. That, we assumed, was the end of that irritant.

We were wrong, of course. The next afternoon, Mary, one of our best friends for years (and no relation to Sara), dropped by for a visit. As we talked, her eyes scanned the veranda. Finally she asked whether we hadn't had a pineapple there yesterday. We said we had, but that we had already eaten it. She commented that it had been a really nice-looking one, and we told her that it had been the best we had eaten in months. Then, after a pause, she asked, "Who brought it to you?" We smiled as we said, "Sara!" because Mary would appreciate our coup—she had commented many times in the past on the fact that Sara only *got* from us and never gave. She was silent for a moment, and then she said, "Well, I'm glad you enjoyed it—my father was waiting until it was fully ripe to harvest it for you, but when it went missing I thought maybe it was the one you had here. I'm glad to see you got it. I thought maybe a thief had eaten it in the bush."

LESSON 3: *Where reciprocity is the rule and gifts are the idiom, you cannot demand a gift, just as you cannot refuse a request.*

It says a great deal about the kindness and patience of the Kaliai people that they have been willing to be our hosts for all these years despite our blunders and lack of good manners. They have taught us a lot, and these three lessons are certainly not the least important things we learned.

From Shells to Money

Ceremonial Exchange among the Simbu of Papua New Guinea

High in the mountains of New Guinea, a transformation is taking place as money becomes increasingly important for the formerly secluded Simbu tribespeople

Karl F. Rambo

Karl F. Rambo is currently conducting research in the Papua New Guinea highlands on the economic consequences of rural migration.

While conducting fieldwork among the Simbu in 1985 and 1986, I occasionally encountered people in the small roadside markets selling crescents of large, old pearl shells, to be worn around the neck. Although the price for these was generally only about U.S. $5, the once highly prized shells drew few interested purchasers. In my discussions with the sellers, they invariably mentioned how—in the past—one such shell would form a substantial portion of the bride-price given by the groom's family to the bride's family in the ceremonial gift given at a marriage. Now money equal to thousands of dollars, collected from many people and displayed on tall bamboo poles, is the valuable supplementing traditional items such as pork. Gifts of purchased cartons of beer, stacked and displayed at the ceremonies, are now much more frequent than the once-common ceremonial gifts of colorful bird of paradise plumes.

This adoption of cash into the ceremonial system has affected the course of economic change and development in the New Guinea highlands in an unusual way. Although the Simbu people now eagerly desire money, what

motivates their actions is more than a desire for material goods.

Until relatively recently, these people were remote from any of the effects of the market economies that link together much of the rest of the world. Prior to contact with the outside world, the Simbu relied almost solely on the products they themselves produced. At that time the New Guinea highlands lay at the end of multistaged trading systems that extended hundreds of kilometers to the coasts, the source of a most precious traditional valuable—seashells. The source of the shells was so remote that some highlanders believed they grew on trees. Prior to the arrival of Australian colonialists, small quantities of shells passed through many hands on their way to the highlands. There, they became one of the most important items needed for the ceremonial gift exchanges.

These ceremonial exchanges were, and continue to be, essential for establishing and maintaining social relationships between the individual members of the small tribes of the region. Today however, this area no longer remains as isolated from the rest of the world as in the past. Money, and goods purchased with money, has for the most part replaced shells and many other traditional goods previously used in these exchanges. The advent of money in the Papua New Guinea highlands and its incorporation into the ceremonial exchange system have resulted in the amalgamation of elements of two

sometimes conflicting economic value systems.

The recent changes in the highlands of Papua New Guinea are of particular interest to anthropologists and other social scientists in that these changes are recent and well documented. People who were for all intents completely isolated from the industrialized and industrializing world become involved in a worldwide economy when they produce goods or sell their labor in a money-linked market. The last three centuries are replete with examples of incorporation of cultures into such a worldwide economy. In many ways, each case recapitulates the earlier adoption of money by peoples who now rely almost exclusively on a monied, market economy. Money has facilitated the incorporation of many far-flung peoples by providing a medium of exchange that translates the value of many material things and services into a common system. Often, however, with the development of a money economy come greatly increased economic stratification and a loss of economic independence. But because the Simbu have maintained their interest in ceremonial exchanges, they have ameliorated some of the negative effects associated with involvement in the cash-oriented market economy.

But before one can understand this interesting economic transformation, one should know something about the environment, culture, and history of the Simbu. The interaction of these

In preparation for a final marriage ceremony, long bamboo poles, covered in money, are placed in the ground. In the wedding ceremony the groom's relatives give money, pigs, and store-bought goods to the bride's relatives.

elements with the introduced cash economy has resulted in a melding of the old with the new to produce a monied economy unlike those commonly found in the industrialized world.

CEREMONIAL EXCHANGE IN TRADITIONAL SIMBU SOCIETY

Lying at the heart of the central highlands of the now independent country of Papua New Guinea, Simbu is the most densely populated province in the country, with more than 180,000 people living in an area slightly larger than the state of Delaware. The majority ethnic group, named the Simbu (or Chimbu) by the first Australian patrol that entered the area, live along the slopes of the mountains bordering the Wahgi River, which runs past some of the highest mountains in the country. In 1933, Australian gold miners and colo-

nial government patrol officers were the first representatives of the outside, Europeanized world to enter the New Guinea mountain valleys the Simbu inhabited. Although little gold was discovered in the area, thousands of tribespeople were found in a locale previously thought to be too rugged for human habitation.

The mountainous, high-altitude terrain that isolated the Simbu and other highland peoples is also responsible for an environment unlike those of the hot coastal and lowland areas with their infertile soils. The climate of this area is temperate, with cool evenings and warm days. Drought conditions are rare. A year-round springlike climate and a lack of many of the tropical diseases found elsewhere in New Guinea contribute to a relatively densely settled population. In most of the northern areas of the province, population densities exceed 150 people per square kilometer.

"Simbu" is the word in the local language first heard by the initial Australian patrol. It is an expression of astonishment called out by the local people when they saw their first white men. Initially, the Simbu people thought the explorers were the reincarnated spirits of their dead relatives. The physical appearance of the early patrol members, as well as their control of a vast quantity of wealth in the form of shells, made them seem otherworldly.

The Simbu like many other cultural groups in the central highlands, are not traditionally a single political group but rather are divided into many tribal units of twenty-five hundred to five thousand people, each identified with discrete territories. The membership of each tribe is further subdivided into patrilineal clans and subclans. Although parliamentary democracy has been practiced for some time, tribal identification and loyalty remain very strong. Today, as in precontact times, warfare breaks out between neighboring tribes. Members of any single clan must find marriage partners outside their own clan. Through marriage, clan members are linked by kinship to members of other clans in their own tribe as well as to people in clans in other tribes. These political, economic, and social links between people are created and maintained through a complex web of ceremonial exchanges of valuables. All important events are marked by the giving of prestations (valuables). The kind of valuables given in these ceremonies has changed over the years with the introduction of money and items purchased with money. Although the Simbu are connected to the rest of the world through the market economy of which they are now a part, the introduction of money and markets has not meant the total abandonment of previously existing economic practices. It is important to

look at the nature and form of these ceremonial exchanges before discussing the changes brought through the introduction of money.

For the Simbu, the bestowing of goods that accompanies ceremonies helps to create social obligations and reciprocal relations with other people and with other clans and tribes. The ceremonies are held in conjunction with a number of events such as marriages, funerals, and the seasonal harvest of particular fruits and vegetables. These events are held regularly. The largest of such events, called *bugla ingu* in the local language, is held once every seven to ten years. In the bugla ingu, entire clans and tribes organize to hold a series of gift prestations culminating in an enormous pig kill, in which thousands of pigs are killed, cooked, and given away to visiting friends and relatives. For the Simbu, maintaining good social relationships

with others, both within and outside the patrilineal clans, is inseparable from such gift exchanges. The amounts given in many such ceremonies require the cooperation of many people.

It is useful to contrast the type of economic transactions that take place in Simbu ceremonial exchange with the types of transaction most familiar to Westerners—barter and trade. Barter and trade consist of discrete economic transactions completed with the giving and receiving of goods, services, or money. Social relationships are often independent of such transactions and, once the deal is completed, there are few continuing social obligations between the parties involved. In addition, forces other than social relationships between the transactors (i.e., supply and demand) regulate the amount of goods or services changing hands.

In ceremonial exchanges such as those in Simbu, however, the exchange

A Simbu man rests from his work in a newly planted sweet potato garden. The slopes on mountain gardens can be as steep as 45 degrees.

is not independent of the social relationship between transactors. Each individual demonstrates his prosperity and ability to produce and shows his willingness and ability to maintain social obligations with each item he gives to an exchange partner. Although there is a general expectation that the recipient will reciprocate with a return presentation at an unspecified future date (and therefore continue the relationship), the purpose of participating in such exchanges is not to maximize a material return from the original gift. In fact, the opposite is closer to reality. Great prestige is gained by giving valuables to an exchange partner. The partner, to maintain the relationship, must return to the original giver at least as much as originally received plus, if he wishes to garner prestige, slightly

more. This amount, over and above the original gift, then becomes debt that must be repaid. Added to this will be any additional goods that become debts incurred by the exchange partner. The competitive nature of these exchanges is acknowledged by the men involved.

In addition to the absence of separation between the giving of the ceremonial prestation and the social relationship between the participants, there is an attempt not to maximize one's economic holdings but to maximize prestige in the community by participating often and generously in the many prestations. Not only is prestige gained, but social ties are maintained with a network of individuals, many of them the affinal relatives (in-laws) acquired at marriage. Although men are the transactors in these situa-

tions, the women are the central links to many of the social/exchange relationships, for it is with the wives' male kin that many of the transactions are arranged.

Each marriage establishes a new exchange relationship between the groom and his close relatives and the bride's father, brothers, and close kin. Gifts must be made to the bride's family at marriage, and this is followed by a lifetime of exchanges at the birth of children, the death of children or the wife, at various points in the wife's children's lives, and at any vegetable exchange (*mogena biri*) or bugla ingu where the wife's group (clan or subclan) is invited. In addition to the relationships with wives' relatives, similar relationships exist with the men's mothers' male kin, their sisters' husbands, and their daughters' husbands. The valuables given in these ceremonies are expected to be returned in the future. An immediate exact equivalence is not expected, but eventually food or goods deemed at least similar in value should be repaid.

The relationships between these men are multi-functional. Ceremonial exchanges serve to distribute certain scarce resources that are not available in a territory—giving forest products and fruits that grow only at lower altitudes, for instance, to people who otherwise would not have access to these things. Mutual aid in work is sometimes extended between exchange partners.

Very important is the support given to men in other tribes in times of war. This is particularly true when there are many such interpersonal relationships between men of two groups. Without the support of others beyond one's clan and tribe, there is danger that if hostilities arise one would not have enough allies to prevent being chased off one's land. If the relationships to men outside one's clan and tribe are not maintained with frequent contributions to ceremonial exchanges, one faces the possibility of not having adequate allies in time of conflict. In fact, long delays in returning goods can add to hostility over other issues, such as marriage disputes and conflicting land claims,

KARL RAMBO

Coffee cherries, the berries containing coffee beans, are handpicked when ripe. Coffee is the major cash crop that finances ceremonial gift presentations. This man's shirt reflects the influence of Christian missions in Simbu.

KARL RAMBO

An unmarried woman, dressed to participate in a dance competition at an Independence Day celebration, surrounded by spectators in modern dress.

turning previous allies into warring enemies.

Although the ceremonial exchange of items is between individuals, individuals are representatives of their clans and subclans. Often the individual prestations are organized and combined so that the men of one clan give goods to their ceremonial exchange partners in another clan in one large display. For example, at a mogena biri, the valuables are placed in a huge pile, twenty to forty feet in diameter, and the recipients, decorated in traditional finery of bird-plume headdresses, dance around the pile chanting, beating drums, and brandishing spears. Speeches are made relating past exchanges and the close relationships between members of each group, and then the entire pile

is disassembled and each parcel given to the proper recipient.

Before contact with the colonial government, most of the items used in ceremonial exchanges were of local origin. Although shells, feathers, stone ax blades, and salt were often imported over long distances, pigs and other locally produced foods predominated in prestations. Each tribe was politically, and in large measure economically, self-contained. Money was unknown in the area. Although in some other non-Western societies shells were used in much the same way we use money, nothing served as such a universal medium of exchange for the precontact Simbu. Pigs, one of the few domesticated animals, were raised on the same sweet potatoes that made up

more than 85 percent of the Simbu people's diet, and pork was the most important item given in the ceremonial exchanges. It was rarely eaten on other occasions. Prior to the arrival of Christian missions, ceremonial sacrifice of pigs not only provided meat to be given to one's exchange partners but also served to appease the ancestral spirits.

MOVEMENT TOWARD A CASH ECONOMY

The initial Western contact with the Simbu was quickly followed by the establishment of a patrol post with a single Australian government officer in residence, and several Catholic and Lutheran missions. Although before the Second World War the changes they brought about were not extreme for most Simbu people, these Westerners did introduce a large quantity of high-quality pearl shell that was flown into the area from the coasts and traded for food and services.

Large-scale economic change did not occur until after the war, when men began to be sent to the coasts to work as laborers on plantations. After finishing their labor contracts, usually after two years, the men returned to their Simbu homes carrying imported manufactured goods such as cloth, metal tools, and cooking pots. These items were valued for their novelty as well as their usefulness.

Opportunities to acquire these sought-after imported goods were limited during this early period because the Simbu lacked the means to earn enough locally for their purchase. This problem was greatly alleviated when, in the late 1950s, coffee was introduced as a cash crop into the Simbu area. Coffee growing was particularly suited to the social and ecological situation of Simbu, and it was quickly adopted by the local people. The cool, temperate conditions were perfect for growing high-quality *arabica* coffee varieties. The poor road network had hampered development by placing delays and weight restrictions on export crops. Dried coffee beans, being durable and of high value for their weight, were perfect for such a situation. In addition, coffee requires relatively little year-round labor and does well as a subsidiary crop to subsistence food crops.

Coffee is still today by far the most important cash crop for the Simbu and the source of most of their money. Other sources of monetary income include growing cardamom, selling vegetables at small markets, and receiving occasional remittances from employed relatives. Average annual household income today approximates U.S. $250 per year.

Although their income is low by American standards, many of the Simbu's basic subsistence needs are satisfied without resorting to the marketplace. Most of the food consumed is produced in family gardens, and many other material needs, like housing and firewood, are obtained with little or no cash expenditure. Much of the money that does pass through the hands of the average Simbu is not spent directly on consumer goods but is channeled first through the now monetized ceremonial gifts.

Because it now requires cash to properly participate in many ceremonial exchange obligations, a man who wishes to obtain a modicum of prestige must have some source of money income. Those who do not contribute to prestations soon become known as insignificant "rubbish" men. The emphasis is, therefore, not on earning cash so as to acquire material goods for oneself, but rather to earn the money necessary to contribute cash to marriage, bride-price, or death compensations, or to buy cartons of beer to present to one's exchange partners at ceremonies. If too much of an individual's income is spent on himself without adequate compensation's being paid to supporters, he gains a reputation as being stingy. In addition to gaining a bad reputation, such an individual may have difficulty obtaining financial and other types of help when needed.

Although the monetization of ceremonial exchanges now encourages participation in activities with cash rewards, for the most part it discourages the accumulation of capital by individuals

for reinvestment into money-making ventures. Small business ventures, such as stores, cattle projects, or commercial trucks, are generally begun with financial help and labor donated by kin and other associates. This help is given like a ceremonial prestation and is treated as such. Great pressure is then put on the leader of a venture to pay back these investments.

Often the response of the owner of a small venture such as a rural trade store is to slowly deplete the stock of the store by giving away store goods or cash receipts to his exchange partners. Since prestige is gained by reimbursing the network of investors, the organizer gains status and maintains a network of content exchange partners even though the business venture fails. Since the Simbu are rarely dependent on money-producing ventures for basic necessities such as food, the economic failure of such enterprises does not have serious consequences for the organizer. In fact, since success in the community depends on maintaining ceremonial exchange relations with other people, the economic failure of a business through its dismantlement and distribution of its assets often has a positive result.

In addition to leveling individual wealth by discouraging accumulation, channeling cash into prestations distributes wealth to a wide circle of people. Thousands of dollars often change hands at such events as weddings or funerals (when death compensation payments, a form of "blood money," are given to a dead person's relatives by the relatives of the person accused of causing the death). After the money is removed from the bamboo poles on which it is displayed, it is distributed widely by the initial receiver, with many individuals receiving only small amounts. So although theoretically as much money is received from the ceremonial exchanges as is put into them, the funds received are often in smaller (but more frequent) amounts. These smaller amounts of money are more prone to be spent quickly on items such as canned fish and bottled beer.

To be sure, there are a few Simbu men who have managed to become

quite wealthy. By being politically savvy and practicing good management, these people have been able to satisfy the demands of their local supporters and exchange partners and succeed in business. In other areas of the Papua New Guinea highlands, where lower population densities allow for greater availability of land and therefore greater individual economic opportunity, other social scientists have reported on a number of such wealthy men. But even in these areas, such people are only a tiny fraction of the population.

So although the pearl shells sold in the markets no longer have the value they once did, and money has become predominant in the Simbu economy, indigenous institutions such as ceremonial gift exchange are maintained. Shells and other imported valuables of the past have been supplanted by another import—cash. But in many ways the economic strategy of maximizing social relationships rather than individual wealth remains intact.

As long as this remains the case, the opportunities for many individuals to achieve long-term capitalistic success, to develop businesses by turning profits back into the businesses rather than toward ceremonial exchanges, remain remote. But the importance of tribal social ties, and the ceremonial prestations that maintain those ties, serves to ameliorate many of the negative side effects of incorporation into the world money-based economy.

ADDITIONAL READING

Paula Brown, *The Chimbu: A Study of Change in the New Guinea Highlands,* Schenkman Press, Cambridge, Mass., 1972.

———, *Highland Peoples of New Guinea,* Cambridge University Press, U.K., 1978.

Bob Connolly and Robin Anderson, *First Contact,* Viking Penguin Inc., New York, 1987.

Ben R. Finney, *Big-Men and Business: Entrepreneurship and Economic Growth in the New Guinea Highlands,* University of Hawaii Press, Honolulu, 1973.

———, *Business Development in the Highlands of New Guinea,* East-West Center, Honolulu, 1987.

Allen Johnson, In Search of the Affluent Society," *Human Nature* 1(9), 1978.

Andrew Strathern, ed., *Inequality in New Guinea Highlands Societies,* Cambridge University Press, 1982.

Life Without Chiefs

Are we forever condemned to a world of haves and have-nots, rulers and ruled?
Maybe not, argues a noted anthropologist—if we can relearn some ancient lessons.

Marvin Harris

Marvin Harris is a graduate research professor of anthropology at the University of Florida and chair of the general anthropology division of the American Anthropological Association. His seventeen books include Cows, Pigs, Wars and Witches *and* Cannibals and Kings.

Can humans exist without some people ruling and others being ruled? To look at the modern world, you wouldn't think so. Democratic states may have done away with emperors and kings, but they have hardly dispensed with gross inequalities in wealth, rank, and power.

However, humanity hasn't always lived this way. For about 98 percent of our existence as a species (and for four million years before then), our ancestors lived in small, largely nomadic hunting-and-gathering bands containing about 30 to 50 people apiece. It was in this social context that human nature evolved. It has been only about ten thousand years since people began to settle down into villages, some of which eventually grew into cities. And it has been only in the last two thousand years that the majority of people in the world have not lived in hunting-and-gathering societies. This brief period of time is not nearly sufficient for noticeable evolution to have taken place. Thus, the few remaining foraging societies are the closest analogues we have to the "natural" state of humanity.

To judge from surviving examples of hunting-and-gathering bands and villages, our kind got along quite well for the greater part of prehistory without so much as a paramount chief. In fact, for tens of thousands of years, life went on without kings, queens, prime ministers, presidents, parliaments, congresses, cabinets, governors, and mayors—not to mention the police officers, sheriffs, marshals, generals, lawyers, bailiffs, judges, district attorneys, court clerks, patrol cars, paddy wagons, jails, and penitentiaries that help keep them in power. How in the world did our ancestors ever manage to leave home without them?

Small populations provide part of the answer. With 50 people per band or 150 per village, everybody knew everybody else intimately. People gave with the expectation of taking and took with the expectation of giving. Because chance played a great role in the capture of animals, collection of wild foodstuffs, and success of rudimentary forms of agriculture, the individuals who had the luck of the catch on one day needed a handout on the next. So the best way for them to provide for their inevitable rainy day was to be generous. As expressed by anthropologist Richard Gould, "The greater the amount of risk, the greater the extent of sharing." Reciprocity is a small society's bank.

In reciprocal exchange, people do not specify how much or exactly what they expect to get back or when they expect to get it. That would besmirch the quality of that transaction and make it similar to mere barter or to buying and selling. The distinction lingers on in societies dominated by other forms of exchange, even capitalist ones. For we do carry out a give-and-take among close kin and friends that is informal, uncalculating, and imbued with a spirit of generosity. Teen-agers do not pay cash for their meals at home or for the use of the family car, wives do not bill their husbands for cooking a meal, and friends give each other birthday gifts and Christmas presents. But much of this is marred by the expectation that our generosity will be acknowledged with expression of thanks.

Where reciprocity really prevails in daily life, etiquette requires that generosity be taken for granted. As Robert Dentan discovered during his field-work among the Semai of Central Malaysia, no one ever says "thank you" for the meat received from another hunter. Having struggled all day to lug the carcass of a pig home through the jungle heat, the hunter allows his prize to be cut up into exactly equal portions, which he then gives away to the entire group. Dentan explains that to express gratitude for the portion received indicates that you are the kind of ungenerous person who calculates how much you give and take: "In this con-

From *New Age Journal*, November/December 1989, pp. 42-45, 205-209. Excerpted from *Our Kind* by Marvin Harris. © 1989 by Marvin Harris. Reprinted by permission of HarperCollins Publishers, Inc.

text, saying 'thank you' is very rude, for it suggests, first, that one has calculated the amount of a gift and, second, that one did not expect the donor to be so generous." To call attention to one's generosity is to indicate that others are in debt to you and that you expect them to repay you. It is repugnant to egalitarian peoples even to suggest that they have been treated generously.

Canadian anthropologist Richard Lee tells how, through a revealing incident, he learned about this aspect of reciprocity. To please the !Kung, the "bushmen" of the Kalahari desert, he decided to buy a large ox and have it slaughtered as a present. After days of searching Bantu agricultural villages for the largest and fattest ox in the region, he acquired what appeared to be a perfect specimen. But his friends took him aside and assured him that he had been duped into buying an absolutely worthless animal. "Of course, we will eat it," they said, "but it won't fill us up—we will eat and go home to bed with stomachs rumbling." Yet, when Lee's ox was slaughtered, it turned out to be covered with a thick layer of fat. Later, his friends explained why they had said his gift was valueless, even though they knew better than he what lay under the animal's skin:

"Yes, when a young man kills much meat he comes to think of himself as a chief or a big man, and he thinks of the rest of us as his servants or inferiors. We can't accept this, we refuse one who boasts, for someday his pride will make him kill somebody. So we always speak of his meat as worthless. This way we cool his heart and make him gentle."

Lee watched small groups of men and women returning home every evening with the animals and wild fruits and plants that they had killed or collected. They shared everything equally, even with campmates who had stayed behind and spent the day sleeping or taking care of their tools and weapons.

"Not only do families pool that day's production, but the entire camp—residents and visitors alike—shares equally in the total quantity of food available," Lee observed. "The evening meal of any one family is made up of portions of food from each of the other families resident. There is a constant flow of nuts, berries, roots, and melons from one family fireplace to another, until each person has received an equitable portion. The following morning a different combination of foragers moves out of camp, and when they return late in the day, the distribution of foodstuffs is repeated."

In small, prestate societies, it was in everybody's best interest to maintain each other's freedom of access to the natural habitat. Suppose a !Kung with a lust for power were to get up and tell his campmates, "From now on, all this land and everything on it belongs to me. I'll let you use it but only with my permission and on the condition that I get first choice of anything you capture, collect, or grow." His campmates, thinking that he had certainly gone crazy, would pack up their few belongings, take a long walk, make a new camp, and resume their usual life of egalitarian reciprocity. The man who would be king would be left by himself to exercise a useless sovereignty.

THE HEADMAN: LEADERSHIP, NOT POWER

To the extent that political leadership exists at all among band-and-village societies, it is exercised by individuals called headmen. These headmen, however, lack the power to compel others to obey their orders. How can a leader be powerful and still lead?

The political power of genuine rulers depends on their ability to expel or exterminate disobedient individuals and groups. When a headman gives a command, however, he has no certain physical means of punishing those who disobey. So, if he wants to stay in "office," he gives few commands. Among the Eskimo, for instance, a group will follow an outstanding hunter and defer to his opinion with respect to choice of hunting spots. But in all other matters, the leader's opinion carries no more weight than any other man's. Similarly, among the !Kung, each band has its recognized leaders, most of whom are males. These men speak out more than others and are listened to

with a bit more deference. But they have no formal authority and can only persuade, never command. When Lee asked the !Kung whether they had headmen—meaning powerful chiefs—they told him, "Of course we have headmen! In fact, we are all headmen. Each one of us is headman over himself."

Headmanship can be a frustrating and irksome job. Among Indian groups such as the Mehinacu of Brazil's Zingu National Park, headmen behave something like zealous scoutmasters on overnight cookouts. The first one up in the morning, the headman tries to rouse his companions by standing in the middle of the village plaza and shouting to them. If something needs to be done, it is the headman who starts doing it, and it is the headman who works harder than anyone else. He sets an example not only for hard work but also for generosity: After a fishing or hunting expedition, he gives away more of his catch than anyone else does. In trading with other groups, he must be careful not to keep the best items for himself.

In the evening, the headman stands in the center of the plaza and exhorts his people to be good. He calls upon them to control their sexual appetites, work hard in their gardens, and take frequent baths in the river. He tells them not to sleep during the day or bear grudges against each other.

COPING WITH FREELOADERS

During the reign of reciprocal exchange and egalitarian headmen, no individual, family, or group smaller than the band or village itself could control access to natural resources. Rivers, lakes, beaches, oceans, plants and animals, the soil and subsoil were all communal property.

Among the !Kung, a core of people born in a particular territory say that they "own" the water holes and hunting rights, but this has no effect on the people who happen to be visiting and living with them at any given time. Since !Kung from neighboring bands are related through marriage, they often visit each other for months at a time and have free use of whatever resources they need without having to ask permission. Though people from distant bands must make a request to use another band's territory, the "owners" seldom refuse them.

The absence of private possession in land and other vital resources means that a form of communism probably existed among prehistoric hunting and collecting bands and small villages. Perhaps I should emphasize that this did not rule out the existence of private property. People in simple band-and-village societies own personal effects such as weapons, clothing, containers, ornaments, and tools. But why should anyone want to steal such objects? People who have a bush camp and move about a lot have no use for extra possessions. And since the group is small enough that everybody knows everybody else, stolen items cannot be used anonymously. If you want something, better to ask for it openly, since by the rules of reciprocity such requests cannot be denied.

I don't want to create the impression that life within egalitarian band-and-village societies unfolded entirely without disputes over possessions. As in every social group, nonconformists and malcontents tried to use the system for their own advantage. Inevitably there were freeloaders, individuals who consistently took more than they gave and lay back in their hammocks while others did the work. Despite the absence of a criminal justice system, such behavior eventually was punished. A widespread belief among band-and-village peoples attributes death and misfortune to the malevolent conspiracy of sorcerers. The task of identifying these evildoers falls to a group's shamans, who remain responsive to public opinion during their divinatory trances. Well-liked individuals who enjoy strong support from their families need not fear the shaman. But quarrelsome, stingy people who do not give as well as take had better watch out.

FROM HEADMAN TO BIG MAN

Reciprocity was not the only form of exchange practiced by egalitarian band-and-village peoples. Our kind long ago found other ways to give and take. Among them the form of exchange known as redistribution played a crucial role in creating distinctions of rank during the evolution of chiefdoms and states.

Redistribution occurs when people turn over food and other valuables to a prestigious figure such as a headman, to be pooled, divided into separate portions, and given out again. The primordial form of redistribution was probably keyed to seasonal hunts and harvests, when more food than usual became available.

True to their calling, headmen-redistributors not only work harder than their followers but also give more generously and reserve smaller and less desirable portions for themselves than for anyone else. Initially, therefore, redistribution strictly reinforced the political and economic equality associated with reciprocal exchange. The redistributors were compensated purely with admiration and in proportion to their success in giving bigger feasts, in personally contributing more than anybody else, and in asking little or nothing for their effort, all of which initially seemed an innocent extension of the basic principle of reciprocity.

But how little our ancestors understood what they were getting themselves into! For if it is a good thing to have a headman give feasts, why not have several headmen give feasts? Or, better yet, why not let success in organizing and giving feasts be the measure of one's legitimacy as a headman? Soon, where conditions permit, there are several would-be headmen vying with each other to hold the most lavish feasts and redistribute the most food and other valuables. In this fashion there evolved the nemesis that Richard Lee's !Kung informants had warned about: the youth who wants to be a "big man."

A classic anthropological study of big men was carried out by Douglas Oliver among the Siuai, a village people who live on the South Pacific island of Bougainville, in the Solomon Islands. In the Siuai language, big men were known as *mumis*. Every Siuai boy's highest ambition was to become

a mumi. He began by getting married, working hard, and restricting his own consumption of meats and coconuts. His wife and parents, impressed with the seriousness of his intentions, vowed to help him prepare for his first feast. Soon his circle of supporters widened and he began to construct a clubhouse in which his male followers could lounge about and guests could be entertained and fed. He gave a feast at the consecration of the clubhouse; if this was a success, the circle of people willing to work for him grew larger still, and he began to hear himself spoken of as a mumi. Larger and larger feasts meant that the mumi's demands on his supporters became more irksome. Although they grumbled about how hard they had to work, they remained loyal as long as their mumi continued to maintain and increase his renown as a "great provider."

Finally the time came for the new mumi to challenge the older ones. He did this at a *muminai* feast, where both sides kept a tally of all the pigs, coconut pies, and sago-almond puddings given away by the host mumi and his followers to the guest mumi and his followers. If the guests could not reciprocate with a feast as lavish as that of the challengers, their mumi suffered a great social humiliation, and his fall from mumihood was immediate.

At the end of a successful feast, the greatest of mumis still faced a lifetime of personal toil and dependence on the moods and inclinations of his followers. Mumihood did not confer the power to coerce others into doing one's bidding, nor did it elevate one's standard of living above anyone else's. In fact, because giving things away was the essence of mumihood, great mumis consumed less meat and other delicacies than ordinary men. Among the Kaoka, another Solomon Islands group, there is the saying, "The giver of the feast takes the bones and the stale cakes; the meat and the fat go to the others." At one great feast attended by 1,100 people, the host mumi, whose name was Soni, gave away thirty-two pigs and a large quantity of sago-almond puddings. Soni himself and some of his closest followers went hungry. "We shall eat Soni's renown," they said.

FROM BIG MAN TO CHIEF

The slide (or ascent?) toward social stratification gained momentum wherever extra food produced by the inspired diligence of redistributors could be stored while awaiting muminai feasts, potlatches, and other occasions of redistribution. The more concentrated and abundant the harvest and the less perishable the crop, the greater its potential for endowing the big man with power. Though others would possess some stored-up foods of their own, the redistributor's stores would be the largest. In times of scarcity, people would come to him, expecting to be fed; in return, he could call upon those who had special skills to make cloth, pots, canoes, or a fine house for his own use. Eventually, the redistributor no longer needed to work in the fields to gain and surpass big-man status. Management of the harvest surpluses, a portion of which continued to be given to him for use in communal feasts and other communal projects (such as trading expeditions and warfare), was sufficient to validate his status. And, increasingly, people viewed this status as an office, a sacred trust, passed on from one generation to the next according to the rules of hereditary succession. His dominion was no longer a small, autonomous village but a large political community. The big man had become a chief.

Returning to the South Pacific and the Trobriand Islands, one can catch a glimpse of how these pieces of encroaching stratification fell into place. The Trobrianders had hereditary chiefs who held sway over more than a dozen villages containing several thousand people. Only chiefs could wear certain shell ornaments as the insignia of high rank, and it was forbidden for commoners to stand or sit in a position that put a chief's head at a lower elevation. British anthropologist Bronislaw Malinowski tells of seeing all the people present in the village of Bwoytalu drop from their verandas "as if blown down by a hurricane" at the sound of a drawn-out cry warning that an important chief was approaching.

Yams were the Trobrianders' staff of life; the chiefs validated their status by storing and redistributing copious quantities of them acquired through donations from their brothers-in-law at harvest time. Similar "gifts" were received by husbands who were commoners, but chiefs were polygymous and, having as many as a dozen wives, received many more yams than anyone else. Chiefs placed their yam supply on display racks specifically built for this purpose next to their houses. Commoners did the same, but a chief's yam racks towered over all the others.

This same pattern recurs, with minor variations, on several continents. Striking parallels were seen, for example, twelve thousand miles away from the Trobrianders, among chiefdoms that flourished throughout the southeastern region of the United States—specifically among the Cherokee, former inhabitants of Tennessee, as described by the eighteenth-century naturalist William Bartram.

At the center of the principal Cherokee settlements stood a large circular house where a council of chiefs discussed issues involving their villages and where redistributive feasts were held. The council of chiefs had a paramount who was the principal figure in the Cherokee redistributive network. At the harvest time a large crib, identified as the "chief's granary," was erected in each field. "To this," explained Bartram, "each family carries and deposits a certain quantity according to his ability or inclination, or none at all if he so chooses." The chief's granaries functioned as a public treasury in case of crop failure, a source of food for strangers or travelers, and as military store. Although every citizen enjoyed free access to the store, commoners had to acknowledge that it really belonged to the supreme chief, who had "an exclusive right and ability . . . to distribute comfort and blessings to the necessitous."

Supported by voluntary donations, chiefs could now enjoy lifestyles that set them increasingly apart from their followers. They could build bigger and finer houses for themselves, eat and dress more sumptuously, and enjoy the sexual favors and personal services of several wives. Despite these harbingers, people in chiefdoms voluntarily invested unprecedented amounts of labor on behalf of communal projects. They dug moats, threw up defensive earthen embankments, and erected great log palisades around their villages. They heaped up small mountains of rubble and soil to form platforms and mounds on top of which they built temples and big houses for their chief. Working in teams and using nothing but levers and rollers, they moved rocks weighing fifty tons or more and set them in precise lines and perfect circles, forming sacred precincts for communal rituals marking the change of seasons.

If this seems remarkable, remember that donated labor created the megalithic alignments of Stonehenge and Carnac, put up the great statues on Easter Island, shaped the huge stone heads of the Olmec in Vera Cruz, dotted Polynesia with ritual precincts set on great stone platforms, and filled the Ohio, Tennessee, and Mississippi valleys with hundreds of large mounds. Not until it was too late did people realize that their beautiful chiefs were about to keep the meat and fat for themselves while giving nothing but bones and stale cakes to their followers.

IN THE END

As we know, chiefdoms would eventually evolve into states, states into empires. From peaceful origins, humans created and mounted a wild beast that ate continents. Now that beast has taken us to the brink of global annihilation.

Will nature's experiment with mind and culture end in nuclear war? No one knows the answer. But I believe it is essential that we understand our past before we can create the best possible future. Once we are clear about the roots of human nature, for example, we can refute, once and for all, the notion that it is a biological imperative for our kind to form hierarchical groups. An observer viewing human life shortly after cultural takeoff would easily have concluded that our species was destined to be irredeemably egalitarian except for distinctions of sex and age. That someday the world would be divided into aristocrats and commoners, masters and slaves, billionaires and homeless beggars would have seemed wholly contrary to human nature as evidenced in the affairs of every human society then on Earth.

Of course, we can no more reverse the course of thousands of years of cultural evolution than our egalitarian ancestors could have designed and built the space shuttle. Yet, in striving for the preservation of mind and culture on Earth, it is vital that we recognize the significance of cultural takeoff and the great difference between biological and cultural evolution. We must rid ourselves of the notion that we are an innately aggressive species for whom war is inevitable. We must reject as unscientific claims that there are superior and inferior races and that the hierarchical divisions within and between societies are the consequences of natural selection rather than of a long process of cultural evolution. We must struggle to gain control over cultural selection through objective studies of the human condition and the recurrent process of history. Not only a more just society, but our very survival as a species may depend on it.

From peaceful origins, humans created and mounted a wild beast that ate continents. Now that beast has taken us to the brink of global annihilation.

Other Families, Other Ways

Since most people in small-scale societies of the past spent their whole lives within a local area, it is understandable that their primary interactions—economic, religious, and otherwise—were with their relatives. It also makes sense that through marriage customs, they strengthened those kinship relationships that clearly defined their mutual rights and obligations. Indeed, the resulting family structure may be surprisingly flexible and adaptive, as witnessed in "When Brothers Share a Wife" by Melvyn Goldstein and in "Arranging a Marriage in India" by Serena Nanda. It is for these reasons that anthropologists have looked upon family and kinship as the key mechanisms through which culture is transmitted from one generation to the next. Social changes may have been slow to take place throughout the world, but as social horizons have widened accordingly, family relationships and community alliances are increasingly based upon new sets of principles. There is no question that kinship networks have diminished in size and strength as we have increasingly become involved with others as coworkers in a market economy. Our associations depend more and more upon factors such as personal aptitudes, educational backgrounds, and job opportunities. Yet, the family is still there. It is smaller, but it still functions in its age-old nurturing and protective role, even under conditions of extreme poverty and a high infant mortality rate (see "Death without Weeping" by Nancy Scheper-Hughes). Beyond the immediate family, the situation is still in a state of flux. Certain ethnic groups, especially those in poverty, still have a need for the broader network, and in some ways seem to be reformulating those ties.

Where the changes described in this section will lead us and which ones will ultimately prevail, we do not know. One thing is certain: anthropologists will be there to document the trends, for the discipline of anthropology has had to change as well. One important feature of the essays in this section is the growing interest of anthropologists in the study of complex societies, where old theoretical perspectives are increasingly inadequate.

Current trends do not necessarily mean the eclipse of the kinship unit, however, as "Young Traders of Northern Nigeria" illustrates. The message is that the large family network is still the best guarantee of individual survival and well-being in an urban setting.

Looking Ahead: Challenge Questions

Why do you think "fraternal polyandry" is socially acceptable in Tibet, but not in our society?

What are the implications of Western education for the ability of Hausa women to earn an income?

How do differences in child care relate to economic circumstances?

What are the pros and cons of arranged marriages versus freedom of choice?

Memories of a !Kung Girlhood

A woman of the hunter-gatherers recalls her childhood; the differences in her way of life fade in the face of basic human similarities.

Marjorie Shostak

Marjorie Shostak is a writer and photographer who first became interested in the !Kung while working with her husband, an anthropologist. For two years, from 1969 to 1971, she lived and worked among the !Kung San of Botswana as a research assistant to Irven DeVore, an anthropologist at Harvard University. After developing fluency in the !Kung language, Shostak began to tape interviews with !Kung women. In 1975 she returned to Botswana for six months to complete the life histories of several women and to correct ambiguous translations. At the same time she collaborated with four other researchers in a study of hormone level and mood fluctuations in relation to menstrual cycles.

I remember when my mother was pregnant with Kumsa. I was still small (about four years old) and I asked, "Mommy, that baby inside you . . . when that baby is born, will it come out from your bellybutton?" She said, "No, it won't come out from there. When you give birth, a baby comes from here." And she pointed to her genitals.

When she gave birth to Kumsa, I wanted the milk she had in her breasts,

and when she nursed him, my eyes watched as the milk spilled out. I cried all night . . . cried and cried.

Once when my mother was with him and they were lying down asleep, I took him away from her and put him down on the other side of the hut. Then I lay down beside her. While she slept I squeezed some milk and started to nurse, and nursed and nursed and nursed. Maybe she thought it was him. When she woke and saw me she cried, "Where . . . tell me . . . what did you do with Kumsa? Where is he?"

I told her he was lying down inside the hut. She grabbed me and pushed me hard away from her. I lay there and cried. She took Kumsa, put him down beside her, and insulted me by cursing my genitals.

"Are you crazy? Nisa-Big Genitals, what's the matter with you? What craziness grabbed you that you took a baby, dropped him somewhere else, and then lay down beside me and nursed? I thought it was Kumsa."

When my father came home, she told him, "Do you see what kind of mind your daughter has? Hit her! She almost killed Kumsa. This little baby, this little thing here, she took from my side and dropped him somewhere else.

I was lying here holding him and fell asleep. She came and took him away, left him by himself, then lay down where he had been and nursed. Now, hit her!"

I said, "You're lying! Me . . . daddy, I didn't nurse. Really I didn't. I don't even want her milk anymore."

He said, "If I ever hear of this again, I'll hit you. Now, don't ever do that again!"

I said, "Yes, he's my little brother, isn't he? My little baby brother and I *love* him. I won't do that again. He can nurse all by himself. Daddy, even if you're not here, I won't try to steal Mommy's breasts. They belong to my brother."

We lived and lived, and as I kept growing, I started to carry Kumsa around on my shoulders. My heart was happy and I started to love him. I carried him everywhere. I would play with him for a while, and whenever he started to cry, I'd take him over to mother to nurse. Then I'd take him back with me and we'd play together again.

That was when Kumsa was still little. But once he was older and started to talk and then to run around, that's when we were mean to each other all the time. Sometimes we hit each other. Other times I grabbed him and bit him and said, "Ooooh . . . what is this thing that has such a horrible face and no brains and is so mean? Why is it so mean to me when I'm not doing anything to it?" Then he said, "I'm going to *hit* you!" And I said, "You're just a *baby!* I, *I* am the one who's going to hit *you*. Why are you so miserable to me?" I insulted him and he insulted me and then I insulted him back. We just stayed together and played like that.

Once, when our father came back carrying meat, we both called out, "Ho, ho, Daddy! Ho, ho, Daddy!" But when I heard him say, "Daddy, Daddy," I yelled, "Why are you greeting my father? He's *my* father, isn't he? You can only say, 'Oh, hello Father.' " But he called out, "Ho, ho . . . Daddy!" I said, "Be quiet! Only *I* will greet him. Is he your father? I'm going to hit you!"

We fought and argued until Mother finally stopped us. Then we just sat around while she cooked the meat.

This was also when I used to take food. It happened over all kinds of food—sweet *nin* berries or *klaru* bulbs . . . other times it was mongongo nuts. Sometimes before my mother left to go gathering, she'd leave food inside a leather pouch and hang it high on one of the branches inside the hut.

But as soon as she was gone, I'd take some of whatever food was left in the bag. If it was *klaru,* I'd find the biggest bulbs and take them. I'd hang the bag back on the branch and go sit somewhere to eat them.

One time I sat down in the shade of a tree while my parents gathered food nearby. As soon as they had moved away from me, I climbed the tree where they had left a pouch hanging, full of *klaru,* and took the bulbs.

I had my own little pouch, the one my father had made me, and I took the bulbs and put them in the pouch. Then I climbed down and sat waiting for my parents to return.

They came back. "Nisa, you ate the *klaru!*" What do you have to say for yourself?" I said, "Uhn uh, I didn't eat them."

I started to cry. Mother hit me and yelled, "Don't take things. You can't seem to understand! I tell you but you don't listen. Don't your ears hear when I talk to you?"

I said, "Uhn uh. Mommy's been making me feel bad for too long now. She keeps saying I steal things and hits me so that my skin hurts. I'm going to stay with Grandma!"

But when I went to my grandmother, she said, "No, I can't take care of you now. If I try you will be hungry. I am old and just go gathering one day at a time. In the morning I just rest. We would sit together and hunger would kill you. Now go back and sit beside your mother and father."

I said, "No, Daddy will hit me. Mommy will hit me. I want to stay with you."

So I stayed with her. Then one day she said, "I'm going to bring you back to your mother and father." She took me to them, saying, "Today I'm giving Nisa back to you. But isn't there someone here who will take good care of

About the !Kung

Nisa is a 50-year-old !Kung woman, one of an estimated 13,000 !Kung San living on the northern fringe of the Kalahari Desert in southern Africa. Much of her life—as daughter, sister, wife, mother, and lover—has been spent in the semi-nomadic pursuit of food and water in the arid savanna.

Like many !Kung, Nisa is a practiced storyteller. The !Kung have no written language with which to record their experiences, and people sit around their fires for hours recounting recent events and those long past. Voices rise and fall, hands move in dramatic gestures, and bird and animal sounds are imitated as stories are told and retold, usually with much exaggeration.

I collected stories of Nisa's life as part of my anthropological effort to record the lives of !Kung women in their own words. Nisa enjoyed working with the machine that "grabs your voice" and the interviews with her produced 25 hours of tape and 425 pages of transcription. The excerpts included here are faithful to her narrative except where awkward or discontinuous passages have been modified or deleted, and where long passages have been shortened.

Although most of Nisa's memories are typical of !Kung life, her early memories, like those of most people, are probably idiosyncratic mixtures of fact and fantasy. Her memories of being hit for taking food are probably not accurate. The !Kung tend to be lenient and indulgent with their children, and researchers have rarely observed any physical punishment or the withholding of food.

Strong feelings of sibling rivalry, like those that Nisa describes, are common. !Kung women wean their children as soon as they find they are pregnant again because they believe the milk belongs to the fetus. Children are not usually weaned until they are three or four years old, which tends to make them resent their younger siblings. Nisa's complaints about being given too little food probably stem from her jealousy of her little brother.

Despite the lack of privacy, !Kung parents are generally discreet in their sexual activity. As children become aware of it, they engage each other in sexual play. Parents say they do not approve of this play but do little to stop it.

Many !Kung girls first marry in their early teens, but these relationships are not consummated until the girls begin menstruating around the age of 16. Early marriages are relatively unstable. Nisa was betrothed twice before marrying Tashay.

The exclamation point at the beginning of !Kung represents one of the many click sounds in the !Kung language. Clicks are made by the tongue breaking air pockets in different parts of the mouth; but the notation for clicks has been eliminated from the translation in all cases except for the name of the !Kung people. Nisa, for instance, should be written as N≠isa.

Marjorie Shostak

her? You don't just hit a child like this one. She likes food and likes to eat. All of you are lazy and you've just left her so she hasn't grown well. You've killed this child with hunger. Look at her now, how small she still is."

Oh, but my heart was happy! Grandmother was scolding Mother! I had so much happiness in my heart that I laughed and laughed. But then, when Grandmother went home and left me there, I cried and cried.

My father started to yell at me. He didn't hit me. His anger usually came out only from his mouth. "You're so senseless! Don't you realize that after you left, everything felt less important? We wanted you to be with us. Yes, even your mother wanted you and missed you. Today, everything will be all right when you stay with us. Your mother will take you where she goes; the two of you will do things together and go gathering together."

Then when my father dug *klaru* bulbs, I ate them, and when he dug *chon* bulbs, I ate them. I ate everything they gave me, and I wasn't yelled at any more.

Mother and I often went to the bush together. The two of us would walk until we arrived at a place where she collected food. She'd set me down in the shade of a tree and dig roots or gather nuts nearby.

Once I left the tree and went to play in the shade of another tree. I saw a tiny steenbok, one that had just been born, hidden in the grass and among the leaves. It was lying there, its little eye just looking out at me.

I thought, "What should I do?" I shouted, *"Mommy!"* I just stood there and it just lay there looking at me.

Suddenly I knew what to do—I ran at it, trying to grab it. But it jumped up and ran away and I started to chase it. It was running and I was running and it was crying as it ran. Finally, I got very close and put my foot in its way, and it fell down. I grabbed its legs and started to carry it back. It was crying, "Ehn . . . ehn . . . ehn. . . ."

Its mother had been close by and when she heard it call, she came running. As soon as I saw her, I started to run again. I wouldn't give it back to its mother!

I called out, "Mommy! Come! Help me with this steenbok! Mommy! The steenbok's mother is coming for me! Run! Come! Take this steenbok from me."

But soon the mother steenbok was no longer following, so I took the baby, held its feet together, and banged it hard against the sand until I killed it. It was no longer crying; it was dead. I felt wonderfully happy. My mother came running and I gave it to her to carry.

The two of us spent the rest of the day walking in the bush. While my mother was gathering, I sat in the shade of a tree, waiting and playing with the dead steenbok. I picked it up. I tried to make it sit up, to open its eyes. I looked at them. After mother had dug enough *sha* roots, we left and returned home.

My father had been out hunting that day and had shot a large steenbok with his arrows. He had skinned it and brought it back hanging on a branch.

"Ho, ho. Daddy killed a steenbok!" I said. "Mommy! Daddy! I'm not going to let anyone have any of *my* steenbok. Now *don't* give it to anyone else. After you cook it, just my little brother and I will eat it, just the two of us."

I remember another time when we were traveling from one place to another and the sun was burning. It was the hot, dry season and there was no water anywhere. The sun was burning! Kumsa had already been born and I was still small.

After we had been walking a long time, my older brother Dau spotted a beehive. We stopped while he and my father chopped open the tree. All of us helped take out the honey. I filled my own little container until it was completely full.

We stayed there, eating the honey, and I found myself getting very thirsty, Then we left and continued to walk, I carrying my honey and my digging stick. Soon the heat began killing us and we were all dying of thirst. I started to cry because I wanted water so badly.

After a while, we stopped and sat down in the shade of a baobab tree. There was still no water anywhere. We just sat in the shade like that.

Finally my father said, "Dau, the rest of the family will stay here under this baobab. But you, take the water

containers and get us some water. There's a well not too far away."

Dau collected the empty ostrich egg-shell containers and the large clay pot and left. I lay there, already dead from thirst and thought, "If I stay with Mommy and Daddy, I'll surely die of thirst. Why don't I follow my big brother and go drink water with him?"

With that I jumped up and ran after him, crying out, calling to him, following his tracks. But he didn't hear me. I kept running . . . crying and calling out.

Finally, he heard something and turned to see. There I was. "Oh, no!" he said. "Nisa's followed me. What can I do with her now that she's here?" He just stood there and waited for me to catch up. He picked me up and carried me high up on his shoulder, and along we went. He really liked me!

The two of us went on together. We walked and walked and walked and walked. Finally, we reached the well. I ran to the water and drank, and soon my heart was happy again. We filled the water containers, put them in a twine mesh sack, and my brother carried it on his back. Then he took me and put me on his shoulder again.

We walked the long way back until we arrived at the baobab where our parents were sitting. They drank the water. Then they said, "How well our children have done, bringing us this water!" We are alive once again!"

We just stayed in the shade of the baobab. Later we left and traveled to another water hole where we settled for a while. My heart was happy . . . eating honey and just living.

We lived there, and after some time passed, we saw the first rain clouds. One came near but just hung in the sky. More rain clouds came over and they too just stood there. Then the rain started to spill itself and it came pouring down.

The rainy season had finally come. The sun rose and set, and the rain spilled itself and fell and kept falling. It fell without ceasing. Soon the water pans were full. And my heart! My heart within me was happy and we lived and ate meat and mongongo nuts. There was more meat and it was all delicious.

And there were caterpillars to eat, those little things that crawl along going "mmm . . . mmmmm . . . mmmmm. . . ." People dug roots and collected nuts and berries and brought home more and more food. There was plenty to eat, and people kept bringing meat back on sticks and hanging it in the trees.

My heart was bursting. I ate lots of food and my tail was wagging, always wagging about like a little dog. I'd laugh with my little tail, laugh with a little donkey's laugh, a tiny thing that is. I'd throw my tail one way and the other, shouting, "Today I'm going to eat caterpillars . . . *cat-er-pillars!*" Some people gave me meat broth to drink, and others prepared the skins of cater-pillars and roasted them for me to eat, and I ate and ate and ate. Then I went to sleep.

But that night, after everyone was dead asleep, I peed right in my sleeping place. In the morning, when everyone got up, I just lay there. The sun rose and had set itself high in the sky, and I was still lying there. I was afraid of people shaming me. Mother said, "Why is Nisa acting like this and refusing to leave her blankets when the sun is sitting up in the sky? Oh . . . she has probably wet herself!"

When I did get up, my heart felt miserable. I thought, "I've peed on myself and now everyone's going to laugh at me." I asked one of my friends, "How come, after I ate all those cater-pillars, when I went to sleep I peed in my bed?" Then I thought, "Tonight, when this day is over, I'm going to lie down separate from the others. If I pee in my bed again, won't mother and father hit me?"

When a child sleeps beside her moth-er, in front, and her father sleeps behind and makes love to her mother, the child watches. Her parents don't fear her, a small child, because even if the child sees, even if she hears, she is unaware of what it is her parents are doing. She is still young and without sense. Perhaps this is the way the child learns. The child is still senseless, without intelli-gence, and just watches.

If the child is a little boy, when he plays with other children, he plays sex with them and teaches it to himself, just like a baby rooster teaches itself. The little girls also learn it by themselves.

Little boys are the first ones to know its sweetness. Yes, a young girl, while she is still a child, her thoughts don't know it. A boy has a penis, and maybe, while he is still inside his mother's belly, he already knows about sex.

When you are a child you play at nothing things. You build little huts and play. Then you come back to the village and continue to play. If people bother you, you get up and play somewhere else.

Once we left a pool of rain water where we had been playing and went to the little huts we had made. We stayed there and played at being hunters. We went out tracking animals, and when we saw one, we struck it with our make-believe arrows. We took some leaves and hung them over a stick and pre-tended it was meat. Then we carried it back to our village. When we got back, we stayed there and ate the meat and then the meat was gone. We went out again, found another animal, and killed it.

Sometimes the boys asked if we wanted to play a game with our genitals and the girls said no. We said we didn't want to play that game, but would like to play other games. The boys told us that playing sex was what playing was all about. That's the way we grew up.

When adults talked to me I listened. Once they told me that when a young woman grows up, she takes a husband. When they first talked to me about it, I said: "What? What kind of thing am I that I should take a husband? Me, when I grow up, I won't marry. I'll just lie by myself. If I married a man, what would I think I would be doing it for?"

My father said: "Nisa, I am old. I am your father and I am old; your mother's old, too. When you get married, you will gather food and give it to your husband to eat. He also will do things for you and give you things you can wear. But if you refuse to take a husband, who will give you food to eat? Who will give you things to have? Who will give you things to wear?"

I said to my father and mother, "No. There's no question in my mind—I refuse a husband. I won't take one. Why should I? As I am now, I am still a child and won't marry."

Then I said to Mother, "Why don't you marry the man you want for me and sit him down beside Father? Then you'll have two husbands."

Mother said: "Stop talking nonsense. I'm not going to marry him; you'll marry him. A husband is what I want to give you. Yet you say I should marry him. Why are playing with me with this talk?"

We just continued to live after that, kept on living and more time passed. One time we went to the village where Old Kantla and his son Tashay were living. My friend Nhuka and I had gone to the water well to get water, and Tashay and his family were there, having just come back from the bush. When Tashay saw me, he decided he wanted to marry me. He called Nhuka over and said, "Nhuka, that young woman, that beautiful young woman . . . what is her name?"

Nhuka told him my name was Nisa, and he said, "That young woman . . . I'm going to tell Mother and Father about her. I'm going to ask them if I can marry her."

The next evening there was a dance at our village, and Tashay and his parents came. We sang and danced into the night. Later his father said, "We have come here, and now that the dancing is finished, I want to speak to you. Give me your child, the child you gave birth to. Give her to me, and I will give her to my son. Yesterday, while we were at the well, he saw your child. When he returned he told me in the name of what he felt that I should come and ask for her today so I could give her to him."

My mother said, "Yes . . . but I didn't give birth to a woman, I bore a child. She doesn't think about marriage, she just doesn't think about the inside of her marriage hut."

Then my father said, "Yes, I also conceived that child, and it is true: She just doesn't think about marriage. When she marries a man, she leaves him and marries another man and leaves him and gets up and marries another man and leaves him. She refuses men com-pletely. There are two men whom she has already refused. So when I look at Nisa today, I say she is not a woman."

Then Tashay's father said, "Yes, I have listened to what you have said.

That, of course, is the way of a child; it is a child's custom to do that. She gets married many times until one day she likes one man. Then they stay together. That is a child's way."

They talked about the marriage and agreed to it. In the morning Tashay's parents went back to their camp, and we went to sleep. When the morning was late in the sky, his relatives came back. They stayed around and his parents told my aunt and my mother that they should all start building the marriage hut. They began building it together, and everyone was talking and talking. There were a lot of people there. Then all the young men went and brought Tashay to the hut. They stayed around together near the fire. I was at Mother's hut. They told two of my friends to get me. But I said to myself, "Ooooh . . . I'll just run away."

When they came, they couldn't find me. I was already out in the bush, and I just sat there by the base of a tree. Soon I heard Nhuka call out, "Nisa . . . Nisa . . . my friend . . . there are things there that will bite and kill you. Now leave there and come back here."

They came and brought me back. Then they laid me down inside the hut. I cried and cried, and people told me: "A man is not something that kills you; he is someone who marries you, and becomes like your father or your older brother. He kills animals and gives you things to eat. Even tomorrow he would do that. But because you are crying, when he kills an animal, he will eat it himself and won't give you any. Beads, too. He will get some beads, but he won't give them to you. Why are you afraid of your husband and why are you crying?"

I listened and was quiet. Later Tashay lay down by the mouth of the hut, near the fire, and I was inside. He came in only after he thought I was asleep. Then he lay down and slept. I woke while it was still dark and thought,

"How am I going to jump over him? How can I get out and go to Mother's hut?" Then I thought, "This person has married me . . . yes." And, I just lay there. Soon the rain came and beat down and it fell until dawn broke.

In the morning, he got up first and sat by the fire. I was frightened. I was so afraid of him, I just lay there and waited for him to go away before I got up.

We lived together a long time and began to learn to like one another before he slept with me. The first time I didn't refuse. I agreed just a little and he lay with me. But the next morning my insides hurt. I took some leaves and wound them around my waist, but it continued to hurt. Later that day I went with the women to gather mongongo nuts. The whole time I thought "Ooooh . . . what has he done to my insides that they feel this way."

That evening we lay down again. But this time I took a leather strap, held my skin apron tightly against me, tied up my genitals with it, and then tied the strap to the hut's frame. I didn't want him to take me again. The two of us lay there and after a while he started to touch me. When he reached my stomach, he felt the leather strap. He felt around to see what it was. He said, "What is this woman doing? Yesterday she lay with me so nicely when I came to her. Why has she tied up her genitals this way?

He sat me up and said, "Nisa . . . Nisa . . . what happened? Why are you doing this?" I didn't answer him.

"What are you so afraid of that you tied your genitals?"

I said, "I'm not afraid of anything."

He said, "No, now tell me what you are afraid of. In the name of what you did, I am asking you."

I said, "I refuse because yesterday when you touched me my insides hurt."

He said, "Do you see me as someone who kills people? Am I going to eat you? I am not going to kill you. I have

married you and I want to make love to you. Have you seen any man who has married a woman and who just lives with her and doesn't have sex with her?"

I said, "No, I still refuse it! I refuse sex. Yesterday my insides hurt, that's why."

He said, "Mmm. Today you will lie there by yourself. But tomorrow I will take you."

The next day I said to him, "Today I'm going to lie here, and if you take me by force, you will have me. You will have me because today I'm just going to lie here. You are obviously looking for some 'food,' but I don't know if the food I have is food at all, because even if you have some, you won't be full."

I just lay there and he did his work.

We lived and lived, and soon I started to like him. After that I was a grown person and said to myself, "Yes, without doubt, a man sleeps with you. I thought maybe he didn't."

We lived on, and then I loved him and he loved me, and I kept on loving him. When he wanted me I didn't refuse and he just slept with me. I thought, "Why have I been so concerned about my genitals? They are, after all, not so important. So why was I refusing them?"

I thought that and gave myself to him and gave and gave. We lay with one another, and my breasts had grown very large. I had become a woman.

FOR FURTHER INFORMATION:

Lee, Richard, B., and Irven DeVore, eds. *Kalahari Hunter-Gatherers: Studies of the !Kung San and Their Neighbors.* Harvard University Press, 1976.

Lee, Richard B., and Irven DeVore, eds. *Man the Hunter.* Aldine, 1968.

Marshall, Lorna. *The !Kung of Nyae Nyae.* Harvard University Press, 1976.

Shostak, Marjorie. "Life before Horticulture: An African Gathering and Hunting Society." *Horticulture*, Vol. 55, No. 2, 1977.

When Brothers Share a Wife

Among Tibetans, the good life relegates many women to spinsterhood

Melvyn C. Goldstein

Melvyn C. Goldstein, now a professor of anthropology at Case Western Reserve University in Cleveland, has been interested in the Tibetan practice of fraternal polyandry (several brothers marrying one wife) since he was a graduate student in the 1960s.

Eager to reach home, Dorje drives his yaks hard over the 17,000-foot mountain pass, stopping only once to rest. He and his two older brothers, Pema and Sonam, are jointly marrying a woman from the next village in a few weeks, and he has to help with the preparations.

Dorje, Pema, and Sonam are Tibetans living in Limi, a 200-square-mile area in the northwest corner of Nepal, across the border from Tibet. The form of marriage they are about to enter—fraternal polyandry in anthropological parlance—is one of the world's rarest forms of marriage but is not uncommon in Tibetan society, where it has been practiced from time immemorial. For many Tibetan social strata, it traditionally represented the ideal form of marriage and family.

The mechanics of fraternal polyandry are simple. Two, three, four, or more brothers jointly take a wife, who leaves her home to come and live with them. Traditionally, marriage was arranged by parents, with children, particularly females, having little or no say. This is changing somewhat nowadays, but it is still unusual for children to marry without their parents' consent. Marriage ceremonies vary by income and region and range from all the brothers sitting together as grooms to only the eldest one formally doing so. The age of the brothers plays an important role in determining this: very young brothers almost never participate in actual marriage ceremonies, although they typically join the marriage when they reach their midteens.

The eldest brother is normally dominant in terms of authority, that is, in managing the household, but all the brothers share the work and participate as sexual partners. Tibetan males and females do not find the sexual aspect of sharing a spouse the least bit unusual, repulsive, or scandalous, and the norm is for the wife to treat all the brothers the same.

Offspring are treated similarly. There is no attempt to link children biologically to particular brothers, and a brother shows no favoritism toward his child even if he knows he is the real father because, for example, his other brothers were away at the time the wife became pregnant. The children, in turn, consider all of the brothers as their fathers and treat them equally, even if they also know who is their real father. In some regions children use the term "father" for the eldest brother and "father's brother" for the others, while in other areas they call all the brothers by one term, modifying this by the use of "elder" and "younger."

Unlike our own society, where monogamy is the only form of marriage permitted, Tibetan society allows a variety of marriage types, including monogamy, fraternal polyandry, and polygyny. Fraternal polyandry and monogamy are the most common forms of marriage, while polygyny typically occurs in cases where the first wife is barren. The widespread practice of fraternal polyandry, therefore, is not the outcome of a law requiring brothers to marry jointly. There is choice, and in fact, divorce traditionally was relatively simple in Tibetan society. If a brother in a polyandrous marriage became dissatisfied and wanted to separate, he simply left the main house and set up his own household. In such cases, all the children stayed in the main household with the remaining brother(s), even if the departing brother was known to be the real father of one or more of the children.

The Tibetans' own explanation for choosing fraternal polyandry is materialistic. For example, when I asked Dorje why he decided to marry with his two brothers rather than take his own wife, he thought for a moment, then said it prevented the division of his family's farm (and animals) and thus facilitated all of them achieving a higher standard of living. And when I later asked Dorje's bride whether it wasn't difficult for her to cope with three brothers as husbands, she laughed and echoed the rationale of avoiding fragmentation of the family and land, adding that she expected to be better off economically, since she would have three husbands working for her and her children.

Exotic as it may seem to Westerners, Tibetan fraternal polyandry is thus in many ways analogous to the way primogeniture functioned in nineteenth-century England. Primogeniture dictated that the eldest son inherited the family estate, while younger sons had to leave home and seek their own employment—for example, in the military or the clergy. Primogeniture maintained family estates intact over generations by permitting only one heir per generation. Fraternal polyandry also accomplishes this but does so by keeping all the brothers together with just one wife so that there is only one *set* of heirs per generation.

While Tibetans believe that in this way fraternal polyandry reduces the risk of family fission, monogamous marriages among brothers need not necessarily precipitate the division of the family estate: brothers could continue to live together, and the family land could continue to be worked jointly. When I asked Tibetans about this, however, they invariably responded that such joint families are unstable because each wife is primarily oriented to her own children and interested in their success and well-being over that of the children of the other wives. For example, if the youngest brother's wife had three sons while the eldest brother's wife had only one daughter, the wife of the youngest brother might begin to demand more resources for her children since, as males, they represent the future of the family. Thus, the children from different wives in the same generation are competing sets of heirs, and this makes such families inherently unstable. Tibetans perceive that conflict will spread from the wives to their husbands and consider this likely to cause family fission. Consequently, it is almost never done.

Although Tibetans see an economic advantage to fraternal polyandry, they do not value the sharing of a wife as an end in itself. On the contrary, they articulate a number of problems inherent in the practice. For example, because authority is customarily exercised by the eldest brother, his younger male siblings have

Family Planning in Tibet

An economic rationale for fraternal polyandry is outlined in the diagram below, which emphasizes only the male offspring in each generation. If every wife is assumed to bear three sons, a family splitting up into monogamous households would rapidly multiply and fragment the family land. In this case, a rule of inheritance, such as primogeniture, could retain the family land intact, but only at the cost of creating many landless male offspring. In contrast, the family practicing fraternal polyandry maintains a steady ratio of persons to land.
Joe LeMonnier

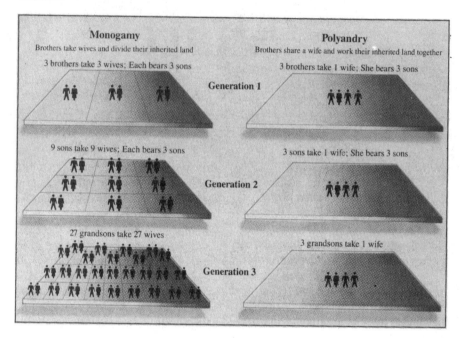

to subordinate themselves with little hope of changing their status within the family. When these younger brothers are aggressive and individualistic, tensions and difficulties often occur despite there being only one set of heirs.

In addition, tension and conflict may arise in polyandrous families because of sexual favoritism. The bride normally sleeps with the eldest brother, and the two have the responsibility to see to it that the other males have opportunities for sexual access. Since the Tibetan subsistence economy requires males to travel a lot, the temporary absence of one or more brothers facilitates this, but there are also other rotation practices. The cultural ideal unambiguously calls for the wife to show equal affection and sexuality to each of the brothers (and vice versa), but deviations from this ideal occur, especially when there is a sizable difference in age between the partners in the marriage.

Dorje's family represents just such a

potential situation. He is fifteen years old and his two older brothers are twenty-five and twenty-two years old. The new bride is twenty-three years old, eight years Dorje's senior. Sometimes such a bride finds the youngest husband immature and adolescent and does not treat him with equal affection; alternatively, she may find his youth attractive and lavish special attention on him. Apart from that consideration, when a younger male like Dorje grows up, he may consider his wife "ancient" and prefer the company of a woman his own age or younger. Consequently, although men and women do not find the idea of sharing a bride or a bridegroom repulsive, individual likes and dislikes can cause familial discord.

Two reasons have commonly been offered for the perpetuation of fraternal polyandry in Tibet: that Tibetans practice female infanticide and therefore have to marry polyandrously, owing to a shortage of females; and that Tibet, lying at extremely high altitudes, is so barren and bleak that Tibetans would starve without resort to this mechanism. A Jesuit who lived in Tibet during the eighteenth century articulated this second view: "One reason for this most odious custom is the sterility of the soil, and the small amount of land that can be cultivated owing to the lack of water. The crops may suffice if the brothers all live together, but if they form separate families they would be reduced to beggary."

Both explanations are wrong, however. Not only has there never been institutionalized female infanticide in Tibet, but Tibetan society gives females considerable rights, including inheriting the family estate in the absence of brothers. In such cases, the woman takes a bridegroom who comes to live in her family and adopts her family's name and identity. Moreover, there is no demographic evidence of a shortage of females. In Limi, for example, there were (in 1974) sixty females and fifty-three males in the fifteen- to thirty-five-year age category, and many adult females were unmarried.

The second reason is also incorrect. The climate in Tibet is extremely harsh, and ecological factors do play a major role perpetuating polyandry, but polyandry is not a means of preventing starvation. It is characteristic, not of the poorest segments of the society, but rather of the peasant landowning families.

In the old society, the landless poor could not realistically aspire to prosperity, but they did not fear starvation. There was a persistent labor shortage throughout Tibet, and very poor families with little or no land and few animals could subsist through agricultural labor, tenant farming, craft occupations such as carpentry, or by working as servants. Although the per person family income could increase somewhat if brothers married polyandrously and pooled their wages, in the absence of inheritable land, the advantage of fraternal polyandry was not generally sufficient to prevent them from setting up their own households. A more skilled or energetic younger brother could do as well or better alone, since he would completely control his income and would not have to share it with his siblings. Consequently, while there was and is some polyandry among the poor, it is much less frequent and more prone to result in divorce and family fission.

An alternative reason for the persistence of fraternal polyandry is that it reduces population growth (and thereby reduces the pressure on resources) by relegating some females to lifetime spinsterhood. Fraternal polyandrous marriages in Limi (in 1974) averaged 2.35 men per woman, and not surprisingly, 31 percent of the females of child-bearing age (twenty to forty-nine) were unmarried. These spinsters either continued to live at home, set up their own households, or worked as servants for other families. They could also become Buddhist nuns. Being unmarried is not synonymous with exclusion from the reproductive pool. Discreet extramarital relationships are tolerated, and actually half of the adult unmarried women in Limi had one or more children. They raised these children as single mothers, working for wages or weaving cloth and blankets for sale. As a group, however, the unmarried woman had far fewer offspring than the married women, averaging only 0.7 children per woman, compared with 3.3 for married women, whether polyandrous, monogamous, or polygynous. While polyandry helps regulate population, this function of polyandry is not consciously perceived by Tibetans and is not the reason they consistently choose it.

If neither a shortage of females nor the fear of starvation perpetuates fraternal polyandry, what motivates brothers, particularly younger brothers, to opt for this system of marriage? From the perspective of the younger brother in a landholding family, the main incentive is the attainment or maintenance of the good life. With polyandry, he can expect a more secure and higher standard of living, with access not only to this family's land and animals but also to its inherited collection of clothes, jewelry, rugs, saddles, and horses. In addition, he will experience less work pressure and much greater security because all responsibility does not fall on one "father." For Tibetan brothers, the question is whether to trade off the greater personal freedom inherent in monogamy for the real or potential economic security, affluence, and social prestige associated with life in a larger, labor-rich polyandrous family.

A brother thinking of separating from his polyandrous marriage and taking his own wife would face various disadvantages. Although in the majority of Tibetan regions all brothers theoretically have rights to their family's estate, in reality Tibetans are reluctant to divide their land into small fragments. Generally, a younger brother who insists on leaving the family will receive only a small plot of land, if that. Because of its power and wealth, the rest of the family usually can block any attempt of the younger brother to increase his share of land through litigation. Moreover, a younger brother may not even get a house and cannot expect to receive much above the minimum in terms of movable possessions, such as furniture, pots, and pans. Thus, a brother contemplating going it on his own must plan on achieving economic security and the good life not through inheritance but through his own work.

The obvious solution for younger brothers—creating new fields from virgin land—is generally not a feasible option. Most Tibetan populations live at high altitudes (above 12,000 feet), where arable land is extremely scarce. For example, in Dorje's village, agriculture ranges only from about 12,900 feet, the lowest point in the area, to 13,300 feet. Above that altitude, early frost and snow destroy the staple barley crop. Furthermore, because of the low rainfall caused by the Himalayan rain shadow, many areas in Tibet and northern Nepal that are within the appropriate altitude range for agriculture have no reliable sources of irrigation. In the end, although there is plenty of unused land in such areas, most of it is either too high or too arid.

Even where unused land capable of being farmed exists, clearing the land and building the substantial terraces necessary for irrigation constitute a great undertaking. Each plot has to be completely dug out to a depth of two to two and half feet so that the large rocks and boulders can be removed. At best, a man might be able to bring a few new fields under cultivation in the first years after separating from his brothers, but he could not expect to acquire substantial amounts of arable land this way.

In addition, because of the limited farmland, the Tibetan subsistence economy characteristically includes a strong emphasis on animal husbandry. Tibetan farmers regularly maintain cattle, yaks, goats, and sheep, grazing them in the areas too high for agriculture. These herds produce wool, milk, cheese, butter, meat, and skins. To obtain these resources, however, shepherds must accompany the animals on a daily basis. When first setting up a monogamous household, a younger brother like Dorje would find it difficult to both farm and manage animals.

In traditional Tibetan society, there was an even more critical factor that operated to perpetuate fraternal polyandry—a form of hereditary servitude somewhat analogous to serfdom in Europe. Peasants were tied to large estates held by aristocrats, monasteries, and the Lhasa government. They were allowed the use of some farmland to produce their own subsistence but were required to provide taxes in kind and corvée (free labor) to their lords. The corvée was a substantial hardship, since a peasant household was in many cases required to furnish the lord with one laborer daily for most of the year and more on specific occasions such as the harvest. This enforced labor, along with the lack of new land and ecological pressure to pursue both agriculture and animal husbandry, made polyandrous families particularly beneficial. The polyandrous family allowed an internal division of adult labor, maximizing economic advantage. For example, while the wife worked the family fields, one brother could perform the lord's corvée, another could look after the animals, and a third could engage in trade.

Although social scientists often discount other people's explanations of why they do things, in the case of Tibetan fraternal polyandry, such explanations are very close to the truth. The custom, however, is very sensitive to changes in its political and economic milieu and, not surprisingly, is in decline in most Tibetan areas. Made less important by the elimination of the traditional serf-based economy, it is disparaged by the dominant non-Tibetan leaders of India, China, and Nepal. New opportunities for economic and social mobility in these countries, such as the tourist trade and government employment, are also eroding the rationale for polyandry, and so it may vanish within the next generation.

Young Traders of Northern Nigeria

Enid Schildkrout

Thirty years ago, Erik Erikson wrote that "the fashionable insistence on dramatizing the dependence of children on adults often blinds us to the dependence of the older generation on the younger one." As a psychoanalyst, Erikson was referring mainly to the emotional bonds between parents and children, but his observation is a reminder that in many parts of the world, adults depend on children in quite concrete ways. In northern Nigeria, children with trays balanced on their heads, carrying and selling a variety of goods for their mothers or themselves, are a common sight in villages and towns. Among the Muslim Hausa, aside from being a useful educational experience, this children's trade, as well as children's performance of household chores and errands, complements the activity of adults and is socially and emotionally significant.

Children's services are especially important to married Hausa women, who, in accordance with Islamic practices, live in purdah, or seclusion. In Nigeria, purdah is represented not so much by the wearing of the veil but by the mud-brick walls surrounding every house or compound and by the absence of women in the markets and the streets. Women could not carry out their domestic responsibilities, not to mention their many income-earning enterprises, without the help of children, who are free from the rigid sexual segregation that so restricts adults.

Except for elderly women, only children can move in and out of their own and other people's houses without violating the rules of purdah. Even children under three years of age are sent on short errands, for example, to buy things for their mothers.

Hausa-speaking people are found throughout West Africa and constitute the largest ethnic group in northern Nigeria, where they number over eighteen million. Their adherence to Islam is a legacy of the centuries during which Arabs came from the north to trade goods of North African and European manufacture. The majority of the Hausa are farmers, but markets and large commercial cities have existed in northern Nigeria since long before the period of British colonial rule. The city of Kano, for example, which was a major emporium for the trans-Saharan caravan trade, dates back to the eighth century. Today it has a population of about one million.

Binta is an eleven-year-old girl who lives in Kano, in a mud-brick house that has piped water, but no electricity. The household includes her father and mother, her three brothers, her father's second wife and her three children, and a foster child, who is the daughter of one of Binta's cousins. By Kano standards, it is a middle-income family. Binta's father sells shoes, and her mother cooks and sells bean cakes and *tuwo*, the stiff porridge made of guinea corn (*Shorghum vulgare*), which is the Hausa's staple. Binta described for me one day's round of activities, which

began very early when she arose to start trading.

"After I woke up, I said my prayers and ate breakfast. Then I went outside the house to sell the bean cakes my mother makes every morning. Soon my mother called me in and asked me to take more bean cakes around town to sell; she spoke to me about making an effort to sell as much as I usually do. I sold forty-eight bean cakes at one kobo each [one kobo is worth one and a half cents]. After I returned home, some people came to buy more cakes from me. Then I went out for a second round of trading before setting out for Arabic school. I study the Koran there every morning from eight to nine.

"When school was over, I washed and prepared to sell *tuwo*. First my mother sent me to another neighborhood to gather the customers' empty bowls. I also collected the money from our regular customers. My mother put the *tuwo* in the bowls and told me the amount of money to collect for each. Then I delivered them to the customers.

"On my way home, a man in the street, whom I know, sent me on an errand to buy him fifteen kobo worth of food; he gave me a reward of one kobo. I then sold some more *tuwo* outside our house by standing there and shouting for customers. When the *tuwo* was finished, I was sent to another house to buy some guinea corn, and one of the women there asked me to bring her one of my mother's big pots. The pot was too heavy for me to carry, but finally one of my brothers helped me take it to her.

"When I returned, my mother was busy pounding some grain, and she sent me out to have some locust beans pounded. She then sent me to pick up three bowls of pounded guinea corn, and she gave me money to take to the woman who had pounded it. The woman told me to remind my mother that she still owed money from the day before.

"When I came home I was sent out to trade again, this time with salt, bouillon cubes, and laundry detergent in small packets. Afterward I prepared some pancakes using ingredients I bought myself—ten kobo worth of flour, one kobo worth of salt, five kobo worth of palm oil, and ten kobo worth of firewood. I took this food outside to sell it to children.

"My mother then gave me a calabash of guinea corn to take for grinding; my younger sister also gave me two calabashes of corn to take. The man who ran the grinding machine advised me that I should not carry so large a load, so I made two trips on the way back. He gave me and my younger brothers, who accompanied me, one kobo each.

"I was then told to take a bath, which I did. After that I was sent to visit a sick relative who was in the hospital. On the way I met a friend, and we took the bus together. I also bought some cheese at the market for five kobo. I met another friend on the way home, and she bought some fish near the market for ten kobo and gave me some. I played on the way to the hospital. When I got home, I found the women of the house preparing a meal. One of them was already eating, and I was invited to eat with her.

"After nightfall, I was sent to take some spices for pounding, and I wasted a lot of time there. The other children and I went to a place where some fruits and vegetables are sold along the street. We bought vegetables for soup for fifty kobo, as my mother had asked me to do. By the time I got home it was late, so I went to sleep."

Binta's many responsibilities are typical for a girl her age. Like many women, Binta's mother relies upon her children in carrying out an occupation

at home. Although purdah implies that a woman will be supported by her husband and need not work, most Hausa women do work, keeping their incomes distinct from the household budget. Women usually cook one main meal a day and purchase their other meals from other women. In this way they are able to use their time earning a living instead of performing only unpaid domestic labor.

Among the Hausa, men and women spend relatively little time together, eating separately and, except in certain ritual contexts, rarely doing the same things. Differences in gender are not as important among children, however. In fact, it is precisely because children's activities are not rigidly defined by sex that they are able to move between the world of women, centered in the inner courtyard of the house, and the world of men, whose activities take place mainly outside the home. Children of both sexes care for younger children, go to the market, and help their mothers cook.

Both boys and girls do trading, although it is more common for girls. From the age of about five until marriage, which is very often at about age twelve for girls, many children like Binta spend part of every day selling such things as fruits, vegetables, and nuts; bouillon cubes, bread, and small packages of detergent, sugar, or salt; and bowls of steaming rice or *tuwo*. If a woman embroiders, children buy the thread and later take the finished product to the client or to an agent who sells it.

Women in purdah frequently change their occupations depending on the availability of child helpers. In Kano, women often trade in small commodities that can be sold in small quantities, such as various kinds of cooked food. Sewing, embroidery, mat weaving, and other craft activities (including, until recently, spinning) are less remunerative occupations, and women pursue them when they have fewer children around to help. Unlike the situation common in the United States, where children tend to hamper a woman's ability to earn money, the Hausa woman finds it difficult to earn income without children's help. Often, if a

woman has no children of her own, a relative's child will come to live with her.

Child care is another service children perform that benefits women. It enables mothers to devote themselves to their young infants, whom they carry on their backs until the age of weaning, between one and two. Even though women are always at home, they specifically delegate the care of young children to older ones. The toddler moves from the mother's back into a group of older children, who take the responsibility very seriously. Until they are old enough, children do not pick up infants or very young children, but by the age of nine, both boys and girls bathe young children, play with them, and take them on errands. The older children do a great deal of direct and indirect teaching of younger ones. As soon as they can walk, younger children accompany their older siblings to Arabic school. There the children sit with their age-mates, and the teacher gives them lessons according to their ability.

Much of a child's activity is directed toward helping his or her parents, but other relatives—grandparents, aunts, uncles, and stepmothers—and adults living in the same house as servants or tenants may call on a child for limited tasks without asking permission of the parents. Like other Muslims, Hausa men may have up to four wives, and these women freely call on each other's children to perform household chores. Even strangers in the street sometimes ask a child to do an errand, such as delivering a message, particularly if the chore requires entering a house to which the adult does not have access. The child will be rewarded with a small amount of money or food.

Adults other than parents also reprimand children, who are taught very early to obey the orders of grownups. Without ever directly refusing to obey a command, however, children do devise numerous strategies of non-compliance, such as claiming that another adult has already co-opted their time or simply leaving the scene and ignoring the command. Given children's greater mobility, there is little an adult can do to enforce compliance.

Besides working on behalf of adults, children also participate in a "children's economy." Children have their own money—from school allowances given to them daily for the purchase of snacks, from gifts, from work they may have done, and even from their own investments. For example, boys make toys for sale, and they rent out valued property, such as slide viewers or bicycles. Just as women distinguish their own enterprises from the labor they do as wives, children regard the work they do for themselves differently from the work they do on behalf of their mothers. When Binta cooks food for sale, using materials she has purchased with her own money, the profits are entirely her own, although she may hand the money over to her mother for safekeeping.

Many girls begin to practice cooking by the age of ten. They do not actually prepare the family meals, for this heavy and tedious work is primarily the wives' responsibility. But they do carry out related chores, such as taking vegetables out for grinding, sifting flour, and washing bowls. Many also cook food for sale on their own. With initial help from their mothers or other adult female relatives, who may given them a cooking pot, charcoal, or a small stove, children purchase small amounts of ingredients and prepare various snacks. Since they sell their products for less than the adult women do, and since the quantities are very small, their customers are mainly children. Child entrepreneurs even extend credit to other children.

Aisha is a ten-year-old girl who was notoriously unsuccessful as a trader. She disliked trading and regularly lost her mother's investment. Disgusted, her mother finally gave her a bit of charcoal, some flour and oil, and a small pot. Aisha set up a little stove outside her house and began making small pancakes, which she sold to very young children. In three months she managed to make enough to buy a new dress, and in a year she bought a pair of shoes. She had clearly chosen her occupation after some unhappy trials at street trading.

Hausa women usually engage in some form of enterprise; most of their profits are invested in their children's marriage expenses. Working at home, a woman weaves a mat for sale.

In the poorest families, as in Aisha's, the profit from children's work goes toward living expenses. This may occur in households that are headed by divorced or widowed women. It is also true for the *almajirai*, or Arabic students, who often live with their teachers. The proceeds of most children's economic activity, however, go to the expenses of marriage. The income contributes to a girl's dowry and to a boy's bridewealth, both of which are considerable investments.

The girl's dowry includes many brightly painted enamel, brass, and glass bowls, collected years before marriage. These utensils are known as *kayan daki*, or "things of the room." After the wedding they are stacked in a large cupboard beside the girl's bed. Very few of them are used, but they are always proudly displayed, except during the mourning period if the husband dies. *Kayan daki* are not simply for conspicuous display, however. They remain the property of the woman unless she sells them or gives them away. In the case of divorce or financial need, they can provide her most important and immediate source of economic security.

Kayan daki traditionally consisted of brass bowls and beautifully carved calabashes. Today the most common form is painted enamel bowls manufactured in Nigeria or abroad. The styles and designs change frequently, and the cost is continually rising.

Among the wealthier urban women and the Western-educated women, other forms of modern household equipment, including electric appliances and china tea sets, are becoming part of the dowry.

The money a young girl earns on her own, as well as the profits she brings home through her trading, are invested by her mother or guardian in *kayan daki* in anticipation of her marriage. Most women put the major part of their income into their daughters' *kayan daki* as well as helping their sons with marriage expenses. When a woman has many children, the burden can be considerable.

For girls, marriage, which ideally coincides with puberty, marks the transition to adult status. If a girl marries as early as age ten, she does not cook for her husband or have sexual relations with him for some time, but she enters purdah and loses the freedom of childhood. Most girls are married by age fifteen, and for many the transition is a difficult one.

Boys usually do not marry until they are over twenty and are able to support a family. They also need to have raised most of the money to cover the cost of getting married. Between the ages of eight and ten, however, they gradually begin to move away from the confines of the house and to regard it as a female domain. They begin taking their food outside and eating it with friends, and they roam much farther than girls in their play activities. By the onset of puberty, boys have begun to observe the rules of purdah by refraining from entering the houses of all but their closest relatives. In general, especially if they have sisters, older boys spend less time than girls doing chores and errands and more time playing and, in recent years, going to school. Traditionally, many boys left home to live and study with an Arabic teacher. Today many also pursue Western education, sometimes in boarding school. Although the transition to adulthood is less abrupt for boys, childhood for both sexes ends by age twelve to fourteen.

As each generation assumes the responsibilities of adulthood and the restrictions of sexual separation, it must rely on the younger members of society who can work around the purdah system. Recently, however, the introduction of Western education has begun to threaten this traditional arrangement, in part just by altering the pattern of children's lives.

The Nigerian government is now engaged in a massive program to provide Western education to all school-age children. This program has been undertaken for sound economic and political reasons. During the colonial period, which ended in the early 1960s, the British had a "hands-off"

policy regarding education in northern Nigeria. They ruled through the Islamic political and judicial hierarchy and supported the many Arabic schools, where the Koran and Islamic law, history, and religion were taught. The British discouraged the introduction of Christian mission schools in the north and spent little on government schools.

The pattern in the rest of Nigeria was very different. In the non-Muslim areas of the country, mission and government schools grew rapidly during the colonial period. The result of this differential policy was the development of vast regional imbalances in the extent and level of Western education in the country. This affected the types of occupational choices open to Nigerians from different regions. Despite a longer tradition of literacy in Arabic in the north, few northerners were eligible for those civil service jobs that required literacy in English, the language of government business. This was one of the many issues in the tragic civil war that tore Nigeria apart in the 1960s. The current goal of enrolling all northern children in public schools, which offer training in English and secular subjects, has, therefore, a strong and valid political rationale.

Western education has met a mixed reception in northern Nigeria. While

it has been increasingly accepted for boys—as an addition to, not a substitute for, Islamic education—many parents are reluctant to enroll their daughters in primary school. Nevertheless, there are already more children waiting to get into school than there are classrooms and teachers to accommodate them. If the trend continues, it will almost certainly have important, if unintended, consequences for purdah and the system of child enterprise that supports it.

Children who attend Western school continue to attend Arabic school, and thus are removed from the household for much of the day. For many women this causes considerable difficulty in doing daily housework. It means increased isolation and a curtailment of income-producing activity. It creates a new concern about where to obtain the income for children's marriages. As a result of these practical pressures, the institution of purdah will inevitably be challenged. Also, the schoolgirl of today may develop new skills and new expectations of her role as a woman that conflict with the traditional ways. As Western education takes hold, today's young traders may witness a dramatic change in Hausa family life—for themselves as adults and for their children.

Death Without Weeping

Has poverty ravaged mother love in the shantytowns of Brazil?

Nancy Scheper-Hughes

Nancy Scheper-Hughes is a professor in the Department of Anthropology at the University of California, Berkeley. She has written Death Without Weeping: Violence of Everyday Life in Brazil *(1992).*

I have seen death without weeping
The destiny of the Northeast is death
Cattle they kill
To the people they do something worse
—Anonymous Brazilian singer (1965)

"Why do the church bells ring so often?" I asked Nailza de Arruda soon after I moved into a corner of her tiny mud-walled hut near the top of the shantytown called the Alto do Cruzeiro (Crucifix Hill). I was then a Peace Corps volunteer and a community development/health worker. It was the dry and blazing hot summer of 1965, the months following the military coup in Brazil, and save for the rusty, clanging bells of N. S. das Dores Church, an eerie quiet had settled over the market town that I call Bom Jesus da Mata. Beneath the quiet, however, there was chaos and panic. "It's nothing," replied Nailza, "just another little angel gone to heaven."

Nailza had sent more than her share of little angels to heaven, and sometimes at night I could hear her engaged in a muffled but passionate discourse with one of them, two-year-old Joana. Joana's photograph, taken as she lay propped up in her tiny cardboard coffin, her eyes open, hung on a wall next to one of Nailza and Ze Antonio taken on the day they eloped.

Nailza could barely remember the other infants and babies who came and went in close succession. Most had died unnamed and were hastily baptized in their coffins. Few lived more than a month or two. Only Joana, properly baptized in church at the close of her first year and placed under the protection of a powerful saint, Joan of Arc, had been expected to live. And Nailza had dangerously allowed herself to love the little girl.

In addressing the dead child, Nailza's voice would range from tearful imploring to angry recrimination: "Why did you leave me? Was your patron saint so greedy that she could not allow me one child on this earth?" Ze Antonio advised me to ignore Nailza's odd behavior, which he understood as a kind of madness that, like the birth and death of children, came and went. Indeed, the premature birth of a stillborn son some months later "cured" Nailza of her "inappropriate" grief, and the day came when she removed Joana's photo and carefully packed it away.

More than fifteen years elapsed before I returned to the Alto do Cruzeiro, and it was anthropology that provided the vehicle of my return. Since 1982 I have returned several times in order to pursue a problem that first attracted my attention in the 1960s. My involvement with the people of the Alto do Cruzeiro now spans a quarter of a century and three generations of parenting in a community where mothers and daughters are often simultaneously pregnant.

The Alto do Cruzeiro is one of three shantytowns surrounding the large market town of Bom Jesus in the sugar plantation zone of Pernambuco in Northeast Brazil, one of the many zones of neglect that have emerged in the shadow of the now tarnished economic miracle of Brazil. For the women and children of the Alto do Cruzeiro the only miracle is that some of them have managed to stay alive at all.

The Northeast is a region of vast proportions (approximately twice the size of Texas) and of equally vast social and developmental problems. The nine states that make up the region are the poorest in the country and are representative of the Third World within a dynamic and rapidly industrializing nation. Despite waves of migrations from the interior to the teeming shantytowns of coastal cities, the majority still live in rural areas on farms and ranches, sugar plantations and mills.

Life expectancy in the Northeast is only forty years, largely because of the appallingly high rate of infant and child mortality. Approximately one million children in Brazil under the age of five die each year. The children of the Northeast, especially those born in shantytowns on the periphery of urban life, are at a very high risk of death. In these areas, children are born without the traditional protection of breast-feeding, subsistence gardens, stable marriages, and multiple adult caretakers that exists in the interior. In the hillside shantytowns that spring up around cities or, in this case, interior market towns, marriages are brittle, single parenting is the norm, and women are frequently forced into the shadow economy of domestic work in the homes of the rich or into unprotected and oftentimes "scab" wage labor on the surrounding sugar plantations, where they clear land for planting and weed for a pittance, sometimes less than a dollar a day. The women of the Alto may not bring their babies with them into the homes of the wealthy, where the often-sick infants are considered sources of contamination, and they cannot carry the little ones to the riverbanks where they wash clothes because the river is heavily infested with schistosomes and other deadly parasites. Nor can they carry their young children to the plantations, which are often several miles away. At wages of a dollar a day, the women of the Alto cannot hire baby sitters. Older children who are not in school will sometimes serve as somewhat indifferent caretakers. But any child not in school is also expected to find wage work. In most cases, babies are simply left at home alone, the door securely fastened. And so many also die alone and unattended.

Bom Jesus da Mata, centrally located in the plantation zone of Pernambuco, is within commuting distance of several sugar plantations and mills. Consequently, Bom Jesus has been a magnet for rural workers forced off their small subsistence plots by large landowners wanting to use every available piece of land for sugar cultivation. Initially, the rural migrants to Bom Jesus were squatters who were given tacit approval by the mayor to put up temporary straw huts on each of the three hills overlooking the town. The Alto do Cruzeiro is the oldest, the largest, and the poorest of the shantytowns. Over the past three decades many of the original migrants have become permanent residents, and the primitive and temporary straw huts have been replaced by small homes (usually of two rooms) made of wattle and daub, sometimes covered with plaster. The more affluent residents use bricks and tiles. In most Alto homes, dangerous kerosene lamps have been replaced by light bulbs. The once tattered rural garb, often fashioned from used sugar sacking, has likewise been replaced by store-bought clothes, often castoffs from a wealthy *patrão* (boss). The trappings are modern, but the hunger, sickness, and death that they conceal are traditional, deeply rooted in a history of feudalism, exploitation, and institutionalized dependency.

My research agenda never wavered. The questions I addressed first crystallized during a veritable "die-off" of Alto babies during a severe drought in 1965. The food and water shortages and the political and economic chaos occasioned by the military coup were reflected in the handwritten entries of births and deaths in the dusty, yellowed pages of the ledger books kept at the public registry office in Bom Jesus. More than 350 babies died in the Alto during 1965 alone—this from a shantytown population of little more than 5,000. But that wasn't what surprised me. There were reasons enough for the deaths in the miserable conditions of shantytown life. What puzzled me was the seeming indifference of Alto women to the death of their infants, and their willingness to attribute to their own tiny offspring an aversion to life that made their death seem wholly natural, indeed all but anticipated.

Although I found that it was possible, and hardly difficult, to rescue infants and toddlers from death by diarrhea and dehydration with a simple sugar, salt, and water solution (even bottled Coca-Cola worked fine), it was more difficult to enlist a mother herself in the rescue of a child she perceived as ill-fated for life or better off dead, or to convince her to take back into her threatened and besieged home a baby she had already come to think of as an angel rather than as a son or daughter.

I learned that the high expectancy of death, and the ability to face child death with stoicism and equanimity, produced patterns of nurturing that differentiated between those infants thought of as thrivers and survivors and those thought of as born already "wanting to die." The survivors were nurtured, while stigmatized, doomed infants were left to die, as mothers say, a mingua, "of neglect." Mothers stepped back and allowed nature to take its course. This pattern, which I call mortal selective neglect, is called passive infanticide by anthropologist Marvin Harris. The Alto situation, although culturally specific in the form that it takes, is not unique to Third World shantytown communities and may have its correlates in our own impoverished urban communities in some cases of "failure to thrive" infants.

I use as an example the story of Zezinho, the thirteen-month-old toddler of one of my neighbors, Lourdes. I became involved with Zezinho when I was called in to help Lourdes in the delivery of another child, this one a fair and robust little tyke with a lusty cry. I noted that while Lourdes showed great interest in the newborn, she totally ignored Zezinho who, wasted and severely malnourished, was curled up in a fetal position on a piece of urine- and feces-soaked cardboard placed under his mother's hammock. Eyes open and vacant, mouth slack, the little boy seemed doomed.

When I carried Zezinho up to the community day-care center at the top of the hill, the Alto women who took turns caring for one another's children (in order to free themselves for part-time work in the cane fields or washing clothes) laughed at my efforts to save Ze, agreeing with Lourdes that here was a baby without a ghost of a chance. Leave him alone, they cautioned. It makes no sense to fight with death. But I did do battle with Ze, and after several weeks of force-feeding (malnourished babies lose their interest in food), Ze began to succumb to my ministrations. He acquired some flesh across his taut chest bones, learned to sit up, and even tried to smile. When he seemed well enough, I returned him to Lourdes in her miserable scrap-material lean-to, but not without guilt about what I had done. I wondered whether returning Ze was at all fair to Lourdes and to his little brother. But I was busy and washed my hands of the matter. And Lourdes did seem more interested in Ze now that he was looking more human.

When I returned in 1982, there was Lourdes among the women who formed my sample of Alto mothers—still struggling to put together some semblance of life for a now grown Ze and her five other surviving children. Much was made of my reunion with Ze in 1982, and everyone enjoyed retelling the story of Ze's rescue and of how his mother had given him up for dead. Ze would laugh the loudest when told how I had had to force-feed him like a fiesta turkey. There was no hint of guilt on the part of Lourdes and no resentment on the part of Ze. In fact, when questioned in private as to who was the best friend he ever had in life, Ze took a long drag on his cigarette and answered without a trace of irony, "Why my mother, of course." "But of course," I replied.

Part of learning how to mother in the Alto do Cruzeiro is learning when to let go of a child who shows that it "wants" to die or that it has no "knack" or no "taste" for life. Another part is learning when it is safe to let oneself love a child. Frequent child death remains a powerful shaper of maternal thinking and practice. In the absence of firm expectation that a child will survive, mother love as we conceptualize it (whether in popular terms or in the psychobiological notion of maternal bonding) is attenuated and delayed with consequences for infant survival. In an environment already precarious to young life, the emotional detachment of mothers toward some of their babies contributes even further to the spiral of high mortality—high fertility in a kind of macabre lock-step dance of death.

The average woman of the Alto experiences 9.5 pregnancies, 3.5 child deaths, and 1.5 stillbirths. Seventy percent of all child deaths in the Alto occur in the first six months of life, and 82 percent by the end of the first year. Of all deaths in the community each year, about 45 percent are of children under the age of five.

Women of the Alto distinguish between child deaths understood as natural (caused by diarrhea and communicable diseases) and those resulting from sorcery, the evil eye, or other magical or supernatural afflictions. They also recognize a large category of infant deaths seen as fated and inevitable. These hopeless cases are classified by mothers under the folk terminology "child sickness" or "child attack." Women say that there are at least fourteen different types of hopeless child sickness, but most can be subsumed under two categories—chronic and acute. The chronic cases refer to infants who are born small and wasted. They are deathly pale, mothers say, as well as weak and passive. They demonstrate no vital force, no liveliness. They do not suck vigorously; they hardly cry. Such babies can be this way at birth or they can be born sound but soon show no resistance, no "fight" against the common crises of infancy: diarrhea, respiratory infections, tropical fevers.

The acute cases are those doomed infants who die suddenly and violently. They are taken by stealth overnight, often following convulsions that bring on head banging, shaking, grimacing, and shrieking. Women say it is horrible to look at such a baby. If the infant begins to foam at the mouth or gnash its teeth or go rigid with its eyes turned back inside its head, there is absolutely no hope. The infant is "put aside"—left alone—often on the floor in a back room, and allowed to die. These symptoms (which accompany high fevers, dehydration, third-stage malnutrition, and encephalitis) are equated by Alto women with madness, epilepsy, and worst of all, rabies, which is greatly feared and highly stigmatized.

Most of the infants presented to me as suffering from chronic child sickness were tiny, wasted famine victims, while those labeled as victims of acute child attack seemed to be infants suffering from the deliriums of high fever or the convulsions that can accompany electrolyte imbalance in dehydrated babies.

Local midwives and traditional healers, praying women, as they are called, advise Alto women on when to allow a baby to die. One midwife explained: "If I can see that a baby was born unfortuitously, I tell the mother that she need not wash the infant or give it a cleansing tea. I tell her just to dust the infant with baby powder and wait for it to die." Allowing nature to take its course is not seen as sinful by these often very devout Catholic women. Rather, it is understood as cooperating with God's plan.

Often I have been asked how consciously women of the Alto behave in this regard. I would have to say that consciousness is always shifting between allowed and disallowed levels of awareness. For example, I was awakened early one morning in 1987 by two neighborhood children who had been sent to fetch me to a hastily organized wake for a two-month-old infant whose mother I had unsuccessfully urged to breast-feed. The infant was being sustained on sugar water, which the mother referred to as *soro* (serum), using a medical term for the infant's starvation regime in light of his chronic diarrhea. I had cautioned the mother that an infant could not live on *soro* forever.

The two girls urged me to console the young mother by telling her that it was "too bad" that her infant was so weak that Jesus had to take him. They were coaching me in proper Alto etiquette. I agreed, of course, but asked, "And what do *you* think?" Xoxa, the eleven-year-old, looked down at her dusty flip-flops and blurted out, "Oh, Dona Nanci, that baby never got enough to eat, but you must never say that!" And so the death of hungry babies remains one of the best kept secrets of life in Bom Jesus da Mata.

Most victims are waked quickly and with a minimum of ceremony. No tears are shed, and the neighborhood children form a tiny procession, carrying the baby to the town graveyard where it will join a multitude of others. Although a few fresh flowers may be scattered over the tiny grave, no stone or wooden cross will mark the place, and the same spot will be reused within a few months' time. The mother will never visit the grave, which soon becomes an anonymous one.

What, then, can be said of these women? What emotions, what sentiments motivate them? How are they able to do what, in fact, must be done? What does mother love mean in this inhospitable context? Are grief, mourning, and melancholia present, although deeply repressed? If so, where shall we look for them? And if not, how are we to understand the moral visions and moral sensibilities that guide their actions?

I have been criticized more than once for presenting an unflattering portrait of poor Brazilian women, women who are, after all, themselves the victims of severe social and institutional neglect. I have described these women as allowing some of their children to die, as if this were an unnatural and inhuman act rather than, as I would assert, the way any one of us might act, reasonably and rationally, under similarly desperate conditions. Perhaps I have not emphasized enough the real pathogens in this environment of high risk: poverty, deprivation, sexism, chronic hunger, and economic exploitation. If mother love is, as many psychologists and some feminists believe, a seemingly natural and universal maternal script, what does it mean to women for whom scarcity, loss, sickness, and deprivation have made that love frantic and robbed them of their grief, seeming to turn their hearts to stone?

Throughout much of human history—as in a great deal of the impoverished Third World today—women have had to give birth and to nurture children under ecological conditions and social arrangements hostile to child survival, as well as to their own well-being. Under circumstances of high childhood mortality, patterns of selective neglect and passive infanticide may be seen as active survival strategies.

They also seem to be fairly common practices historically and across cultures. In societies characterized by high childhood mortality and by a correspondingly high (replacement) fertility, cultural practices of infant and child care tend to be organized primarily around survival goals. But what this means is a pragmatic recognition that not all of one's children can be expected to live. The nervousness about child survival in areas of northeast Brazil, northern India, or Bangladesh, where a 30 percent or 40 percent mortality rate in the first years of life is common, can lead to forms of delayed attachment and a casual or benign neglect that serves to weed out the worst

bets so as to enhance the life chances of healthier siblings, including those yet to be born. Practices similar to those that I am describing have been recorded for parts of Africa, India, and Central America.

Life in the Alto do Cruzeiro resembles nothing so much as a battlefield or an emergency room in an overcrowded inner-city public hospital. Consequently, morality is guided by a kind of "lifeboat ethics," the morality of triage. The seemingly studied indifference toward the suffering of some of their infants, conveyed in such sayings as "little critters have no feelings," is understandable in light of these women's obligation to carry on with their reproductive and nurturing lives.

In their slowness to anthropomorphize and personalize their infants, everything is mobilized so as to prevent maternal overattachment and, therefore, grief at death. The bereaved mother is told not to cry, that her tears will dampen the wings of her little angel so that she cannot fly up to her heavenly home. Grief at the death of an angel is not only inappropriate, it is a symptom of madness and of a profound lack of faith.

Infant death becomes routine in an environment in which death is anticipated and bets are hedged. While the routinization of death in the context of shantytown life is not hard to understand, and quite possible to empathize with, its routinization in the formal institutions of public life in Bom Jesus is not as easy to accept uncritically. Here the social production of indifference takes on a different, even a malevolent, cast.

In a society where triplicates of every form are required for the most banal events (registering a car, for example), the registration of infant and child death is informal, incomplete, and rapid. It requires no documentation, takes less than five minutes, and demands no witnesses other than office clerks. No questions are asked concerning the circumstances of the death, and the cause of death is left blank, unquestioned and unexamined. A neighbor, grandmother, older sibling, or common-law husband may register the

death. Since most infants die at home, there is no question of a medical record.

From the registry office, the parent proceeds to the town hall, where the mayor will give him or her a voucher for a free baby coffin. The full-time municipal coffinmaker cannot tell you exactly how many baby coffins are dispatched each week. It varies, he says, with the seasons. There are more needed during the drought months and during the big festivals of Carnaval and Christmas and São Joao's Day because people are too busy, he supposes, to take their babies to the clinic. Record keeping is sloppy.

Similarly, there is a failure on the part of city-employed doctors working at two free clinics to recognize the malnutrition of babies who are weighed, measured, and immunized without comment and as if they were not, in fact, anemic, stunted, fussy, and irritated starvation babies. At best the mothers are told to pick up free vitamins or a health "tonic" at the municipal chambers. At worst, clinic personnel will give tranquilizers and sleeping pills to quiet the hungry cries of "sick-to-death" Alto babies.

The church, too, contributes to the routinization of, and indifference toward, child death. Traditionally, the local Catholic church taught patience and resignation to domestic tragedies that were said to reveal the imponderable workings of God's will. If an infant died suddenly, it was because a particular saint had claimed the child. The infant would be an angel in the service of his or her heavenly patron. It would be wrong, a sign of a lack of faith, to weep for a child with such good fortune. The infant funeral was, in the past, an event celebrated with joy. Today, however, under the new regime of "liberation theology," the bells of N. S. das Dores parish church no longer peal for the death of Alto babies, and no priest accompanies the procession of angels to the cemetery where their bodies are disposed of casually and without ceremony. Children bury children in Bom Jesus da Mata. In this most Catholic of communities, the coffin is handed to the disabled and irritable municipal gravedigger, who often chides the children for one reason or another. It may be that the coffin is larger than expected and the gravedigger can find no appropriate space. The children do not wait for the gravedigger to complete his task. No prayers are recited and no sign of the cross made as the tiny coffin goes into its shallow grave.

When I asked the local priest, Padre Marcos, about the lack of church ceremony surrounding infant and childhood death today in Bom Jesus, he replied: "In the old days, child death was richly celebrated. But those were the baroque customs of a conservative church that wallowed in death and misery. The new church is a church of hope and joy. We no longer celebrate the death of child angels. We try to tell mothers that Jesus doesn't want all the dead babies they send him." Similarly, the new church has changed its baptismal customs, now often refusing to baptize dying babies brought to the back door of a church or rectory. The mothers are scolded by the church attendants and told to go home and take care of their sick babies. Baptism, they are told, is for the living; it is not to be confused with the sacrament of extreme unction, which is the anointing of the dying. And so it appears to the women of the Alto that even the church has turned away from them, denying the traditional comfort of folk Catholicism.

The contemporary Catholic church is caught in the clutches of a double bind. The new theology of liberation imagines a kingdom of God on earth based on justice and equality, a world without hunger, sickness, or childhood mortality. At the same time, the church has not changed its official position on sexuality and reproduction, including its sanctions against birth control, abortion, and sterilization. The padre of Bom Jesus da Mata recognizes this contradiction intuitively, although he shies away from discussions on the topic, saying that he prefers to leave questions of family planning to the discretion and the "good consciences" of his impoverished parishioners. But this, of course, sidesteps the extent to which those good consciences have been shaped by traditional church teachings in Bom Jesus, especially by his recent predecessors. Hence, we can begin to see that the seeming indifference of Alto mothers toward the death of some of their infants is but a pale reflection of the official indifference of church and state to the plight of poor women and children.

Nonetheless, the women of Bom Jesus are survivors. One woman, Biu, told me her life history, returning again and again to the themes of child death, her first husband's suicide, abandonment by her father and later by her second husband, and all the other losses and disappointments she had suffered in her long forty-five years. She concluded with great force, reflecting on the days of Carnaval '88 that were fast approaching:

No, Dona Nanci, I won't cry, and I won't waste my life thinking about it from morning to night. . . . Can I argue with God for the state that I'm in? No! And so I'll dance and I'll jump and I'll play Carnaval! And yes, I'll laugh and people will wonder at a *pobre* like me who can have such a good time.

And no one did blame Biu for dancing in the streets during the four days of Carnaval—not even on Ash Wednesday, the day following Carnaval '88 when we all assembled hurriedly to assist in the burial of Mercea, Biu's beloved *casula,* her last-born daughter who had died at home of pneumonia during the festivities. The rest of the family barely had time to change out of their costumes. Severino, the child's uncle and godfather, sprinkled holy water over the little angel while he prayed: "Mercea, I don't know whether you were called, taken, or thrown out of this world. But look down at us from your heavenly home with tenderness, with pity, and with mercy." So be it.

Arranging a Marriage in India

Serena Nanda

John Jay College of Criminal Justice

Sister and doctor brother-in-law invite correspondence from North Indian professionals only, for a beautiful, talented, sophisticated, intelligent sister, 5′ 3″, slim, M.A. in textile design, father a senior civil officer. Would prefer immigrant doctors, between 26–29 years. Reply with full details and returnable photo.

A well-settled uncle invites matrimonial correspondence from slim, fair, educated South Indian girl, for his nephew, 25 years, smart, M.B.A., green card holder, 5′ 6″. Full particulars with returnable photo appreciated.

Matrimonial Advertisements,
India Abroad

In India, almost all marriages are arranged. Even among the educated middle classes in modern, urban India, marriage is as much a concern of the families as it is of the individuals. So customary is the practice of arranged marriage that there is a special name for a marriage which is not arranged: It is called a "love match."

On my first field trip to India, I met many young men and women whose parents were in the process of "getting them married." In many cases, the bride and groom would not meet each other before the marriage. At most they might meet for a brief conversation, and this meeting would take place only after their parents had decided that the match was suitable. Parents do not compel their children to marry a person who either marriage partner finds objectionable. But only after one match is refused will another be sought.

As a young American woman in India for the first time, I found this custom of arranged marriage oppressive. How could any intelligent young person agree to such a marriage without great reluctance? It was contrary to everything I believed about the importance of romantic love as the only basis of a happy marriage. It also clashed with my strongly held notions that the choice of such an intimate and permanent relationship could be made only by the individuals involved. Had anyone tried to arrange my marriage, I would have been defiant and rebellious!

At the first opportunity, I began, with more curiosity than tact, to question the young people I met on how they felt about this practice. Sita, one of my young informants, was a college graduate with a degree in political science. She had been waiting for over a year while her parents were arranging a match for her. I found it difficult to accept the docile manner in which this well-educated young woman awaited the outcome of a process that would result in her spending the rest of her life with a man she hardly knew, a virtual stranger, picked out by her parents.

"How can you go along with this?" I asked her, in frustration and distress. "Don't you care who you marry?"

"Of course I care," she answered. "This is why I must let my parents choose a boy for me. My marriage is too important to be arranged by such an inexperienced person as myself. In such matters, it is better to have my parents' guidance."

I had learned that young men and women in India do not date and have very little social life involving members of the opposite sex. Although I could not disagree with Sita's reasoning, I continued to pursue the subject.

"But how can you marry the first man you have ever met? Not only have you missed the fun of meeting a lot of different people, but you have not given yourself the chance to know who is the right man for you."

"Meeting with a lot of different people doesn't sound like any fun at all," Sita answered. "One hears that in America the girls are spending all their time worrying about whether they will meet a man and get married. Here we have the chance to enjoy our life and let our parents do this work and worrying for us."

She had me there. The high anxiety of the competition to "be popular" with the opposite sex certainly was the most prominent feature of life as an American teenager in the late fifties. The endless worrying about the rules that governed our behavior and about our popularity ratings sapped both our self-esteem and our enjoyment of adolescence. I reflected that absence of this competition in India most certainly may have contributed to the self-confidence and natural charm of so many of the young women I met.

And yet, the idea of marrying a perfect stranger, whom one did not know and did not "love," so offended my American ideas of individualism and romanticism, that I persisted with my objections.

"I still can't imagine it," I said. "How can you agree to marry a man you hardly know?"

"But of course he will be known. My parents would never arrange a marriage for me without knowing all about the boy's family background. Naturally we will not rely only on what the family tells us. We will check the particulars out ourselves. No one will want their daughter to marry into a family that is not good. All these things we will know beforehand."

Impatiently, I responded, "Sita, I don't mean know the family, I mean, know the man. How can you marry someone you don't know personally and don't love? How can you think of spending your life with someone you may not even like?"

"If he is a good man, why should I not like him?" she said. "With you people, you know the boy so well before you marry, where will be the fun to get married? There will be no mystery and no romance. Here we have the whole of our married life to get to know and love our husband. This way is better, is it not?"

Her response made further sense, and I began to have second thoughts on the matter. Indeed, during months of

meeting many intelligent young Indian people, both male and female, who had the same ideas as Sita, I saw arranged marriages in a different light. I also saw the importance of the family in Indian life and realized that a couple who took their marriage into their own hands was taking a big risk, particularly if their families were irreconcilably opposed to the match. In a country where every important resource in life—a job, a house, a social circle—is gained through family connections, it seemed foolhardy to cut oneself off from a supportive social network and depend solely on one person for happiness and success.

Six years later I returned to India to again do fieldwork, this time among the middle class in Bombay, a modern, sophisticated city. From the experience of my earlier visit, I decided to include a study of arranged marriages in my project. By this time I had met many Indian couples whose marriages had been arranged and who seemed very happy. Particularly in contrast to the fate of many of my married friends in the United States who were already in the process of divorce, the positive aspects of arranged marriages appeared to me to outweigh the negatives. In fact, I thought I might even participate in arranging a marriage myself. I had been fairly successful in the United States in "fixing up" many of my friends, and I was confident that my matchmaking skills could be easily applied to this new situation, once I learned the basic rules. "After all," I thought, "how complicated can it be? People want pretty much the same things in a marriage whether it is in India or America."

An opportunity presented itself almost immediately. A friend from my previous Indian trip was in the process of arranging for the marriage of her eldest son. In India there is a perceived shortage of "good boys," and since my friend's family was eminently respectable and the boy himself personable, well educated, and nice looking, I was sure that by the end of my year's fieldwork, we would have found a match.

The basic rule seems to be that a family's reputation is most important.

It is understood that matches would be arranged only within the same caste and general social class, although some crossing of subcastes is permissible if the class positions of the bride's and groom's families are similar. Although dowry is now prohibited by law in India, extensive gift exchanges took place with every marriage. Even when the boy's family do not "make demands," every girl's family nevertheless feels the obligation to give the traditional gifts, to the girl, to the boy, and to the boy's family. Particularly when the couple would be living in the joint family—that is, with the boy's parents and his married brothers and their families, as well as with unmarried siblings—which is still very common even among the urban, upper-middle class in India, the girl's parents are anxious to establish smooth relations between their family and that of the boy. Offering the proper gifts, even when not called "dowry," is often an important factor in influencing the relationship between the bride's and groom's families and perhaps, also, the treatment of the bride in her new home.

In a society where divorce is still a scandal and where, in fact, the divorce rate is exceedingly low, an arranged marriage is the beginning of a lifetime relationship not just between the bride and groom but between their families as well. Thus, while a girl's looks are important, her character is even more so, for she is being judged as a prospective daughter-in-law as much as a prospective bride. Where she would be living in a joint family, as was the case with my friend, the girl's ability to get along harmoniously in a family is perhaps the single most important quality in assessing her suitability.

My friend is a highly esteemed wife, mother, and daughter-in-law. She is religious, soft-spoken, modest, and deferential. She rarely gossips and never quarrels, two qualities highly desirable in a woman. A family that has the reputation for gossip and conflict among its womenfolk will not find it easy to get good wives for their sons. Parents will not want to send their daughter to a house in which there is conflict.

My friend's family were originally from North India. They had lived in Bombay, where her husband owned a business, for forty years. The family had delayed in seeking a match for their eldest son because he had been an Air Force pilot for several years, stationed in such remote places that it had seemed fruitless to try to find a girl who would be willing to accompany him. In their social class, a military career, despite its economic security, has little prestige and is considered a drawback in finding a suitable bride. Many families would not allow their daughters to marry a man in an occupation so potentially dangerous and which requires so much moving around.

The son had recently left the military and joined his father's business. Since he was a college graduate, modern, and well traveled, from such a good family, and, I thought, quite handsome, it seemed to me that he, or rather his family, was in a position to pick and choose. I said as much to my friend.

While she agreed that there were many advantages on their side, she also said, "We must keep in mind that my son is both short and dark; these are drawbacks in finding the right match." While the boy's height had not escaped my notice, "dark" seemed to me inaccurate; I would have called him "wheat" colored perhaps, and in any case, I did not realize that color would be a consideration. I discovered, however, that while a boy's skin color is a less important consideration than a girl's, it is still a factor.

An important source of contacts in trying to arrange her son's marriage was my friend's social club in Bombay. Many of the women had daughters of the right age, and some had already expressed an interest in my friend's son. I was most enthusiastic about the possibilities of one particular family who had five daughters, all of whom were pretty, demure, and well educated. Their mother had told my friend, "You can have your pick for your son, whichever one of my daughters appeals to you most."

I saw a match in sight. "Surely," I said to my friend, "we will find one there. Let's go visit and make our choice." But my friend held back; she did not seem to share my enthusiasm, for reasons I could not then fathom.

When I kept pressing for an explanation of her reluctance, she admitted, "See, Serena, here is the problem. The family has so many daughters, how will they be able to provide nicely for any of them? We are not making any demands, but still, with so many daughters to marry off, one wonders whether she will even be able to make a proper wedding. Since this is our eldest son, it's best if we marry him to a girl who is the only daughter, then the wedding will truly be a gala affair." I argued that surely the quality of the girls themselves made up for any deficiency in the elaborateness of the wedding. My friend admitted this point but still seemed reluctant to proceed.

"Is there something else," I asked her, "some factor I have missed?" "Well," she finally said, "there is one other thing. They have one daughter already married and living in Bombay. The mother is always complaining to me that the girl's in-laws don't let her visit her own family often enough. So it makes me wonder, will she be that kind of mother who always wants her daughter at her own home? This will prevent the girl from adjusting to our house. It is not a good thing." And so, this family of five daughters was dropped as a possibility.

Somewhat disappointed, I nevertheless respected my friend's reasoning and geared up for the next prospect. This was also the daughter of a woman in my friend's social club. There was clear interest in this family and I could see why. The family's reputation was excellent; in fact, they came from a subcaste slightly higher than my friend's own. The girl, who was an only daughter, was pretty and well educated and had a brother studying in the United States. Yet, after expressing an interest to me in this family, all talk of them suddenly died down and the search began elsewhere.

"What happened to that girl as a prospect?" I asked one day. "You

Even today, almost all marriages in India are arranged. It is believed that parents are much more effective at deciding who their daughters should marry.

never mention her any more. She is so pretty and so educated, what did you find wrong?"

"She is too educated. We've decided against it. My husband's father saw the girl on the bus the other day and thought her forward. A girl who 'roams about' the city by herself is not the girl for our family." My disappointment this time was even greater, as I thought the son would have liked the girl very much. But then I thought, my friend is right, a girl who is going to live in a joint family cannot be too independent or she will make life miserable for everyone. I also learned that if the family of the girl has even a slightly higher social status than the family of the boy, the bride may think herself too good for them, and this too will cause problems. Later my friend admitted to me that this had been an important factor in her decision not to pursue the match.

The next candidate was the daughter of a client of my friend's husband. When the client learned that the family was looking for a match for their son, he said, "Look no further, we have a daughter." This man then invited my friends to dinner to see the girl. He had already seen their son at the office and decided that "he liked the boy." We all went together for tea, rather than dinner—it was less of a commitment—and while we were there, the girl's mother showed us around the house. The girl was studying for her exams and was briefly introduced to us.

After we left, I was anxious to hear my friend's opinion. While her husband liked the family very much and was impressed with his client's business accomplishments and reputation, the wife didn't like the girl's looks. "She is short, no doubt, which is an important plus point, but she is also fat and wears glasses." My friend obviously thought she could do better for her son and asked her husband to make his excuses to his client by saying that they had decided to postpone the boy's marriage indefinitely.

By this time almost six months had passed and I was becoming impatient. What I had thought would be an easy matter to arrange was turning out to be quite complicated. I began to believe that between my friend's desire for a girl who was modest enough to fit into her joint family, yet attractive and educated enough to be an acceptable partner for her son, she would not find anyone suitable. My friend laughed at my impatience: "Don't be so much in a hurry," she said. "You Americans want everything done so quickly. You get married quickly and then just as quickly get divorced. Here we take marriage more seriously. We must take all the factors into account. It is not enough for us to learn by our mistakes. This is too serious a business. If a mistake is made we have not only ruined the life of our son or daughter, but we have spoiled the reputation of our family as well. And that will make it much harder for their brothers and sisters to get married. So we must be very careful."

What she said was true. and I promised myself to be more patient, though it was not easy. I had really hoped and expected that the match would be made before my year in India was up. But it was not to be. When I left India my friend seemed no further along in finding a suitable match for her son than when I had arrived.

Two years later, I returned to India and still my friend had not found a girl for her son. By this time, he was close to thirty, and I think she was a little worried. Since she knew I had friends all over India, and I was going to be there for a year, she asked me to "help her in this work" and keep an eye out for someone suitable. I was flattered that my judgment was respected, but knowing now how complicated the process was, I had lost my earlier confidence as a matchmaker. Nevertheless, I promised that I would try.

It was almost at the end of my year's stay in India that I met a family with a marriageable daughter whom I felt might be a good possibility for my friend's son. The girl's father was related to a good friend of mine and by coincidence came from the same village as my friend's husband. This new family had a successful business in a medium-sized city in central India and were from the same subcaste as my friend. The daughter was pretty and chic; in fact, she had studied fashion design in college. Her parents would not allow her to go off by herself to any of the major cities in India where she could make a career, but they had compromised with her wish to work by allowing her to run a small dressmaking boutique from their home. In spite of her desire to have a career, the daughter was both modest and home-loving and had had a traditional, sheltered upbringing. She had only one other sister, already married, and a brother who was in his father's business.

I mentioned the possibility of a match with my friend's son. The girl's parents were most interested. Although their daughter was not eager to marry just yet, the idea of living in Bombay—a sophisticated, extremely fashion-conscious city where she could continue her education in clothing design—was a great inducement. I gave the girl's father my friend's address and suggested that when they went to Bombay on some business or whatever, they look up the boy's family.

Returning to Bombay on my way to New York, I told my friend of this newly discovered possibility. She seemed to feel there was potential but, in spite of my urging, would not make any moves herself. She rather preferred to wait for the girl's family to call upon them. I hoped something would come of this introduction, though by now I had learned to rein in my optimism.

A year later I received a letter from my friend. The family had indeed come to visit Bombay, and their daughter and my friend's daughter, who were near in age, had become very good friends. During that year, the two girls had frequently visited each other. I thought things looked promising.

Last week I received an invitation to a wedding: My friend's son and the girl were getting married. Since I had found the match, my presence was particularly requested at the wedding. I was thrilled. Success at last! As I prepared to leave for India, I began thinking, "Now, my friend's younger son, who do I know who has a nice girl for him . . .?"

Gender and Status

The feminist movement in the United States has had a significant impact upon the development of anthropology. Feminists have rightly charged that anthropologists have tended to gloss over the lives of women in studies of society and culture. In part, this is because, up until recent times, most anthropologists have been men. The result has been an undue emphasis upon male activities as well as male perspectives in descriptions of particular societies.

These changes, however, have proven to be a firm corrective. In the last few years, anthropologists have begun to study women and, more particularly, the sexual division of labor and its relation to biology as well as to social and political status. In addition, these changes in emphasis have been accompanied by an increase in the number of women in the field.

Feminist anthropologists have begun to critically attack many of the established anthropological truths. They have shown, for example, that field studies of nonhuman primates, which were often used to demonstrate the evolutionary basis of male dominance, distorted the actual evolutionary record by focusing primarily on baboons. (Male baboons are especially dominant and aggressive.) Other, less-quoted primate studies show how dominance and aggression are highly situational phenomena, sensitive to ecological variation. Feminist anthropologists have also shown that the subsistence contribution of women has likewise been ignored by anthropologists. A classic case is that of the !Kung, a hunting and gathering people in Southern Africa, where women provide the bulk of the foodstuffs, including most of the available protein, and who, not coincidentally, enjoy a more egalitarian relationship with men. Even when the issue has to do with premarital virginity for women, Alice Schlegel (in "Status, Property, and the Value on Virginity") shows that the concern for biological paternity may have more to do with maintaining or enhancing a family's social status than with male domination per se.

The most common occurrence, at least in recent history, has been male domination over women. Recent studies have concerned themselves with why there has been such gender inequality. Although the subordination of women can be extreme (as seen in "The Little Emperors" by Daniela Deane), Ernestine Friedl, in "Society and Sex Roles," explains that the sex that controls the valued goods of exchange in a society is the dominant gender and, since this is a matter of cultural variation, male authority is not biologically predetermined. Indeed, women have played visibly prominent roles in many cultures, as addressed in "Yellow Woman and a Beauty of the Spirit." Even so, sexual equality is still far from being a reality in many parts of the world (see "The War against Women"), and, as we are shown in "The Initiation of a Maasai Warrior" and in "Female Circumcision," gender relationships are deeply embedded in social experience.

Looking Ahead: Challenge Questions

What is it about foraging societies that encourages an egalitarian relationship between the sexes? Why are the Eskimos an exception?

What kinds of shifts in the social relations of production are necessary for women to achieve equality with men?

What was meant by "beauty" in the old-time Pueblo culture?

How and why is diversity valued in Pueblo culture?

What are bridewealth and dowry and under what circumstances do they occur?

How does female circumcision differ from male circumcision in terms of its social functions?

What kinds of personal dilemmas do women face in a changing society?

What kinds of historical, religious, and legal legacies have contributed to violence against women around the world?

How may a culture's political and religious ideology serve to justify sex role differences?

What have been the unforeseen consequences of China's one-child policy?

Does China's one-child policy represent the wave of the future for the world?

Society and Sex Roles

Ernestine Friedl

Ernestine Friedl is a professor of anthropology at Duke University; a former president of the American Anthropological Association, a fellow of the American Academy of Arts and Sciences, and an advisory editor to Human Nature. She received her Ph.D. from Columbia University in 1950. Until recently, Friedl was a firm believer in the relative equality of women in the field of anthropology and had little interest in the anthropological study of women. None of her field work among the Pomo and Chippewa Indians of North America, or in rural and urban Greece was concerned with women's issues.

In the early 1970s, while serving on the American Anthropological Association Committee on the Status of Women, Friedl became convinced that women were discriminated against as much in anthropology as in the other academic disciplines. Since that time, she has devoted her efforts to the cross-cultural study of sex roles and has written one book on the topic, Women and Men: An Anthropologist's View. *Friedl now accounts for her own success in part by the fact that she attended an all-women's college and taught for many years at the City University of New York, a university system that included a women's college.*

"Women must respond quickly to the demands of their husbands," says anthropologist Napoleon Chagnon describing the horticultural Yanomamo Indians of Venezuela. When a man returns from a hunting trip, "the woman, no matter what she is doing, hurries home and quietly but rapidly prepares a meal for her husband. Should the wife be slow in doing this, the husband is within his rights to beat her. Most reprimands...take the form of blows with the hand or with a piece of firewood. . . .Some of them chop their wives with the sharp edge of a machete or axe, or shoot them with a barbed arrow in some nonvital area, such as the buttocks or leg."

Among the Semai agriculturalists of central Malaya, when one person refuses the request of another, the offended party suffers *punan,* a mixture of emotional pain and frustration. "Enduring *punan* is commonest when a girl has refused the victim her sexual favors," reports Robert Dentan. "The jilted man's 'heart becomes sad.' He loses his energy and his appetite. Much of the time he sleeps, dreaming of his lost love. In this state, he is in fact very likely to injure himself 'accidentally.' " The Semai are afraid of violence; a man would never strike a woman.

The social relationship between men and women has emerged as one of the principal disputes occupying the attention of scholars and the public in recent years. Athough the discord is sharpest in the United States, the controversy has spread throughout the world. Numerous national and international conferences, including one in Mexico sponsored by the United Nations, have drawn together delegates from all walks of life to discuss such questions as the social and political rights of each sex, and even the basic nature of males and females.

Whatever their position, partisans often invoke examples from other cultures to support their ideas about the proper role of each sex. Because women are clearly subservient to men in many societies, like the Yanomamo, some experts conclude that the natural pattern is for men to dominate. But among the Semai no one has the right to command others, and in West Africa women are often chiefs. The place of women in these societies supports the argument of those who believe that sex roles are not fixed, that if there is a natural order, it allows for many different arrangements.

The argument will never be settled as long as the opposing sides toss examples from the world's cultures at each other like intellectual stones. But the effect of biological differences on male and female behavior can be clarified by looking at known examples of the earliest forms of human society and examining the relationship between technology, social organization, environment, and

From *Human Nature* magazine, April 1978. © 1978 by Human Nature, Inc. Reprinted by permission of Harcourt Brace & Company.

sex roles. The problem is to determine the conditions in which different degrees of male dominance are found, to try to discover the social and cultural arrangements that give rise to equality or inequality between the sexes, and to attempt to apply this knowledge to our understanding of the changes taking place in modern industrial society.

As Western history and the anthropological record have told us, equality between the sexes is rare; in most known societies females are subordinate. Male dominance is so widespread that it is virtually a human universal; societies in which women are consistently dominant do not exist and have never existed.

Evidence of a society in which women control all strategic resources like food and water, and in which women's activities are the most prestigious has never been found. The Iroquois of North America and the Lovedu of Africa came closest. Among the Iroquois, women raised food, controlled its distribution, and helped to choose male political leaders. Lovedu women ruled as queens, exchanged valuable cattle, led ceremonies, and controlled their own sex lives. But among both the Iroquois and the Lovedu, men owned the land and held other positions of power and prestige. Women were equal to men; they did not have ultimate authority over them. Neither culture was a true matriarchy.

Patriarchies are prevalent, and they appear to be strongest in societies in which men control significant goods that are exchanged with people outside the family. Regardless of who produces food, the person who gives it to others creates the obligations and alliances that are at the center of all political relations. The greater the male monopoly on the distribution of scarce items, the stronger their control of women seems to be. This is most obvious in relatively simple hunter-gatherer societies.

Hunter-gatherers, or foragers, subsist on wild plants, small land animals, and small river or sea creatures gathered by hand; large land animals and sea mammals hunted

with spears, bows and arrows, and blow guns; and fish caught with hooks and nets. The 300,000 hunter-gatherers alive in the world today include the Eskimos, the Australian aborigines, and the Pygmies of Central Africa.

Foraging has endured for two million years and was replaced by farming and animal husbandry only 10,000 years ago; it covers more than 99 percent of human history. Our foraging ancestry is not far behind us and provides a clue to our understanding of the human condition.

Hunter-gatherers are people whose ways of life are technologically simple and socially and politically egalitarian. They live in small groups of 50 to 200 and have neither kings, nor priests, nor social classes. These conditions permit anthropologists to observe the essential bases for inequalities between the sexes without the distortions induced by the complexities of contemporary industrial society.

The source of male power among hunter-gatherers lies in their control of a scarce, hard to acquire, but necessary nutrient—animal protein. When men in a hunter-gatherer society return to camp with game, they divide the meat in some customary way. Among the !Kung San of Africa, certain parts of the animal are given to the owner of the arrow that killed the beast, to the first hunter to sight the game, to the one who threw the first spear and to all men in the hunting party. After the meat has been divided, each hunter distributes his share to his blood relatives and his in-laws, who in turn share it with others. If an animal is large enough, every member of the band will receive some meat.

Vegetable foods, in contrast, are not distributed beyond the immediate household. Women give food to their children, to their husbands, to other members of the household, and rarely, to the occasional visitor. No one outside the family regularly eats any of the wild fruits and vegetables that are gathered by the women.

The meat distributed by the men is a public gift. Its source is widely

known, and the donor expects a reciprocal gift when other men return from a successful hunt. He gains honor as a supplier of a scarce item and simultaneously obligates others to him.

These obligations constitute a form of power or control over others, both men and women. The opinions of hunters play an important part in decisions to move the village; good hunters attract the most desirable women; people in other groups join camps with good hunters; and hunters, because they already participate in an internal system of exchange, control exchange with other groups for flint, salt, and steel axes. The male monopoly on hunting unites men in a system of exchange and gives them power; gathering vegetable food does not give women equal power even among foragers who live in the tropics, where the food collected by women provides more than half the hunter-gatherer diet.

If dominance arises from a monopoly on big-game hunting, why has the male monopoly remained unchallenged? Some women are strong enough to participate in the hunt and their endurance is certainly equal to that of men. Dobe San women of the Kalahari Desert in Africa walk an average of 10 miles a day carrying from 15 to 33 pounds of food plus a baby.

Women do not hunt, I believe, because of four interrelated factors: variability in the supply of game; the different skills required for hunting and gathering; the incompatibility between carrying burdens and hunting; and the small size of semi-nomadic foraging populations.

Because the meat supply is unstable, foragers must make frequent expeditions to provide the band with gathered food. Environmental factors such as seasonal and annual variation in rainful often affect the size of the wildlife population. Hunters cannot always find game, and when they do encounter animals, they are not always successful in killing their prey. In northern latitudes, where meat is the primary food, periods of starvation are known in every generation. The irregularity of the game supply leads hunter-gatherers in areas where plant foods are available to depend on these predictable foods a good part of the time. Someone must gather the fruits, nuts, and roots and carry them back to camp to feed unsuccessful hunters, children, the elderly, and anyone who might not have gone foraging that day.

Foraging falls to the women because hunting and gathering cannot be combined on the same expedition. Although gatherers sometimes notice signs of game as they work, the skills required to track game are not the same as those required to find edible roots or plants. Hunters scan the horizon and the land for traces of large game; gatherers keep their eyes to the ground, studying the distribution of plants and the texture of the soil for hidden roots and animal holes. Even if a woman who was collecting plants came across the track of an antelope, she could not follow it; it is impossible to carry a load and hunt at the same time. Running with a heavy load is difficult, and should the animal be sighted, the hunter would be off balance and could neither shoot an arrow nor throw a spear accurately.

Pregnancy and child care would also present difficulties for a hunter. An unborn child affects a woman's body balance, as does a child in her arms, on her back, or slung at her side. Until they are two years old, many hunter-gatherer children are carried at all times, and until they are four, they are carried some of the time.

An observer might wonder why young women do not hunt until they become pregnant, or why mature women and men do not hunt and gather on alternate days, with some women staying in camp to act as wet nurses for the young. Apart from the effects hunting might have on a mother's milk production, there are two reasons. First, young girls begin to bear children as soon as they are physically mature and strong enough to hunt, and second, hunter-gatherer bands are so small that there are unlikely to be enough lactating women to serve as wet nurses. No hunter-gatherer group could afford to maintain a specialized female hunting force.

Because game is not always available, because hunting and gathering are specialized skills, because women carrying heavy loads cannot hunt, and because women in hunter-gatherer societies are usually either pregnant or caring for young children, for most of the last two million years of human history men have hunted and women have gathered.

If male dominance depends on controlling the supply of meat, then the degree of male dominance in a society should vary with the amount of meat available and the amount supplied by the men. Some regions, like the East African grasslands and the North American woodlands, abounded with species of large mammals; other zones, like tropical forests and semi-deserts, are thinly populated with prey. Many elements affect the supply of game, but theoretically, the less meat provided exclusively by the men, the more egalitarian the society.

All known hunter-gatherer societies fit into four basic types; those in which men and women work together in communal hunts and as teams gathering edible plants, as did the Washo Indians of North America; those in which men and women each collect their own plant foods although the men supply some meat to the group, as do the Hadza of Tanzania; those in which male hunters and female gatherers work apart but return to camp each evening to share their acquisitions, as do the Tiwi of North Australia; and those in which the men provide all the food by hunting large game, as do the Eskimo. In each case the extent of male dominance increases directly with the proportion of meat supplied by individual men and small hunting parties.

Among the most egalitarian of hunter-gatherer societies are the Washo Indians, who inhabited the valleys of the Sierra Nevada in what is now southern California and Nevada. In the spring they moved north to Lake Tahoe for the large fish runs of sucker and native trout. Everyone—men, women, and children—participated in the fishing. Women spent the summer gathering edible berries and seeds while the men continued to fish. In the fall some men hunted deer but the most important source of animal protein was the jack rabbit, which was captured in communal hunts. Men and women together drove the rabbits into nets tied end to end. To provide food for the winter, husbands and wives worked as teams in the late fall to collect pine nuts.

Since everyone participated in most food-gathering activities, there were no individual distributors of food and relatively little difference in male and female rights. Men and women were not segregated from each other in daily activities; both were free to take lovers after marriage; both had the right to separate whenever they chose; menstruating women were not isolated from the rest of the group; and one of the two major Washo rituals celebrated hunting while the other celebrated gathering. Men were accorded more prestige if they had killed a deer, and men directed decisions about the seasonal movement of the group. But if no male leader stepped forward, women were permitted to lead. The distinctive feature of groups such as the Washo is the relative equality of the sexes.

The sexes are also relatively equal among the Hadza of Tanzania but this near-equality arises because men and women tend to work alone to feed themselves. They exchange little food. The Hadza lead a leisurely life in the seemingly barren environment of the East African Rift Gorge that is, in fact, rich in edible berries, roots, and small game. As a result of this abundance, from the time they are 10 years old, Hadza men and women gather much of their own food. Women take their young children with them into the bush, eating as they forage, and collect only enough food for a light family meal in the evening. The men eat berries and roots as they hunt for small game, and should they bring down a rabbit or a hyrax, they eat the meat on the spot. Meat is

In the maritime Inuit (Eskimo) societies, inequality between the sexes is matched by the ability to supply food for the group. The men hunt for meat and control the economy. Women perform all the other duties that support life in the community, and are virtually treated as objects. (Photo credit: American Museum of Natural History—Dr. F. Rainey)

carried back to the camp and shared with the rest of the group only on those rare occasions when a poisoned arrow brings down a large animal—an impala, a zebra, an eland, or a giraffe.

Because Hadza men distribute little meat, their status is only slightly higher than that of the women. People flock to the camp of a good hunter and the camp might take on his name because of his popularity, but he is in no sense a leader of the group. A Hadza man and a woman have an equal right to divorce and each can repudiate a marriage simply by living apart for a few weeks. Couples tend to live in the same camp as the wife's mother but they sometimes make long visits to the camp of the husband's mother. Although a man may take more than one wife, most Hadza males cannot afford to

indulge in this luxury. In order to maintain a marriage, a man must supply both his wife and his mother-in-law with some meat and trade goods, such as beads and cloth, and the Hadza economy gives few men the wealth to provide for more than one wife and mother-in-law. Washo equality is based on cooperation; Hadza equality is based on independence.

In contrast to both these groups, among the Tiwi of Melville and Bathurst Islands off the northern coast of Australia, male hunters dominate female gatherers. The Tiwi are representative of the most common form of foraging society, in which the men supply large quantities of meat, although less than half the food consumed by the group. Each morning Tiwi women, most with babies on

their backs, scatter in different directions in search of vegetables, grubs, worms, and small game such as bandicoots, lizards, and opossums. To track the game, they use hunting dogs. On most days women return to camp with some meat and with baskets full of *korka*, the nut of a native palm, which is soaked and mashed to make a porridge-like dish. The Tiwi men do not hunt small game and do not hunt every day, but when they do they often return with kangaroo, large lizards, fish, and game birds.

The porridge is cooked separately by each household and rarely shared outside the family, but the meat is prepared by a volunteer cook, who can be male or female. After the cook takes one of the parts of the animal traditionally reserved for him or her, the animal's "boss," the one who caught it, distributes the rest to all near kin and then to all others residing with the band. Although the small game supplied by the women is distributed in the same way as the big game supplied by the men, Tiwi men are dominant because the game they kill provides most of the meat.

The power of the Tiwi men is clearest in their betrothal practices. Among the Tiwi, a woman must always be married. To ensure this, female infants are betrothed at birth and widows are remarried at the gravesides of their late husbands. Men form alliances by exchanging daughters, sisters, and mothers in marriage and some collect as many as 25 wives. Tiwi men value the quantity and quality of the food many wives can collect and the many children they can produce.

The dominance of the men is offset somewhat by the influence of adult women in selecting their next husbands. Many women are active strategists in the political careers of their male relatives, but to the exasperation of some sons attempting to promote their own futures, widowed mothers sometimes insist on selecting their own partners. Women also influence the marriages of their daughters and granddaughters, especially when the selected husband dies before the bestowed child moves to his camp.

Among the Eskimo, representative of the rarest type of forager society, inequality between the sexes is matched by inequality in supplying the group with food. Inland Eskimo men hunt caribou throughout the year to provision the entire society, and maritime Eskimo men depend on whaling, fishing, and some hunting to feed their extended families. The women process the carcasses, cut and sew skins to make clothing, cook, and care for the young; but they collect no food of their own and depend on the men to supply all the raw materials for their work. Since men provide all the meat, they also control the trade in hides, whale oil, seal oil, and other items that move between the maritime and inland Eskimos.

Eskimo women are treated almost exclusively as objects to be used, abused, and traded by men. After puberty all Eskimo girls are fair game for any interested male. A man shows his intentions by grabbing the belt of a woman and if she protests, he cuts off her trousers and forces himself upon her. These encounters are considered unimportant by the rest of the group. Men offer their wives' sexual services to establish alliances with trading partners and members of hunting and whaling parties.

Despite the consistent pattern of some degree of male dominance among foragers, most of these societies are egalitarian compared with agricultural and industrial societies. No forager has any significant opportunity for political leadership. Foragers, as a rule, do not like to give or take orders, and assume leadership only with reluctance. Shamans (those who are thought to be possessed by spirits) may be either male or female. Public rituals conducted by women in order to celebrate the first menstruation of girls are common, and the symbolism in these rituals is similar to that in the ceremonies that follow a boy's first kill.

In any society, status goes to those who control the distribution of valued goods and services outside the family. Equality arises when both sexes work side by side in food production, as do the Washo, and the products are simply distributed among the workers. In such circumstances, no person or sex has greater access to valued items than do others. But when women make no contribution to the food supply, as in the case of the Eskimo, they are completely subordinate.

When we attempt to apply these generalizations to contemporary industrial society, we can predict that as long as women spend their discretionary income from jobs on domestic needs, they will gain little social recognition and power. To be an effective source of power, money must be exchanged in ways that require returns and create obligations. In other words, it must be invested.

Jobs that do not give women control over valued resources will do little to advance their general status. Only as managers, executives, and professionals are women in a position to trade goods and services, to do others favors, and therefore to obligate others to them. Only as controllers of valued resources can women achieve prestige, power, and equality.

Within the household, women who bring in income from jobs are able to function on a more nearly equal basis with their husbands. Women who contribute services to their husbands and children without pay, as do some middle-class Western housewives, are especially vulnerable to dominance. Like Eskimo women, as long as their services are limited to domestic distribution they have little power relative to their husbands and none with respect to the outside world.

As for the limits imposed on women by their procreative functions in hunter-gatherer societies, child-bearing and child care are organized around work as much as work is organized around reproduction. Some foraging groups space their children three to four years apart and have an average of only four to six children, far fewer than many women in other cultures. Hunter-gatherers nurse their infants for extended periods, sometimes for as long as four years. This custom suppresses ovulation and limits the size of their families. Sometimes, although rarely, they practice infanticide. By limiting reproduction, a woman who is gathering food has only one child to carry.

Different societies can and do adjust the frequency of birth and the care of children to accommodate whatever productive activities women customarily engage in. In horticultural societies, where women work long hours in gardens that may be far from home, infants get food to supplement their mothers' milk, older children take care of younger children, and pregnancies are widely spaced. Throughout the world, if a society requires a woman's labor, it finds ways to care for her children.

In the United States, as in some other industrial societies, the accelerated entry of women with preschool children into the labor force has resulted in the development of a variety of child-care arrangements. Individual women have called on friends, relatives, and neighbors. Public and private child-care centers are growing. We should realize that the declining birth rate, the increasing acceptance of childless or single-child families, and a de-emphasis on motherhood are adaptations to a sexual division of labor reminiscent of the system of production found in hunter-gatherer societies.

In many countries where women no longer devote most of their productive years to childbearing, they are beginning to demand a change in the social relationship of the sexes. As women gain access to positions that control the exchange of resources, male dominance may become archaic, and industrial societies may one day become as egalitarian as the Washo.

REFERENCES

Friedl, Ernestine, *Women and Men: An Anthropologist's View,* Holt, Rinehart and Winston, 1975.

Martin, M. Kay, and Barbara Voorhies, eds., *Female of the Species,* Columbia University Press, 1977.

Murphy, Yolanda, and Robert Murphy, *Women of the Forest,* Columbia University Press, 1974.

Reiter, Rayna, ed., *Toward an Anthropology of Women,* Monthly Review Press, 1975.

Rosaldo, M.Z., and Louise Lamphere, eds., *Women, Culture, and Society,* Stanford University Press, 1974.

Schlegel, Alice, ed., *Sexual Stratification; A Cross-Cultural View,* Columbia University Press, 1977.

Strathern, Marilyn, *Women in Between: Female Roles in a Male World,* Academic Press, 1972.

Yellow Woman and a Beauty of the Spirit

For a Laguna Pueblo Child Who Looked 'Different,' There Was Comfort in the Old Ways—A World in Which Faces and Bodies Could Not Be Separated From Hearts and Souls

Leslie Marmon Silko

Leslie Marmon Silko's most recent book is "Almanac of the Dead," published by Simon & Schuster. She lives in Tucson, Ariz.

From the time I was a small child, I was aware that I was different. I looked different from my playmates. My two sisters looked different too. We didn't look quite like the other Laguna Pueblo children, but we didn't look quite white either. In the 1880s, my great grandfather had followed his older brother west from Ohio to the New Mexico territory to survey the land for the U.S. government. The two Marmon brothers came to the Laguna Pueblo Reservation because they had an Ohio cousin who already lived there. The Ohio cousin was involved in sending Indian children thousands of miles away from their families to the War Department's big Indian boarding school in Carlisle, Pa. Both brothers married "full blood" Laguna Pueblo women. My great-grandfather had first married my great-grandmother's older sister, but she died in childbirth and left two small children. My great-grandmother was 15 or 20 years younger than my great-grandfather. She had attended Carlisle Indian School and spoke and wrote English beautifully.

I called her Grandma A'mooh because that's what I heard her say whenever she saw me. "A'mooh" means "granddaughter" in the Laguna language. I remember this word because her love and her acceptance of me as a small child were so important. I had sensed immediately that something about my appearance was not acceptable to some people, white and Indian. But I did not see any signs of that strain or anxiety in the face of my beloved Grandma A'mooh.

Younger people, people my parents' age, seemed to look at the world in a more "modern" way. The "modern" way included racism. My physical appearance seemed not to matter to the old-time people. They looked at the world very differently; a person's appearance and possessions did not matter nearly as much as a person's behavior. For them, a person's value lies in how that person interacts with other people, how that person behaves toward the animals and the Earth. That is what matters most to the old-time people. The Pueblo people believed this long before the Puritans arrived with their notions of sin and damnation, and racism. The old-time beliefs persist today; thus I will refer to the old-time people in the present tense as well as the past. Many worlds may coexist here.

I spent a great deal of time with my great-grandmother. Her house was next to our house, and I used to wake up at dawn, hours before my parents or younger sisters, and I'd go wait on the porch swing or on the back steps by her kitchen door. She got up at dawn, but she was more than 80 years old so she needed a little while to get dressed and to get the fire going in the cookstove. I had been carefully instructed by my parents not to bother her and to behave, and to try to help her any way I could. I always loved the early mornings when the air was so cool with a hint of rain smell in the breeze. In the dry New Mexico air, the least hint of dampness smells sweet.

My great-grandmother's yard was planted with lilac bushes and iris; there were four o'clocks, cosmos, morning glories and hollyhocks and old-fashioned rose bushes that I helped her water. If the garden hose got stuck on one of the big rocks that lined the path in the yard, I ran and pulled it free. That's what I came to do early every morning: to help Grandma water the plants before the heat of the day arrived.

Grandma A'mooh would tell about the old days, family stories about relatives who had been killed by Apache raiders who stole the sheep our relatives had been herding near Swahnee.

From the *Los Angeles Times Magazine*, December 19, 1993, pp. 52-66. © 1993 by Leslie Marmon Silko. Reprinted by permission of Wylie, Aitken & Stone, Inc.

Sometimes she read the Bible stories that we kids liked because of the illustrations of Jonah in the mouth of a whale and Daniel surrounded by lions. Grandma A'mooh would send me home when she took her nap, but when the sun got low and the afternoon began to cool off, I would be back on the porch swing, waiting for her to come out to water the plants and to haul in firewood for the evening. When Grandma was 85, she still chopped her own kindling. She used to let me carry in the coal bucket for her, but she would not allow me to use the ax. I carried armloads of kindling too, and I learned to be proud of my strength.

I was allowed to listen quietly when Aunt Susie or Aunt Alice came to visit Grandma. When I got old enough to cross the road alone, I went and visited them almost daily. They were vigorous women who valued books and writing. They were usually busy chopping world or cooking but never hesitated to take time to answer my questions. Best of all they told me the "hummah-hah" stories, about an earlier time when animals and humans shared a common language. In the old days, the Pueblo people had educated their children in this manner; adults took time out to talk to and teach young people. Everyone was a teacher, and every activity had the potential to teach the child.

But as soon as I started kindergarten at the Bureau of Indian Affairs day school, I began to learn more about the difference between the Laguna Pueblo world and the outside world. It was at school that I learned just how different I looked from my classmates. Sometimes tourists driving past on Route 66 would stop by Laguna Day School at recess time to take photographs of us kids. One day, when I was in the first grade, we all crowded around the smiling white tourists who peered at our faces. We all wanted to be in the picture because afterward the tourists sometimes gave us each a penny. Just as we were all posed and ready to have our picture taken, the tourist man looked at me. "Not you," he said and motioned for me to step away from my classmates. I felt so embarrassed that I wanted to disappear. My classmates were puzzled by the tourists' behavior, but I knew the tourists didn't want me in their snapshot because I looked different, because I was part white.

In the view of the old-time people, we are all sisters and brothers because the Mother Creator made all of us—all colors and all sizes. We are sisters and brothers, clanspeople of all the living beings around us. The plants, the birds, fish, clouds, water, even the clay—they all are related to us. The old-time people believe that all things, even rocks and water, have spirit and being. They understood that all things only want to continue being as they are; they need only to be left as they are. Thus the old folks used to tell us kids not to disturb the earth unnecessarily. All things as they were created exist already in harmony with one another as long as we do not disturb them.

As the old story tells us, Tse'its'i'na-ko, Thought Woman, the Spider, thought of her three sisters, and as she thought of them, they came into being. Together with Thought Woman, they thought of the sun and the stars and the moon. The Mother Creators imagined the earth and the oceans, the animals and the people, and the kat'sina spirits that reside in the mountains. The Mother Creators imagined all the plants that flower and the trees that bear fruit. As Thought Woman and her sisters thought of it, the whole universe came into being. In this universe, there is no absolute good or absolute bad; there are only balances and harmonies that ebb and flow. Some years the desert receives abundant rain, other years there is too little rain, and sometimes there is so much rain that floods cause destruction. But rain itself is neither innocent or guilty. The rain is simply itself.

My great-grandmother was dark and handsome. Her expression in photographs is one of confidence and strength. I do not know if white people then or now would consider her beautiful. I do not know if the old-time Laguna Pueblo people considered her beautiful or if the old-time people even thought in those terms. To the Pueblo way of thinking, the act of comparing one living being with another was silly, because each being or thing is unique and therefore incomparably valuable because it is the only one of its kind. The old-time people thought it was crazy to attach such importance to a person's appearance. I understood very early that there were two distinct ways of interpreting the world. There was the white people's way, and there was the Laguna way. In the Laguna way, it was bad manners to make comparisons that might hurt another person's feelings.

In everyday Pueblo life, not much attention was paid to one's physical appearance or clothing. Ceremonial clothing was quite elaborate but was used only for the sacred dances. The traditional Pueblo societies were communal and strictly egalitarian, which means that no matter how well or how poorly one might have dressed, there was no "social ladder" to fall from. All food and other resources were strictly shared so that no one person or group had more than another. I mention social status because it seems to me that most of the definitions of beauty in contemporary Western culture are really codes for determining social status. People no longer hide their face-lifts, and they discuss their liposuctions because the point of the procedures isn't just cosmetic, it is social. It says to the world, "I have enough spare cash that I can afford surgery for cosmetic purposes."

In the old-time Pueblo world, beauty was manifested in behavior and in one's relationships with other living beings. Beauty was as much a feeling of harmony as it was a visual, aural or sensual effect. The whole person had to be beautiful, not just the face or the body; faces and bodies could not be separated from hearts and souls. Health was foremost in achieving this sense of well-being and harmony; in the old-time Pueblo world, a person who did not look healthy inspired feelings of worry and anxiety, not feelings of well-being. A healthy person, of course, is in harmony with the world around her; she is at peace with herself too. Thus an unhappy person or spiteful person would not be considered beautiful.

In the old days, strong, sturdy women were most admired. One of my most vivid preschool memories is of the crew of Laguna women, in their 40s and 50s, who came to cover our house with adobe plaster. They handled the ladders with great ease, and while two women ground the adobe mud on stones and added straw, another woman loaded the hod with mud and passed it up to the two women on ladders, who were smoothing the plaster on the wall with their hands. Since women owned the houses, they did the plastering. At Laguna, men did the basket-making and the weaving of fine textiles; men helped a great deal with the child-care too. Because the Creator is female, there is no stigma on being female; gender is not used to control behavior. No job was a "man's job" or a "woman's job"; the most able person did the work.

My Grandma Lily had been a Ford Model A mechanic when she was a teen-ager. I remember when I was young, she was always fixing broken lamps and appliances. She was small and wiry, but she could lift her weight in rolled roofing or boxes of nails. When she was 75, she was still repairing washing machines in my uncle's coin-operated laundry.

The old-time people paid no attention to birthdays. When a person was ready to do something, she did it. When she no longer was able, she stopped. Thus the traditional Pueblo people did not worry about aging or about looking old because there were no social boundaries drawn by the passage of years. It was not remarkable for young men to marry women as old as their mothers. I never heard anyone talk about "women's work" until after I left Laguna for college. Work was there to be done by any able-bodied person who wanted to do it. At the same time, in the old-time Pueblo world, identity was acknowledged to be always in a flux; in the old stories, one minute Spider Woman is a little spider under a yucca plant, and the next instant she is a spritely grandmother walking down the road.

When I was growing up, there was a young man from a nearby village who wore nail polish and women's blouses and permed his hair. People paid little attention to his appearance; he was always part of a group of other young men from his village. No one ever made fun of him. Pueblo communities were, and still are, very interdependent, but they also have to be tolerant of individual eccentricities because survival of the group means everyone has to cooperate.

In the old Pueblo world, differences were celebrated as signs of the Mother Creators' grace. Persons born with exceptional physical or sexual differences were highly respected and honored because their physical differences gave them special positions as mediators between this world and the spirit world. The great Navajo medicine man of the 1920s, the Crawler, had a hunchback and could not walk upright, but he was able to heal even the most difficult cases. Before the arrival of Christian missionaries, a man could dress as a woman and work with the women and even marry a man without any fanfare. Likewise, a woman was free to dress like a man, to hunt and go to war with the men and to marry a woman. In the old Pueblo world view, we are all a mixture of male and female, and this sexual identity is changing constantly. Sexual inhibition did not begin until the Christian missionaries arrived. For the old-time people, marriage was about teamwork and social relationships, not about sexual excitement. In the days before the Puritans came, marriage did not mean an end to sex with people other than your spouse. Women were just as likely as men to have a "si'ash," or lover.

New life was so precious that pregnancy was always appropriate, and pregnancy before marriage was celebrated as a good sign. Since the children belonged to the mother and her clan, and women owned and bequeathed the houses and farmland, the exact determination of paternity wasn't critical. Although fertility was prized, infertility was no problem because mothers with unplanned pregnancies gave their babies to childless couples

within the clan in open adoption arrangements. Children called their mother's sisters "mother" as well, and a child became attached to a number of parent figures.

In the sacred kiva ceremonies, men mask and dress as women to pay homage and to be possessed by the female energies of the spirit beings. Because differences in physical appearance were so highly valued, surgery to change one's face and body to resemble a model's face and body would be unimaginable. To be different, to be unique was blessed and was best of all.

The traditional clothing of Pueblo women emphasized a woman's sturdiness. Buckskin leggings wrapped around the legs protected her from scratches and injuries while she worked. The more layers of buckskin, the better. All those layers gave her legs the appearance of strength, like sturdy tree trunks. To demonstrate sisterhood and brotherhood with the plants and animals, the old-time people make masks and costumes that transform the human figures of the dancers into the animal beings they portray. Dancers paint their exposed skin; their postures and motions are adapted from their observations. But the motions are stylized. The observer sees not an actual eagle or actual deer dancing, but witnesses a human being, a dancer, gradually changing into a woman/buffalo or a man/deer. Every impulse is to reaffirm the urgent relationships that human beings have with the plant and animal world.

In the high desert plateau country, all vegetation, even weeds and thorns, becomes special, and all life is precious and beautiful because without the plants, the insects and the animals, human beings living here cannot survive. Perhaps human beings long ago noticed the devastating impact human activity can have on the plants and animals; maybe this is why tribal cultures devised the stories about humans and animals intermarrying, and the clans that bind humans to animals and plants through a whole complex of duties.

We children were always warned not to harm frogs or toads, the beloved children of the rain clouds, because terrible floods would occur. I remember in the summer the old folks used to stick big bolls of cotton on the outside of their screen doors as bait to keep the flies from going in the house when the door was opened. The old folks staunchly resisted the killing of flies because once, long, long ago, when human beings were in a great deal of trouble, green bottle fly carried the desperate messages of human beings to the Mother Creator in the Fourth World below this one. Human beings had outraged the Mother Creator by neglecting the Mother Corn altar while they dabbled with sorcery and magic. The Mother Creator disappeared, and with her disappeared the rain clouds, and the plants and the animals too. The people began to starve, and they had no way of reaching the Mother Creator down below. The green bottle fly took the message to the Mother Creator, and the people were saved. To show their gratitude, the old folks refused to kill any flies.

The old stories demonstrate the interrelationships that the Pueblo people have maintained with their plant and animal clanspeople. Kochininako, Yellow Woman, represents all women in the old stories. Her deeds span the spectrum of human behavior and are mostly heroic acts, though in at least one story, she chooses to join the secret Destroyer Clan, which worships destruction and death. Because Laguna Pueblo cosmology features a female creator, the status of women is equal with the status of men, and women appear as often as men in the old stories as hero figures. Yellow Woman is my favorite because she dares to cross traditional boundaries of ordinary behavior during times of crisis in order to save the Pueblo; her power lies in her courage and in her uninhibited sexuality, which the old-time Pueblo stories celebrate again and again because fertility was so highly valued.

The old stories always say that Yellow Woman was beautiful, but remember that the old-time people were not so much thinking about physical appearances. In each story, the beauty that Yellow Woman possesses is the beauty of her passion, her daring and her sheer strength to act when catastrophe is imminent.

In one story, the people are suffering during a great drought and accompanying famine. Each day, Kochininako has to walk farther and farther from the village to find fresh water for her husband and children. One day she travels far, far to the east, to the plains, and she finally locates a freshwater spring. But when she reaches the pool, the water is churning violently as if something large had just gotten out of the pool. Kochininako does not want to see what huge creature had been at the pool, but just as she fills her water jar and turns to hurry away, a strong, sexy man in buffalo skin leggings appears by the pool. Little drops of water glisten on his chest. She cannot help but look at him because he is so strong and so good to look at. Able to transform himself from human to buffalo in the wink of an eye, Buffalo Man gallops away with her on his back. Kochininako falls in love with Buffalo Man, and because of this liaison, the Buffalo People agree to give their bodies to the hunters to feed the starving Pueblo. Thus Kochininako's fearless sensuality results in the salvation of the people of her village, who are saved by the meat the Buffalo people "give" to them.

My father taught me and my sisters to shoot .22 rifles when we were 7; I went hunting with my father when I was 8, and I killed my first mule deer buck when I was 13. The Kochininako stories were always my favorite because Yellow Woman had so many adventures. In one story, as she hunts rabbits to feed her family, a giant monster pursues her, but she has the courage and presence of mind to outwit it.

In another story, Kochininako has a fling with Whirlwind Man and returns to her husband 10 months later with twin baby boys. The twin boys grow up to be great heroes of the people. Once again, Kochininako's vibrant sexuality benefits her people.

The stories about Kochininako made me aware that sometimes an individual must act despite disapproval, or concern for "appearances" or "what others may say." From Yellow Woman's adventures, I learned to be comfortable with my differences. I even imagined that Yellow Woman had yellow skin, brown hair and green eyes like mine, although her name does not refer to her color, but rather to the ritual color of the East.

There have been many other moments like the one with the camera-toting tourist in the schoolyard. But the old-time people always say, remember the stories, the stories will help you be strong. So all these years I have depended on Kochininako and the stories of her adventures.

Kochininako is beautiful because she has the courage to act in times of great peril, and her triumph is achieved by her sensuality, not through violence and destruction. For these qualities of the spirit, Yellow Woman and all women are beautiful.

Status, Property, and the Value on Virginity

Alice Schlegel

One way to assess a woman's autonomy is to ask whether she controls her own sexuality. Thus, the prohibition on premarital sex for females is often considered a measure of men's control over women's lives. There are certain difficulties with this assumption, however. First, the way a people feels about premarital sex is not necessarily consonant with its attitude toward extramarital sex, as many people allow premarital freedom but condemn adultery, while others, such as the South African Lovedu (Sacks 1979), insist on premarital virginity but turn a blind eye to discreet extramarital affairs.

Second, this assumption fails to recognize that in most societies, the value placed on virginity applies to adolescent girls, not to adult women. With few exceptions worldwide, girls are still physically adolescent when they marry, generally within three or four years after puberty. More important, young people are generally not social adults until they marry, so that the premarital female is socially an adolescent girl. Some societies, such as our own and that of 17th-century England (Stone 1977), for example, are exceptions to this, having a stage that I call "youth" intervening between adolescence and full adulthood. However, in most parts of the world the bride is a teenage girl who in most aspects of her life is still very much under the authority of her parents.

If virginity is not, then, a very good measure of female subordination, we must look for other aspects of girls' and young women's lives that are associated with the proscription of premarital sex. One common notion is that virginity is valued when men have to "pay" for wives by transferring goods in the form of bridewealth to the women's families. This notion is based on the assumption that there is some innate preference for virgins which can be activated when men have the upper hand, so to speak, because they are paying for the bride. It must be noted, of course, that there is no universal preference for virgin brides. Such an assumption projects onto other cultures the attitudes that have developed historically in our own. Moreover, the belief that when men give bridewealth they pay for virgin brides is shaken when we read in Goody (1973:25) that dowry-giving societies, in which the bride's family pays, are generally intolerant of premarital sex for girls. Here the family pays to give, not to receive, a virgin bride.

There is a connection between marriage transactions—the movement of goods or services at the time of a marriage—and the value on virginity, but it is not obvious what that connection is. In this paper, I argue that the virginity of daughters protects the interests of brides' families when they use marital alliances to maintain or enhance their social status. To illuminate this issue, it is necessary to understand the varying effects that marriage transactions have on the transmission or retention of property and on the social debts thus incurred.

MARRIAGE TRANSACTIONS

The form of marriage transaction that has received the most attention in the anthropological literature is *bridewealth,* goods given by the groom, usually with the assistance of his kin, to the family of the bride. Bridewealth generally does not remain with the family that receives it: it or its equivalent is used to obtain wives for brothers of the bride or an additional wife for her father. Thus, goods and women circulate and countercirculate. In the large majority of bridewealth-giving societies, which are patrilocal, households end up with as many women as they have produced, by replacing daughters with daughters-in-law and sisters with wives.

Women exchange is also a form of replacement, the exchange being direct rather than mediated by a transfer of property. Women exchange and bridewealth are most frequently found where women have economic value through their large contribution to subsistence (cf. Schlegel and Barry 1986). In each case the result is a kind of social homeostasis, both among the families through which women and goods circulate and within the household that sooner or later gains a woman to replace each one it has lost.

Brideservice is often considered to be analogous to bridewealth, with payment in labor rather than goods. They differ significantly, however, in that the benefit of brideservice goes directly to the bride's household and is not circulated as are bridewealth goods. Thus, families with many daughters receive much free labor, while families with few get little.

While *gift exchange,* in which relatively equal amounts are exchanged between the families of the bride and groom, can occur at all levels of social complexity, it is often found in societies with important status differences in rank or wealth; it occurs most often in Asia, native North America, and the Pacific. Since residence is predominantly patrilocal in gift-exchanging societies, the bride-receiving household is socially, although not economically, in debt to the bride-giving one. The exchange of equivalent goods is a way of ensuring that the intermarrying families are of the same social status, as indicated by the wealth that they own or can call up from among their kin and dependents.

Status is a major consideration in dowry-giving societies. The bride's dowry is sometimes matched against the groom's settlement, thus ensuring equivalence, a usual practice among European land-owning peasants or elites. Dowry can also be used to "buy" a high status son-in-law, a common practice in South Asia and one also known in Europe. Dowry or a bride's anticipated inheritance can be used to attract a poor but presentable groom, a client son-in-law whose allegiance will be primarily to the house into which he has married and on which he is dependent. This strategy seems to have been practiced by mercantile families in Europe and Latin America. Dowry was associated historically with the property-owning classes of the Old High Culture areas such as the Mediterranean (ancient Mesopotamia, Greece, and Rome) and Asia (India, China, and Japan), and was the common form throughout Europe until recently.

The final form of marriage transaction to be examined here is *indirect dowry,* which contains some features of both bridewealth, in that goods are given by the groom's family, and dowry, in that the goods end up with the new conjugal couple. Sometimes the groom's kin give goods directly to the bride, but more often they give goods to her father, who then gives goods to the new couple. The latter form has frequently been confused with bridewealth, as in the Islamic *mahr.* Indirect dowry tends to be found both on the fringes of and within the Old High Culture areas, such as Egypt, where it has been introduced along with conversion to Islam, replacing the simple dowry of earlier times. In its classic form, indirect dowry appears to be a way of establishing the properly rights of the conjugal couples that make up larger households, in anticipation of eventual fission. In addition, it allows for status negotiation without either family being put in the other's economic or social debt.

There are variations within these major types, and there are additional features (such as the European dower) that are secondary and limited in distribution. In complex societies, the form of transaction may vary according to region or class. In prerevolutionary China, for example, the landed or mercantile elite gave dowry while the landless peasantry gave indirect dowry. In modern China, marriage transactions have disappeared from urban areas, whereas bridewealth has replaced indirect dowry among peasants (Fang 1990).

WHY VALUE VIRGINITY?

Since the burden of controlling a girl's sexuality through socialization or surveillance falls upon her family, it is instructive to consider what benefits are to be derived from preserving the virginity of daughters and sisters. Goody (1976) sees restrictiveness as a way of avoiding inappropriate marriages: by controlling a girl's sexuality, her family can better control her marriage choice, for the loss of virginity may "diminish a girl's honour and reduce her marriage chances" (Goody 1976:14). However, this presupposes that preserving virginity has some inherent value, whereas that value is precisely what needs to be explained.

I argue that virginity is valued in those societies in which young men may seek to better their chances in life by allying themselves through marriage to a wealthy or powerful family. In preserving a daughter's virginity, a family is protecting her from seduction, impregnation, and paternity claims on her child. This is most critical when certain kinds of property transactions are involved. In societies in which dowry is given (or daughters inherit), it would be attractive to seduce a dowered daughter (or heiress), demanding her as wife along with her property. Her parents would be reluctant to refuse, since the well-being of their grandchildren would depend upon their inheritance from both of their parents, and another man would be unlikely to marry the mother if it meant that he had not only to support her children but also to make them his heirs. (The widow with children would be a different matter, since these children would have received property through their father and would make no claims on their stepfather beyond support, for which their labor would provide compensation.)

To illustrate that upward mobility through marriage with a dowered daughter or heiress is known in dowry-giving societies, let us consider a common theme of European fairy tales. A poor but honest young man goes through trials to win the hand of the princess, who inherits her father's kingdom. Or, he wins her heart, and through the good offices of a fairy godmother or other spirit helper, they evade her wrathful father and are eventually reconciled with him. This more or less legitimate means to upward mobility is not so different from the illegitimate one, by which he wins the girl through seduction.

This line of reasoning was familiar to the seventeenth- and eighteenth-century English, as Trumbach tells it:

> Stealing a son . . . was not the great crime. It was, rather, the theft of a daughter that was the real nightmare. For a woman's property became her husband's and she took his social standing. . . . To steal an heiress was therefore the quickest way to make a man's fortune—this was the common

doctrine of the stage before 1710—and it had a special appeal to younger sons (1978:101–102).

As the table shows, the value on virginity is statistically associated with the type of economic exchange linked to the marriage transaction.

All of the dowry-giving societies in the sample value virginity except the Haitians. Nevertheless, as Herskovits, writing about Haiti, points out: "Even though pre-marital relations are commonplace, . . . the pregnancy of an unmarried girl is regarded as both reprehensible and unfortunate, and she is severely beaten for it by her family" (1971:111). Their fear of her seduction is well founded, for if they disapprove of a suitor and reject him, the young man "uses all persuasion to give her a child and, this achieved, abandons her to show his contempt for the family that has formally refused to accept him as a son-in-law" (Herskovits 1971:110). To avoid childbearing, women and girls resort to magical means of contraception and the more effective abortion.

The majority of societies that exchange gifts and give indirect dowry also expect brides to be virgins. This is particularly true in the case of gift exchange, in which a bride's family gives quantities of property along with her, receiving a more or less equivalent amount from the family of the groom. As noted earlier, gift exchange is a way of ensuring that the two families are of equal wealth or of equal social power. Impregnating a girl would give a boy and his family a claim on that girl and an alliance with her family, even though they would have to come up with something themselves for the exchange (not necessarily equivalent to what a more appropriate suitor would give; see the case of the Omaha, discussed below). As in dowry-giving societies, an emphasis on virginity discourages a man who is tempted to jump the status barrier by claiming fatherhood of a woman's child. The sample does, however, include three exceptions to the general requirement of virginity in gift-exchanging societies, and it is instructive to examine these deviant cases.

Malinowski (1932) has discussed at some length the sexual freedom of girls in the Trobriand Islands in Melanesia. However, we must recall that the Trobriand Islanders do not, at least ideologically, associate sexual intercourse with pregnancy. Weiner (1976:122) relates two cases in which pregnancy was attributed to magic, and her informants maintained that women could conceive without male assistance. No boy, then, can make a claim on a girl simply because he has been sleeping with her and she has become pregnant. Fatherhood can only be attained after marriage, when it is socially defined.

Among the Omaha Indians of the Great Plains, virginity was not considered important for most girls (as coded in Broude and Greene [1980]), but according to Fletcher and LaFlesche (1911), virgins were held in greater esteem than those who had lost their virginity. It was a special privilege to marry a girl who had been tattooed with the "mark of honor," which was given to a virgin of a prominent family on the occasion of her father's or another close relative's initiation into one of the ceremonial societies. Only the marriages in prominent families involved significant gift exchange. In ordinary marriages, the young husband was expected to work a year or two for his father-in-law, making brideservice a more common feature than gift exchange. Thus, it was in the important marriages, accompanied by the exchange of goods of much value, that the bride was expected to be a virgin. Omaha elite families faced the danger that a daughter might be seduced by a youth who would persuade her to elope. As long as his family recognized the marriage and brought some gifts to the bride's father, the marriage was legitimate in the eyes of the community. Maintaining the virginity of high-status girls protected their families from unwanted alliances.

In the Polynesian islands of Samoa, similarly, girls from untitled families had sexual freedom (as coded in Broude and Greene [1980]) but the daughters of titled chiefs did not. Samoa had an ambilineal descent system, in that children could be affiliated either to the mother's or the father's group. If the mother's rank was higher than the father's, the children's status would be elevated above their father's. High-status families would wish to guard their daughters against potential social climbers, who might be tempted to improve their children's position in life by seducing and marrying socially superior girls. It appears that only the arranged marriages, generally of high-status people, involved much gift exchange. Most marriages were of the "elopement" type and were much less expensive than the arranged ones (Shore 1981). Thus, as in the case of the Omaha, intracultural comparison demonstrates a correlation between the type of marriage transaction and the value on virginity.

It is clear that when no property accompanies the marriage, virginity is of little interest. If the groom gives goods or labor, the picture is mixed, but fewer societies are restrictive than permissive. In societies in which the bride's side gives considerable property, as with gift exchange, dowry, and, in many cases, indirect dowry, virginity is most likely to be valued. Thus, there is an association between the giving of property, particularly from the bride's side, and control of the girl's sexuality. I have interpreted this as a means by which the families of girls prevent their being seduced by ineligible boys, resulting in alliances that could be an embarrassment. This is particularly the case when status negotiation is a prominent feature of marital alliances, in those societies in which families use the marriages of their daughters to maintain or enhance their social position. Such considerations are likely to be found only in rank or class societies.

VIRGINITY AND FATHERHOOD

The question of the value on virginity revolves around two issues: whether premarital sexual intercourse leads to pregnancy, and whether biological fatherhood alone gives a man a claim on a child and its mother. There should be less concern over virginity when sexual intercourse is not likely to lead to pregnancy than when it is. Safe, so-

**Correlations of value on virginity
with type of marriage transaction[1]**

Virginity valued	Marriage transaction					
	None	Bride-wealth[2]	Bride-service	Gift exchange	Dowry and indirect dowry	Total
Yes	3	16	6	9	18	52
No	26	27	10	3	7	73

N = 125; Chi-square = 27.13; p <.0001

[1] Information on attitudes toward premarital sex for females comes primarily from the code "Attitude Toward Premarital Sex (Female)" in Broude and Greene (1980), which is based on the Standard Sample of 186 preindustrial societies. I have altered the code established by Broude and Greene for four societies based on the ethnographic literature. The second source is a body of data collected by Herbert Barry and me on adolescent socialization in Standard Sample societies not coded by Broude and Greene.
[2] Includes token bridewealth.

cially condoned abortion is a reliable way of preventing unwanted births, and virginity is not such an issue if abortion is freely available, as it has been in Southeast Asia since at least the sixteenth century. Even there, however, the elite have secluded their daughters, possibly in imitation of the Hindu, Buddhist, or Moslem aristocrats whom they have emulated in other ways (cf. Reid 1988:163).

Although abortive techniques are widely known and practiced, even where proscribed (Devereux 1976), there is little evidence to indicate the extent to which illicit abortions are available to unmarried girls. Desperate girls, with the help of their mothers, surely must resort to them, as anecdotal information indicates; but whether or not they are successful, and whether or not the girls can keep them secret, are open to question. Illicit abortion is a last-ditch measure for preventing unwanted births and must take a distant second place to the maintenance of virginity.

Impregnating a girl does not automatically give a boy or man a claim to her child or to her. In the Trobriand Islands, as we have seen, biological fatherhood alone is simply not recognized. In other places, it may be recog-

nized without giving the impregnator a paternity claim. Such a claim may have to be paid for either directly or indirectly through bridewealth and marriage to the mother; if it is not, the child is absorbed into the mother's kin group. This practice appears to be more common in Africa than in other regions, although the question requires a study in its own right. I suggest that the acceptance of illegitimate children is greater when children are a distinct economic asset. They are likely to be so in underpopulated areas, such as are found throughout much of Africa (Kopytoff 1987). In such places, the availability of labor rather than of land is the major constraint on the economic success and expansion of the productive unit, the family and the kin group, and illegitimate origins do not detract from the potential labor value of a child. A similar explanation may hold for some European peasantries.

Where land is in short supply in preindustrial societies and family resources consist of private property, heirship is a central concern. A bastard is less likely to be welcomed, since it is totally dependent on the mother's family and does not draw in resources from the father. Bastards may be better received when the father is of much

higher status than the mother—when he is, for example, a king or the noble impregnator of a peasant girl. In such cases, so long as paternity is acknowledged, the child provides a left-handed link to wealth and power, one that otherwise would be beyond the reach of the mother's family.

If children are not an unqualified asset to the mother's family, the rules of social life are likely to include the prescription that fathers take responsibility for their children, thus bringing biological and social fatherhood closer together. The responsibility for one's child can be restated as the right to that child, and biological fatherhood becomes a claim on social fatherhood. When the status of the mother is equal to or lower than that of the impregnator, it is to her advantage to use the rule of responsibility to press for marriage or at least support, so long as the impregnator is willing (or is unable to escape). Turning this on its head, when the mother is of greater wealth or higher status, particularly when her status or property will be inherited by her child, it is to the advantage of the impregnator to use the rule of responsibility to press *his* claim on the child and its mother. It is in precisely such situations, I propose, that virginity is valued, as it is the surest way of preventing such claims.

This is not to deny that virginity may acquire secondary meanings. In its extreme form, a value on virginity can lead to a value on chastity so great that widows are discouraged from remarriage. Such was the case in India for the higher castes (Ullrich 1977), throughout prerevolutionary China (Chiao 1971), and in early Christian Europe (Verdon 1988). In such places celibacy comes to be seen as a spiritually higher state than married sexuality. In this form, the ideal of virginity has been incorporated into some religions and has been diffused along with conversion.

While the eighteenth-century English, living at a time of expanding wealth and social mobility, were aware of the social advantage of seducing an heiress and spoke freely about it, it is improbable that most peoples would give this as the reason for keeping their daughters virginal. In Eurasia, at any rate, one is much more likely to get explanations involving purity and the shame that follows its loss. We weave significance around the hard facts of existence, and virginity, a practical concern, can be a sign of spiritual purity when the invasion of the body implies the invasion of the spirit or when the seduction of female kin comes to symbolize the violability of the lineage.

The idealization of virginity is most common in Eurasia, and it is found in some other areas, such as Polynesia or native North America, where certain categories of girls are expected to be virginal. It is noteworthy that belief in the purity or spiritual power of virginity, chastity, and celibacy developed in those regions where dowry or gift-exchange was the established form or the form practiced by the elite and aspired to by those who would imitate them. Ideology does not arise *de novo* but is grounded in existential concerns and issues. I suggest that the ideology of virginity has its source in pragmatic concerns about status maintenance and improvement.

As a practical matter, ensuring that daughters and sisters remain virginal puts a heavy burden of surveillance on parents and brothers. The effort required is worthwhile when the stakes are high, as when considerable property and status are involved, or the secondary meanings of virginity are such that the purity of the girl and thus the honor of her family are at issue. In many parts of the Mediterranean world, control over female sexuality is a lived metaphor for control over social relations. The transgressing girl is defying her male kin and giving away what only they have the right to bestow (cf. Schneider 1971).

Elsewhere, particularly among poorer people in societies that value virginity, the daughter's choice of husband is of minor consequence. Thus, there is no point in restricting her. Even when virginity is generally accorded a high value, it may be an ideal to which only a minority aspire. Recognizing this makes it easier to reconcile the seeming contradiction between the high value placed on virginity and the high rate of bastardy at various times and places throughout European history.

IMPLICATIONS OF THE PROPOSITION

Regarding a value on virginity is a way of forestalling male social climbing through seduction causes us to take a fresh look at the interest, in some places, in seducing virgins and the self-congratulation or acclaim by peers that accompanies the successful boy or man in this pursuit. It has nothing to do with sexual pleasure, for the experienced girl or woman is a more satisfying sexual partner than the virgin. What, then, is the point?

First, of course, is the thrill of the forbidden. However, seducing a virgin can be as much of a coup in sexually permissive societies like Samoa as it is in the restrictive ones. In a discussion of adolescent sexuality in the Trobriand Islands, Weiner (1988:71) has pointed out that attracting lovers is not a frivolous pastime but rather "the first step toward entering the adult world of strategies, where the line between influencing others while not allowing others to gain control of oneself must be carefully learned." If the game of seduction is serious business, then how much more is this true when seduction can lead to status improvement. We can understand the Cinderella story and its variants as a tale of upward mobility for women through sexual attraction—but what about upwardly mobile men?

Winning the heart of a high-status woman as a path to a better life may be a male fantasy in all societies that are divided by rank or class, or at least those in which men will not be killed or severely punished for the attempt. Boys and youths have nothing to lose and much to gain if they can make a paternity claim on the child of a high-status girl. In such a setting, where only a few can succeed, all boys will be tempted to refine their skills with virgins of their own rank while hoping for their big chance with a *taupou* (the Samoan "village princess") or her equivalent.

It is well recognized that women use their sexual attractiveness to try to improve their position through a socially advantageous marriage or liaison, when such possibilities are open to them. (The seclusion of girls not only protects daughters against seduction but also protects sons against inconvenient romantic attachments, thus reinforcing parental control over the marriages of children of both sexes.) It should not surprise us that men and boys do the same if the opportunity arises. When sexual success can be translated into social success, it is predictable that men and boys will make themselves attractive to women and that sexual exploits will become a major topic of discussion, teasing, and boasting. In such cases, male competitiveness is channeled into overt sexual competition. The man who seduces a dowered virgin has his fortune made.

CONCLUSION

The trend in the modern world follows the pattern established for the preindustrial societies in the sample. With readily available contraception and abortion, extramarital sexual relations do not have to result in pregnancy or illegitimate birth. Even if a paternity claim is pressed, there is no obligation in our individual-centered society to honor it, as economic opportunities for women as well as welfare payments by the state make it possible to support a child without a husband.

Equally important, the dowry has lapsed in most European and European-derived cultures. Parental investment in daughters is increasingly in the form of education, not dowry. Furthermore, the daughter's choice of a husband does not have the significance for the family today that it did in earlier times. For most people in the industrial world, there is little in the way of a family estate to preserve. Even among the rich, a rebellious daughter and her husband can be cut out of the will, since in modern societies the disposal of assets is up to the individual with legal ownership of them. Thus, a daughter's choice of a husband is not critical to the well-being of the family and the maintenance of its assets.

Most commentators on the "sexual revolution" point to the availability of new contraception and abortion technology as the deciding factor in the changing of our sexual habits. But contraception and abortion have a long history in civilization; techniques to reduce fertility have been known and used in Europe and elsewhere for centuries, albeit clandestinely. Technology alone, without significant changes in social relations, is not enough to alter such deep-seated cultural values as the value on virginity. As marriage transactions disappear and social status is gained more through achievement than through the family into which one is born or marries, parental control over marriage declines and disappears. The choice of a son-in-law is no longer a central concern, and the virginity of daughters loses its salience.

Female Circumcision

Not Just Another Bit of Exotic Ethnographic Trivia

Katherine A. Dettwyler

In Africa today, women's voices are being raised for the first time against genital mutilations still practiced on babies, little girls, and women. These voices belong to a few women, who, from Egypt to Mali, from the Sudan and Somalia to Senegal, remain closely attached to their identity and heritage, but are prepared to call it in question when traditional practices endanger their lives and their health. They are beginning the delicate task of helping women free themselves from customs which have no advantage and many risks for their physical and psychological well-being, without at the same time destroying the supportive and beneficial threads of their cultural fabric.

—Scilla McLean and Efua Graham

Moussa and I sat on low stools in the small patch of shade cast by a locust tree in a compound near the market shared by two brothers, Tamasheqs from northern Mali. We had come to remeasure two girls from the original sample. The morning light was already harsh and promised another blistering day, unrelieved by even a breath of wind. I watched the dark opening of the small kitchen hut across the compound, into which the father of one of the girls had disappeared some minutes before. Finally, two spectral figures emerged from the doorway of the hut and shuffled gingerly toward us across the dusty courtyard. Both girls were dressed oddly, with long capes draped over their heads. Their eyes were downcast, their steps uncertain. Their skin was a dusty gray color, not at all the normal rich, vibrant brown of healthy Malian children.

I turned to Moussa in concern and whispered, "What's the matter with them?"

"Nothing," he explained, "but they've just been circumcised."

"When?" I asked, horrified.

Moussa turned to their fathers and asked, then told me: "They did it this morning."

"Please, you can go back and sit down," I called to the girls in a shaky voice. "We can come back another day."

"It's OK, you can go ahead," one of the mothers insisted.

"No. No. I think we need to go," I said hastily, getting up and heading toward the compound gate.

Moussa made apologies to all concerned and hurried after me. He knew me well enough to know that I was very upset. We hurried away down the narrow alleyway toward the morning market. Once we reached the open spaces and the noise and bustle of the market, I stopped to catch my breath.

"Oh Lord, Moussa, do you think they'll be OK?" I asked.

He paused. "I don't know. We usually circumcise girls much younger. It's hard on them when they're this old. They didn't look good."

"What can we do?" I implored.

"Nothing. There's nothing we can do. You know that. Why don't we come back in a few weeks, and if they've survived, we can measure them then."

"All right. Let's go visit someone else this morning."

"How about the Fat Lady from Timbuktu?" Moussa suggested. "She always makes you laugh."

"That's a great idea! We can also check and see how Daouda is doing."

During my dissertation research I had, more or less, gotten used to the fact that the Bambara practice female circumcision, generally what can be called the relatively mild form, involving clitoridectomy (removal of the clitoris). The even milder form, involving removal of the hood of the clitoris, is anatomically analogous to male circumcision in the United States. Clitoridectomy in females would be analogous to cutting off the head of the penis in males. Clitoridectomy is mild only relative to infibulation, the more severe form of genital mutilation.

Infibulation involves clitoridectomy plus cutting off the outer edges of the labia majora, which are then stitched together across the midline to form a permanent layer of scar tissue, preventing sexual intercourse. When a woman is married, the scar tissue is cut open, allowing the husband sexual intercourse. Infibulation is generally understood by anthropologists as a particularly severe, physical means of male control of female sexual behavior, which is accomplished in other societies by practices such as purdah, veils, or social censure for "loose" women. However, circumcision is explained in a variety of ways by the different cultures, mostly African and Asian, that practice it. Often, a religious explanation is offered, such as that found among the Dogon of northern Mali, who believe that all children are born with the potential to be either sex. A boy must have his foreskin removed to make him truly male, and girl must have her clitoris removed to make her truly female, capable, as an adult, of sexual intercourse with men and safe childbirth.

Among the residents of Magnambougou, female circumcision (clitoridectomy) is usually performed when a girl is about six months old. In this community, girls have clitoridectomies because "It's our tradition. We all do this." No amount of probing revealed any religious justification for the practice, and people seemed to accept it without question. Once, when Moussa wasn't available and I was just spending a lazy afternoon chatting with my good friend Agnes (her European name reveals that she was Christian, not Muslim), we discussed the topic of why the Bambara circumcise their daughters. In response to all of my questions, she just kept saying "tradition." "Well," I told her, "I read in a book about the Bambara [*African Folk Medicine*, by Pascal James Imperato] that the Bambara think that if you don't cut the clitoris off, it will grow to become almost as long as a man's penis." She looked at me as if I were absolutely nuts.

"*Who* told you that?" she asked.

"I read it in a book. Some people here in Mali told that to the author."

"Who?"

"His name is Pascal Imperato. He's a medical doctor. He was here during the smallpox vaccination campaign," I explained.

"No, I mean, who told him that we believe that?"

"I don't know who, specifically, he travelled all over Mali."

"Well, I never heard of that. That's stupid."

"So, what do you think does happen if you don't cut it off?"

"I don't know. Everyone has theirs removed, so I don't know what happens. It's just our tradition."

"Would you like to see what it looks like in an adult woman if you don't remove it? Would you like to see mine?" I asked, half in jest.

"You aren't circumcised?" she blurted out in surprise.

"No, of course not."

"Why 'of course not'?" she mocked me.

"We just don't do it in my culture."

"Why not?"

"Tradition," I admitted, starting to chuckle. "Seriously, let's go in the house, and I'll show you mine if you'll show me yours."

"Oh, sure!" Agnes doubled over with laughter, slapping the ground in front of her with both palms.

"I'm serious," I protested.

"You mean to tell me that American women aren't circumcised, but they still find husbands?"

"Yes."

"Your husband knew you weren't circumcised, and he married you anyway?"

"Yes."

"Well, is your husband circumcised?"

"Yes, most boys in the United States are circumcised as infants."

"Was your daughter circumcised as an infant?"

"No, of course not!"

"But your son was?"

"Well, yes," I admitted. "But it's hardly the same thing! We only remove the foreskin of the penis, not the head of the penis, which would be the equivalent of clitoridectomy for a female. I don't think it takes away from a man's sexual pleasure to be circumcised."

"Strange people, you American toubabs," she chided. "You circumcise the boys but not the girls. How can you do that to your own daughter? Don't you know people will shun her?"

"Not in my culture," I explained.

"You know," she confided, looking around furtively, "the French toubabs don't circumcise boys *or* girls!"

"Come on, don't you want to see what an uncircumcised woman looks like? Let's go in the house, right now.

But you have to show me yours as well."

She howled with laughter again. We went around and around; I never convinced her that I was serious, and she never agreed to my suggestion. My interest in female circumcision was a source of much amusement to Agnes, and whenever I saw her after that, she would remind me of our "silly conversation." Usually I didn't have to think about circumcision, and I would put it out of my mind. I told Miranda that if anyone ever asked her if she was circumcised, she was just to tell them "Yes, of course." I knew they wouldn't be so rude as to try and check it out for themselves.

Few Westerners know about female circumcision, and those who do often have difficulty understanding it because they can't fully comprehend the lack of importance that people attach to sex and sexual pleasure (especially female sexual pleasure) in some cultures. When I tried to determine the impact of clitoridectomy on women's sexual pleasure, women didn't understand my questions, telling me "sex is a woman's duty to her husband; it doesn't matter if it feels good for her."

Likewise, the concept of sexual foreplay seemed completely foreign to the Malian women I talked to. They did complain that they couldn't use spermicidal sponges as birth control options, but not because their husbands were particularly opposed to birth control (though many were, the number of children a man has being a direct indication of his wealth and power). Rather, sponges were impractical because their use necessitated that the couple wait for several minutes after the insertion of the sponge before having intercourse. Most husbands couldn't, or wouldn't, wait the required two or three minutes after the insertion of the sponge. "What if it hurts because you aren't ready?" I asked one young woman. "You just turn your face to the wall, and endure," she replied, not really understanding the point of my question.

If I stayed on the subject of clitoridectomy or sexual pleasure too long, women would invariably chastise me, saying, "We Malian women have more important things to worry about than whether or not sex feels good." Whenever the topic of circumcision depressed me, I had only to visit the compound of my friend, the Fat Lady from Timbuktu, whose jolly good spirits never failed to lighten my mood. At the same time, the plight of her house servant and the servant's son, Daouda, epitomized the reality expressed by so many women: they had other problems to worry about; they couldn't concern themselves with the issue of sexual pleasure, or the lack thereof.

Several weeks before the day of these clitoridectomies, as Moussa and I hiked the narrow back streets of Magnambougou looking for my earlier informants, we passed by a compound with a big, red metal door and Moussa asked "Do you remember the Fat Lady from Timbuktu?"

"Of course, now that you mention her!" I replied in delight. "I had forgotten all about her."

"Well, this is where she lives. Shall we see if she is at home?" he asked.

"Yes, let's do."

In 1982, one of the young children in my growth study was a little girl who was visiting her grandmother. The grandmother, a woman of perhaps 50 years, was very much interested in my research. Ethnically, she was a Moor, and she had moved to Bamako from Timbuktu. She was intelligent, articulate, and friendly, and she had a highly developed sense of humor. She was also enormously obese, and came to be known in my field notes as the Fat Lady from Timbuktu. Whenever I had occasion to be in her part of the community, I would stop by just to chat. Her daughter and granddaughter went back to their home village after

several months, but I continued to visit the grandmother's compound because I enjoyed her company so much. She used to tease me all the time about not having a son yet for my husband (Miranda was almost three years old at the time, and a typical Malian woman would have had another infant by then). She told me that I should wean Miranda so that I could get pregnant again and have a son for Steven. Malian women know that breastfeeding has a contraceptive effect, although they are not aware of the mechanism. When a baby nurses, the mother's pituitary releases the hormone prolactin, which aids in milk production, and also suppresses ovulation, preventing another pregnancy. But this contraceptive effect, known as lactational amenorrhea or lactational anovulation, only works when the baby nurses very often around the clock. At three years of age, Miranda was only nursing a few times a day, not enough to maintain lactational amenorrhea. In fact, my menstrual periods had returned when Miranda was 23 months old. It didn't seem to occur to the Fat Lady that I might want to prevent another pregnancy, or that I would have the means to do so.

Other women in Magnambougou told me I should wean Miranda when she turned two years old, because nursing longer would make her stupid. I knew from my dissertation research that this belief had been reported in several cultures. However, I also knew that most children around the world are nursed until they are two or three years old, and some longer. According to several of my elderly female informants, traditional rural Malians nursed their children until they weaned by themselves, usually between three and four years of age. This was much more in keeping with our species' primate heritage, and what human babies had

evolved to expect, and I intended to do the same with my children.

Of course, the Fat Lady also teased that Steven probably wasn't that interested in me sexually anymore because I was too old and not fat enough. Tongue firmly in cheek, she offered her 12-year-old daughter as Steven's second wife, pointing out that not only was she beautiful (she was), but she was a very hard worker and an obedient child who would do whatever I told her. Every time I saw her, either at her compound, or at the market, she would say, "Bring your husband over to take a look. He won't be able to resist."

When I returned to visit her in 1989, she was overjoyed to see me again. She immediately called over her daughter, now 18 years old and even more beautiful than before, and said, "Look, your cowife has come to claim you." The girl blushed and ran away. She was glad to hear that I had had a son "for Steven" and chided me for still being "skinny." At 5 feet 8 inches tall, I weighed about 160 pounds when I first arrived in Mali in 1989, hardly skinny by American standards.

The Fat Lady herself was, if anything, even bigger than she had been in 1983. Standing only about 5 feet tall, she weighed close to 300 pounds. The ethnic group to which she belongs, the Moors, like their Saharan neighbors, the Tamasheq, value obesity in their women above all other signs of beauty. To have a fat wife signifies to the world that a man is wealthy, is able to provide plenty of food for his family to eat, and has slaves or servants to do the physical labor so that his wife can relax, lounging around and visiting with her friends and eating sweets. To be fat is to be healthy. Even more importantly, to be fat is to be sexy. . . .

The War Against Women

In much of the world, political and economic 'progress' has been dragging them backward

Twenty-five years ago, a band of militant women picketed the Miss America Pageant in Atlantic City, tossed bras, girdles and other "boob-girlie symbols" into the trash and added an epithet (bra burners) and a rallying cry (women's liberation) to the English language. A quarter of a century later, few countries are without a women's movement; few governments are immune to women's demands. Traditional notions of a woman's place are eroding, and gender gaps are narrowing.

Yet much of the world is still waging war against women. In 1980, the United Nations summed up the burden of inequality: Women, half the world's population, did two thirds of the world's work, earned one tenth of the world's income and owned one hundredth of the world's property. Fourteen years later, despite the fall of repressive regimes, a decade of high growth, the spread of market economics and the rise of female prime ministers and CEOs, women remain victims of abuse and discrimination just about everywhere. The 1993 U.N. Human Development Report found that there still is no country that treats its women as well as its men.

Not only have the political and economic gains of the past decade not always benefited women; in many places "progress" has dragged them backward:

■ **Victims of freedom.** The collapse of communism in the former Soviet Union has thrown women out of work in disproportionate numbers, chan-

neled them into second-rate jobs and revived prerevolutionary attitudes about a woman's place. Women applying for office jobs in the new Russia often are told that their duties include sleeping with the boss.

■ **Victims of democracy.** The new democratically elected assemblies of Eastern Europe have far fewer women members than their puppet predecessors did, and abortion rights are under fire in Germany, Poland and Romania.

■ **Victims of prosperity.** China's economy is growing at a double-digit clip, but most of the workers in the sweatshops that are helping to power the boom are women. And Beijing has subordinated women's health, employment and education needs to its goal of keeping the birthrate low.

■ **Victims of holy war.** Islamic militants are crusading against Western-style women's rights, issuing death threats against feminists and making headway even in traditionally tolerant Muslim lands such as Egypt.

■ **Victims of progress.** In China, India and other nations where sons are still valued more highly than daughters, medical technology has provided a new means of disposing of unwanted baby girls.

■ **Victims of violence.** Despite the toppling of military dictatorships in Latin America, the deregulation of India's economy and the end of apartheid in South Africa, there has been no halt to what the U.N. has called "a global epidemic of violence against women."

■ **Victims of success.** In America and Western Europe, women have made great strides in politics and in some professions. But even in Norway, where women now dominate the political scene, women are still hired last, fired first, paid less than men and held back from the top jobs. In America, a growing number of "separate sisters," including black women and other minorities, women in traditional "women's jobs" and both elderly and young women, charge that the feminist movement has ignored them and their concerns.

The collapse of communism, unlamented almost everywhere, has hurt women in unexpected ways. Gender equality was always more rhetorical than real under Marxism, but women have been hard hit by the implosion of old command economies, the end of guaranteed employment and the unraveling of the social safety net. In Russia, 70 percent of those laid off in the first two post-Communist years were women.

Birthrates in Russia and eastern Germany have dropped to all-time lows as benefits have evaporated and state-financed kindergartens have closed. Abortion rights are under fire in Germany and have been all but extinguished in Poland. In Romania, where abortion was banned for 23 years, abortion rates have hit a global high and the Orthodox Church is pushing to restore the ban.

Even robust economic growth is no guarantee that women will prosper. In China, where Communists still rule but capitalism is taking command, women are no longer being hired for secure, benefit-buffered jobs in state enterprises. Instead, they are being channeled into jobs as secretaries, tour guides and hostesses, for which they dress in traditional, tight *cheongsams* with thigh-high slits. Prof. Ma Xiaonian of the Beijing Women's Hotline says that when women ask how to deal with sexual harassment on the job he advises them to give in if they want to get ahead.

Small bandwagon. Even where female politicians have made gains, women's rights have not always followed. Twenty-five years ago, only three women had run a modern country: India's Indira Gandhi, Israel's Golda Meir and Sri Lanka's Sirimavo Bandaranaike. Since then, 25 more women have been elected head of state or government. Six women prime ministers and three presidents hold office today, as do 300 women ministers in 142 countries. But until recently, when Pakistan's Benazir Bhutto jumped on their small bandwagon, only Prime Minister Gro Harlem Brundtland of Norway and President Mary Robinson of Ireland had strongly pushed women's causes or candidacies.

Bhutto, the first woman to lead a Muslim country, was criticized in her first term for failing women. Back in power, she has a women's agenda, including separate women's police stations and courts, a 10 percent quota for government jobs and the expansion of education for girls. But a litmus test

will be whether she challenges an Islamic ordinance that allows rape victims to be charged with adultery; some 2,000 women languish in Pakistani jails under the law.

Across the Muslim world, women are feeling the heat from Islamic militants. The government of Bangladesh's female Prime Minister Khaleda Zia took away the passport of the country's leading feminist writer, Taslima Nasreen, because "her books were against religion." This encouraged local Islamic zealots to issue a Salman Rushdie-style *fatwa,* or religious edict, calling for Nasreen, who writes about taboo subjects such as sexual abuse, to be put to death for blasphemy. Two Egyptian feminists have received similar death threats.

Western feminists have learned to be cautious about rushing to the aid of endangered women where oppressors can claim cultural or religious sanction. Even local women activists sometimes turn defensive when traditional practices such as genital mutilation in Africa come under foreign attack. The U.N.'s Human Rights Commission tiptoed into that minefield earlier this month by calling for "the eradication of the harmful effects of certain traditional or customary practices." Next month, the commission will name a special investigator to look into violence against women.

As a club of governments, the U.N. is an unlikely catalyst for a feminist revolution. Three U.N. women's con-

ferences, in 1975, 1980 and 1985, served as transmission belts for the message of women s liberation. Now the world is gearing up for a fourth women's conference in Beijing next year and a fourth global plan for righting wrongs against the second sex.

High among them is what Health and Human Services Secretary Donna Shalala calls "terrorism in the home." Anthropology confirms that if there is anything universal about the female condition it is vulnerability to assault. In the United States in 1991, the FBI recorded 106,593 rapes. And a survey of Third World women's groups in the late 1980s found violence the top common concern. A woman is raped in South Africa every 83 seconds. In Latin America, where macho culture breeds high levels of abuse, more than 100 women's projects are dedicated to fighting it.

Violence has been a potent mobilizing force for feminists. Indian women date the takeoff of their movement to protests against rape and "bride burning" in the late 1970s. Today some American women's groups are promoting an antiviolence campaign that would replace abortion rights as the unifying thrust of the feminist movement.

The National Organization for Women is planning a national march against violence this summer while Congress considers a bill that would make violence against women a civil rights offense. But some prominent dissenters oppose making violence a priority be-

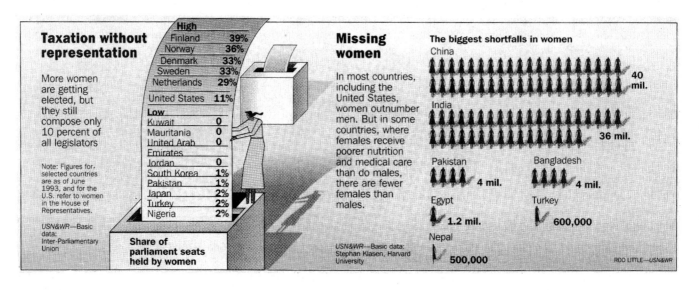

Taxation without representation

More women are getting elected, but they still compose only 10 percent of all legislators

Note: Figures for selected countries are as of June 1993, and for the U.S. refer to women in the House of Representatives.

USN&WR—Basic data: Inter-Parliamentary Union

High	
Finland	39%
Norway	36%
Denmark	33%
Sweden	33%
Netherlands	29%
United States	11%
Low	
Kuwait	0
Mauritania	0
United Arab Emirates	0
Jordan	0
South Korea	1%
Pakistan	1%
Japan	2%
Turkey	2%
Nigeria	2%

Share of parliament seats held by women

Missing women

In most countries, including the United States, women outnumber men. But in some countries, where females receive poorer nutrition and medical care than do males, there are fewer females than males.

USN&WR—Basic data: Stephan Klasen, Harvard University

The biggest shortfalls in women

China 40 mil.

India 36 mil.

Pakistan 4 mil.

Bangladesh 4 mil.

Egypt 1.2 mil.

Turkey 600,000

Nepal 500,000

ROD LITTLE—USN&WR

cause, like the drives against pornography and sexual harassment, it fosters "victim feminism."

While rape, harassment and battering hog the headlines, the vital issues for most women in most countries continue to be bread-and-butter ones. A recent survey by *Ms.* magazine found equal pay and job discrimination the top concerns of American women.

More women are working: They do so in industrial nations at 77 percent of the men's rate in 1991, up from 59 percent 20 years earlier. But women's pay still averages two thirds of men's, mainly because women are clustered in low-wage "women's jobs." In the United States, year-round full-time working women earned 71 percent of the male wage in 1992, up from 62 percent a decade earlier. But women high school graduates earn slightly less than do men who dropped out of school before ninth grade.

Basic burdens. For poor women—and the majority of women are poor—needs are more basic: food, shelter, work. Third World women get nothing like equal pay. Most of their work, on family farms or crafts, does not even count as paid labor, and they rarely inherit or control property. Their burdens have eased somewhat as birth control has become widely available. Mothers are producing fewer children, but every year half a million women still die from pregnancy-related problems, including botched abortions.

The other big shackle on poor women is illiteracy. Although the literacy gap is shrinking, two thirds of the world's illiterates are female; 600 million women cannot read, and 90 million school-age girls are not in school. Uneducated women everywhere have high birthrates, low earnings and short lives. Yet even a few years of education for girls can be a magic bullet, leading to smaller, healthier families, less economic dependence and less vulnerability to abusive husbands.

Natural hardiness has made females the majority in all Western countries and in most of the poorest. But nearly half the world's women live in countries where males are more numerous. In these places, as Harvard economist Amartya Sen points out, girls and women get less food and health care than their brothers and husbands and often die of neglect.

A measure of this extreme prejudice is the number of missing women. China and India together have 75 million fewer women than they should have, according to calculations by Harvard scholar Stephan Klasen. Premature death from neglect is the main cause, but there are others. In China, many girls are not counted because their families hide them from the birth control police. Both Asian giants have traditions of female infanticide, which continues in small pockets. And now technology offers a modern alternative in the form of sex-selective abortions.

Even villagers have access to ultrasound machines that can detect the sex of a fetus in time for a late abortion. Selective abortion is producing a big deficit in newborn girls, but it also leaves feminists in a moral quandary: Can abortion-rights advocates demand that limits be placed on a woman's right to choose? This dilemma may be the international abortion hot potato of the 1990s.

Now that American feminists are looking beyond abortion, their priorities may be more relevant to the forgotten women at home and overseas. Since feisty women tend to flourish best where speech is free, it may be that a rising tide of political and economic freedom eventually will lift women's boats, too. Russian women are beginning to meet in informal groups similar to those that coalesced into America's women's movement three decades ago. South African women are beginning to fight for equal rights now that majority rights are nearly won. In China, where women are just raising their heads above the parapet, there was not even a word for feminism until a few weeks ago, when women academics in Beijing settled on *nuquanzhuyi*—"women's rightsism." Just in time, too, before regiments of women's rightsists descend on Beijing for the womanpower fest next year.

By Emily MacFarquhar with Jennifer Seter, Susan V. Lawrence in Beijing, Robin Knight in London and Joannie M. Schrof

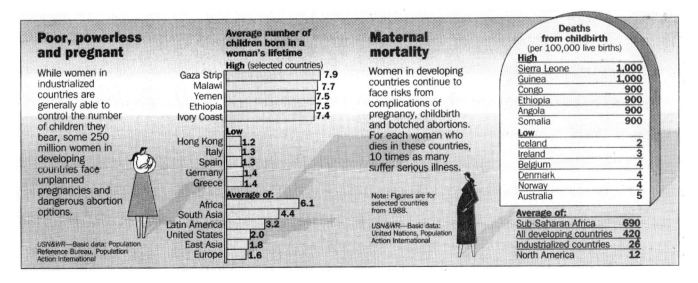

Poor, powerless and pregnant

While women in industrialized countries are generally able to control the number of children they bear, some 250 million women in developing countries face unplanned pregnancies and dangerous abortion options.

USN&WR—Basic data: Population Reference Bureau, Population Action International

Average number of children born in a woman's lifetime

High (selected countries)

Country	
Gaza Strip	7.9
Malawi	7.7
Yemen	7.5
Ethiopia	7.5
Ivory Coast	7.4

Low

Country	
Hong Kong	1.2
Italy	1.3
Spain	1.3
Germany	1.4
Greece	1.4

Average of:

Africa	6.1
South Asia	4.4
Latin America	3.2
United States	2.0
East Asia	1.8
Europe	1.6

Maternal mortality

Women in developing countries continue to face risks from complications of pregnancy, childbirth and botched abortions. For each woman who dies in these countries, 10 times as many suffer serious illness.

Note: Figures are for selected countries from 1988.

USN&WR—Basic data: United Nations, Population Action International

Deaths from childbirth (per 100,000 live births)

High

Country	
Sierra Leone	1,000
Guinea	1,000
Congo	900
Ethiopia	900
Angola	900
Somalia	900

Low

Country	
Iceland	2
Ireland	3
Belgium	4
Denmark	4
Norway	4
Australia	5

Average of:

Sub-Saharan Africa	690
All developing countries	420
Industrialized countries	26
North America	12

The Initiation of a Maasai Warrior

Tepilit Ole Saitoti

"Tepilit, circumcision means a sharp knife cutting into the skin of the most sensitive part of your body. You must not budge; don't move a muscle or even blink. You can face only one direction until the operation is completed. The slightest movement on your part will mean you are a coward, incompetent and unworthy to be a Maasai man. Ours has always been a proud family, and we would like to keep it that way. We will not tolerate unnecessary embarrassment, so you had better be ready. If you are not, tell us now so that we will not proceed. Imagine yourself alone remaining uncircumcised like the water youth [white people]. I hear they are not circumcised. Such a thing is not known in Maasailand; therefore, circumcision will have to take place even if it means holding you down until it is completed."

My father continued to speak and every one of us kept quiet. "The pain you will feel is symbolic. There is a deeper meaning in all this. Circumcision means a break between childhood and adulthood. For the first time in your life, you are regarded as a grownup, a complete man or woman. You will be expected to give and not just to receive. To protect the family always, not just to be protected yourself. And your wise judgment will for the first time be taken into consideration. No family affairs will be discussed without your being consult-

ed. If you are ready for all these responsibilities, tell us now. Coming into manhood is not simply a matter of growth and maturity. It is a heavy load on your shoulders and especially a burden on the mind. Too much of this—I am done. I have said all I wanted to say. Fellows, if you have anything to add, go ahead and tell your brother, because I am through. I have spoken."

After a prolonged silence, one of my half-brothers said awkwardly, "Face it, man . . . it's painful. I won't lie about it, but it is not the end. We all went through it, after all. Only blood will flow, not milk." There was laughter and my father left.

My brother Lellia said, "Men, there are many things we must acquire and preparations we must make before the ceremony, and we will need the cooperation and help of all of you. Ostrich feathers for the crown and wax for the arrows must be collected."

"Are you *orkirekenyi?*" one of my brothers asked. I quickly replied no, and there was laughter. *Orkirekenyi* is a person who has transgressed sexually. For you must not have sexual intercourse with any circumcised woman before you yourself are circumcised. You must wait until you are circumcised. If you have not waited, you will be fined. Your father, mother, and the circumciser will take a cow from you as punishment.

Just before we departed, one of my closest friends said, "If you kick the knife, you will be in trouble." There was laughter. "By the way, if you have decided to kick the circumciser, do it well. Silence him once and for all." "Do it the way you kick a football in school." "That will fix him," another added, and we all laughed our heads off again as we departed.

The following month was a month of preparation. I and others collected wax, ostrich feathers, honey to be made into honey beer for the elders to drink on the day of circumcision, and all the other required articles.

Three days before the ceremony my head was shaved and I discarded all my belongings, such as my necklaces, garments, spear, and sword. I even had to shave my pubic hair. Circumcision in many ways is similar to Christian baptism. You must put all the sins you have committed during childhood behind and embark as a new person with a different outlook on a new life.

The circumciser came the following day and handed the ritual knives to me. He left drinking a calabash of beer. I stared at the knives uneasily. It was hard to accept that he was going to use them on my organ. I was to sharpen them and protect them from people of ill will who might try to blunt them, thus rendering them inefficient during the ritual and thereby bringing shame on our family. The knives threw a chill down my spine; I was not sure I was sharpening them properly, so I took them to my closest brother for him to check out, and he assured me that the knives were all right. I hid them well and waited.

Tension started building between me and my relatives, most of whom worried that I wouldn't make it through the ceremony valiantly. Some even snarled at me, which was their way of encouraging me. Others threw insults and abusive words my way. My sister Loiyan in particular was more troubled by the whole affair than anyone in the whole family. She had to assume my mother's role during the circumcision. Were I to fail my initiation, she would have to face the consequences. She would be spat upon and even beaten for representing the mother of an unworthy son. The same fate would befall my father, but he seemed unconcerned. He had this weird belief that because I was not particularly handsome, I must be brave. He kept saying, "God is not so bad as to have made him ugly and a coward at the same time."

Failure to be brave during circumcision would have other unfortunate consequences: the herd of cattle belonging to the family still in the compound would be beaten until they stampeded; the slaughtered oxen and honey beer prepared during the month before the ritual would go to waste; the initiate's food would be spat upon and he would have to eat it or else get a severe beating. Everyone would call him Olkasiodoi, the knife kicker.

Kicking the knife of the circumciser would not help you anyway. If you struggle and try to get away during the ritual, you will be held down until the operation is completed. Such failure of nerve would haunt you in the future. For example, no one will choose a person who kicked the knife for a position of leadership. However, there have been instances in which a person who failed to go through circumcision successfully became very brave afterwards because he was filled with anger over the incident; no one dares to scold him or remind him of it. His agemates, particularly the warriors, will act as if nothing had happened.

During the circumcision of a woman, on the other hand, she is allowed to cry as long as she does not hinder the operation. It is common to see a woman crying and kicking during circumcision. Warriors are usually summoned to help hold her down.

For woman, circumcision means an end to the company of Maasai warriors. After they recuperate, they soon get married, and often to men twice their age.

The closer it came to the hour of truth, the more I was hated, particularly by those closest to me. I was deeply troubled by the withdrawal of all the support I needed. My annoyance turned into anger and resolve. I decided not to budge or blink, even if I were to see my intestines flowing before me. My resolve was hardened when newly circumcised warriors came to sing for me. Their songs were utterly insulting, intended to annoy me further. They tucked their wax arrows under my crotch and rubbed them on my nose. They repeatedly called me names.

By the end of the singing, I was fuming. Crying would have meant I was a coward. After midnight they left me alone and I went into the house and tried to sleep but could not. I was exhausted and numb but remained awake all night.

At dawn I was summoned once again by the newly circumcised warriors. They piled more and more insults on me. They sang their weird songs with even more vigor and excitement than before. The songs praised warriorhood and encouraged one to achieve it at all costs. The songs continued until the sun shone on the cattle horns clearly. I was summoned to the main cattle gate, in my hand a ritual cowhide from a cow that had been properly slaughtered during my naming ceremony. I went past Loiyan, who was milking a cow, and she muttered something. She was shaking all over. There was so much tension that people could hardly breathe.

I laid the hide down and a boy was ordered to pour ice-cold water, known as *engare entolu* (ax water), over my head. It dripped all over my naked body and I shook furiously. In a matter of seconds I was summoned to sit down. A large crowd of boys and men formed a semicircle in front of me; women are

not allowed to watch male circumcision and vice-versa. That was the last thing I saw clearly. As soon as I sat down, the circumciser appeared, his knives at the ready. He spread my legs and said, "One cut," a pronouncement necessary to prevent an initiate from claiming that he had been taken by surprise. He splashed a white liquid, a ceremonial paint called *enturoto*, across my face. Almost immediately I felt a spark of pain under my belly as the knife cut through my penis' foreskin. I happened to choose to look in the direction of the operation. I continued to observe the circumciser's fingers working mechanically. The pain became numbness and my lower body felt heavy, as if I were weighed down by a heavy burden. After fifteen minutes or so, a man who had been supporting from behind pointed at something, as if to assist the circumciser. I came to learn later that the circumciser's eyesight had been failing him and that my brothers had been mad at him because the operation had taken longer than was usually necessary. All the same, I remained pinned down until the operation was over. I heard a call for milk to wash the knives, which signaled the end, and soon the ceremony was over.

With words of praise, I was told to wake up, but I remained seated. I waited for the customary presents in appreciation of my bravery. My father gave me a cow and so did my brother Lillia. The man who had supported my back and my brother-in-law gave me a heifer. In all I had eight animals given to me. I was carried inside the house to my own bed to recuperate as activities intensified to celebrate my bravery.

I laid on my own bed and bled profusely. The blood must be retained within the bed, for according to Maasai tradition, it must not spill to the ground. I was drenched in my own blood. I stopped bleeding after about half an hour but soon was in intolerable pain. I was supposed to squeeze my organ and force blood to flow out of the wound, but no one had told me, so the blood coagulated and caused unbearable pain. The circumciser was brought to my aid and showed me what to do, and soon the pain subsided.

The following morning, I was escorted by a small boy to a nearby valley to walk and relax, allowing my wound to drain. This was common for everyone who had been circumcised, as well as for women who had just given birth. Having lost a lot of blood, I was extremely weak. I walked very slowly, but in spite of my caution I fainted. I tried to hang on to bushes and shrubs, but I fell, irritating my wound. I came out of unconsciousness quickly, and the boy who was escorting me never realized what had happened. I was so scared that I told him to lead me back home. I could have died without there being anyone around who could have helped me. From that day on, I was selective of my company while I was feeble.

In two weeks I was able to walk and was taken to join other newly circumcised boys far away from our settlement. By tradition Maasai initiates are required to decorate their headdresses with all kinds of colorful birds they have killed. On our way to the settlement, we hunted birds and teased girls by shooting them with our wax blunt arrows. We danced and ate and were well treated wherever we went. We were protected from the cold and rain during the healing period. We were not allowed to touch food, as we were regarded as unclean, so whenever we ate we had to use specially prepared sticks instead. We remained in this pampered state until our wounds healed and our headdresses were removed. Our heads were shaved, we discarded our black cloaks and bird headdresses and embarked as newly shaven warriors, Irkeleani.

As long as I live I will never forget the day my head was shaved and I emerged a man, a Maasai warrior. I felt a sense of control over my destiny so great that no words can accurately describe it. I now stood with confidence, pride, and happiness of being, for all around me I was desired and loved by beautiful, sensuous Maasai maidens. I could now interact with women and even have sex with them, which I had not been allowed before. I was now regarded as a responsible person.

In the old days, warriors were like gods, and women and men wanted only to be the parent of a warrior. Everything else would be taken care of as a result. When a poor family had a warrior, they

ceased to be poor. The warrior would go on raids and bring cattle back. The warrior would defend the family against all odds. When a society respects the individual and displays confidence in him the way the Maasai do their warriors, the individual can grow to his fullest potential. Whenever there was a task requiring physical strength or bravery, the Maasai would call upon their warriors. They hardly ever fall short of what is demanded of them and so are characterized by pride, confidence, and an extreme sense of freedom. But there is an old saying in Maasai: "You are never a free man until your father dies." In other words, your father is paramount while he is alive and you are obligated to respect him. My father took advantage of this principle and held a tight grip on all his warriors, including myself. He always wanted to know where we all were at any given time. We fought against his restrictions, but without success. I, being the youngest of my father's five warriors, tried even harder to get loose repeatedly, but each time I was punished severely.

Roaming the plains with other warriors in pursuit of girls and adventure was a warrior's pastime. We would wander from one settlement to another, singing, wrestling, hunting, and just playing. Often I was ready to risk my father's punishment for this wonderful freedom.

One clear day my father sent me to take sick children and one of his wives to the dispensary in the Korongoro Highlands. We rode in the L.S.B. Leakey lorry. We ascended the highlands and were soon attended to in the local hospital. Near the conservation offices I met several acquaintances, and one of them told me of an unusual circumcision that was about to take place in a day or two. All the local warriors and girls were preparing to attend it.

The highlands were a lush green from the seasonal rains and the sky was a purple-blue with no clouds in sight. The land was overflowing with milk, and the warriors felt and looked their best, as they always did when there was plenty to eat and drink. Everyone was at ease. The demands the community usually made on warriors during the dry sea-

son when water was scarce and wells had to be dug were now not necessary. Herds and flocks were entrusted to youths to look after. The warriors had all the time for themselves. But my father was so strict that even at times like these he still insisted on overworking us in one way or another. He believed that by keeping us busy, he would keep us out of trouble.

When I heard about the impending ceremony, I decided to remain behind in the Korongoro Highlands and attend it now that the children had been treated. I knew very well that I would have to make up a story for my father upon my return, but I would worry about that later. I had left my spear at home when I boarded the bus, thinking that I would be coming back that very day. I felt lighter but now regretted having left it behind; I was so used to carrying it wherever I went. In gales of laughter resulting from our continuous teasing of each other, we made our way toward a distant kraal. We walked at a leisurely pace and reveled in the breeze. As usual we talked about the women we desired, among other things.

The following day we were joined by a long line of colorfully dressed girls and warriors from the kraal and the neighborhood where we had spent the night, and we left the highland and headed to Ingorienito to the rolling hills on the lower slopes to attend the circumcision ceremony. From there one could see Oldopai Gorge, where my parents lived, and the Inaapi hills in the middle of the Serengeti Plain.

Three girls and a boy were to be initiated on the same day, an unusual occasion. Four oxen were to be slaughtered, and many people would therefore attend. As we descended, we saw the kraal where the ceremony would take place. All those people dressed in red seemed from a distance like flamingos standing in a lake. We could see lines of other guests heading to the settlements. Warriors made gallant cries of happiness known as *enkiseer*. Our line of warriors and girls responded to their cries even more gallantly.

In serpentine fashion, we entered the gates of the settlement. Holding spears in our left hands, we warriors walked proudly, taking small steps, swaying like palm trees, impressing our girls, who walked parallel to us in another line, and of course the spectators, who gazed at us approvingly.

We stopped in the center of the kraal and waited to be greeted. Women and children welcomed us. We put our hands on the children's heads, which is how children are commonly saluted. After the greetings were completed, we started dancing.

Our singing echoed off the kraal fence and nearby trees. Another line of warriors came up the hill and entered the compound, also singing and moving slowly toward us. Our singing grew in intensity. Both lines of warriors moved parallel to each other, and our feet pounded the ground with style. We stamped vigorously, as if to tell the next line and the spectators that we were the best.

The singing continued until the hot sun was overhead. We recessed and ate food already prepared for us by other warriors. Roasted meat was for those who were to eat meat, and milk for the others. By our tradition, meat and milk must not be consumed at the same time, for this would be a betrayal of the animal. It was regarded as cruel to consume a product of the animal that could be obtained while it was alive, such as milk, and meat, which was only available after the animal had been killed.

After eating we resumed singing, and I spotted a tall, beautiful *esiankiki* (young maiden) of Masiaya whose family was one of the largest and richest in our area. She stood very erect and seemed taller than the rest.

One of her breasts could be seen just above her dress, which was knotted at the shoulder. While I was supposed to dance generally to please all the spectators, I took it upon myself to please her especially. I stared at and flirted with her, and she and I danced in unison at times. We complemented each other very well.

During a break, I introduced myself to the *esiankiki* and told her I would like to see her after the dance. "Won't you need a warrior to escort you home later when the evening threatens?" I said. She replied, "Perhaps, but the evening is still far away."

I waited patiently. When the dance ended, I saw her departing with a group of other women her age. She gave me a sidelong glance, and I took that to mean come later and not now. With so many others around, I would not have been able to confer with her as I would have liked anyway.

With another warrior, I wandered around the kraal killing time until the herds returned from pasture. Before the sun dropped out of sight, we departed. As the kraal of the *esiankiki* was in the lowlands, a place called Enkoloa, we descended leisurely, our spears resting on our shoulders.

We arrived at the woman's kraal and found that cows were now being milked. One could hear the women trying to appease the cows by singing to them. Singing calms cows down, making it easier to milk them. There were no warriors in the whole kraal except for the two of us. Girls went around into warriors' houses as usual and collected milk for us. I was so eager to go and meet my *esiankiki* that I could hardly wait for nightfall. The warriors' girls were trying hard to be sociable, but my mind was not with them. I found them to be childish, loud, bothersome, and boring.

As the only warriors present, we had to keep them company and sing for them, at least for a while, as required by custom. I told the other warrior to sing while I tried to figure out how to approach my *esiankiki*. Still a novice warrior, I was not experienced with women and was in fact still afraid of them. I could flirt from a distance, of course. But sitting down with a woman and trying to seduce her was another matter. I had already tried twice to approach women soon after my circumcision and had failed. I got as far as the door of one woman's house and felt my heart beating like a Congolese drum; breathing became difficult and I had to turn back. Another time I managed to get in the house and suceeded in sitting on the bed, but then I started trembling until the whole bed was shaking, and conversation became difficult. I left the house and the woman, amazed and speechless, and never went back to her again.

Tonight I promised myself I would be brave and would not make any silly, ridiculous moves. "I must be mature and not afraid," I kept reminding myself, as I remembered an incident involving one of my relatives when he was still very young and, like me, afraid of women. He went to a woman's house and sat on a stool for a whole hour; he was afraid to awaken her, as his heart was pounding and he was having difficulty breathing.

When he finally calmed down, he woke her up, and their conversation went something like this:

"Woman, wake up."

"Why should I?"

"To light the fire."

"For what?"

"So you can see me."

"I already know who you are. Why don't *you* light the fire, as you're nearer to it than me?"

"It's your house and it's only proper that you light it yourself."

"I don't feel like it."

"At least wake up so we can talk, as I have something to tell you."

"Say it."

"I need you."

"I do not need one-eyed types like yourself."

"One-eyed people are people too."

"That might be so, but they are not to my taste."

They continued talking for quite some time, and the more they spoke, the braver he became. He did not sleep with her that night, but later on he persisted until he won her over. I doubted whether I was as strong-willed as he, but the fact that he had met with success encouraged me. I told my warrior friend where to find me should he need me, and then I departed.

When I entered the house of my *esiankiki*, I called for the woman of the house, and as luck would have it, my lady responded. She was waiting for me. I felt better, and I proceeded to talk to her like a professional. After much talking back and forth, I joined her in bed.

The night was calm, tender, and loving, like most nights after initiation ceremonies as big as this one. There must have been a lot of courting and lovemaking.

Maasai women can be very hard to deal with sometimes. They can simply reject a man outright and refuse to change their minds. Some play hard to get, but in reality are testing the man to see whether he is worth their while. Once a friend of mine while still young was powerfully attracted to a woman nearly his mother's age. He put a bold move on her. At first the woman could not believe his intention, or rather was amazed by his courage. The name of the warrior was Ngengeiya, or Drizzle.

"Drizzle, what do you want?"

The warrior stared her right in the eye and said, "You."

"For what?"

"To make love to you."

"I am your mother's age."

"The choice was either her or you."

This remark took the woman by surprise. She had underestimated the saying "There is no such thing as a young warrior." When you are a warrior, you are expected to perform bravely in any situation. Your age and size are immaterial.

"You mean you could really love me like a grown-up man?"

"Try me, woman."

He moved in on her. Soon the woman started moaning with excitement, calling out his name. "Honey Drizzle, Honey Drizzle, you *are* a man." In a breathy, stammering voice, she said, "A real man."

Her attractiveness made Honey Drizzle ignore her relative old age. The Maasai believe that if an older and a younger person have intercourse, it is the older person who stands to gain. For instance, it is believed that an older woman having an affair with a young man starts to appear younger and healthier, while the young man grows older and unhealthy.

The following day when the initiation rites had ended, I decided to return home. I had offended my father by staying away from home without his consent, so I prepared myself for whatever punishment he might inflict on me. I walked home alone.

The Little Emperors

A generation of spoiled brats, a tidal wave of abortions and thousands of missing girls—these are some of the unintended consequences of China's revolutionary one-child policy

Daniela Deane

Daniela Deane, who has two sons and lives in Hong Kong, is a free-lance writer who contributes to the Washington Post *and* Newsweek. *Her last article for this magazine was "The Vanishing Border," about the growing integration of southern China and Hong Kong.*

XU MING SITS ON THE WORN SOFA WITH his short, chubby arms and legs splayed, forced open by fat and the layers of padded clothing worn in northern China to ward off the relentless chill. To reach the floor, the tubby 8-year-old rocks back and forth on his big bottom, inching forward slowly, eventually ending upright. Xu Ming finds it hard to move.

"He got fat when he was about 3," says his father, Xu Jianguo, holding the boy's bloated, dimpled hand. "We were living with my parents and they were very good to him. He's the only grandson. It's a tradition in China that boys are very loved. They love him very much, and so they feed him a lot. They give him everything he wants."

Xu Ming weighs 135 pounds, about twice what he should at his age. He's one of hundreds of children who have sought help in the past few years at the Beijing Children's Hospital, which recently began the first American-style fat farm for obese children in what was once the land of skin and bones.

"We used to get a lot of cases of malnutrition," says Dr. Ni Guichen, director of endocrinology at the hospital and founder of the weight-reduction classes. "But in the last 10 years, the problem has become obese children. The number of fat children in China is growing very fast. The main reason is the one-child policy," she says, speaking in a drab waiting room. "Because parents can only have one child, the families take extra good care of that one child, which means feeding him too much."

Bulging waistlines are one result of China's tough campaign to curb its population. The one-child campaign, a strict national directive that seeks to limit each Chinese couple to a single son or daughter, has other dramatic consequences: millions of abortions, fewer girls and a generation of spoiled children.

The 10-day weight-reduction sessions—a combination of exercise, nutritional guidance and psychological counseling—are very popular. Hundreds of children—some so fat they can hardly walk—are turned away for each class.

According to Ni, about 5% of children in China's cities are obese, with two obese boys for every overweight girl, the traditional preference toward boys being reflected in the amount of attention lavished on the child. "Part of the course is also centered on the parents. We try to teach them how to bring their children up properly, not just by spoiling them," Ni says.

Ming's father is proud that his son, after two sessions at the fat farm, has managed to halve his intake of *jiaozi*, the stodgy meat-filled dumplings that are Ming's particular weakness, from 30 to 15 at a sitting. "Even if he's not full, that's all he gets," he says. "In the beginning, it was very difficult. He would put his arms around our necks and beg us for more food. We couldn't bear it, so we'd give him a little more."

Ming lost a few pounds but hasn't been able to keep the weight off. He's a bit slimmer now, but only because he's taller. "I want to lose weight," says Ming, who spends his afternoons snacking at his grandparents' house and his evenings plopped in front of the television set at home. "The kids make fun of me, they call me a fat pig. I hate the nicknames. In sports class, I can't do what the teacher says. I can run a little bit, but after a while I have to sit down. The teacher puts me at the front of the class where all the other kids can see me. They all laugh and make fun of me."

The many fat children visible on China's city streets are just the most obvious example of 13 years of the country's one-child policy. In the vast countryside, the policy has meant shadowy lives as second-class citizens for thousands of girls, or, worse, death. It has made abortion a way of life and a couple's sexual intimacy the government's concern. Even women's menstrual cycles are monitored. Under the directive, couples literally have to line up for permission to procreate. Second children are sometimes possible, but only on payment of a heavy fine.

The policy is an unparalleled intrusion into the private lives of a nation's citizens, an experiment on a scale never attempted elsewhere in the world. But no expert will argue that China—by far the world's most populous country with 1.16 billion people—could continue without strict curbs on its population.

China's communist government adopted the one-child policy in 1979 in response to the staggering doubling of the country's population during Mao Tse-tung's rule. Mao, who died in 1976, was convinced that the country's masses were a strategic asset and vigorously encouraged the Chinese to produce even-larger families.

But large families are now out for the Chinese—20% of the world's population living on just 7% of the arable land. "China has to have a population policy," says Huang Baoshan, deputy director of the State Family Planning Commission. With the numbers ever growing, "how can we feed these people, clothe them, house them?"

DINNER TIME FOR ONE 5-YEAR-OLD GIRL consists of granddad chasing her through the house, bowl and spoon in hand, barking like a dog or mewing like a cat. If he performs authentically enough, she rewards him by accepting a mouthful of food. No problem, insists granddad, "it's good exercise for her."

An 11-year-old boy never gets up to go to the toilet during the night. That's because his mother, summoned by a shout, gets up instead and positions a bottle under the covers for him. "We wouldn't want him to have to get up in the night," his mother says.

Another mother wanted her 16-year-old to eat some fruit, but the teen-ager was engrossed in a video game. Not wanting him to get his fingers sticky or daring to interrupt, she peeled several grapes and popped one after another into his mouth. "Not so fast," he snapped. "Can't you see I have to spit out the seeds?"

Stories like these are routinely published in China's newspapers, evidence that the government-imposed birth-control policy has produced an emerging generation of spoiled, lazy, selfish, self-centered and overweight children. There are about 40 million only chil-

dren in China. Dubbed the country's "Little Emperors," their behavior toward their elders is likened to that of the young emperor Pu Yi, who heaped indignities on his eunuch servants while making them cater to his whims, as chronicled in Bernardo Bertolucci's film "The Last Emperor."

Many studies on China's only children have been done. One such study confirmed that only children generally are not well liked. The study, conducted by a team of Chinese psychologists, asked a group of 360 Chinese children, half who have siblings and half who don't, to rate each other's behavior. The only children were, without fail, the least popular, regardless of age or social background. Peers rated them more uncooperative and selfish than children with brothers and sisters. They bragged more, were less helpful in group activities and more apt to follow their own selfish interests. And they wouldn't share their toys.

The Chinese lay a lot of blame on what they call the "4-2-1" syndrome—four doting grandparents, two overindulgent parents, all pinning their hopes and ambitions on one child.

Besides stuffing them with food, Chinese parents have very high expectations of their one *bao bei,* or treasured object. Some have their still-in-strollers babies tested for IQ levels. Others try to teach toddlers Tang Dynasty poetry. Many shell out months of their hard-earned salaries for music lessons and instruments for children who have no talent or interest in playing. They fill their kids' lives with lessons in piano, English, gymnastics and typing.

The one-child parents, most of them from traditionally large Chinese families, grew up during the chaotic, 10-year Cultural Revolution, when many of the country's cultural treasures were destroyed and schools were closed for long periods of time. Because many of that generation spent years toiling in the fields rather than studying, they demand—and put all their hopes into—academic achievement for their children.

"We've already invested a lot of money in his intellectual development," Wang Zhouzhi told me in her Spartan home in a tiny village of Changping

county outside Beijing, discussing her son, Chenqian, an only child. "I don't care how much money we spend on him. We've bought him an organ and we push him hard. Unfortunately, he's only a mediocre student," she says, looking toward the 10-year-old boy. Chenqian, dressed in a child-sized Chinese army uniform, ate 10 pieces of candy during the half-hour interview and repeatedly fired off his toy pistol, all without a word of reproach from his mother.

Would Chenqian have liked a sibling to play with? "No," he answers loudly, firing a rapid, jarring succession of shots. His mother breaks in: "If he had a little brother or sister, he wouldn't get everything he wants. Of course he doesn't want one. With only one child, I give my full care and concern to him."

But how will these children, now entering their teen-age years and moving quickly toward adulthood, become the collectivist-minded citizens China's hard-line communist leadership demands? Some think they never will. Ironically, it may be just these overindulged children who will change Chinese society. After growing up doing as they wished, ruling their immediate families, they're not likely to obey a central government that tells them to fall in line. This new generation of egotists, who haven't been taught to take even their parents into consideration, simply may not be able to think of the society as a whole—the basic principle of communism.

THE NEED FOR FAMILY PLANNING IS OBvious in the cities, where living space is limited and the one-child policy is strictly enforced and largely successful. City dwellers are slowly beginning to accept the notion that smaller families are better for the country, although most would certainly want two children if they could have them. However, in the countryside, where three of every four Chinese live—nearly 900 million people—the goal of limiting each couple to only one child has proved largely elusive.

In the hinterlands, the policy has become a confusing patchwork of special cases and exceptions. Provincial authorities can decide which couples can have a second child. In the southern province of Guangdong, China's richest, two children are allowed and many couples can afford to pay the fine to have even a third or fourth child. The amounts of the fines vary across the country, the highest in populous Sichuan province, where the fine for a second child can be as much as 25% of a family's income over four years. Special treatment has been given to China's cultural minorities such as the Mongolians and the Tibetans because of their low numbers. Many of them are permitted three or four children without penalty, although some Chinese social scientists have begun to question the privilege.

"It's really become a two-child policy in the countryside," says a Western diplomat. "Because of the traditional views on labor supply, the traditional bias toward the male child, it's been impossible for them to enforce a one-child policy outside the cities. In the countryside, they're really trying to stop that third child."

Thirteen years of strict family planning have created one of the great mysteries of the vast and remote Chinese countryside: Where have all the little girls gone? A Swedish study of sex ratios in China, published in 1990, and based on China's own census data, concluded that several million little girls are "missing"—up to half a million a year in the years 1985 to 1987—since the policy was introduced in late 1979.

In the study, and in demographic research worldwide, sex ratio at birth in humans is shown to be very stable, between 105 and 106 boys for every 100 girls. The imbalance is thought to be nature's way of compensating for the higher rates of miscarriage, stillbirth and infant mortality among boys.

In China, the ratio climbed consistently during the 1980s, and it now rests at more than 110 boys to 100 girls. "The imbalance is evident in some areas of the country," says Stirling Scruggs, director of the United Nations Population Fund in China. "I don't think the reason is widespread

infanticide. They're adopting out girls to try for a boy, they're hiding their girls, they're not registering them. Throughout Chinese history, in times of famine, and now as well, people have been forced to make choices between boys and girls, and for many reasons, boys always win out."

With the dismantling of collectives, families must, once again, farm their own small plots and sons are considered necessary to do the work. Additionally, girls traditionally "marry out" of their families, transferring their filial responsibilities to their in-laws. Boys carry on the family name and are entrusted with the care of their parents as they age. In the absence of a social security system, having a son is the difference between starving and eating when one is old. To combat the problem, some innovative villages have begun issuing so-called "girl insurance," an old-age insurance policy for couples who have given birth to a daughter and are prepared to stop at that.

"People are scared to death to be childless and penniless in their old age," says William Hinton, an American author of seven books chronicling modern China. "So if they don't have a son, they immediately try for another. When the woman is pregnant, they'll have a sex test to see if it's a boy or a girl. They'll abort a girl, or go in hiding with the girl, or pay the fine, or bribe the official or leave home. Anything. It's a game of wits."

Shen Shufen, a sturdy, round-faced peasant woman of 33, has two children—an 8-year-old girl and a 3-year-old boy—and lives in Sihe, a dusty, one-road, mud-brick, village in the countryside outside Beijing. Her husband is a truck driver. "When we had our girl, we knew we had to have another child somehow. We saved for years to pay the fine. It was hard giving them that money, 3,000 yuan ($550 in U.S. dollars), in one night. That's what my husband makes in three years. I was so happy when our second child was a boy."

The government seems aware of the pressure its policies put on expectant parents, and the painful results, but has not shown any flexibility. For instance,

Beijing in 1990 passed a law forbidding doctors to tell a couple the results of ultrasound tests that disclose the sex of their unborn child. The reason: Too many female embryos were being aborted.

And meanwhile, several hundred thousand women—called "guerrilla moms"—go into hiding every year to have their babies. They become part of China's 40-million-strong floating population that wanders the country, mostly in search of work, sleeping under bridges and in front of railway stations. Tens of thousands of female children are simply abandoned in rural hospitals.

And although most experts say female infanticide is not widespread, it does exist. "I found a dead baby girl," says Hinton. "We stopped for lunch at this mountain ravine in Shaanxi province. We saw her lying there, at the bottom of the creek bed. She was all bundled up, with one arm sticking out. She had been there a while, you could tell, because she had a little line of mold growing across her mouth and nostrils."

Death comes in another form, too: neglect. "It's female neglect, more than female infanticide, neglect to the point of death for little girls," says Scruggs of the U.N. Population Fund. "If you have a sick child, and it's a girl," he says, "you might buy only half the dose of medicine she needs to get better."

Hundreds of thousands of unregistered little girls—called "black children"—live on the edge of the law, unable to get food rations, immunizations or places in school. Many reports are grim. The government-run China News Service reported last year that the drowning of baby girls had revived to such an extent in Guangxi province that at least 1 million boys will be unable to find wives in 20 years. And partly because of the gender imbalance, the feudalistic practice of selling women has been revived.

The alarming growth of the flesh trade prompted authorities to enact a law in January that imposes jail sentences of up to 10 years and heavy fines for people caught trafficking. The government also recently began broadcasting a television dramatization to warn women against the practice. The public-service message shows two women, told that they would be given high-paying jobs, being lured to a suburban home. Instead, they are locked in a small, dark room, and soon realize that they have been sold.

LI WANGPING IS NERVOUS. SHE KEEPS looking at the air vents at the bottom of the office door, to see if anyone is walking by or, worse still, standing there listening. She rubs her hands together over and over. She speaks in a whisper. "I'm afraid to get into trouble talking to you," Li confides. She says nothing for a few minutes.

"After my son was born, I desperately wanted another baby," the 42-year-old woman finally begins. "I just wanted to have more children, you understand? Anyway, I got pregnant three times, because I wasn't using any birth control. I didn't want to use any. So, I had to have three abortions, one right after the other. I didn't want to at all. It was terrible killing the babies I wanted so much. But I had to."

By Chinese standards, Li (not her real name) has a lot to lose if she chooses to follow her maternal yearnings. As an office worker at government-owned CITIC, a successful and dynamic conglomerate, she has one of the best jobs in Beijing. Just being a city-dweller already puts her ahead of most of the population.

"One of my colleagues had just gotten fired for having a second child. I couldn't afford to be fired," continues Li, speaking in a meeting room at CITIC headquarters. "I had to keep everything secret from the family-planning official at CITIC, from everyone at the office. Of course, I'm supposed to be using birth control. I had to lie. It was hard lying, because I felt so bad about everything."

She rubs her hands furiously and moves toward the door, staring continuously at the air slats. "I have to go now. There's more to say, but I'm afraid to tell you. They could find me."

China's family-planning officials wield awesome powers, enforcing the policy through a combination of incentives and deterrents. For those who comply, there are job promotions and small cash awards. For those who resist, they suffer stiff fines and loss of job and status within the country's tightly knit and heavily regulated communities. The State Family Planning Commission is the government ministry entrusted with the tough task of curbing the growth of the world's most populous country, where 28 children are born every minute. It employs about 200,000 full-time officials and uses more than a million volunteers to check the fertility of hundreds of millions of Chinese women.

"Every village or enterprise has at least one family-planning official," says Zhang Xizhi, a birth-control official in Changping county outside Beijing. "Our main job is propaganda work to raise people's consciousness. We educate people and tell them their options for birth control. We go down to every household to talk to people. We encourage them to have only one child, to marry late, to have their child later."

China's population police frequently keep records of the menstrual cycles of women of childbearing age, on the type of birth control they use and the pending applications to have children. If they slip up, street committees—half-governmental, half-civilian organizations that have sprung up since the 1949 Communist takeover—take up the slack. The street committees, made up mostly of retired volunteers, act as the central government's ear to the ground, snooping, spying and reporting on citizens to the authorities.

When a couple wants to have a child—even their first, allotted one—they must apply to the family-planning office in their township or workplace, literally lining up to procreate. "If a woman gets pregnant without permission, she and her husband will get fined, even if it's their first," Zhang says. "It is fair to fine her, because she creates a burden on the whole society by jumping her place in line."

If a woman in Nanshao township, where Zhang works, becomes pregnant with a second child, she must terminate her pregnancy unless she or her husband or their first child is disabled or if both parents are only children. Her local family-planning official will repeatedly visit her at home to pressure her to comply. "Sometimes I have to go to people's homes five or six times to explain everything to them over and over to get them to have an abortion," says Zhang Cuiqing, the family-planning official for Sihe village, where there are 2,900 married women of childbearing age, of which 2,700 use some sort of birth control. Of those, 570 are sterilized and 1,100 have IUDs. Zhang recites the figures proudly, adding, "If they refuse, they will be fined between 20,000 and 50,000 yuan (U.S. $3,700 to $9,500)." The average yearly wage in Sihe is 1,500 yuan ($285).

The lack of early sexual education and unreliable IUDs are combining to make abortion—which is free, as are condoms and IUDs—a cornerstone of the one-child policy. Local officials are told not to use force, but rather education and persuasion, to meet their targets. However, the desire to fulfill their quotas, coupled with pressure from their bosses in Beijing, can lead to abuses by overzealous officials.

"Some local family-planning officials are running amok, because of the targets they have to reach," a Western health specialist says, "and there are a bunch of people willing to turn a blind eye to abuses because the target is so important."

The official Shanghai Legal Daily last year reported on a family-planning committee in central Sichuan province that ordered the flogging of the husbands of 10 pregnant women who refused to have abortions. According to the newspaper, the family-planning workers marched the husbands one by one into an empty room, ordered them to strip and lie on the floor and then beat them with a stick, once for every day their wives were pregnant.

"In some places, yes, things do happen," concedes Huang of the State Family Planning Commission. "Sometimes, family-planning officials do carry it too far."

THE YOUNG WOMAN LIES STILL ON THE narrow table with her eyes shut and her legs spread while the doctor quickly performs a suction abortion. A few moments, and the fetus is removed. The woman lets out a short, sharp yell. "OK, next," the doctor says.

She gets off the table and, holding a piece of cloth between her legs to catch the blood and clutching her swollen womb, hobbles over to a bed and collapses. The next patient gets up and walks toward the abortion table. No one notices a visitor watching. "It's very quick, it only takes about five minutes per abortion," says Dr. Huang Xiaomiao, chief physician at Beijing's Maternity Hospital. "No anesthetic. We don't use anesthetic for abortions or births here. Only for Cesarean sections, we use acupuncture."

Down the hall, 32-year-old Wu Guobin waits to be taken into the operating room to have her Fallopian tubes untied—a reversal of an earlier sterilization. "After my son was killed in an accident last year, the authorities in my province said I could try for another." In the bed next to Wu's, a dour-faced woman looks ready to cry. "She's getting sterilized," the nurse explains. "Her husband doesn't want her to, but her first child has mental problems."

Although it's a maternity hospital, the Family Planning Unit—where abortions, sterilizations, IUD insertions and the like are carried out—is the busiest department. "We do more abortions than births," says Dr. Fan Huimin, head of the unit. "Between 10 and 20 a day."

Abortions are a way of life in China, where about 10.5 million pregnancies are terminated each year. (In the United States, 1.6 million abortions are performed a year, but China's population is four to five times greater than the United States'.) One fetus is aborted for about every two children born and Chinese women often have several abortions. Usually, abortions are performed during the first trimester. But because some women resist, only to cave in under mental bullying further into their terms, abortions are also done in the later months of pregnancy, sometimes up till the eighth month.

Because of their population problem, the Chinese have become pioneers in contraceptive research. China will soon launch its own version of the controversial French abortion pill RU-486, which induces a miscarriage. They have perfected a non-scalpel procedure for male sterilization, with no suture required, allowing the man to "ride his bicycle home within five minutes." This year, the government plans to spend more than the $34 million it spent last year on contraception. The state will also buy some 961 million condoms to be distributed throughout the country, 11% more than in 1991.

But even with a family-planning policy that sends a chill down a Westerner's spine and touches every Chinese citizen's life, 64,000 babies are born every day in China and overpopulation continues to be a paramount national problem. Officials have warned that 24 million children will be born in 1992—a number just slightly less than the population of Canada. "The numbers are staggering," says Scruggs, the U.N. Population Fund official, noting that "170 million people will be added in the 1990s, which is the current population of England, France and Italy combined. There are places in China where the land can't feed that many more people as it is."

China estimates that it has prevented 200 million births since the one-child policy was introduced. Women now are having an average of 2.4 children as compared to six in the late '60s. But the individual sacrifice demanded from every Chinese is immense.

Large billboards bombard the population with images of happy families with only one child. The government is desperately trying to convince the masses that producing only one child leads to a wealthier, healthier and happier life. But foreigners in China tell a different story, that the people aren't convinced. They tell of being routinely approached—on the markets, on the streets, on the railways—and asked about the contraceptive policies of their countries. Expatriate women in Beijing all tell stories of Chinese women enviously asking them how many sons they have and how many children they plan to have. They explain that they only have one child because the government allows them only one.

"When I'm out with my three children on the weekend," says a young American father who lives in Beijing, "people are always asking me why am I allowed to have three children. You can feel when they ask you that there is envy there. There's a natural disappointment among the people. They just want to have more children. But there's a resigned understanding, an acceptance that they just can't."

Religion, Belief, and Ritual

The anthropological concern for religion, belief, and ritual does not have to do with the scientific validity of such phenomena, but rather the way in which people relate various concepts of the "supernatural" to their everyday lives. With this more practical perspective, some anthropologists have found that traditional spiritual healing is just as helpful in the treatment of illness as modern medi-cine, that voodoo is a form of social control, and that the ritual and spiritual preparation for playing the game of baseball can be just as important as spring training.

Every society is composed of feeling, thinking, and acting human beings who at one time or another are either conforming to or altering the social order into which they were born. Religion is an ideological framework that gives special legitimacy and validity to human experience within any given sociocultural system. In this way, monogamy as a marriage form or monarchy as a political form ceases to be simply one of many alternative ways in which a society can be organized, but becomes, for the believer, the only legitimate way. Religion renders certain human values and activities as sacred and inviolable, and it is this "mythic" function that helps to explain the strong ideological attachments that some people have regardless of the scientific merits of their points of view.

While under some conditions religion may in fact be "the opiate of the masses," under other conditions such a belief system may be a rallying point for social and economic protest. A contemporary example of the former might be the "Moonies" (members of the Unification Church founded by Sun Myung Moon), while a good example of the latter is the role of the black church in the American civil rights movement, along with the prominence of such religious figures as Martin Luther King Jr. and Jesse Jackson.

Finally, a word of caution must be set forth concerning attempts to understand belief systems of other cultures. At times the prevailing attitude seems to be that "what I believe in is religion and what you believe in is superstition." While anthropologists generally do not subscribe to this view, there is a tendency within the field to explain that which seems, on the surface, to be incomprehensible, impractical behavior as some form of "religious ritual." The unit articles should serve as a strong warning concerning the pitfalls of that approach.

"Psychotherapy in Africa" shows how important traditional belief systems, combined with community involvement, can be to the physical and psychological well-being of the individual. This perspective is so important that the treatment of illness is hindered without it. The hunters of Amazonia (in "No Pain, No Game") use magic to enhance their hunting success. "The Mbuti Pygmies: Change and Adaptation" involves ritual that is subtle, informal, and yet absolutely necessary for social harmony and stability. The emphasis in "The Secrets of Haiti's Living Dead" is upon both individual conformity and community solidarity.

Mystical beliefs and ritual are not absent from the modern world. Cargo Cults (in "Cargo Cults") are an expression of both frustration and hope in the face of the overwhelming modern market economy. "Rituals of Death" draws striking parallels between capital punishment in the United States and human sacrifice among the Aztecs of Mexico. "Body Ritual among the Nacirema" reveals that even our daily routines have mystic overtones. Finally, "Superstition and Ritual in American Baseball" examines the need for ritual and taboo in the "great American pastime."

In summary, the articles in this section will show religion, belief, and ritual in relationship to practical human affairs.

Looking Ahead: Challenge Questions

How can modern medicine be combined with traditional healing to take advantage of the best aspects of both?

In what respects do perceptions of disease affect treatment and recovery?

How does ritual contribute to a sense of personal security, individual responsibility, and social equality.

How has voodoo become such an important form of social control in rural Haiti?

In what ways can capital punishment be seen as a ritual with social functions?

In what ways are magic rituals practical and rational?

How do rituals and taboos get established in the first place?

How important are ritual and taboo in our modern industrial society?

Why do people engage in "cargo cults," and what happens when the cargo does not come?

Psychotherapy in Africa

Thomas Adeoye Lambo

Thomas Adeoye Lambo is deputy director-general of the World Health Organization in Geneva and an advisory editor of Human Nature. *He was born in Abeokuta, Nigeria, in 1923 and lived there until he finished secondary school. He studied medicine at the University of Birmingham in England, later specializing in psychiatry. Lambo first received international acclaim in 1954 when he published reports on the neuropsychiatric problems of Nigeria's Yoruba tribe and on the establishment of the Aro village hospital. Lambo served as medical director of Aro until 1962, when he was appointed to the first Chair of Psychiatry at Nigeria's Ibadan University; in 1968 he became vice-chancellor of the University. Lambo's psychiatric research and approach to therapy have consistently blended biology, culture, and social psychology.*

Some years ago, a Nigerian patient came to see me in a state of extreme anxiety. He had been educated at Cambridge University and was, to all intents and purposes, thoroughly "Westernized." He had recently been promoted to a top-level position in the administrative service, bypassing many of his able peers. A few weeks after his promotion, however, he had had an unusual accident from which he barely escaped with his life. He suddenly became terrified that his colleagues had formed a conspiracy and were trying to kill him.

His paranoia resisted the usual methods of Western psychiatry, and he had to be sedated to relieve his anxiety. But one day he came to see me, obviously feeling much better. A few nights before, he said, his grandfather had appeared to him in a dream and had assured him of a long and healthy life. He had been promised relief from fear and anxiety if he would sacrifice a goat. My patient bought a goat the following day, carried out all of the detailed instructions of his grandfather, and quickly recovered. The young man does not like to discuss this experience because he feels it conflicts with his educational background, but occasionally, in confidence, he says: "There is something in these native things, you know."

To the Western eye, such lingering beliefs in ritual and magic seem antiquated and possibly harmful—obstacles in the path of modern medicine. But the fact is that African cultures have developed indigenous forms of psychotherapy that are highly effective because they are woven into the social fabric. Although Western therapeutic methods are being adopted by many African therapists, few Africans are simply substituting new methods for traditional modes of treatment. Instead, they have attempted to combine the two for maximum effectiveness.

The character and effectiveness of medicine for the mind and the body always and everywhere depend on the culture in which the medicine is practiced. In the West, healing is often considered to be a private matter between patient and therapist. In

Africa, healing is an integral part of society and religion, a matter in which the whole community is involved. To understand African psychotherapy one must understand African thought and its social roots.

It seems impossible to speak of a single African viewpoint because the continent contains a broad range of cultures. The Ga, the Masai, and the Kikuyu, for example, are as different in their specific ceremonies and customs as are the Bantus and the Belgians. Yet in sub-Saharan black Africa the different cultures do share a consciousness of the world. They have in common a characteristic perception of life and death that makes it possible to describe their overriding philosophy. (In the United States, Southern Baptists and Episcopalians are far apart in many of their rituals and beliefs, yet one could legitimately say that both share a Christian concept of life.)

The basis of most African value systems is the concept of the unity of life and time. Phenomena that are regarded as opposites in the West exist on a single continuum in Africa. African thought draws no sharp distinction between animate and inanimate, natural and supernatural, material and mental, conscious and unconscious. All things exist in dynamic correspondence, whether they are visible or not. Past, present, and future blend in harmony; the world does not change between one's dreams and the daylight.

Essential to this view of the world is the belief that there is continuous communion between the dead and the living. Most African cultures share the idea that the strength and influence of every clan is anchored by the spirits of its deceased heroes. These heroes are omnipotent and indestructible, and their importance is comparable to that of the Catholic saints. But to Africans, spirits and deities are ever present in human affairs; they are the guardians of the established social order.

The common element in rituals throughout the continent—ancestor cults, deity cults, funeral rites, agricultural rites—is the unity of the people with the world of spirits, the mystical and emotional bond between the natural and supernatural worlds.

Because of the African belief in deities and ancestral spirits, many Westerners think that African thought is more concerned with the supernatural causes of events than with their natural causes. On one level this is true. Africans attribute nearly all forms of illness and disease, as well as personal and communal catastrophes, accidents, and deaths to the magical machinations of their enemies and to the intervention of gods and ghosts. As a result there is a deep faith in the power of symbols to produce the effects that are desired. If a man finds a hair, or a piece of material, or a bit of a fingernail belonging to his enemy, he believes he has only to use the object ritualistically in order to bring about the enemy's injury or death.

As my educated Nigerian patient revealed by sacrificing a goat, the belief in the power of the supernatural is not confined to uneducated Africans. In a survey of African students in British universities conducted some years ago, I found that the majority of them firmly believed that their emotional problems had their origin in, or could at least be influenced by, charms and diabolical activities of other African students or of people who were still in Africa. I recently interviewed the student officers at the Nigeria House in London and found no change in attitude.

The belief in the power of symbols and magic is inculcated at an early age. I surveyed 1,300 elementary-school children over a four-year period and found that 85 percent used native medicine of some sort—incantations, charms, magic to help them pass exams, to be liked by teachers, or to ward off the evil effects of other student "medicines." More than half of these children came from Westernized homes, yet they held firmly to the power of magic ritual.

Although most Africans believe in supernatural forces and seem to deny natural causality, their belief system is internally consistent. In the Western world, reality rests on the human ability to master things, to conquer objects, to subordinate the outer world to human will. In the African world, reality is found in the soul, in a religious acquiescence to life, not in its mastery. Reality rests on the relations between one human being and another, and between all people and spirits.

The practice of medicine in Africa is consistent with African philosophy. Across the African continent, sick people go to acknowledged diviners and healers—they are often called witch doctors in the West—in order to discover the nature of their illness. In almost every instance, the explanation involves a deity or an ancestral spirit. But this is only one aspect of the diagnosis, because the explanation given by the diviner is also grounded in natural phenomena. As anthropologist Robin Horton observes: "The diviner who diagnoses the intervention of a spiritual agency is also expected to give some acceptable account of what moved the agency in question to intervene. And this account very commonly involves reference to some event in the world of visible, tangible happenings. Thus if a diviner diagnoses the action of witchcraft influence or lethal medicine spirits, it is usual for him to add something about the human hatreds, jealousies, and misdeeds that have brought such agencies into play. Or, if he diagnoses the wrath of an ancestor, it is usual for him to point to the human breach of kinship morality which has called down this wrath."

The causes of illness are not simply attributed to the unknown or dropped into the laps of the gods. Causes are always linked to the patient's immediate world of social events. As Victor Turner's study of the Ndembu people of central Africa revealed, diviners believe a patient "will not get better until all the tensions and aggressions in the group's interrelations have been brought to light and exposed to ritual treatment." In my work with the Yoruba culture, I too found that supernatural forces are regarded as the agents and consequences of human will. Sickness is the natural effect of some social mistake—breaching a taboo or breaking a kinship rule.

African concepts of health and illness, like those of life and death, are intertwined. Health is not regarded as an isolated phenomenon but reflects the integration of the community. It is not the mere absence of disease but a sign that a person is living in peace and harmony with his neighbors, that he is keeping the laws of the gods and the tribe. The practice of medicine is more than the administration of drugs and potions. It encompasses all activities—personal and communal—that are directed toward the promotion of human well-being. As S.R. Burstein wrote, to be healthy requires "averting the wrath of gods or spirits, making rain, purifying streams or habitations, improving sex potency or fecundity or the fertility of fields and crops—in short, it is bound up with the whole interpretation of life."

Native healers are called upon to treat a wide range of psychiatric disorders, from schizophrenia to neurotic syndromes. Their labels may not be the same, but they recognize the difference between an incapacitating psychosis and a temporary neurosis, and between a problem that can be cured (anxiety) and one that cannot (congenital retardation or idiocy). In many tribes a person is defined as mad when he talks nonsense, acts foolishly and irresponsibly, and is unable to look after himself.

It is often assumed that tribal societies are a psychological paradise and that mental illness is the offspring of modern civilization and its myriad stresses. The African scenes in Alex Haley's *Roots* tend to portray a Garden of Eden, full of healthy

tribesmen. But all gardens have snakes. Small societies have their own peculiar and powerful sources of mental stress. Robin Horton notes that tribal societies have a limited number of roles to be filled, and that there are limited choices for individuals. As a result each tribe usually has a substantial number of social misfits. Traditional communities also have a built-in set of conflicting values: aggressive ambition versus a reluctance to rise above one's neighbor; ruthless individualism versus acceptance of one's place in the lineage system. Inconsistencies such as these, Horton believes, "are often as sharp as those so well known in modern industrial societies. . . .One may even suspect that some of the young Africans currently rushing from the country to the towns are in fact escaping from a more oppressive to a less oppressive psychological environment."

Under typical tribal conditions, traditional methods are perfectly effective in the diagnosis and treatment of mental illness. The patient goes to the tribal diviner, who follows a complex procedure. First the diviner (who may be a man or a woman) determines the "immediate" cause of the illness—that is, whether it comes from physical devitalization or from spiritual possession. Next he or she diagnoses the "remote" cause of the ailment: Had the patient offended one of his ancestor spirits or gods? Had a taboo been violated? Was some human agent in the village using magic or invoking the help of evil spirits to take revenge for an offense?

The African diviner makes a diagnosis much as a Western psychoanalyst does: through the analysis of dreams, projective techniques, trances and hypnotic states (undergone by patient and healer alike), and the potent power of words. With these methods, the diviner defines the psychodynamics of the patient and gains insight into the complete life situation of the sick person.

One projective technique of diagnosis—which has much in common with the Rorschach test—occurs in *Ifa* divination, a procedure used by Yoruba healers. There are 256 *Odus* (incantations) that are poetically structured; each is a dramatic series of words that evoke the patient's emotions. Sometimes the power of the *Odus* lies in the way the words are used, the order in which they are arranged, or the starkness with which they express a deep feeling. The incantations are used to gain insight into the patient's problem. Their main therapeutic value, as in the case with the Rorschach ink blots, is to interpret omens, bring up unconscious motives, and make unknown desires and fears explicit.

Once the immediate and remote causes are established, the diagnosis is complete and the healer decides on the course of therapy. Usually this involves an expiatory sacrifice meant to restore the unity between man and deity. Everyone takes part in the treatment; the ritual involves the healer, the patient, his family, and the community at large. The group rituals —singing and dancing, confessions, trances, storytelling, and the like— that follow are powerful therapeutic measures for the patient. They release tensions and pressures and promote positive mental health by tying all individuals to the larger group. Group rituals are effective because they are the basis of African social life, an essential part of the lives of "healthy" Africans.

Some cultures, such as the N'jayei society of the Mende in Sierra Leone and the Yassi society of the Sherbro, have always had formal group therapy for their mentally ill. When one person falls ill, the whole tribe attends to his physical and spiritual needs.

Presiding over all forms of treatment is the healer, or *nganga*. My colleagues and I have studied and worked with these men and women for many years, and we are consistently impressed by their abilities.

Many of those we observed are extraordinary individuals of great common sense, eloquence, boldness, and charisma. They are highly respected within their communities as people who through self-denial, dedication, and prolonged meditation and training have discovered the secrets of the healing art and its magic (a description of Western healers as well, one might say).

The traditional *nganga* has supreme self-confidence, which he or she transmits to the patient. By professing an ability to commune with supernatural beings—and therefore to control or influence them—the healer holds boundless power over members of the tribe. Africans regard the *nganga*'s mystical qualities and eccentricities fondly, and with awe. So strongly do people believe in the *nganga*'s ability to find out which ancestral spirit is responsible for the psychological distress of the patient, that pure suggestion alone can be very effective.

For centuries the tribal practice of communal psychotherapy served African society well. Little social stigma was attached to mental illness; even chronic psychotics were tolerated in their communities and were able to function at a minimal level. (Such tolerance is true of many rural cultures.) But as the British, Germans, French, Belgians, and Portuguese colonized many African countries, they brought a European concept of mental illness along with their religious, economic, and educational systems.

They built prisons with special sections set aside for "lunatics"— usually vagrant psychotics and criminals with demonstrable mental disorders—who were restricted with handcuffs and ankle shackles. The African healers had always drawn a distinction between mental illness and criminality, but the European colonizers did not.

In many African cultures today, the traditional beliefs in magic and religion are dying. Their remaining influence serves only to create anxiety and ambivalence among Africans who are living through a period of rapid social and economic change. With the disruption and disorganization of family units, we have begun to see clinical problems that once were rare: severe depression, obsessional neurosis, and emotional incapacity. Western medicine has come a long way from the shackle solution, but it is not the best kind of therapy for people under such stress. In spite of its high technological and material advancement, modern science does not satisfy the basic metaphysical and social needs of many people, no matter how sophisticated they are.

In 1954 my colleagues and I established a therapeutic program designed to wed the best practices of traditional and contemporary psychology. Our guiding premise was to make use of the therapeutic practices that already existed in the indigenous culture, and to recognize the power of the group in healing.

We began our experiment at Aro, a rural suburb of the ancient town of Abeokuta, in western Nigeria. Aro consists of four villages that lie in close proximity in the beautiful rolling countryside. The villages are home Yoruba tribesmen and their relatives, most of whom are peasant farmers, fishermen, and craftsmen.

Near these four villages we built a day hospital that could accommodate up to 300 patients, and then we set up a village care system for their treatment. Our plan was to preserve the fundamental structure of African culture: closely knit groups, well-defined kin networks, an interlocking system of mutual obligations and traditional roles.

Patients came to the hospital every morning for treatment and spent their afternoons in occupational therapy, but they were not confined to the hospital. Patients lived in homes in the four villages or, if necessary, with hospital staff members who lived on hospital grounds—ambulance drivers, clerks, dispensary attendants, and gardeners. (This boarding-out procedure resembles a system that has been practiced for several hundred years in Gheel, a town in Belgium, where the mentally ill live in local households surrounding a central institution.)

We required the patients, who came from all over Nigeria, to arrive at the village hospital with at least one relative—a mother, sister, brother, or aunt—who would be able to cook for them, wash their clothes, take them to the hospital in the morning, and pick them up in the afternoon.

These relatives, along with the patients, took part in all the social activities of the villages: parties, plays, dances, storytelling. Family participation was successful from the beginning. We were able to learn about the family influences and stresses on the patient, and the family members learned how to adjust to the sick relative and deal with his or her emotional needs.

The hospital staff was drawn from the four villages, which meant that the hospital employees were the "landlords" of most of the patients, in constant contact with them at home and at work. After a while, the distinction between the two therapeutic arenas blurred and the villages became extensions of the hospital wards.

Doctors, nurses, and superintendents visited the villages every day and set up "therapy" groups—often for dancing, storytelling, and other rituals—as well as occupational programs that taught patients traditional African crafts.

It is not enough to treat patients on a boarding-out or outpatient basis. If services are not offered to them outside of the hospital, an undue burden is placed on their families and neighbors. This increases the tension to which patients are exposed. An essential feature of our plan was to regard the villages as an extension of the hospital, subject to equally close supervision and control.

But we neither imposed the system

on the local people nor asked them to give their time and involvement without giving them something in return. We were determined to inflict no hardships. The hosptial staff took full responsibility for the administration of the villages and for the health of the local people. They held regular monthly meetings with the village elders and their councils to give the villagers a say in the system. The hospital also arranged loans to the villagers to expand, repair, or build new houses to take care of the patients; it paid for the installation of water pipes and latrines; it paid for a mosquito eradication squad; it offered jobs to many local people and paid the "landlords" a small stipend.

Although these economic benefits aided the community, no attempt was ever made to structure the villages in any way, or to tell the villagers what to do with the patients or how to treat them. As a result of economic benefits, hospital guidance, and a voice in their own management, village members supported the experiment.

In a study made after the program began, we learned that patients who were boarded out under this system adapted more quickly and responded more readily to treatment than patients who lived in the hospital. Although the facilities available in the hospital were extensive—drug medication, group therapy sessions, modified insulin therapy, electro-convulsive shock treatments—we found that the most important therapeutic factor was the patient's social contacts, especially with people who were healthier than the patient. The village groups, unlike the hospital group, were unrehearsed, unexpected, and voluntary. Patients could choose their friends and activities; they were not thrown together arbitrarily and asked to "work things out." We believe that the boarded-out patients improved so quickly because of their daily contact with settled, tolerant, healthy people. They learned to function in society again without overwhelming anxiety.

One of the more effective and controversial methods we used was to colaborate with native healers. Just as New Yorkers have faith in their psychoanalysts, and pilgrims have faith in their priests, the Yoruba have faith in the *nganga;* and faith, as we are learning, is half the battle toward cure.

Our unorthodox alliance proved to be highly successful. The local diviners and religious leaders helped many of the patients recover, sometimes through a simple ceremony at a village shrine, sometimes in elaborate forms of ritual sacrifice, sometimes by interpreting the spiritual or magical causes of their dreams and illnesses.

At the beginning of the program patients were carefully selected for admission, but now patients of every sort are accepted: violent persons, catatonics, schizophrenics, and others whose symptoms make them socially unacceptable or emotionally withdrawn. The system is particularly effective with emotionally disturbed and psychotic children, who always come to the hospital with a great number of concerned relatives. Children who have minor neurotic disorders are kept out of the hospital entirely and treated exclusively and successfully in village homes.

The village care system was designed primarily for the acutely ill and for those whose illness was manageable, and the average stay for patients at Aro was, and is, about six months. But patients who were chronically ill and could not recover in a relatively short time posed a problem. For one thing, their relatives could not stay with them in the villages because of family and financial obligations in their home communities. We are working out solutions for such people on a trial-and-error basis. Some of the incapacitated psychotic patients now live on special farms; others live in Aro villages near the hospital and earn their keep while receiving regular supervision. The traditional

healers keep watch over these individuals and maintain follow-up treatment.

We have found many economic, medical, and social advantages to our program. The cost has been low because we have concentrated on using human resources in the most effective and strategic manner. Medically and therapeutically, the program provides a positive environment for the treatment of character disorders, sociopathy, alcoholism, neuroses, and anxiety. Follow-up studies show that the program fosters a relatively quick recovery for these problems and that the recidivism rate and the need for aftercare are significantly reduced. The length of stay at Aro, and speed of recovery, is roughly one third of the average stay in other hospitals, especially for all forms of schizophrenia. Patients with neurotic disorders respond most rapidly. Because of its effectiveness, the Aro system has been extended to four states in Nigeria and to five countries in Africa, including Kenya, Ghana, and Zambia. At each new hospital the program is modified to fit local conditions.

Some observers of the Aro system argue that it can operate only in nonindustrial agrarian communities, like those in Africa and Asia, where families and villages are tightly knit. They say that countries marked by high alienation and individualism could not import such a program. Part of this argument is correct. The Aro approach to mental health rests on particularly African traditions, such as the *nganga*, and on the belief in the continuum of life and death, sickness and health, the natural and the supernatural.

But some lessons of the Aro plan have already found their way into Western psychotherapy. Many therapists recognize the need to place the sick person in a social context; a therapist cannot heal the patient without attending to his beliefs, family, work, and environment. Various forms of group therapy are being developed in an attempt to counteract the Western emphasis on curing the individual in isolation. Lately, family therapy has been expanded into a new procedure called network therapy in which the patient's entire network of relatives, coworkers, and friends become involved in the treatment.

Another lesson of Aro is less obvious than the benefits of group support. It is the understanding that treatment begins with a people's indigenous beliefs and their world view, which underlie psychological functioning and provide the basis for healing. Religious values that give meaning and coherence to life can be the healthiest route for many people. As Jung observed years ago, religious

factors are inherent in the path toward healing, and the native therapies of Africa support his view.

A supernatural belief system, Western or Eastern, is not a sphere of arbitrary dreams but a sphere of laws that dictate the rules of kinship, the order of the universe, the route of happiness. The Westerner sees only part of the African belief system, such as the witch doctor, and wonders how wild fictions can take root in a reasonable mind. (His own fictions seem perfectly reasonable, of course.) But to the African, the religious-magical system is a great poem, allegorical of human experience, wise in its portrayal of the world and its creatures. There is more method, more reason,

in such madness than in the sanity of most people today.

REFERENCES

Burstein, S.R. "Public Health and Prevention of Disease in Primitive Communities." *The Advancement of Science,* Vol. 9, 1952, pp. 75- 81.
Horton, Robin. "African Traditional Thought and Western Science." *Africa,* Vol. 37, 1967, pp. 50-71.
Horton, Robin. *The Traditional Background of Medical Practice in Nigeria.* Institute of Africa Studies, 1966.
Lambo, T.A. "A World View of Mental Health: Recent Developments and Future Trends." *American Journal of Orthopsychiatry,* Vol. 43, 1973, pp. 706-716.
Lambo, T.A. "Psychotherapy in Africa." *Psychotherapy and Psychosomatics,* Vol. 24, 1974, pp. 311-326.

The Mbuti Pygmies: Change and Adaptation

Colin M. Turnbull

THE EDUCATIONAL PROCESS

. . . In the first three years of life every Mbuti alive experiences almost total security. The infant is breast-fed for those three years, and is allowed almost every freedom. Regardless of gender, the infant learns to have absolute trust in both male and female parent. If anything, the father is just another kind of mother, for in the second year the father formally introduces the child to its first solid food. There used to be a beautiful ritual in which the mother presented the child to the father in the middle of the camp, where all important statements are made (anyone speaking from the middle of the camp must be listened to). The father took the child and held it to his breast, and the child would try to suckle, crying "*ema, ema,*" or "mother." The father would shake his head, and say "no, father . . . *eba*," but like a mother (the Mbuti said), then give the child its first solid food.

At three the child ventures out into the world on its own and enters the *bopi*, what we mght call a playground, a tiny camp perhaps a hundred yards from the main camp, often on the edge of a stream. The *bopi* were indeed playgrounds, and often very noisy ones, full of fun and high spirits. But they were also rigorous training grounds for eventual economic responsibility. On entry to the *bopi*, for one thing, the child discovers the importance of age as a structural principle, and the relative unimportance of gender and biological kinship. The *bopi* is the private world of the children. Younger youths may occasionally venture in, but if adults or elders try, as they sometimes do when angry at having their afternoon snooze interrupted, they invariably get driven out, taunted, and ridiculed. Children, among the Mbuti, have rights, but they also learn that they have responsibilities. Before the hunt sets out each day it is the children, sometimes the younger youths, who light the hunting fire.

Ritual among the Mbuti is often so informal and apparently casual that it may pass unnoticed at first. Yet insofar as ritual involves symbolic acts that represent unspoken, perhaps even unthought, concepts or ideals, or invoke other states of being, alternative frames of mind and reference, then Mbuti life is full of ritual. The hunting fire is one of the more obvious of such rituals. Early in the morning children would take firebrands from the *bopi*, where they always lit their own fire with embers from their family hearths, and set off on the trail by which the hunt was to leave that day (the direction of each day's hunt was always settled by discussion the night before). Just a short distance from the camp they lit a fire at the base of a large tree, and covered it with special leaves that made it give off a column of dense smoke. Hunters leaving the camp, both men and women, and such youths and children as were going with them, had to pass by this fire. Some did so casually, without stopping or looking, but passing through the smoke. Others reached into the smoke with their hands as they passed, rubbing the smoke into their bodies. A few always stopped, for a moment, and let the smoke envelop them, only then almost dreamily moving off.

And indeed is *was* a form of intoxication, for the smoke invoked the spirit of the forest, and by passing through it the hunters sought to fill themselves with that spirit, not so much to make the hunt successful as to minimize the sacrilege of killing. Yet they, the hunters, could not light the fire themselves. After all, they were already contaminated by death. Even youths, who daily joined the hunt at the edges, catching any game that escaped the nets, by hand, if they could, were not pure enough to invoke the spirits of forestness. But young children were uncontaminated, as yet untainted by contact with the original sin of the Mbuti. It was their responsibility to light the fire, and if it was not lit then the hunt would not take place, or as the Mbuti put it, the hunt *could* not take place.

In this way even the children in Mbuti society, at the first of the four age levels that dominate Mbuti social structure, are given very real social responsibility and see themselves as a part of that structure, by virtue of their purity. After all, they have just been born from the source of all purity, the forest itself. By the same reasoning, the elders, who are about to return to that ultimate source of all being, through death, are at least closer to purity than the adults, who are daily contaminated by killing. Elders no longer go on the hunt. So, like the children, the elders have important sacred ritual responsibilities in the Mbuti division of labor by age.

In the *bopi* the children play, but they have no "games" in the strict sense of the word. Levi-Strauss has perceptively compared games with rituals, suggesting that whereas in a game the players start theoretically equal but end up unequal, in a ritual just the reverse takes place. All are equalized. Mbuti children could be seen every day playing in the *bopi*, but not once did I see a game, not one activity that smacked of any kind of competition, except perhaps that competition that it is necessary for us all to feel from time to time, competition with our own private and personal inadequacies. One such pastime (rather than game) was tree climbing. A dozen or so children would climb up a young sapling. Reaching the top, their weight brought the sapling bending down until it almost touched the ground. Then all the children leapt off together, shrieking as the young tree sprang upright again with a rush. Sometimes one child, male or female, might stay on a

little too long, either out of fear, or out of bravado, or from sheer carelessness or bad timing. Whatever the reason, it was a lesson most children only needed to be taught once, for the result was that you got flung upward with the tree, and were lucky to escape with no more than a few bruises and a very bad fright.

Other pastimes taught the children the rules of hunting and gathering. Frequently elders, who stayed in camp when the hunt went off, called the children into the main camp and enacted a mock hunt with them there. Stretching a discarded piece of net across the camp, they pretended to be animals, showing the children how to drive them into the nets. And, of course, the children played house, learning the patterns of cooperation that would be necessary for them later in life. They also learned the prime lesson of egality, other than for purposes of division of labor making no distinction between male and female, this nuclear family or that. All in the *bopi* were *apua'i* to each other, and so they would remain throughout their lives. At every age level—childhood, youth, adulthood, or old age—everyone of that level is *apua'i* to all the others. Only adults sometimes (but so rarely that I think it was only done as a kind of joke, or possibly insult) made the distinction that the Bira do, using *apua'i* for male and *amua'i* for female. Male or female, for the Mbuti, if you are the same age you are *apua'i*, and that means that you share everything equally, regardless of kinship or gender.

YOUTH AND POLITICS

Sometime before the age of puberty boys or girls, whenever they feel ready, move back into the main camp from the *bopi* and join the youths. This is when they must assume new responsibilities, which for the youths are primarily political. Already, in the *bopi*, the children become involved in disputes, and are sometimes instrumental in settling them by ridicule, for nothing hurts an adult more than being ridiculed by children. The art of reason, however, is something they learn from the youths,

and it is the youths who apply the art of reason to the settlement of disputes.

When puberty comes it separates them, for the first time in their experience, from each other as *apua'i*. Very plainly girls are different from boys. When a girl has her first menstrual period the whole camp celebrates with the wild *elima* festival, in which the girl, and some of her chosen girl friends, are the center of all attention, living together in a special *elima* house. Male youths sit outside the *elima* house and wait for the girls to come out, usually in the afternoon, for the *elima* singing. They sing in antiphony, the girls leading, the boys responding. Boys come from neighboring territories all around, for this is a time of courtship. But there are always eligible youths within the camp as well, and the *elima* girl may well choose girls from other territories to come and join her, so there is more than enough excuse for every youth to carry on several flirtations, legitimate or illegitimate. I have known even first cousins to flirt with each other, but learned to be prudent enough not to pull out my kinship charts and point this out—well, not in public anyway.

The *elima* is more than a premarital festival, more than a joint initiation of youth into adulthood, and more than a rite of passage through puberty, though it is all those things. It is a public recognition of the opposition of male and female, and every *elima* is used to highlight the *potential* for conflict that lies in that opposition. As at other times of crisis, at puberty, a time of change and uncertainty, the Mbuti bring all the major forms of conflict out into the open. And the one that evidently most concerns them is the male/female opposition.

The adults begin to play a special form of "tug of war" that is clearly a ritual rather than a game. All the men are on one side, the women on the other. At first it looks like a game, but quickly it becomes clear that the objective is for *neither* side to win. As soon as the women begin to win, one of them will leave the end of the line and run around to join the men, assuming a deep male voice and in other ways ridicul-

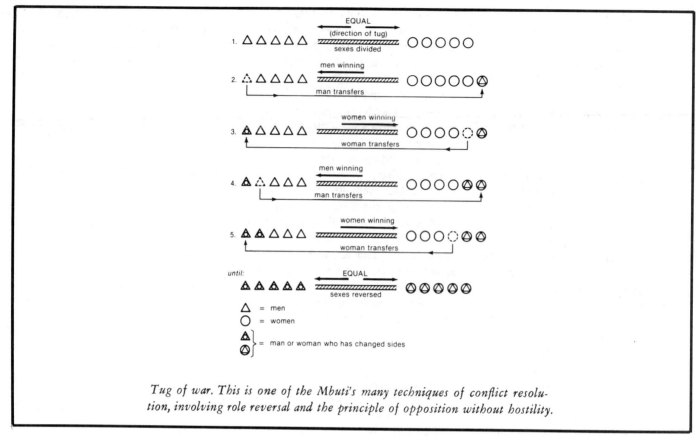

Tug of war. This is one of the Mbuti's many techniques of conflict resolution, involving role reversal and the principle of opposition without hostility.

ing manhood. Then, as the men begin to win, a male will similarly join the women, making fun of womanhood as he does so. Each adult on changing sides attempts to outdo all the others in ridiculing the opposite sex. Finally, when nearly all have switched sides, and sexes, the ritual battle between the genders simply collapses into hysterical laughter, the contestants letting go of the rope, falling onto the ground, and rolling over with mirth. Neither side wins, both are equalized very nicely, and each learns the essential lesson, that there should be *no* contest. . . .

No Pain, No Game

For the Mayoruna and Matses of the Amazonian forest,
preparing for the hunt can be an ordeal

Katharine Milton

Katharine Milton has returned again and again to Brazil to record the lives of little-known groups of human inhabitants. She is especially concerned with how different indigenous peoples use the forest's resources, and with the nutritional components of their tropical plant foods and the significance of local food taboos. Milton is a professor of physical anthropology at the University of California at Berkeley.

Early in my study of diet and ecology in Lobo, a village of 110 Mayoruna Indians in Brazil's Amazonian forest, I noticed that the men and adolescent boys had neat rows of small scars on their upper arms and chest. At first I thought these might be the result of cigarette burns, and although this seemed a bit odd, I didn't really question my interpretation until it dawned on me that the Mayoruna had no cigarettes. Not conversant in Panoan, the Mayoruna language, I finally pointed to the scars and indicated that I wanted to know what had caused them. Several youths smiled at me and then ran into the forest. After twenty or thirty minutes, they returned bearing a leafy branch on which sat a large, handsome, green frog.

I thought it very kind of the boys to show me this wonderful frog, but I had no idea that it was connected to my question about the burn marks. I wondered if the boys thought I was hungry and were offering the frog to me for my supper. They allowed me to admire it for some minutes as it sat calmly on the branch and then on the shoulder and arm of one young man. It was a vivid green, with striking yellow mottling on the underside of its limbs and body, and it moved with an exaggeratedly slow gait, similar to that of the African chameleon. But then the boys took the frog and began to prepare it for some kind of procedure. I finally realized that the frog did have something to do with the burns after all.

Without touching the animal, the boys looped slender cords made of vines around all four of its limbs. They then drove small stakes into the ground and stretched the frog out, firmly attaching the cords to the stakes. At that point, several of them picked up wooden splinters and began to harass the frog, poking it particularly around the eyes and nostrils. In response, the terrified frog began to exude a clear, glossy secretion from its skin that began to settle in a cloudy, mucuslike film around its feet. I had no doubt that this was some kind of potent substance that the frog used for defense. Did contact with it cause burns? Using a splinter, the boys scraped the secretion off the head, back, sides, and limbs of the frog.

After the frog had been poked and scraped for some minutes, its ability to produce the secretion evidently was exhausted. At that point, the captors carefully removed the cords from the frog's limbs and permitted it to walk away. The frog was not physically damaged, only frightened. One boy who briefly touched the frog while removing the cords ran to the nearby river to wash his hands.

The secretion had been collected on a clean, flat piece of wood, which was placed near a fire to dry. The wood with the dried secretion—which looked like shiny glue—was then wrapped in cloth and stored in a secure, dry area in the thatch of a nearby house. On four occasions I observed how the frog's secretion was used in a type of hunting magic.

Traditionally, the Mayoruna live by horticulture (sweet manioc, plantain), hunting (tapir, peccary, woolly monkey, spider monkey), and some supplementary fishing. The men's skills with bow and arrow are impressive: "I pity the animal that crosses the path of a Mayoruna," remarked a visitor who had done considerable hunting with them. Yet hunting game in the forests of the Amazon Basin is always an unpredictable venture, a hunter never knowing whether on any given day he will have good luck, moderate luck, or no luck at all. Anthropologists have long noted that important activities with uncertain outcomes are the most likely to be surrounded with magical practices.

Detailed cave paintings, animal figurines, and stylized caches of animal bones found in Europe suggest that more than 30,000 years ago, human hunters were carrying out a wide variety of magical practices, possibly to improve hunting success. Ethnographic accounts of many past as well as present-day hunter-gatherer groups throughout the world describe a rich array of magical practices involving smoke, blood, bark, leaves, roots, and other substances, which the hunters believe improve their hunting prowess and luck, increase the numbers of prey, or propitiate animal spirits.

The Mayoruna use the frog secretion as a drug and regard its effects as a potent form of hunting magic. On two occasions when I observed the procedure, the drug was taken on a day of heavy rain—perhaps a bad day to hunt but a good day to practice hunting magic in preparation for more opportune conditions. I never saw a hunter take the drug by himself: two, three, or more men took it together.

To get the frog secretion into the body, the hunters heat a vine twig on a burning log until the twig is white hot. One man then takes the twig and applies it to the arm or chest of a person wishing to take the drug. The white-hot twig is allowed to rest on the surface of the skin for less than a second, then removed and reheated; each individual ultimately receives three to six burns, placed in a neat row, one under the other. At this point, the frog secretion is taken from its storage site and unwrapped. One hunter mixes his saliva with it, stirring it with a splinter to make a whitish, soft paste. The individual receiving the drug then uses his fingernail to carefully scrape away the small burned patches of skin, leaving open wounds. A small mound of the paste is then applied to each open burn.

Before receiving the burns, participants drink an impressive amount of manioc, banana, or other gruel. The first time I witnessed this, I didn't know why they did it, but I soon found out. The drug apparently enters the bloodstream through the open wounds very rapidly; within minutes it induces heavy, repeated vomiting. The Indians told me, through an interpreter, that the gruel lessens the pain. Another visible result is swelling of the lips and face; other rapid effects are headache and a burning sensation in the anal mucosa.

After vomiting several times, each participant sits quietly, often holding his head in his hands. Later he gets into his hammock and falls into a "sleep," during which he may babble and make other sounds. The sleep was described to me as exciting, rather than restful. Men say they think of "nothing" while in this sleep; that it is very similar to being very drunk. If they take the secretion about eight in the morning, they are recovering from its effects by five or six in the evening of the same day, although they may still lie about in their hammocks and act somewhat groggy. I was told, however, that if someone who is under the influence of the drug is thrown in the river or forced to bathe, he will rapidly shake off his somnolence.

I asked various Mayoruna why they took the drug since it appeared to be so unpleasant. The men replied that taking the frog secretion "made them hunt better." Taking it was said "to get rid of bad luck, help you to keep good luck, and help your arrows find the game animals." Men also stated that taking the secretion made them physically much more powerful—their senses keener, their stamina greater, their aim with the arrow more precise.

I was told that Mayoruna boys are first given the frog secretion when they are about seven or eight years of age "so that they will become accustomed to taking it." Women occasionally take the frog secretion so that "they will work harder." I estimated that most or all adult male hunters in Lobo take the frog secretion at least once a month.

The Mayoruna Indians in Lobo have another type of painful hunting magic. Men seek out large "fire" caterpillars, whose three-inch bodies are covered with long, white, stinging hairs. My one contact with one of these caterpillars produced such immediate, excruciating pain that for months afterward I flinched at the mere thought of white, fuzzy objects. As caterpillars are soft-bodied, small organisms, they apparently require a very rapid-acting chemical defense against potential predators that would crush or ingest them.

Some Mayoruna keep these white caterpillars on banana plants in their gardens so they will be readily available. To use them for hunting magic, they pick up the caterpillar on a twig and rub it on the bare upper arm. This practice, which is supposed to make a man a better hunter, leaves additional areas of scar tissue on the Mayoruna men and boys who take the frog secretion.

The Mayoruna I visited live in western Brazil, near the border with Peru. Steven Romanoff, an American anthropologist, has spent some fifteen months living with the Mayoruna of Peru, where they are referred to as Matses. His description of how the frog secretion is used for hunting magic matches what I saw almost completely, but he also mentions that the drug is sometimes administered to individuals (men, women, or children) who are lazy or are having problems or even as a punishment. Among the Matses, a dab of the paste may even be placed on the nose of a favored hunting dog to improve its hunting abilities.

Romanoff also observed a number of other energy-inducing rituals among the Matses. In these, an older man, respected for his knowledge or energy, blows tobacco smoke or uses stinging nettles or other painful materials to magically imbue younger individuals, usually men, with energy, strength, or knowledge.

While working with the Amahuaca Indians in a Peruvian headwater area of the Rio Inuya near the Brazilian border, anthropologist Robert Carneiro of the American Museum of Natural History also observed similar hunting magic. The Amahuaca, like the Mayoruna, are Panoan-speakers, and the two groups may be closely related. The Amahuaca men take a frog secretion (almost certainly from the same species of frog used by the Mayoruna) and place it in burns using the same technique. Carneiro, however, reports that in their case the effects last for some three days rather than a single day, and that Amahuaca men claim to experience vivid hallucinations while under the effects of the drug.

Amahuaca men also deliberately seek out wasps' nests and let numerous wasps sting them, believing that they will emerge from this ordeal better hunters. Youths may have strips of highly caustic tree bark tied around their wrists or forearms to insure that when they are hunting "no animal will escape."

Some years ago, Delvair Montagner Melatti, a Brazilian anthropologist, began to work with another Panoan-speaking group in Brazil, the Marubo, who live to the south of the Mayoruna and are one of their traditional enemies. The Marubo used the frog secretion extensively during her earlier visits, giving it to children as young as three years of age. Children typically did not like to take the secretion, which is unpleasant for anyone and which, in a small child, can produce very powerful effects. According to Montagner, taking the frog secretion appeared to be a daily or even twice daily ritual; however, the Marubo bathed very shortly after the secretion was administered. In some manner, the shock of the cold water and action of the bath curtailed much of the effect of the secretion, so the Marubo did not spend the rest of the day lying in a hammock

A Mayoruna boy, below, holding his family's catch from the river, and a Mayoruna teenager with his pet fawn, below right, belong to a much more isolated group.
Katharine Milton

but rather were able to hunt, work, or carry out other activities with vigor.

The Marubo stated that they used the secretion for two principal reasons—to rid the body of harmful impurities, including such things as bad luck, and to imbue the body with power, energy, and good luck. Children were given the secretion not only for these reasons but also as a punishment to correct improper behavior. In the past, the area of the body on which the burns were placed was apparently related to the type of effect desired. To cure laziness, for example, burns would be placed on the back of the neck, while to rid oneself of weakness and become powerful and quick, burns were placed on the stomach or upper arms. To improve hunting success, burns were placed on the chest and upper arms. To kill people in warfare, they were placed near the sternum. Painful, stinging herbs were also rubbed on the skin to augment the effects of the frog secretion. In her later visits, Montagner noted far fewer scars on the bodies of the Marubo and concluded that the practice was gradually dying out owing to the influence of missionaries and other outside forces.

The Mayoruna and others obtain the secretion from *Phyllomedusa bicolor,* a large tree frog that lives high in trees near rivers and streams. Curious about the chemical composition of the frog

secretion, I obtained a dried sample and brought it back to the United States for analysis. I sent it to the laboratory of John Daly, a chemist at the National Institutes of Health, who along with his associate Charles Myers, a herpetologist at the American Museum of Natural History, is well known for studies of the chemical compounds in secretions of the so-called poison dart frogs.

Poison dart frogs of the genus *Phyllobates* produce among the most potent of all naturally occurring, nonprotein toxins—the batrachotoxin alkaloids. Some Indian groups smear the secretions from these frogs on blowgun darts in order to kill game. The poison leads rapidly to cardiac failure in wounded game, but the meat of such animals is safe for humans to consume.

The secretion from the hunting magic frog, *Phyllomedusa bicolor,* is very different from those of poison dart frogs. Daly and his colleagues were able to isolate a previously unknown peptide, which they named adenoregulin. Earlier work by Vittorio Erspamer had shown that the skin of the frog contained a variety of vasoactive and opioid peptides. All these peptides presumably interact to produce the variety of symptoms and sensations noted in individuals who take the frog secretion. When some of the frog secretion was administered to mice at the National Institutes of Health, the mice

Katharine Milton

fell into a drowsy trance. When the mice were stimulated, however, the effects of the trance could be rapidly dissipated—the same pattern of behavior noted in the Marubo, who bathe in the river after taking the secretion and then are able to carry out their daily activities with increased enthusiasm.

No one knows how tropical forest-dwelling people first acquired knowledge about the plant and animal compounds they use as medicines, stimulants, and magic. Most such discoveries were probably the result of some chance observation of the effect of contact with, or ingestion of, some leaf, bark, insect, or animal. The observer may have noted this effect on himself or on another person or animal. A series of trial-and-error experiments may then have helped determine how best to administer and use the chemical substances involved. To the best of my knowledge, the Mayoruna, and related Panoan-speaking groups among whom the procedure has been observed, are the only Amazonian Indians who introduce a drug into their bloodstream through a deliberate break in the skin. Elsewhere, such chemical substances are generally inhaled or swallowed.

Why many hunting magic procedures are painful or unpleasant is another mystery. Perhaps, as practitioners claim, the experience leaves them feeling energized and refreshed. The pain or stimulation brought on by frog secretions, wasp stings, stinging caterpillars, and caustic bark conceivably causes the release of brain peptide endorphins that ultimately lead to enhanced alertness, physical strength, and endurance.

Or more simply, hunters may believe that by subjecting themselves to some form of ordeal or discipline they are earning favor or investing themselves with extra power derived from animal spirits, deities, or ancestors. This added confidence and determination could enhance their hunting success. The limits of the human mind's influence over physical reality, at least over the body and health, are far from settled. Whether through a prayer, a fetish, or a frog, people throughout the world find ways to harness this resource.

CARGO CULTS

Peter M. Worsley

Patrols of the Australian Government venturing into the "uncontrolled" central highlands of New Guinea in 1946 found the primitive people there swept up in a wave of religious excitement. Prophecy was being fulfilled: The arrival of the Whites was the sign that the end of the world was at hand. The natives proceeded to butcher all of their pigs—animals that were not only a principal source of subsistence but also symbols of social status and ritual preeminence in their culture. They killed these valued animals in expression of the belief that after three days of darkness "Great Pigs" would appear from the sky. Food, firewood and other necessities had to be stock-piled to see the people through to the arrival of the Great Pigs. Mock wireless antennae of bamboo and rope had been erected to receive in advance the news of the millennium. Many believed that with the great event they would exchange their black skins for white ones.

This bizarre episode is by no means the single event of its kind in the murky history of the collision of European civilization with the indigenous cultures of the southwest Pacific. For more than 100 years traders and missionaries have been reporting similar disturbances among the peoples of Melanesia, the group of Negro-inhabited islands (including New Guinea, Fiji, the Solomons and the New Hebrides) lying between Australia and the open Pacific Ocean. Though their technologies were based largely upon stone and wood, these peoples had highly developed cultures, as measured by the standards of maritime and agricultural

ingenuity, the complexity of their varied social organizations and the elaboration of religious belief and ritual. They were nonetheless ill prepared for the shock of the encounter with the Whites, a people so radically different from themselves and so infinitely more powerful. The sudden transition from the society of the ceremonial stone ax to the society of sailing ships and now of airplanes has not been easy to make.

After four centuries of Western expansion, the densely populated central highlands of New Guinea remain one of the few regions where the people still carry on their primitive existence in complete independence of the world outside. Yet as the agents of the Australian Government penetrate into ever more remote mountain valleys, they find these backwaters of antiquity already deeply disturbed by contact with the ideas and artifacts of European civilization. For "cargo"—Pidgin English for trade goods—has long flowed along the indigenous channels of communication from the seacoast into the wilderness. With it has traveled the frightening knowledge of the white man's magical power. No small element in the white man's magic is the hopeful message sent abroad by his missionaries: the news that a Messiah will come and that the present order of Creation will end.

The people of the central highlands of New Guinea are only the latest to be gripped in the recurrent religious frenzy of the "cargo cults." However variously embellished with details from native myth and Christian belief, these cults all advance the

same central theme: the world is about to end in a terrible cataclysm. Thereafter God, the ancestors or some local culture hero will appear and inaugurate a blissful paradise on earth. Death, old age, illness and evil will be unknown. The riches of the white man will accrue to the Melanesians.

Although the news of such a movement in one area has doubtless often inspired similar movements in other areas, the evidence indicates that these cults have arisen independently in many places as parallel responses to the same enormous social stress and strain. Among the movements best known to students of Melanesia are the "Taro Cult" of New Guinea, the "Vailala Madness" of Papua, the "Naked Cult" of Espiritu Santo, the "John Frum Movement" of the New Hebrides and the "Tuka Cult" of the Fiji Islands.

At times the cults have been so well organized and fanatically persistent that they have brought the work of government to a standstill. The outbreaks have often taken the authorities completely by surprise and have confronted them with mass opposition of an alarming kind. In the 1930s, for example, villagers in the vicinity of Wewak, New Guinea, were stirred by a succession of "Black King" movements. The prophets announced that the Europeans would soon leave the island, abandoning their property to the natives, and urged their followers to cease paying taxes, since the government station was about to disappear into the sea in a great earthquake. To the tiny community of Whites in charge of the region, such talk was dangerous. The authorities jailed four of the prophets and exiled three others. In yet another movement that sprang up in declared opposition to the local Christian mission, the cult leader took Satan as his god.

Troops on both sides in World War II found their arrival in Melanesia heralded as a sign of the Apocalypse. The G.I.'s who landed in the New Hebrides, moving up for the bloody fighting on Guadalcanal, found the natives furiously at work preparing airfields, roads and docks for the magic ships and planes that they believed were coming from "Rusefel" (Roosevelt), the friendly king of America.

The Japanese also encountered millenarian visionaries during their southward march to Guadalcanal. Indeed, one of the strangest minor military actions of World War II occurred in Dutch New Guinea, when Japanese forces had to be turned against the local Papuan inhabitants of the Geelvink Bay region. The Japanese had at first been received with great joy, not because their "Greater East Asia Co-Prosperity Sphere" propaganda had made any great impact upon the Papuans, but because the natives regarded them as harbingers of the new world that was dawning, the flight of the Dutch having already given the first sign. Mansren, creator of the islands and their peoples, would now return, bringing with him the ancestral dead. All this had been known, the cult leaders declared, to the crafty Dutch, who had torn out the first page of the Bible where these truths were inscribed. When Mansren returned, the existing world order would be entirely overturned. White men would turn black like Papuans, Papuans would become Whites; root crops would grow in trees, and coconuts and fruits would grow like tubers. Some of the islanders now began to draw together into large "towns"; others took Biblical names such as "Jericho" and "Galilee" for their villages. Soon they adopted military uniforms and began drilling. The Japanese, by now highly unpopular, tried to disarm and disperse the Papuans; resistance in-

evitably developed. The climax of this tragedy came when several canoe-loads of fanatics sailed out to attack Japanese warships, believing themselves to be invulnerable by virtue of the holy water with which they had sprinkled themselves. But the bullets of the Japanese did not turn to water, and the attackers were mowed down by machine-gun fire.

Behind this incident lay a long history. As long ago as 1857 missionaries in the Geelvink Bay region had made note of the story of Mansren. It is typical of many Melanesian myths that became confounded with Christian doctrine to form the ideological basis of the movements. The legend tells how long ago there lived an old man named Manamakeri ("he who itches"), whose body was covered with sores. Manamakeri was extremely fond of palm wine, and used to climb a huge tree every day to tap the liquid from the flowers. He soon found that someone was getting there before him and removing the liquid. Eventually he trapped the thief, who turned out to be none other than the Morning Star. In return for his freedom, the Star gave the old man a wand that would produce as much fish as he liked, a magic tree and a magic staff. If he drew in the sand and stamped his foot, the drawing would become real. Manamakeri, aged as he was, now magically impregnated a young maiden; the child of this union was a miracle-child who spoke as soon as he was born. But the maiden's parents were horrified, and banished her, the child and the old man. The trio sailed off in a canoe created by Mansren ("The Lord"), as the old man now became known. On this journey Mansren rejuvenated himself by stepping into a fire and flaking off his scaly skin, which changed into valuables. He then sailed around Geelvink Bay, creating islands where he stopped, and peopling them with the ancestors of the present-day Papuans.

The Mansren myth is plainly a creation myth full of symbolic ideas relating to fertility and rebirth. Comparative evidence—especially the shedding of his scaly skin—

confirms the suspicion that the old man is, in fact, the Snake in another guise. Psychoanalytic writers argue that the snake occupies such a prominent part in mythology the world over because it stands for the penis, another fertility symbol. This may be so, but its symbolic significance is surely more complex than this. It is the "rebirth" of the hero, whether Mansren or the Snake, that exercises such universal fascination over men's minds.

The 19th-century missionaries thought that the Mansren story would make the introduction of Christianity easier, since the concept of "resurrection," not to mention that of the "virgin birth" and the "second coming," was already there. By 1867, however, the first cult organized around the Mansren legend was reported.

Though such myths were widespread in Melanesia, and may have sparked occasional movements even in the pre-White era, they took on a new significance in the late 19th century, once the European powers had finished parceling out the Melanesian region among themselves. In many coastal areas the long history of "blackbirding"—the seizure of islanders for work on the plantations of Australia and Fiji—had built up a reservoir of hostility to Europeans. In other areas, however, the arrival of the Whites was accepted, even welcomed, for it meant access to bully beef and cigarettes, shirts and paraffin lamps, whisky and bicycles. It also meant access to the knowledge behind these material goods, for the Europeans brought missions and schools as well as cargo.

Practically the only teaching the natives received about European life came from the missions, which emphasized the central significance of religion in European society. The Melanesians already believed that man's activities—whether gardening, sailing canoes or bearing children—needed magical assistance. Ritual without human effort was not enough. But neither was human effort on its own. This outlook was reinforced by mission teaching.

The initial enthusiasm for European rule, however, was speedily dispelled. The rapid growth of the plantation economy removed the bulk of the able-bodied men from the villages, leaving women, children and old men to carry on as best they could. The splendid vision of the equality of all Christians began to seem a pious deception in face of the realities of the color bar, the multiplicity of rival Christian missions and the open irreligion of many Whites.

For a long time the natives accepted the European mission as the means by which the "cargo" would eventually be made available to them. But they found that acceptance of Christianity did not bring the cargo any nearer. They grew disillusioned. The story now began to be put about that it was not the Whites who made the cargo, but the dead ancestors. To people completely ignorant of factory production, this made good sense. White men did not work; they merely wrote secret signs on scraps of paper, for which they were given shiploads of goods. On the other hand, the Melanesians labored week after week for pitiful wages. Plainly the goods must be made for Melanesians somewhere, perhaps in the Land of the Dead. The Whites, who possessed the secret of the cargo, were intercepting it and keeping it from the hands of the islanders, to whom it was really consigned. In the Madang district of New Guinea, after some 40 years' experience of the missions, the natives went in a body one day with a petition demanding that the cargo secret should now be revealed to them, for they had been very patient.

So strong is this belief in the existence of a "secret" that the cargo cults generally contain some ritual in imitation of the mysterious European customs which are held to be the clue to the white man's extraordinary power over goods and men. The believers sit around tables with bottles of flowers in front of them, dressed in European clothes, waiting for the cargo ship or airplane to materialize;

other cultists feature magic pieces of paper and cabalistic writing. Many of them deliberately turn their backs on the past by destroying secret ritual objects, or exposing them to the gaze of uninitiated youths and women, for whom formerly even a glimpse of the sacred objects would have meant the severest penalties, even death. The belief that they were the chosen people is further reinforced by their reading of the Bible, for the lives and customs of the people in the Old Testament resemble their own lives rather than those of the Europeans. In the New Testament they find the Apocalypse, with its prophecies of destruction and resurrection, particularly attractive.

Missions that stress the imminence of the Second Coming, like those of the Seventh Day Adventists, are often accused of stimulating millenarian cults among the islanders. In reality, however, the Melanesians themselves rework the doctrines the missionaries teach them, selecting from the Bible what they themselves find particularly congenial in it. Such movements have occurred in areas where missions of quite different types have been dominant, from Roman Catholic to Seventh Day Adventist. The reasons for the emergence of these cults, of course, lie far deeper in the life-experience of the people.

The economy of most of the islands is very backward. Native agriculture produces little for the world market, and even the European plantations and mines export only a few primary products and raw materials: copra, rubber, gold. Melanesians are quite unable to understand why copra, for example, fetches 30 pounds sterling per ton one month and but 5 pounds a few months later. With no notion of the workings of world-commodity markets, the natives see only the sudden closing of plantations, reduced wages and unemployment, and are inclined to attribute their insecurity to the whim or evil in the nature of individual planters.

Such shocks have not been confined to the economic order. Govern-

ments, too, have come and gone, especially during the two world wars: German, Dutch, British and French administrations melted overnight. Then came the Japanese, only to be ousted in turn largely by the previously unknown Americans. And among these Americans the Melanesians saw Negroes like themselves, living lives of luxury on equal terms with white G.I.'s. The sight of these Negroes seemed like a fulfillment of the old prophecies to many cargo cult leaders. Nor must we forget the sheer scale of this invasion. Around a million U.S. troops passed through the Admiralty Islands, completely swamping the inhabitants. It was a world of meaningless and chaotic changes in which anything was possible. New ideas were imported and given local twists. Thus in the Loyalty Islands people expected the French Communist Party to bring the millennium. There is no real evidence, however, of any Communist influence in these movements, despite the rather hysterical belief among Solomon Island planters that the name of the local "Masinga Rule" movement was derived from the word "Marxian"! In reality the name comes from a Solomon Island tongue, and means "brotherhood."

Europeans who have witnessed outbreaks inspired by the cargo cults are usually at a loss to understand what they behold. The islanders throw away their money, break their most sacred taboos, abandon their gardens and destroy their precious livestock; they indulge in sexual license or, alternatively, rigidly separate men from women in hugh communal establishments. Sometimes they spend days sitting gazing at the horizon for a glimpse of the long-awaited ship or airplane; sometimes they dance, pray and sing in mass congregations, becoming possessed and "speaking with tongues."

Observers have not hesitated to use such words as "madness," "mania," and "irrationality" to characterize the cults. But the cults reflect quite logical and rational attempts to make sense out of a social order that appears senseless and chaotic. Given the ignorance of the Melanesians about the wider European society, its economic organization and its highly developed technology, their reactions form a consistent and understandable pattern. They wrap up all their yearning and hope in an amalgam that combines the best counsel they can find in Christianity and their native belief. If the world is soon to end, gardening or fishing is unnecessary; everything will be provided. If the Melanesians are to be part of a much wider order, the taboos that prescribe their social conduct must now be lifted or broken in a newly prescribed way.

Of course the cargo never comes. The cults nonetheless live on. If the millennium does not arrive on schedule, then perhaps there is some failure in the magic, some error in the ritual. New breakaway groups organize around "purer" faith and ritual. The cult rarely disappears, so long as the social situation which brings it into being persists.

At this point it should be observed that cults of this general kind are not peculiar to Melanesia. Men who feel themselves oppressed and deceived have always been ready to pour their hopes and fears, their aspirations and frustrations, into dreams of a millennium to come or of a golden age to return. All parts of the world have had their counterparts of the cargo cults, from the American Indian ghost dance to the communist-millenarist "reign of the saints" in Münster during the Reformation, from medieval European apocalyptic cults to African "witch-finding" movements and Chinese Buddhist heresies. In some situations men have been content to wait and pray; in others they have sought to hasten the day by using their strong right arms to do the Lord's work. And always the cults serve to bring together scattered groups, notably the peasants and urban plebeians of agrarian societies and the peoples of "stateless" societies where the cult unites separate (and often hostile) villages, clans and tribes into a wider religio-political unity.

Once the people begin to develop secular political organizations, however, the sects tend to lose their importance as vehicles of protest. They begin to relegate the Second Coming to the distant future or to the next world. In Melanesia ordinary political bodies, trade unions and native councils are becoming the normal media through which the islanders express their aspirations. In recent years continued economic prosperity and political stability have taken some of the edge off their despair. It now seems unlikely that any major movement along cargo-cult lines will recur in areas where the transition to secular politics has been made, even if the insecurity of prewar times returned. I would predict that the embryonic nationalism represented by cargo cults is likely in future to take forms familiar in the history of other countries that have moved from subsistence agriculture to participation in the world economy.

The Secrets of Haiti's Living Dead

A Harvard botanist investigates mystic potions, voodoo rites, and the making of zombies.

Gino Del Guercio

Gino Del Guercio is a national science writer for United Press International.

Five years ago, a man walked into l'Estère, a village in central Haiti, approached a peasant woman named Angelina Narcisse, and identified himself as her brother Clairvius. If he had not introduced himself using a boyhood nickname and mentioned facts only intimate family members knew, she would not have believed him. Because, eighteen years earlier, Angelina had stood in a small cemetery north of her village and watched as her brother Clairvius was buried.

The man told Angelina he remembered that night well. He knew when he was lowered into his grave, because he was fully conscious, although he could not speak or move. As the earth was thrown over his coffin, he felt as if he were floating over the grave. The scar on his right cheek, he said, was caused by a nail driven through his casket.

The night he was buried, he told Angelina, a voodoo priest raised him from the grave. He was beaten with a sisal whip and carried off to a sugar plantation in northern Haiti where, with other zombies, he was forced to work as a slave. Only with the death of the zombie master were they able to escape, and Narcisse eventually returned home.

Legend has it that zombies are the living dead, raised from their graves and animated by malevolent voodoo sorcerers, usually for some evil purpose. Most Haitians believe in zombies, and Narcisse's claim is not unique. At about the time he reappeared, in 1980, two women turned up in other villages saying they were zombies. In the same year, in northern Haiti, the local peasants claimed to have found a group of zombies wandering aimlessly in the fields.

But Narcisse's case was different in one crucial respect; it was documented. His death had been recorded by doctors at the American-directed Schweitzer Hospital in Deschapelles. On April 30, 1962, hospital records show, Narcisse walked into the hospital's emergency room spitting up blood. He was feverish and full of aches. His doctors could not diagnose his illness, and his symptoms grew steadily worse. Three days after he entered the hospital, according to the records, he died. The attending physicians, an American among them, signed his death certificate. His body was placed in cold storage for twenty hours, and then he was buried. He said he remembered hearing his doctors pronounce him dead while his sister wept at his bedside.

At the Centre de Psychiatrie et Neurologie in Port-au-Prince, Dr. Lamarque Douyon, a Haitian-born, Canadian-trained psychiatrist, has been systematically investigating all reports of zombies since 1961. Though convinced zombies were real, he had been unable to find a scientific explanation for the phenomenon. He did not believe zombies were people raised from the dead, but that did not make them any less interesting. He speculated that victims were only made to *look* dead, probably by means of a drug that dramatically slowed metabolism. The victim was buried, dug up within a few hours, and somehow reawakened.

The Narcisse case provided Douyon with evidence strong enough to warrant a request for assistance from colleagues in New York. Douyon wanted to find an ethnobotanist, a traditional-medicines expert, who could track down the zombie potion he was sure existed. Aware of the medical potential of a drug that could dramatically lower metabolism, a group organized by the late Dr. Nathan Kline—a New York psychiatrist and pioneer in the field of psychopharmacology—raised the funds necessary to send someone to investigate.

The search for that someone led to the Harvard Botanical Museum, one of the world's foremost institutes of ethnobiology. Its director, Richard Evans Schultes, Jeffrey professor of biology, had spent thirteen years in the tropics studying native medicines. Some of his best-known work is the investigation of curare, the substance used by the nomadic people of the Amazon to poison their darts. Refined into a powerful muscle relaxant called D-tubocurarine, it is now an essential component of the anesthesia used during almost all surgery.

Schultes would have been a natural for the Haitian investigation, but he was too busy. He recommended another Harvard ethnobotanist for the assignment, Wade Davis, a 28-year-old Canadian pursuing a doctorate in biology.

Davis grew up in the tall pine forests of British Columbia and entered Harvard in 1971, influenced by a Life magazine story on the student strike of 1969. Before Harvard, the only Americans he had known were draft dodgers, who seemed very exotic. "I used to fight forest fires with them," Davis says. "Like everybody else, I thought America was where it was at. And I wanted to go to Harvard because of that Life article. When I got there, I realized it wasn't quite what I had in mind."

Davis took a course from Schultes, and when he decided to go to South America to study plants, he approached his professor for guidance. "He was an extraordinary figure," Davis remembers. "He was a man who had done it all. He had lived alone for years in the Amazon." Schultes sent Davis to the rain forest with two letters of introduction and two pieces of advice: wear a pith helmet and try ayahuasca, a powerful hallucinogenic vine. During that expedition and others, Davis proved himself an "outstanding field man," says his mentor. Now, in early 1982, Schultes called him into his office and asked if he had plans for spring break.

"I always took to Schultes's assignments like a plant takes to water," says Davis, tall and blond, with inquisitive blue eyes. "Whatever Shultes told me to do, I did. His letters of introduction opened up a whole world." This time the world was Haiti.

Davis knew nothing about the Caribbean island—and nothing about African traditions, which serve as Haiti's cultural basis. He certainly did not believe in zombies. "I thought it was a lark," he says now.

Davis landed in Haiti a week after his conversation with Schultes, armed with a hypothesis about how the zombie drug—if it existed—might be made. Setting out to explore, he discovered a country materially impoverished, but rich in culture and mystery. He was impressed by the cohesion of Haitian society; he found none of the crime,

social disorder, and rampant drug and alcohol abuse so common in many of the other Caribbean islands. The cultural wealth and cohesion, he believes, spring from the country's turbulent history.

During the French occupation of the late eighteenth century, 370,000 African-born slaves were imported to Haiti between 1780 and 1790. In 1791, the black population launched one of the few successful slave revolts in history, forming secret societies and overcoming first the French plantation owners and then a detachment of troops from Napoleon's army, sent to quell the revolt. For the next hundred years Haiti was the only independent black republic in the Caribbean, populated by people who did not forget their African heritage. "You can almost argue that Haiti is more African than Africa," Davis says. "When the west coast of Africa was being disrupted by colonialism and the slave trade, Haiti was essentially left alone. The amalgam of beliefs in Haiti is unique, but it's very, very African."

Davis discovered that the vast majority of Haitian peasants practice voodoo, a sophisticated religion with African roots. Says Davis, "It was immediately obvious that the stereotypes of voodoo weren't true. Going around the countryside, I found clues to a whole complex social world." Vodounists believe they communicate directly with, indeed are often possessed by, the many spirits who populate the everyday world. Vodoun society is a system of education, law, and medicine; it embodies a code of ethics that regulates social behavior. In rural areas, secret vodoun societies, much like those found on the west coast of Africa, are as much or more in control of everyday life as the Haitian government.

Although most outsiders dismissed the zombie phenomenon as folklore, some early investigators, convinced of its reality, tried to find a scientific explanation. The few who sought a zombie drug failed. Nathan Kline, who helped finance Davis's expedition, had searched unsuccessfully, as had Lamarque Douyon, the Haitian psychiatrist. Zora Neale Hurston, an American black woman, may have come closest. An anthropological pioneer, she went to Haiti in the Thirties, studied vodoun

society, and wrote a book on the subject, *Tell My Horse,* first published in 1938. She knew about the secret societies and was convinced zombies were real, but if a powder existed, she too failed to obtain it.

Davis obtained a sample in a few weeks.

He arrived in Haiti with the names of several contacts. A BBC reporter familiar with the Narcisse case had suggested he talk with Marcel Pierre. Pierre owned the Eagle Bar, a bordello in the city of Saint Marc. He was also a voodoo sorcerer and had supplied the BBC with a physiologically active powder of unknown ingredients. Davis found him willing to negotiate. He told Pierre he was a representative of "powerful but anonymous interests in New York," willing to pay generously for the priest's services, provided no questions were asked. Pierre agreed to be helpful for what Davis will only say was a "sizable sum." Davis spent a day watching Pierre gather the ingredients—including human bones—and grind them together with mortar and pestle. However, from his knowledge of poison, Davis knew immediately that nothing in the formula could produce the powerful effects of zombification.

Three weeks later, Davis went back to the Eagle Bar, where he found Pierre sitting with three associates. Davis challenged him. He called him a charlatan. Enraged, the priest gave him a second vial, claiming that this was the real poison. Davis pretended to pour the powder into his palm and rub it into his skin. "You're a dead man," Pierre told him, and he might have been, because this powder proved to be genuine. But, as the substance had not actually touched him, Davis was able to maintain his bravado, and Pierre was impressed. He agreed to make the poison and show Davis how it was done.

The powder, which Davis keeps in a small vial, looks like dry black dirt. It contains parts of toads, sea worms, lizards, tarantulas, and human bones. (To obtain the last ingredient, he and Pierre unearthed a child's grave on a nocturnal trip to the cemetery.) The poison is rubbed into the victim's skin. Within hours he begins to feel nauseated and has difficulty breathing. A pins-

and-needles sensation afflicts his arms and legs, then progresses to the whole body. The subject becomes paralyzed; his lips turn blue for lack of oxygen. Quickly—sometimes within six hours—his metabolism is lowered to a level almost indistinguishable from death.

As Davis discovered, making the poison is an inexact science. Ingredients varied in the five samples he eventually acquired, although the active agents were always the same. And the poison came with no guarantee. Davis speculates that sometimes instead of merely paralyzing the victim, the compound kills him. Sometimes the victim suffocates in the coffin before he can be resurrected. But clearly the potion works well enough often enough to make zombies more than a figment of Haitian imagination.

Analysis of the powder produced another surprise. "When I went down to Haiti originally," says Davis, "my hypothesis was that the formula would contain *concombre zombi*, the 'zombie's cucumber,' which is a *Datura* plant. I thought somehow *Datura* was used in putting people down." *Datura* is a powerful psychoactive plant, found in West Africa as well as other tropical areas and used there in ritual as well as criminal activities. Davis had found *Datura* growing in Haiti. Its popular name suggested the plant was used in creating zombies.

But, says Davis, "there were a lot of problems with the *Datura* hypothesis. Partly it was a question of how the drug was administered. *Datura* would create a stupor in huge doses, but it just wouldn't produce the kind of immobility that was key. These people had to appear dead, and there aren't many drugs that will do that."

One of the ingredients Pierre included in the second formula was a dried fish, a species of puffer or blowfish, common to most parts of the world. It gets its name from its ability to fill itself with water and swell to several times its normal size when threatened by predators. Many of these fish contain a powerful poison known as tetrodotoxin. One of the most powerful nonprotein poisons known to man, tetrodotoxin turned up in every sample of zombie powder that Davis acquired.

Numerous well-documented accounts of puffer fish poisoning exist, but the most famous accounts come from the Orient, where *fugu* fish, a species of puffer, is considered a delicacy. In Japan, special chefs are licensed to prepare *fugu*. The chef removes enough poison to make the fish nonlethal, yet enough remains to create exhilarating physiological effects—tingles up and down the spine, mild prickling of the tongue and lips, euphoria. Several dozen Japanese die each year, having bitten off more than they should have.

"When I got hold of the formula and saw it was the *fugu* fish, that suddenly

Richard Schultes

His students continue his tradition of pursuing botanical research in the likeliest of unlikely places.

Richard Evans Schultes, Jeffrey professor of biology emeritus, has two homes, and they could not be more different. The first is Cambridge, where he served as director of the Harvard Botanical Museum from 1970 until last year, when he became director emeritus. During his tenure he interested generations of students in the exotic botany of the Amazon rain forest. His impact on the field through his own research is worldwide. The scholarly ethnobotanist with steel-rimmed glasses, bald head, and white lab coat is as much a part of the Botanical Museum as the thousands of plant specimens and botanical texts on the museum shelves.

In his austere office is a picture of a crew-cut, younger man stripped to the waist, his arms decorated with tribal paint. This is Schultes's other persona. Starting in 1941, he spent thirteen years in the rain forests of South America, living with the Indians and studying the plants they use for medicinal and spiritual purposes.

Schultes is concerned that many of the people he has studied are giving up traditional ways. "The people of so-called primitive societies are becoming civilized and losing all their forefathers' knowledge of plant lore," he says. "We'll be losing the tremendous amounts of knowledge they've gained over thousands of years. We're interested in the practical aspects with the hope that new medicines and other things can be developed for our own civilization."

Schultes's exploits are legendary in the biology department. Once, while gathering South American plant specimens hundreds of miles from civilization, he contracted beriberi. For forty days he fought creeping paralysis and overwhelming fatigue as he paddled back to a doctor. "It was an extraordinary feat of endurance," says disciple Wade Davis. "He is really one of the last nineteenth-century naturalists."

Hallucinogenic plants are one of Schultes's primary interests. As a Harvard undergraduate in the Thirties, he lived with Oklahoma's Kiowa Indians to observe their use of plants. He participated in their peyote ceremonies and wrote his thesis on the hallucinogenic cactus. He has also studied other hallucinogens, such as morning glory seeds, sacred mushrooms, and ayahuasca, a South American vision vine. Schultes's work has led to the development of anesthetics made from curare and alternative sources of natural rubber.

Schultes's main concern these days is the scientific potential of plants in the rapidly disappearing Amazon jungle. "If chemists are going to get material on 80,000 species and then analyze them, they'll never finish the job before the jungle is gone," he says. "The short cut is to find out what the [native] people have learned about the plant properties during many years of living in the very rich flora."

—G.D.G.

threw open the whole Japanese literature," says Davis. Case histories of *fugu* poisoning read like accounts of zombification. Victims remain conscious but unable to speak or move. A man who had "died" after eating *fugu* recovered seven days later in the morgue. Several summers ago, another Japanese poisoned by *fugu* revived after he was nailed into his coffin. "Almost all of Narcisse's symptoms correlated. Even strange things such as the fact that he said he was conscious and could hear himself pronounced dead. Stuff that I thought had to be magic, that seemed crazy. But, in fact, that is what people who get *fugu*-fish poisoning experience."

Davis was certain he had solved the mystery. But far from being the end of his investigation, identifying the poison was, in fact, its starting point. "The drug alone didn't make zombies," he explains. "Japanese victims of pufferfish poisoning don't become zombies, they become poison victims. All the drug could do was set someone up for a whole series of psychological pressures that would be rooted in the culture. I wanted to know why zombification was going on," he says.

He sought a cultural answer, an explanation rooted in the structure and beliefs of Haitian society. Was zombification simply a random criminal activity? He thought not. He had discovered that Clairvius Narcisse and "Ti Femme," a second victim he interviewed, were village pariahs. Ti Femme was regarded as a thief. Narcisse had abandoned his children and deprived his brother of land that was rightfully his. Equally suggestive, Narcisse claimed that his aggrieved brother had sold him to a *bokor,* a voodoo priest who dealt in black magic; he made cryptic reference to having been tried and found guilty by the "masters of the land."

Gathering poisons from various parts of the country, Davis had come into direct contact with the vodoun secret societies. Returning to the anthropological literature on Haiti and pursuing his contacts with informants, Davis came to understand the social matrix within which zombies were created.

Davis's investigations uncovered the importance of the secret societies. These groups trace their origins to the bands of escaped slaves that organized the revolt against the French in the late eighteenth century. Open to both men and women, the societies control specific territories of the country. Their meetings take place at night, and in many rural parts of Haiti the drums and wild celebrations that characterize the gatherings can be heard for miles.

Davis believes the secret societies are responsible for policing their communities, and the threat of zombification is one way they maintain order. Says Davis, "Zombification has a material basis, but it also has a societal logic." To the uninitiated, the practice may appear a random criminal activity, but in rural vodoun society, it is exactly the opposite—a sanction imposed by recognized authorities, a form of capital punishment. For rural Haitians, zombification is an even more severe punishment than death, because it deprives the subject of his most valued possessions: his free will and independence.

The vodounists believe that when a person dies, his spirit splits into several different parts. If a priest is powerful enough, the spiritual aspect that controls a person's character and individuality, known as *ti bon ange,* the "good little angel," can be captured and the corporeal aspect, deprived of its will, held as a slave.

From studying the medical literature on tetrodotoxin poisoning, Davis discovered that if a victim survives the first few hours of the poisoning, he is likely to recover fully from the ordeal. The subject simply revives spontaneously. But zombies remain without will, in a trance-like state, a condition vodounists attribute to the power of the priest. Davis thinks it possible that the psychological trauma of zombification may be augmented by *Datura* or some other drug; he thinks zombies may be fed a *Datura* paste that accentuates their disorientation. Still, he puts the material basis of zombification in perspective: "Tetrodotoxin and *Datura* are only templates on which cultural forces and beliefs may be amplified a thousand times."

Davis has not been able to discover how prevalent zombification is in Haiti.

"How many zombies there are is not the question," he says. He compares it to capital punishment in the United States: "It doesn't really matter how many people are electrocuted, as long as it's a possibility." As a sanction in Haiti, the fear is not of zombies, it's of becoming one.

Davis attributes his success in solving the zombie mystery to his approach. He went to Haiti with an open mind and immersed himself in the culture. "My intuition unhindered by biases served me well," he says. "I didn't make any judgments." He combined this attitude with what he had learned earlier from his experiences in the Amazon. "Schultes's lesson is to go and live with the Indians as an Indian." Davis was able to participate in the vodoun society to a surprising degree, eventually even penetrating one of the Bizango societies and dancing in their nocturnal rituals. His appreciation of Haitian culture is apparent. "Everybody asks me how did a white person get this information? To ask the question means you don't understand Haitians—they don't judge you by the color of your skin."

As a result of the exotic nature of his discoveries, Davis has gained a certain notoriety. He plans to complete his dissertation soon, but he has already finished writing a popular account of his adventures. To be published in January by Simon and Schuster, it is called *The Serpent and the Rainbow,* after the serpent that vodounists believe created the earth and the rainbow spirit it married. Film rights have already been optioned; in October Davis went back to Haiti with a screenwriter. But Davis takes the notoriety in stride. "All this attention is funny," he says. "For years, not just me, but all Schultes's students have had extraordinary adventures in the line of work. The adventure is not the end point, it's just along the way of getting the data. At the Botanical Museum, Schultes created a world unto itself. We didn't think we were doing anything above the ordinary. I still don't think we do. And you know," he adds, "the Haiti episode does not begin to compare to what others have accomplished—particularly Schultes himself."

Rituals of Death

Capital Punishment and Human Sacrifice

Elizabeth D. Purdum and J. Anthony Paredes

We were perplexed by the resurgence of enthusiasm for the death penalty in the United States. According to a 1986 *Gallup Report,* support for the death penalty in America has reached a near-record high in 50 years of polling, with 70 percent of Americans favoring execution of convicted murderers (Gallup, 1986). In a 1983 poll conducted in Florida, 72 percent of respondents were found to support the death penalty, compared with 45 percent in 1964 (Cambridge Survey Research, 1985). Still more perplexing is the finding that nearly half of those supporting the death penalty agree that "only the poor and unfortunate are likely to be executed" (Ellsworth and Ross, 1983:153). Equally startling is the revelation that although deterrence is often given as a primary justification for the death penalty, most people would continue to support it even if convinced that it had no greater deterrent effect than that of a life sentence (P. Harris, 1986). In addition, there is little if any evidence that capital punishment reduces the crime rate; there seems, rather, to be some historical evidence for a reverse correlation. Pickpocketing, a crime then punishable by hanging, was rampant among spectators at executions in England circa 1700 (Lofland, 1977). Bowers and Pierce (1980) argue, on the basis of increased murder rates in New York State in the month following executions, that capital punishment has a "brutalizing" effect and leads to more, not less, violence. Why, then, does capital punishment receive such widespread support in modern America?

Capital Punishment—Another "Riddle of Culture"

In theory, capital punishment should be no more a puzzle than any other seemingly bizarre, nonrational custom. Either human cultures are amenable to scientific explanation or they are not. And we anthropologists have not been timid about tackling everything from Arunta penile subincision to Hindu cow love as problems for scientific explication. As a first step in this task, we will compare capital punishment in Florida, the leader in the United States in death sentencing since Florida's 1972 capital punishment statute was affirmed by the U.S. Supreme Court in 1976, with certain forms of human sacrifice as practiced by the Aztecs of Mexico in the sixteenth century. This is not a capricious comparison. John Cooper (1976) pointedly seeks the "socio-religious origins of capital punishment" in ancient rites of, to use his term, "propitiatory death." But his study is narrowly constrained by canons of Western philosophy and history. By making a more exotic comparison, we hope to point the way to more nomothetic principles for understanding state-sanctioned homicide in complex societies. Albert Camus (1959) also perceived elements of religious ritual in French capital punishment, but argued that the practice continued only because hidden from the view of the general public. Anticipating our comparisons here, anthropologist Colin Turnbull concludes in his article "Death by Decree" that the key to understanding capital punishment is to be found in its ritual element (1978). John Lofland (1977) has compared the dramaturgy of state executions circa 1700 in England with those of contemporary America, concluding that modern executions in their impersonal, unemotional, and private aspects appear humane, yet deny the reality of death and strip the condemned of any opportunity to die with dignity or courage.

It was the public media spectacle surrounding recent executions in Florida that triggered the thoughts leading to this paper. Detailed, minute-by-minute accounts of Florida's first post–1976 execution, widely reported press conferences with death row inmates, television images of the ambulance bearing the body of an executed criminal, news photos of mourners and revelers outside the prison on the night before an execution—all these served to transform a closely guarded, hidden expression of the ultimate power of the state into a very public ceremonial event. We were reminded of the pomp and circumstance for the masses accompanying the weird rites of Tenochtitlan that greeted sixteenth-century Spaniards. In such similarities, we thought, might lie the key to a dispassionate, anthropological understanding of capital punishment in modern America.

Before proceeding we must note that the Aztec state itself imposed capital punishment for a variety of crimes, ranging from murder to fornication to violations of the dress code for commoners. The available sources indicate, however, that among the Aztecs capital punishment was swift, rather unceremonious, and even brutish. It is the high drama of Aztec rituals of human sacrifice that shows the closest parallels with the bureaucratically regulated procedures for electrocution of the condemned at Starke, Florida, in the 1980s.

The Victims of Execution and Sacrifice

The death penalty is imposed on only a small percentage of Americans convicted of homicide—5 percent, according to a 1980 Georgia study (Baldus et al., 1983). Today there are 2,182 people on death row in the United States; 296 of these are in Florida (NAACP Legal Defense and Educational Fund, 1988). Since 1976, 18 persons have been executed in Florida. Prior to 1972, when the Supreme Court voided state death penalty statutes, it was clear that the death penalty was disproportionately applied to black men. Fifty-four percent of the 3,859 people executed in the United States between 1930 and 1967 were nonwhite. Among those executed for rape during the same period, 405 of 455 were black (U.S. Department of Justice, 1986). Nakell and Hardy's study of homicide cases in North Carolina from 1977 and 1978 revealed the effects of race of victim and race of defendant throughout the criminal justice process (1987). The relationship between race and execution consistently holds even when one controls for such factors as differential conviction rates and the relationship between the defendant and the victim (Radelet, 1981).

Recent studies (for example, Baldus et al., 1983a; Bowers and Pierce, 1980b; Gross and Mauro, 1984; Pasternoster, 1983; and Radelet, 1981) suggest that the defendant's race, since the reinstatement of the death penalty in 1976, is less important than it once was

in predicting death sentences. These studies conclude that a more significant factor is the race of the victim: that is, people who kill whites are more likely to receive the death penalty than people who kill blacks.

Statistics aside, people familiar with death row inmates readily acknowledge that they are marginal members of society—economically, socially, and, even, in the case of Florida, geographically. Many come from backgrounds of extreme poverty and abuse. Michael Radelet and his colleagues (1983) report one common denominator among families who have members in prison: low socioeconomic status. Poverty makes it hard, if not impossible, for families to maintain ties with prisoners. Many inmates on death row have few family or social ties. Only about 15 of the 208 men on death row in Florida in 1983 had visitors each week; 60 others had visitors about once a month; and fewer than half received a visitor in any given year (Radelet et al., 1983). Many of Florida's inmates are from out of state. More than a few of Florida's death row inmates are also crazy, retarded, or both. For instance, Arthur Goode, who was convicted of murdering a nine-year-old boy, ate a half-gallon of butter pecan ice cream, his requested "last meal," then gave as his final statement his desire to marry a young boy. In the three weeks before his execution, Goode wrote letters to the governor and other prominent officials complaining of the lack of toilet paper to blow his nose (Radelet and Barnard, 1986). There is an inmate who believes that one of the people helping him with his court appeals is alternately a dead disc jockey or one of his own seven wives. Or, there is James Douglas Hill, a 26-year-old with an IQ of 66 and a serious speech impediment, who, having learned to read and write while in prison, sent to his mother this message:

Hi mom me hour are you doing to day fine i hope i am doing ok for now But i miss you so varry varry much that i can cry But i am to Big to cry. . . . i miss you i miss you love James all way. By now. (Sherrill, 1984:555)

In 1987 James Douglas Hill was released on bail when substantial doubt about his guilt surfaced.

Detailed statistics on *whom* the Aztecs put to death in their rites of human sacrifice are not available, nor is the exact number of sacrificial victims. Nonetheless, the Aztecs of Central Mexico sacrificed humans on a scale unprecedented in any other society. Putting aside the question of whether the Aztecs were nutritionally motivated toward this human slaughter (Harner, 1977), annual estimates for central Mexico in the first decades of the sixteenth century vary from 20,000 (Cortes, as quoted by Fagan, 1984:230) to 250,000 sacrificed victims (Woodrow Borah, as quoted by Harner, 1977:119).

Most of the sacrificial victims were able-bodied male war captives from neighboring kingdoms, but the Aztecs reportedly also sacrificed large numbers of children—sold to the priests by the poor. The children's tears were believed to be particularly appealing to Tlaloc, the rain god. Women were also sometimes sacrificed, some of them presented as impersonations of certain female deities. Similarly, one of the most frequently recounted, and often highly romanticized, forms of Aztec human sacrifice was that in which a flawless young war captive was pampered and indulged for a year as the embodiment of a god, then killed with great ritual and sadness while the victim dutifully played his role in the deicidal drama. Most Aztec war captives enjoyed no such protracted special treatment. How god-impersonators were selected we do not know. Neither do we know how many war captives' lives were spared, if any, nor how many were doomed to a life of slavery.

Paralleling the numerous means of execution employed in the United States—electrocution, hanging, firing squad, deadly gas, lethal injection—the Aztecs sacrificed their victims with a variety of techniques. These included beheading, burning, and flights of arrows, but the most common method was to spread the victim on a large, elaborately carved stone, cut open his chest with an obsidian knife, then tear out his heart. We present here a brief, composite account of "ordinary" war captive sacrifice using the method of coronary excision.

Announcement of Death

According to Fray Diego Duran's account of the aftermath of a battle between the Aztecs and the Tepeacas, the Tepeacan captives were taken back to the Aztec capital, Tenochtitlan, with collars around their necks and their hands bound behind them. The captives "went along singing sadly, weeping and lamenting their fate," knowing they were to be sacrificed. Once they were in the capital, priests threw incense on them, offered them maize bread, and said:

We welcome you
To this city of Mexico Tenochtitlan
. . . .
Do you think that you have come to live;
You have come to die.
. . . .
We salute you and comfort you with these words:
You have not come because of weakness,
But because of your manliness.
You will die here but your fame will live forever.
(Duran, 1964:101)

The announcement of a Florida death row inmate's impending death comes with the signing of a death warrant by the state governor, once all routine appeals and bids for clemency have failed. The criteria by which the decision is made to sign a warrant against a particular person at a particular time are not publicly known.

A death warrant is a single-page document in legal language, bordered in black. Each one bears the state seal and is officially witnessed by the secretary of state—not by some seemingly more likely authority such as the attorney general. Each death warrant is publicized by a news release issued shortly after the governor signs. Between 1972 and the end of 1988, Florida's three governors signed over two hundred death warrants. Once the warrant is signed in Tallahassee, the superintendent of Florida State Prison at Starke, 150 miles away, is immediately notified. Prison guards are sent to get the person named in the warrant from his or her cell. They bring the prisoner, who may have no forewarning of what is about to happen, to the assistant superintendent's office. There the superintendent or his designee reads the warrant aloud to the condemned. Following a string of "whereas's" tracing the history of the case, the warrant concludes:

Now, therefore, I, [names governor], as Governor of the State of Florida and pursuant to the authority and responsibility vested by the Constitution and the laws of Florida do hereby issue this warrant directing the Superintendent of the Florida State Prison to cause the sentence of death to be executed upon [names person] on some day of the week beginning [for instance] Noon, Tuesday, the 29th day of October, 1989, and ending Noon, Tuesday, the 5th day of November, 1989, in accord with the provisions of the laws of the State of Florida.

The warrant is usually dated four weeks before the last day the warrant is in effect. Reportedly, warrants are never issued for executions to take place during the time the state supreme court is not in session or during the Christmas season. After the warrant is read, the prisoner is permitted to telephone a lawyer and a family member, if he or she has any.

Treatment After Announcement of Death

Aztec war captives were served "Divine Wine" (probably pulque) and paraded past images of the Aztec gods and past the emperor, Montezuma. They were given cloaks, loincloths, and sandals—sandals being a mark of nobility. Next, the prisoners were taken to the central marketplace, where they were given flowers and "shields of splendid featherwork" and forced to dance upon a platform. The condemned were also given tobacco to smoke, which, according to Duran, "comforted them greatly" (Duran, 1964:102).

The war captives were dispersed among the several wards of the city, and men were assigned to guard and maintain them with the charge:

Take care that they do not escape
Take care that they do not die!
Behold, they are children of the Sun!
Feed them well; let them be fat and desirable for the sacrifice
. . . (Duran, 1964:108)

Duran (1964) reports that captives were treated well and honored as if they were gods.

Many days passed during which craftsmen were instructed to carve a stone for the sacrificial altar. A few days later the altar was ready, and temple youths were given instructions about how the sacrifice was to be conducted. Guests were invited from neighboring states, and booths were decorated for spectators.

In Florida, the reading of the death warrant initiates a period officially designated as "death watch," marked by moving the person to a cell in "Q Wing," where he or she will be closer to the electric chair and isolated from other death row inmates. Most of the person's possessions are taken away, including photographs and tennis shoes, the only personally owned item of apparel that inmates are ordinarily allowed; the condemned is allowed to retain only those items listed in the "Execution Guidelines," a 39-page single-spaced document (Florida State Prison, 1983). The only books on the list are "religious tracts as distributed by Institution Chaplain, maximum possession ten (10)." Magazine and newspaper subscriptions may continue, but no new periodicals may be ordered. In a curious specific parallel with Aztec practice, there are no special restrictions on tobacco for prisoners on Q Wing. Three meals a day are fed to all "condemned inmates," and dietary restrictions for "medical reasons" continue to be observed. Indeed, meticulous, detailed instructions are given to prison personnel to ensure that the condemned person is kept in good health and not provided with any item that might be used to harm himself or attempt suicide. Moreover, under current procedures if a prisoner is determined to have become insane on death row, he or she is spared execution until restored to mental health (Radelet and Barnard, 1986).

6. RELIGION, BELIEF, AND RITUAL

Once death watch begins, social visits are "noncontact" and held in the "maximum security visiting park" any two days, Monday through Friday, 9 A.M. to 3 P.M. Other death row inmates are permitted "contact" social visits for six hours on Saturdays or Sundays. Legal visits for the condemned may continue to be the "contact" type during the death warrant, but only until one week before execution, when these visits, too, become noncontact. Media visits are scheduled through prison officials on Tuesday, Wednesday, and Thursday until Phase II of death watch begins, five days before the execution is scheduled to occur.

With Phase II of death watch, more property is taken from the prisoner. The condemned is allowed only a few so-called comfort items: "one TV located outside cell, 1 radio, 1 deck of cards, 1 Bible, 1 book, periodical, magazine or newspaper." Very specific day-by-day regulations and procedures now go into effect, beginning with "Execution Day–Minus Five (5)," when the "execution squad" is identified. Likewise, on Execution Day–Minus Four (4), testing of the electrical equipment to be used for execution begins. During Phase II the inmate is subjected to further limitations on visits, but during the 48 hours before the scheduled execution, the condemned may have an interview with a media representative of his or her choice. Execution Day–Minus Four (4) is a particularly busy day: the condemned reinventories his or her property and specifies in writing its disposition; specifies in writing his or her funeral arrangements; and is measured for a suit of clothing—the suit will be cheap—in which the condemned will, if he or she wants, be buried. On Day–Minus Three (3) there are "no activities," and Day–Minus Two (2) is devoted primarily to testing the equipment and "execution squad drill." On Execution Day–Minus One (1) the pace quickens, and it is on this day that the chef takes the person's order for the last meal.

Each time the prisoner is moved during Phase II of death watch, the entire prison is locked down and the condemned undergoes a complete body search upon being returned to his or her cell. A guard sits outside the condemned inmate's cell, as one always does during an active death warrant, but now the guard records every 15 minutes what the prisoner is doing.

Final Preparations for Death

On the day of an Aztec sacrifice, the visiting nobles were seated in their decorated booths and the prisoners were placed in a line before them and made to dance. The victims were smeared with plaster; white feathers were tied to their hair; their eyelids were blackened and their lips painted red. Priests who would perform the actual sacrifice stood in a long row according to their rank. Each priest was disguised as a god and carried a richly decorated sword and shield. The priests sat under a beautifully adorned arbor erected at the summit of a large, truncated pyramid. Chanters came forth and began to dance and sing.

In Florida, sometime around midnight on the night before an execution, the condemned is usually allowed a last one-hour contact visit. The person is permitted to see his own clergyman if he has one, but only the prison chaplain will be permitted to accompany the inmate to the place of execution. At 4:30 A.M. the prisoner is served his or her last meal, to be eaten on a paper plate with a spoon; if the prisoner has requested a steak, the chef has cut the meat into bite-sized pieces beforehand and arranged them to appear to be an intact steak. No later than 5:30 A.M., the official witnesses to the execution, 12 in number (one of whom may be designated by the condemned), must assemble at the main prison gate. At 5:50 A.M. the media witnesses, also 12 in number, are picked up at the "media onlooker area." Both types of witnesses will later be "escorted to the witness room of the execution chamber." At 6:00 A.M. an administrative assistant, three designated electricians, a physician, and a physician's assistant are assembled in the death chamber. The administrative assistant establishes

telephone contact with the state governor's office. Meanwhile, the condemned inmate has his or her head and right calf shaved (to better conduct electricity), takes a shower under the supervision of a high-ranking prison official, and is dressed in his or her new burial clothes, omitting the suit jacket and shoes. Until recently, by informal custom the prison superintendent would then have a drink of whiskey with the condemned in his cell, but public outcry was so great that the practice was discontinued. At 6:50 "conducting gel" is applied to the person's head and leg. The superintendent reads the death warrant to the condemned a final time.

The Moment of Death

Each Aztec victim was taken singly to the sacrificial stone and tethered to it by a rope. In one form of sacrifice, in a mockery of self-defense, the victim was then given a sword edged with feathers rather than obsidian. The high priest rose and descended to the stone, walked around it twice and returned to his seat. Next, an old man disguised as an ocelot gave the captive four wooden balls and a drink of "Divine Wine" and instructed him to defend himself. Many victims tried to defend themselves against a series of ceremonially garbed priest-warriors, but others "unwilling to undergo such ceremony cast themselves upon the stone seeking a quick death" (Duran, 1964:112). Death was inevitable: as soon as the captive was wounded, four priests painted black, with long braided hair and garments resembling chasubles, spread-eagled the victim on the stone, each priest holding a limb. The high priest cut open the victim's chest with an obsidian knife, pulled out the victim's heart and offered the organ to the sun. The heart was deposited in a jar or placed on a brazier, and the next victim was brought forward.

The superintendent of Florida State Prison at Starke and two other prison officials escort the condemned inmate to the death chamber at 6:56 A.M. The person is strapped into the electric chair. At 7:00 A.M. the condemned is permitted to make a last statement. The governor directs the superintendent to proceed with the execution, traditionally concluding with the words "God save us all." The witnesses have been seated in their peculiarly carved, white high-backed chairs. The electrician places the sponge and cap on the inmate's head. The assistant superintendent engages the circuit breaker. The electrician activates the panel, the superintendent signals the executioner to throw the switch, and the "automatic cycle will begin." The actual executioner is an anonymous private citizen dressed in a black hood and robe who will be paid $150 for his services. Once the automatic cycle has run its course, the superintendent invites the doctor to conduct the examination. If all has gone well, the condemned is pronounced dead and the time recorded. A designated prison official proclaims, "The sentence of _____ has been carried out. Please exit to the rear at this time." By custom, someone in attendance waves a white cloth just outside the prison to signal the crowd assembled in a field across from it—reporters, death penalty opponents and proponents, and any others—that the deed is done. Official guidelines for the execution of more than one inmate on a single day exist, but we will dispense with those here.

After Death

Fray Bernardino de Sahagun (1951:24) reports that after each Aztec captive had been slain, the body was taken gently away and rolled down the stairs of the sacrificial pyramid. At the bottom, the victim's head was cut off for display on a rack and the remainder of the corpse was taken to one of the special houses, *calpulli*, where "they divided [the bodies] up in order to eat them." Meanwhile, those who had taken part in the sacrifice entered a temple, removed their ritual garb, and were rewarded with fine clothes and a feast. The lords from the provinces who had been brought to observe were

"shocked and bewildered."

As soon as a Florida inmate is pronounced dead in the electric chair, ambulance attendants are called into the chamber; they remove the inmate from the chair and take the body to a waiting ambulance, which transports the corpse to the medical examiner's office. There an autopsy is performed. Until recently, portions of the brain were removed for secret study by a University of Florida researcher investigating the relationship between "head trauma and violent behavior." This procedure was followed for 11 of the 13 men executed between 1979 and 1985, but was stopped in response to negative publicity. Once the autopsy is completed, the corpse is released to the funeral home for cremation or burial. If the deceased has made no arrangements for a private funeral, his or her body is interred on the prison grounds. The executioner, meanwhile, is returned to his secret pick-up point and compensated. There is a "debriefing" at the prison of all the other participants in the execution save one.

The Native Explanations

What explanations are given by Aztecs and modern Americans for these decidedly gruesome acts? While we will probably never know what the Aztec man in the street thought of the sacrificial murders committed by his priests and nobles, official theology, if we may trust the sources, held that the gods had to be fed and placated to keep the crops growing, the sun high, and the universe in healthy order. Unfortunately for war captives, one of the gods' favorite foods was human hearts.

The explanations given by Americans for capital punishment generally are clothed in more pragmatic, secular terms. Most commonly, supporters of capital punishment invoke stimulus-response psychology and declare that such punishment will prevent others from committing heinous crimes. For instance, following the execution of an admitted child-murderer, Florida's governor declared that "he hoped the execution would be a warning to others

who harbored the desire to mistreat children" (Sherrill, 1984:553). Other explanations emphasize the lower cost of execution as compared with long-term imprisonment, the need to provide families of murder victims with a sense of justice and mental repose, and what might be called the "social hygiene" approach: "[S]ome people just ought to be eliminated—we kill rattlesnakes, we don't keep them as pets," declared one Florida Supreme Court justice (*Tallahassee Democrat*, 15 Sept. 1985).

Despite the rationalistic cast of the most common public explanations for capital punishment, at least some of the explanations, or justifications, that surface into public view are unabashedly religious. The author of a letter to the *Tallahassee Democrat* (6 Feb. 1985) cited scripture to argue that earthly governments have the God-given right and authority "to make and enforce laws, including the right to take human life." He urged his readers to submit " 'to every ordinance of man for the Lord's sake,' " for in so doing evildoers will be punished, those who do well will be praised, and " 'ye will put to silence the ignorance of foolish men' (I Peter 2:13–15)." We suspect that beneath more sophisticated explanations for capital punishment there is, if not an outright appeal to supernatural authority, the same deep-seated set of nameless fears and anxieties that motivate humans everywhere to commit ceremonial acts that reassure and give substance to the Durkheimian view that "religion is society collectively worshipping itself."

Conclusion

The perceptive reader will have recognized the sometimes startling points of similarity between the conduct of some forms of Aztec human sacrifice and capital punishment in Florida. There are, of course, some profoundly important points of difference as well. We will not belabor the obvious here, but given the many commonalities in the organization, procedures, and even physical appurtenances between Aztec human sacrifice and Florida capital punishment, it is reasonable to propose that whatever psychosocial functions human sacrifice might have served in the Aztec empire, they are matched by similar functions for capital punishment in the United States. Just as Aztec ripping out of human hearts was couched in mystical terms of maintaining universal order and well-being of the state (putting aside the question of the utility of such practices as terror tactics with which to intimidate neighboring societies), we propose that capital punishment in the United States serves to assure many that society is not out of control after all, that the majesty of the Law reigns, and that God is indeed in his heaven. Precise, emic ("native") corroboration of our interpretation of capital punishment as the ultimate validator of law is provided by an automobile bumper sticker first seen in Tallahassee in 1987, shortly after the Florida legislature passed a controversial statute requiring automobile passengers to wear safety belts:

I'LL BUCKLE UP—
WHEN BUNDY DOES
IT'S THE LAW

"Bundy" is Theodore Bundy, Florida's most famous prisoner sentenced to be "buckled up" in the electric chair.

Sources as diverse as the populist *National Enquirer* (Mitteager, 1985) and the eminent legal scholar Lawrence Friedman (1973) instruct their readers that the crime rate is actually far lower today than 100 years ago. But through the mass media, the average American is subjected to a daily diet of fanatical terrorists, crazed rapists, revolting child molesters, and ghoulish murderers, to say nothing of dishonest politicians, unruly protestors, welfare and tax cheats, greedy gurus and philandering preachers, marauding street gangs, sexual perverts, and drug fiends, while all the time having to deal with the everyday personal irritations of a society in which, as Marvin Harris (1981) tells us, nothing works, mothers leave home, and gays come out of the closet. In an ironic twist on the anthropological debate (e.g., Isaac, 1983; Ortiz de Montellano, 1982; Price, 1978) over Harner's proposed materialist ex-

planation of Aztec human sacrifice, we hypothesize that the current groundswell of support for capital punishment in the United States springs from the universal, ancient human impulse to do something in times of stress, even if it is only ritual. Bronislaw Malinowski observed that "there are no peoples however primitive without religion and magic" (1954:17); neither are there peoples so civilized that they are devoid of magic. All peoples turn to magic when knowledge, technology, and experience fail (Malinowski, 1954). In the face of all the evidence that capital punishment does no more to deter crime than the bloody rituals of Tenochtitlan did to keep the sun in the sky, we must seek some broader, noninstrumental function that the death penalty serves. We propose, in short, that modern capital punishment is an institutionalized *magical* response to perceived disorder in American life and in the world at large, an attempted magical solution that has an especial appeal to the beleaguered, white, God-fearing men and women of the working class. And in certain aspiring politicians they find their sacrificial priests.

References

Baldus, David C.; Charles A. Pulaski, Jr.; and George Woodworth. 1983. "Comparative Review of Death Sentences: An Empirical Study of the Georgia Experience." *Journal of Criminal Law and Criminology* 74:661–753.

Bowers, William, J., and Glenn L. Pierce. 1980. "Deterrence or Brutalization: What Is the Effect of Executions?" *Crime and Delinquency* 26:453–84.

—————. 1980. "Arbitrariness and Discrimination Under Post-*Furman* Capital Statutes." *Crime and Delinquency* 26:563–635.

Cambridge Survey Research. 1985. "An Analysis of Attitudes Toward Capital Punishment in Florida." Prepared for Amnesty International.

Camus, Albert. 1959. *Reflections on the Guillotine.* Michigan City, Ind.: Fridtjof-Karla.

Cooper, John W. 1976. "Propitiation as Social Maintenance: A Study of Capital Punishment Through the Sociology of Religion." M.A. thesis, Florida State University.

Duran, Fray Diego. 1964. *The Aztecs.* New

York: Orion Press.

Ellsworth, Phoebe C., and Lee Ross. 1983. "Public Opinion and Capital Punishment: A Close Examination of the Views of Abolitionists and Retentionists." *Crime and Delinquency* 29:116–69.

Fagan, Brian M. 1984. *The Aztecs.* New York: W. H. Freeman.

Florida State Prison. 1983. "Execution Guidelines During Active Death Warrant." Starke: Florida State Prison. Reprinted in part at pp. 235–40 of Amnesty International, *United States of America: The Death Penalty.* London: Amnesty International, 1987.

Friedman, Lawrence M. 1973. *A History of American Law.* New York: Simon and Schuster.

Gallup, George. 1986. "The Death Penalty." *Gallup Report* 244–45 (Jan.–Feb.) 10–16.

Gross, Samuel R., and Robert Mauro. 1984. "Patterns of Death: An Analysis of Racial Disparities in Capital Sentencing and Homicide Victimization." *Stanford Law Review* 37:27–153.

Harner, Michael. 1977. "The Ecological Basis for Aztec Sacrifice." *American Ethnologist* 4:117–35.

Harris, Marvin. 1981. *America Now: The Anthropology of a Changing Culture.* New York: Simon and Schuster.

Harris, Philip W. 1986. "Over-Simplification and Error in Public Opinion Surveys on Capital Punishment." *Justice Quarterly* 3:429–55.

Isaac, Barry L. 1983. "The Aztec 'Flowery War': A Geopolitical Explanation." *Journal of Anthropological Research* 39:415–32.

Lofland, John. 1977. "The Dramaturgy of State Executions." Pp. 275–325 in *State Executions Viewed Historically and Sociologically,* by Horace Bleackley. Montclair, N.J.: Patterson Smith.

Malinowski, Bronislaw. 1954. *Magic, Science and Religion and Other Essays.* Garden City, N.Y.: Doubleday.

Mitteager, James. 1985. "Think Crime Is Bad Now? It Was Much Worse 100 Years Ago." *National Enquirer,* 25 Nov., p. 25.

NAACP Legal Defense and Educational Fund. 1988. "Death Row, U.S.A." Unpublished compilation, available from 99 Hudson St., New York, N.Y. 10013.

Nakell, Barry, and Kenneth A. Hardy. 1987. *The Arbitrariness of the Death Penalty.* Philadelphia: Temple University Press.

Ortiz de Montellano, Bernard R. 1982. "The Body Dangerous: Physiology and Social Stratification." *Reviews in Anthropology* 9:97–107.

Paternoster, Raymond. 1983. "Race of Victim and Location of Crime: The Decision to Seek the Death Penalty in South Carolina." *Journal of Criminal Law and Criminology* 74:754–85.

Price, Barbara J. 1978. "Demystification, Enriddlement and Aztec Cannibalism: A

Materialist Rejoinder to Harner." *American Ethnologist* 5:98–115.

Radelet, Michael L. 1981. "Racial Characteristics and the Imposition of the Death Penalty." *American Sociological Review* 46:918–27.

Radelet, Michael L., and George W. Barnard. 1986. "Ethics and the Psychiatric Determination of Competency to Be Executed." *Bulletin of the American Academy of Psychiatry and the Law* 14:37–53.

Radelet, Michael L.; Margaret Vandiver; and Felix M. Berardo. 1983. "Families, Prisons, and Men with Death Sentences: The Human Impact of Structured Uncertainty." *Journal of Family Issues* 4:593–612.

Sahagun, Fray Bernardino de. 1951. *General History of the Things of New Spain*,

Santa Fe, N.M.: School of American Research and the University of Utah.

Sherrill, Robert. 1984. "In Florida, Insanity Is No Defense." *The Nation* 239:539, 552–56.

Turnbull, Colin. 1978. "Death by Decree." *Natural History* 87 (May):51–66.

U.S. Department of Justice. 1986. *Capital Punishment, 1984.* Washington, D.C.: U.S. Government Printing Office.

Body Ritual Among the Nacirema

Horace Miner
University of Michigan

The anthropologist has become so familiar with the diversity of ways in which different peoples behave in similar situations that he is not apt to be surprised by even the most exotic customs. In fact, if all of the logically possible combinations of behavior have not been found somewhere in the world, he is apt to suspect that they must be present in some yet undescribed tribe. This point has, in fact, been expressed with respect to clan organization by Murdock (1949:71). In this light, the magical beliefs and practices of the Nacirema present such unusual aspects that it seems desirable to describe them as an example of the extremes to which human behavior can go.

Professor Linton first brought the ritual of the Nacirema to the attention of anthropologists twenty years ago (1936:326), but the culture of this people is still very poorly understood. They are a North American group living in the territory between the Canadian Cree, the Yaqui and Tarahumare of Mexico, and the Carib and Arawak of the Antilles. Little is known of their origin, though tradition states that they came from the east. According to Nacirema mythology, their nation was originated by a culture hero, Notgnishaw, who is otherwise known for two great feats of strength—the throwing of a piece of wampum across the river Pa-To-Mac and the chopping down of a cherry tree in which the Spirit of Truth resided.

Nacirema culture is characterized by a highly developed market economy which has evolved in a rich natural habitat. While much of the people's time is devoted to economic pursuits, a large part of the fruits of these labors and a considerable portion of the day are spent in ritual activity. The focus of this activity is the human body, the appearance and health of which loom as a dominant concern in the ethos of the people. While such a concern is certainly not unusual, its ceremonial aspects and associated philosophy are unique.

The fundamental belief underlying the whole system appears to be that the human body is ugly and that its natural tendency is to debility and disease. Incarcerated in such a body, man's only hope is to avert these characteristics through the use of the powerful influences of ritual and ceremony. Every household has one or more shrines devoted to this purpose. The more powerful individuals in the society have several shrines in their houses and, in fact, the opulence of a house is often referred to in terms of the number of such ritual centers it possesses. Most houses are of wattle and daub construction, but the shrine rooms of the more wealthy are walled with stone. Poorer families imitate the rich by applying pottery plaques to their shrine walls.

While each family has at least one such shrine, the rituals associated with it are not family ceremonies but are private and secret. The rites are normally only discussed with children, and then only during the period when they are being initiated into these mysteries. I was able, however, to establish sufficient rapport with the natives to examine these shrines and to have the rituals described to me.

The focal point of the shrine is a box or chest which is built into the wall. In this chest are kept the many charms and magical potions without which no native believes he could live. These preparations are secured from a variety of specialized practitioners. The most powerful of these are the medicine men, whose assistance must be rewarded with substantial gifts. However, the medicine men do not provide the curative potions for their clients, but decide what the ingredients should be and then write them down in an ancient and secret language. This writing is understood only by the medicine men and by the herbalists who, for another gift, provide the required charm.

The charm is not disposed of after it has served its purpose, but is placed in the charm-box of the household shrine. As these magical materials are specific for certain ills, and the real or imagined maladies of the people are many, the charm-box is usually full to overflowing. The magical packets are so numerous that people forget what their purposes were and fear to use them again. While the natives are very vague on this point, we can only assume that the idea in retaining all the old magical materials is that their presence in

From *American Anthropologist*, June 1956, pp. 503-507. Reprinted by permission of the American Anthropological Association. Not for further reproduction.

the charm-box, before which the body rituals are conducted, will in some way protect the worshipper.

Beneath the charm-box is a small font. Each day every member of the family, in succession, enters the shrine room, bows his head before the charm-box, mingles different sorts of holy water in the font, and proceeds with a brief rite of ablution. The holy waters are secured from the Water Temple of the community, where the priests conduct elaborate ceremonies to make the liquid ritually pure.

In the hierarchy of magical practitioners, and below the medicine men in prestige, are specialists whose designation is best translated "holy-mouth-men." The Nacirema have an almost pathological horror and fascination with the mouth, the condition of which is believed to have a supernatural influence on all social relationships. Were it not for the rituals of the mouth, they believe that their teeth would fall out, their gums bleed, their jaws shrink, their friends desert them, and their lovers reject them. (They also belive that a strong relationship exists between oral and moral characteristics. For example, there is a ritual ablution of the mouth for children which is supposed to improve their moral fiber.)

The daily body ritual performed by everyone includes a mouth-rite. Despite the fact that these people are so punctilious about care of the mouth, this rite involves a practice which strikes the uninitiated stranger as revolting. It was reported to me that the ritual consists of inserting a small bundle of hog hairs into the mouth, along with certain magical powders, and then moving the bundle in a highly formalized series of gestures.

In addition to the private mouth-rite, the people seek out a holy-mouth-man once or twice a year. These practitioners have an impressive set of paraphernalia, consisting of a variety of augers, awls, probes, and prods. The use of these objects in the exorcism of the evils of the mouth involves almost unbelievable ritual torture of the client. The holy-mouth-man opens the client's mouth and, using the above mentioned tools, enlarges any holes which decay may have created in the teeth. Magical materials are put into these holes. If there are no naturally occurring holes in the teeth, large sections of one or more teeth are gouged out so that the supernatural substance can be applied. In the client's view, the purpose of these ministrations is to arrest decay and to draw friends. The extremely sacred and traditional character of the rite is evident in the fact that the natives return to the holy-mouth-men year after year, despite the fact that their teeth continue to decay.

It is to be hoped that, when a thorough study of the Nacirema is made, there will be a careful inquiry into the personality structure of these people. One has but to watch the gleam in the eye of a holy-mouth-man, as he jabs an awl into an exposed nerve, to suspect that a certain amount of sadism is involved. If this can be established, a very interesting pattern emerges, for most of the population shows definite masochistic tendencies. It was to these that Professor Linton referred in discussing a distinctive part of the daily body ritual which is performed only by men. This part of the rite involves scraping and lacerating the surface of the face with a sharp instrument. Special women's rites are performed only four times during each lunar month, but what they lack in frequency is made up in barbarity. As part of this ceremony, women bake their heads in small ovens for about an hour. The theoretically interesting point is that what seems to be a preponderantly masochistic people have developed sadistic specialists.

The medicine men have an imposing temple, or *latipso*, in every community of any size. The more elaborate ceremonies required to treat very sick patients can only be performed at this temple. These ceremonies involve not only the thaumaturge but a permanent group of vestal maidens who move sedately about the temple chambers in distinctive costume and headdress.

The *latipso* ceremonies are so harsh that it is phenomenal that a fair proportion of the really sick natives who enter the temple ever recover. Small children whose indoctrination is still incomplete have been known to resist attempts to take them to the temple because "that is where you go to die." Despite this fact, sick adults are not only willing but eager to undergo the protracted ritual purification, if they can afford to do so. No matter how ill the supplicant or how grave the emergency, the guardians of many temples will not admit a client if he cannot give a rich gift to the custodian. Even after one has gained admission and survived the ceremonies, the guardians will not permit the neophyte to leave until he makes still another gift.

The supplicant entering the temple is first stripped of all his or her clothes. In every-day life the Nacirema avoids exposure of his body and its natural functions. Bathing and excretory acts are performed only in the secrecy of the household shrine, where they are ritualized as part of the body-rites. Psychological shock results from the fact that body secrecy is suddenly lost upon entry into the *latipso*. A man, whose own wife has never seen him in an excretory act, suddenly finds himself naked and assisted by a vestal maiden while he performs his natural functions into a sacred vessel. This sort of ceremonial treatment is necessitated by the fact that the excreta are used by a diviner to ascertain the course and nature of the client's sickness. Female clients, on the other hand, find their naked bodies are subjected to the scrutiny, manipulation and prodding of the medicine men.

Few supplicants in the temple are well enough to do anything but lie on their hard beds. The daily ceremonies, like the rites of the holy-mouth-men, involve discomfort and torture. With ritual precision, the vestals awaken their miserable charges each dawn and roll them about on their beds of pain while performing ablutions, in the formal movements of which the maidens are highly trained. At other times they insert magic wands in the supplicant's mouth or force him to eat substances which are supposed to be healing. From time to time the medicine men come to their clients and jab magically treated needles into their flesh. The fact that these temple ceremonies may not cure, and may even kill the neophyte, in no way decreases the people's faith in the medicine men.

There remains one other kind of practioner, known as a "listener." This witch-doctor has the power to exorcise the devils that lodge in the heads of people who have been bewitched. The Nacirema believe that parents bewitch their own children. Mothers are particularly suspected of putting a curse on children while teaching them the secret body rituals. The counter-magic of the witch-doctor is unusual in its lack of ritual. The patient simply tells the "listener" all his troubles and fears, beginning with the earliest difficulties he can remember. The memory displayed by the Nacirema in these exorcism sessions is truly remarkable. It is not uncommon for the patient to bemoan the rejection he felt upon being weaned as a babe, and a few individuals even see their troubles going back to the traumatic effects of their own birth.

In conclusion, mention must be made of certain practices which have their base in native esthetics but which depend upon the pervasive aversion to the natural body and its functions. There are ritual fasts to make fat people thin and ceremonial feasts to make thin people fat. Still other rites are used to make women's breasts large if they are small, and smaller if they are large. General dissatisfaction with breast shape is symbolized in the fact that the ideal form is virtually outside the range of human variation. A few women afflicted with almost inhuman hypermammary development are so idolized that they make a handsome living by simply going from village to village and permitting the natives to stare at them for a fee.

Reference has already been made to the fact that excretory functions are ritualized, routinized, and relegated to secrecy. Natural reproductive functions are similarly distorted. Intercourse is taboo as a topic and scheduled as an act. Efforts are made to avoid pregnancy by the use of magical materials or by limiting intercourse to certain phases of the moon. Conception is actually very infre-

quent. When pregnant, women dress so as to hide their condition. Parturition takes place in secret, without friends or relatives to assist, and the majority of women do not nurse their infants.

Our review of the ritual life of the Nacirema has certainly shown them to be a magic-ridden people. It is hard to understand how they have managed to exist so long under the burdens which they have imposed upon themselves. But even such exotic customs as these take on real meaning when they are viewed with the insight provided by Malinowski when he wrote (1948:70):

Looking from far and above, from our high places of safety in the developed civilization, it is easy to see all the crudity and irrelevance of magic. But without its power and guidance early man could not have mastered his practical difficulties as he has done, nor could man have advanced to the higher stages of civilization.

REFERENCES

Linton, Ralph. 1936. *The Study of Man*. New York, D. Appleton-Century Co.

Malinowski, Bronislaw. 1948. *Magic, Science, and Religion*. Glencoe, The Free Press.

Murdock, George P. 1949. *Social Structure*. New York, The Macmillan Co.

Superstition and Ritual in American Baseball

George Gmelch

George Gmelch teaches anthropology at Union College in Schenectady, New York. He has just completed a book on Caribbean migration, Double Passage, *from the University of Michigan Press. He is currently doing research for a book tentatively entitled* Culture Change and Professional Baseball in America: 1960–1990.

On each pitching day for the first three months of a winning season, Dennis Grossini, a pitcher on a Detroit Tiger farm team, arose from bed at exactly 10:00 A.M. At 1:00 P.M. he went to the nearest restaurant for two glasses of iced tea and a tuna fish sandwich. Although the afternoon was free he changed into the sweatshirt and supporter he wore during his last winning game, and one hour before the game he chewed a wad of Beech-Nut chewing tobacco. During the game he touched his letters (the team name on his uniform) after each pitch and straightened his cap after each ball. Before the start of each inning he replaced the pitcher's rosin bag next to the spot where it was the inning before. And after every inning in which he gave up a run, he would wash his hands.

I asked him which part of the ritual was most important. He responded, "You can't really tell what's most important so it all becomes important. I'd be afraid to change anything. As long as I'm winning, I do everything the same. Even when I can't wash my hands (this would occur when he had to bat), it scares me going back to the mound. . . . I don't feel quite right."

Trobriand Islanders, according to anthropologist Bronislaw Malinowski, felt the same way about their fishing magic. Among the Trobrianders, fishing took two forms. In the inner lagoon fish were plentiful and there was little danger; on the open sea fishing was dangerous and yields varied widely. Malinowski found that magic was not used in lagoon fishing, where men could rely solely on their knowledge and skill. But when fishing on the open sea, Trobrianders used a great deal of magical ritual to ensure safety and increase their catch.

Baseball, the American national sport, is an arena in which the players behave remarkably like Malinowski's Trobriand fishermen. To professional baseball players, baseball is more than a game. It is an occupation. Since their livelihood depends on how well they perform, they use magic to try to control or eliminate the chance and uncertainty built into baseball.

To control uncertainty Chicago White Sox shortstop Ozzie Guillen doesn't wash his underclothes after a good game. The Boston Red Sox's Wade Boggs eats chicken before every game (that's 162 meals of chicken per year). Ex-San Francisco Giant pitcher Ron Bryant added a new stick of bubble gum to the collection in his bulging back pocket after each game he won. Jim Ohms, my teammate on the Daytona Beach Islanders in 1966, used to put another penny in the pouch of his supporter after each win. Clanging against the hard plastic genital cup, the pennies made an audible sound as the pitcher ran the bases toward the end of a winning season.

Whether they are professional baseball players, Trobriand fishermen, soldiers, or farmers, people resort to magic in situations of chance, when they believe they have limited control over the success of their activities. In technologically advanced societies that pride themselves on a scientific approach to problem solving, as well as in simple societies, rituals of magic are common. Magic is a human attempt to impose order and certainty on a chaotic, uncertain situation. This attempt is irrational in that there is no causal connection between the instruments of magic and the desired consequences of the magical practice. But it is rational in that it creates in the practitioner a sense of confidence, competence, and control, which in turn is important to successfully executing a specific activity and achieving a desired result.

I have long had a close relationship with baseball, first as a participant and then as an observer. I devoted much of my youth to the game and played professionally as first baseman for five teams in the Detroit Tiger organization over three years. I also spent two years in the Quebec Provincial League. For

Originally appeared in *Elysian Fields Quarterly: The Baseball Review,* All Star Issue, 1992, Vol. 11, No. 3, pp. 25-36, P.O. Box 45618, Madison, WI 53744, 1-800-273-1444. © 1992 by George Gmelch. Reprinted by permission.

additional information about baseball magic I interviewed twenty-eight professional ballplayers and sportswriters.

There are three essential activities in baseball—pitching, hitting, and fielding. The first two, pitching and hitting, involve a great deal of chance and are comparable to the Trobriand fishermen's open sea; in them, players use magic and ritual to increase their chances for success. The third activity, fielding, involves little uncertainty and is similar to the Trobriander inner lagoon; fielders find it unnecessary to resort to magic.

The pitcher is the player least able to control the outcome of his own efforts. His best pitch may be hit for a home run, and his worst pitch may be hit directly into the hands of a fielder for an out or be swung at and missed for a third strike. He may limit the opposing team to a few hits yet lose the game, or he may give up a dozen hits and win. Frequently pitchers perform well and lose, and perform poorly and win. One has only to look at the frequency with which pitchers end a season with poor won-lost records but good earned run averages, or vice versa. For example, in 1990 Dwight Gooden gave up more runs per game than his teammate Sid Fernandez but had a won-lost record nearly twice as good. Gooden won nineteen games and lost only seven, one of the best in the National League, while Sid Fernandez won only nine games while losing fourteen. They pitched for the same team—the New York Mets—and therefore had the same fielders behind them. Regardless of how well he performs, on every outing the pitcher depends upon the proficiency of his teammates, the inefficiency of the opposition, and caprice.

An incredible example of bad luck in pitching occurred some years ago involving former Giant outfielder Willie Mays. Mays intentionally "dove for the dirt" to avoid being hit in the head by a fastball. While he was falling the ball hit his bat and went shooting down the left field line. Mays jumped up and ran, turning the play into a double. Players shook their heads in amazement—most players can't hit when they try to, but Mays couldn't avoid

hitting even when he tried not to. The pitcher looked on in disgust.

Hitting is also full of risk and uncertainty—Red Sox outfielder and Hall of Famer Ted Williams called it the most difficult single task in the world of sports. Consider the forces and time constraints operating against the batter. A fastball travels from the pitcher's mound to the batter's box, just sixty and one-half feet, in three to four tenths of a second. For only three feet of the journey, an absurdly short two-hundredths of a second, the ball is in a position where it can be hit. And to be hit well the ball must be neither too close to the batter's body nor too far from the "meat" of his bat. Any distraction, any slip of a muscle or change in stance, can throw a swing off. Once the ball is hit chance plays a large role in determining where it will go—into a waiting glove, whistling past a fielder's diving stab, or into the wide open spaces. While the pitcher who threw the fastball to Mays was suffering, Mays was collecting the benefits of luck.

Batters also suffer from the fear of being hit by a pitch—specifically, by a fastball that often travels at speeds exceeding ninety miles per hour. Throughout baseball history the great fastball pitchers like Sandy Koufax, Bob Gibson, Nolan Ryan, and Roger Clemens have thrived on this fear and on the level of distraction it causes hitters. The well-armed pitcher inevitably captures the advantage in the psychological war of nerves that characterizes the ongoing tension between pitcher and hitter, and that determines who wins and loses the game. If a hitter is crowding the plate in order to reach balls on the outside corner, or if the batter has been hitting unusually well, pitchers try to regain control of their territory. Indeed, many pitchers intentionally throw at or "dust" a batter in order to instill this sense of fear (what hitters euphemistically call "respect") in him. On one occasion Dock Ellis of the Pittsburgh Pirates, having become convinced that the Cincinnati Reds were dominating his team, intentionally hit the first three Reds batters he faced before his manager removed him from the game.

In fielding, on the other hand, the player has almost complete control over the outcome. Once a ball has been hit in his direction, no one can intervene and ruin his chances of catching it for an out. Infielders have approximately three seconds in which to judge the flight of the fall, field it cleanly, and throw it to first base. Outfielders have almost double that amount of time to track down a fly ball. The average fielding percentage (or success rate) of .975, compared with a .250 success rate for hitters (the average batting percentage), reflects the degree of certainty in fielding. Compared with the pitcher or the hitter, the fielder has little to worry about. He knows that in better than 9.7 times out of 10, he will execute his task flawlessly.

In keeping with Malinowski's hypothesis about the relationship between magic and uncertainty, my research shows that baseball players associate magic with hitting and pitching, but not with fielding. Despite the wide assortment of magic—which includes rituals, taboos, and fetishes—associated with both hitting and pitching, I have never observed any directly connected to fielding. In my experience I have known only one player, a shortstop with fielding problems, who reported any ritual even remotely connected with fielding.

The most common form of magic in professional baseball is personal ritual—a prescribed form of behavior that players scrupulously observe in an effort to ensure that things go their way. These rituals, like those of Malinowski's Trobriand fishermen, are performed in a routine, unemotional manner, much as players do nonmagical things to improve their play: rubbing pine tar on the hands to improve a grip on the bat, or rubbing a new ball to make it more comfortable and responsive to the pitcher's grip. Rituals are infinitely varied since ballplayers may formalize any activity that they consider important to performing well.

Rituals usually grow out of exceptionally good performances. When a player does well he seldom attributes his success to skill alone. Although his skill remains constant, he may go hit-less in one game and in the next get three or four hits. Many players attribute the inconsistencies in their performances to an object, item of food, or form of behavior outside their play. Through ritual, players seek to gain control over their performance. In the 1920s and 1930s sportswriters reported that a player who tripped en route to the field would often retrace his steps and carefully walk over the stumbling block for "insurance."

The word taboo comes from a Polynesian term meaning prohibition. Failure to observe a taboo or prohibition leads to undesirable consequences or bad luck. Most players observe a number of taboos. Taboos usually grow out of exceptionally poor performances, which players often attribute to a particular behavior or food. Certain uniform numbers may become taboo. If a player has a poor spring training season or an unsuccessful year, he may refuse to wear the same number again. During my first season of professional baseball I ate pancakes before a game in which I struck out four times. Several weeks later I had a repeat performance, again after eating pancakes. The result was a pancake taboo—I never ate pancakes during the season from that day on. Another personal taboo, against holding a baseball during the national anthem (the usual practice for first basemen, who must warm up the other infielders), had a similar origin.

In earlier decades some baseball players believed that it was bad luck to go back and fasten a missed buttonhole after dressing for a game. They simply left missed buttons on shirts or pants undone. This taboo is not practiced by modern ballplayers.

Fetishes or charms are material objects believed to embody supernatural powers that aid or protect the owner. Good luck fetishes are standard equipment for many ballplayers. They include a wide assortment of objects: horsehide covers from old baseballs, coins, crucifixes, and old bats. Ordinary objects acquire power by being connected to exceptionally hot batting or pitching streaks, especially ones in which players get all the breaks. The

object is often a new possession or something a player finds and holds responsible for his new good fortune. A player who is in a slump might find a coin or an odd stone just before he begins a hitting streak, attribute an improvement in his performance to the influence of the new object, and regard it as a fetish.

While playing for Spokane, a Dodger farm team, Alan Foster forgot his baseball shoes on a road trip and borrowed a pair from a teammate. That night he pitched a no-hitter, which he attributed to the borrowed shoes. After he bought them from his teammate, they became a prized possession.

During World War II American soldiers used fetishes in much the same way. Social psychologist Samuel Stouffer and his colleagues found that in the face of great danger and uncertainty, soldiers developed magical practices, particularly the use of protective amulets and good-luck charms (crosses, Bibles, rabbits' feet, medals), and jealously guarded articles of clothing they associated with past experiences of escape from danger. Stouffer also found that prebattle preparations were carried out in a fixed "ritual" order, much as ballplayers prepare for a game.

Because most pitchers play only once every four days, they perform rituals less frequently than hitters. The rituals they do perform, however, are just as important. A pitcher cannot make up for a poor performance the next day, and having to wait three days to redeem oneself can be miserable. Moreover, the team's win or loss depends more on the performance of the pitcher than on any other single player. Considering the pressures to do well, it is not surprising that pitchers' rituals are often more complex than those of hitters.

A seventeen-game winner in the Texas Rangers organization, Mike Griffin begins his ritual preparation a full day before he pitches, by washing his hair. The next day, although he does not consider himself superstitious, he eats bacon for lunch. When Griffin dresses for the game he puts on his clothes in the same order, making certain he puts the slightly longer of his

two outer, or "stirrup," socks on his right leg. "I just wouldn't feel right mentally if I did it the other way around," he explains. He always wears the same shirt under his uniform on the day he pitches. During the game he takes off his cap after each pitch, and between innings he sits in the same place on the dugout bench.

Tug McGraw, formerly a relief pitcher for the Phillies, slapped his thigh with his glove with each step he took leaving the mound at the end of an inning. This began as a means of saying hello to his wife in the stands, but it then became ritual as McGraw slapped his thigh whether his wife was there or not.

Many of the rituals pitchers engage in—tugging their caps between pitches, touching the rosin bag after each bad pitch, smoothing the dirt on the mound before each new batter or inning—take place on the field. Most baseball fans observe this behavior regularly, never realizing that it may be as important to the pitcher as actually throwing the ball.

Uniform numbers have special significance for some pitchers. Many have a lucky number which they request. Since the choice is usually limited, pitchers may try to get a number that at least contains their lucky number, such as fourteen, four, thirty-four, or forty-four for the pitcher whose lucky number is four. Oddly enough, there is no consensus about the effect of wearing number thirteen. Some pitchers will not wear it; others such as the Mets' David Cone and Oakland's John "Blue Moon" Odom prefer it. (During a pitching slump, however, Odom asked for a new number. Later he switched back to thirteen.)

The way in which number preferences emerge varies. Occasionally a pitcher requests the number of a former professional star, hoping that—in a form of imitative magic—it will bring him the same measure of success. Or he may request a favorite number that he has always associated with good luck. Vida Blue, former Athletic and Giant, changed his uniform number from thirty-five to fourteen, the number he wore as a high-school quarterback. When the new number did not produce the better pitching performance he was looking for, he switched back to his old number.

One of the sources of his good fortune, Blue believed, was the baseball hat he had worn—since 1974. Several American League umpires refused to let him wear the faded and soiled cap. When Blue persisted he was threatened with a fine and suspension from a game. Finally he conceded, but not before he ceremoniously burned the hat on the field before a game. On the days they are scheduled to appear, many pitchers avoid activities that they believe sap their strength and therefore detract from their effectiveness, or that they otherwise generally link with poor performance. (Many pitchers avoid eating certain foods on their pitching days; actually, some food taboos make good physiological sense). Some pitchers do not shave on the day of a game. In fact, Oakland's Dave Stewart and St. Louis's Todd Worrell don't shave as long as they are winning. Early in the 1989 season Stewart had six consecutive victories and a beard before he finally lost. Ex-St. Louis Cardinal Al Hrabosky took this taboo to extreme lengths; Samsonlike, he refused to cut his hair or beard during the entire season—hence part of the reason for his nickname, the "Mad Hungarian." Many hitters go through a series of preparatory rituals before stepping into the batter's box. These include tugging on their caps, touching their uniform letters or medallions, crossing themselves, tapping or bouncing the bat on the plate, swinging the weighted warm-up bat a prescribed number of times, and smoothing the dirt in the box.

There were more than a dozen individual elements in the batting ritual of Mike Hargrove, former Cleveland Indian first baseman. And after each pitch he would step out of the batter's box and repeat the entire sequence. His rituals were so time consuming that he was called "the human rain delay."

Clothing, both the choice of clothes and the order in which they are put on, is often ritualized. During a batting streak many players wear the same clothes and uniforms for each game and put them on in exactly the same order. Once I changed sweatshirts midway through the game for seven consecutive games to keep a hitting streak going. During a sixteen-game winning streak in 1954, the New York Giants wore the same clothes in each game and refused to let them be cleaned for fear that their good fortune might be washed away with the dirt. Taking this ritual to the extreme, Leo Durocher, managing the Brooklyn Dodgers to a pennant in 1941, spent three and a half weeks in the same black shoes, gray slacks, blue coat, and knitted blue tie.

The opposite may also occur. Several of the Oakland A's players bought new street clothing in an attempt to break a fourteen-game losing streak. Most players, however, single out one or two lucky articles or quirks of dress rather than ritualizing all items of clothing. After hitting two home runs in a game, infielder Jim Davenport of the San Francisco Giants discovered that he had missed a buttonhole while dressing for the game. For the remainder of his career he left the same button undone.

A popular ritual associated with hitting is tagging a base when leaving and returning to the dugout during each inning. Mickey Mantle was in the habit of tagging second base on the way to or from the outfield. During a successful month of the season, one player stepped on third base on his way to the dugout after the third, sixth, and ninth innings of each game. Asked if he ever purposely failed to step on the bag, he replied, "Never! I wouldn't dare. It would destroy my confidence to hit." A hitter who is playing poorly may try different combinations of tagging and not tagging particular bases in an attempt to find a successful combination.

When their players are not hitting some managers will rattle the bat bin, the large wooden box containing the team's bats, as if the bats were in a stupor and could be aroused by a good shaking. Similarly, some hitters rub their hands along the handles of the bats protruding from the bin, presumably in hopes of picking up some power or luck from bats that are getting hits for their owners.

There is a taboo against crossing bats, against permitting one bat to rest on top of another. Although this superstition appears to be dying out among ballplayers today, it was religiously observed by some of my teammates. And in some cases it was elaborated even further. One former Detroit minor leaguer became quite annoyed when a teammate tossed a bat from the batting cage and it landed on top of his bat. Later he explained that the top bat might steal hits from the lower one. In his view, bats contained a finite number of hits, a sort of baseball "image of limited good." For Pirate shortstop Honus Wagner, a charter member of baseball's Hall of Fame, each bat contained only a certain number of hits, and never more than 100. Regardless of the quality of the bat, he would discard it after its 100th hit.

Hall of Famer Johnny Evers, of the Cub double-play trio Tinker to Evers to Chance, believed in saving his luck. If he was hitting well in practice, he would suddenly stop and retire to the bench to "save" his batting for the game. One player told me that many of his teammates on the Asheville Tourists in the Class A Western Carolinas League would not let pitchers touch or swing their bats, not even to loosen up. The traditionally poor-hitting pitchers were believed to pollute or weaken the bats.

Food often forms part of a hitter's ritual repertoire. Eating certain foods before a game is supposed to give the ball "eyes," that is, the ability to seek the gaps between fielders after being hit. In hopes of maintaining a batting streak I once ate chicken every day at 4:00 P.M. until the streak ended. Yankee catcher Jim Leyritz eats turkey before every game. Hitters, like pitchers, also avoid certain foods that are believed to sap their strength during the game.

There are other examples of hitters' ritualized behavior. I once kept my eyes closed during the national anthem in an effort to prolong a batting streak. A friend of mine refused to read anything on the day of a game because he believed that reading weakened his eyesight when batting.

These are personal taboos. There are some taboos, however, that all players hold and that do not develop out of individual experiences or misfortunes. These taboos are learned, some as early as Little League. Mentioning a no-hitter while one is in progress is a widely known example. It is believed that if a pitcher hears the words "no-hitter," the spell will be broken and the no-hitter lost. This taboo is still observed by many sports broadcasters, who use various linguistic subterfuges to inform their listeners that the pitcher had not given up a hit, never mentioning "no-hitter."

But superstitions, like most everything else, change over time. Many of the rituals and beliefs of early baseball are no longer remembered. A century ago players spent time off the field and on looking for items that would bring them luck. For example, to find a hairpin on the street assured a batter of hitting safely in that day's game (today women don't wear hairpins—a good reason why the belief has died out). To catch sight of a white horse or a wagonload of barrels were also good omens. In 1904 the manager of the New York Giants, John McGraw, hired a driver and a team of white horses to drive past the Polo Grounds around the time his players were arriving at the ballpark. He knew that if his players saw white horses they'd have more confidence and that could only help them play better. Belief in the power of white horses survived in a few backwaters until the 1960s. A gray haired manager of a team I played for in Quebec would drive around the countryside before important games and during the playoffs looking for a white horse. When he was successful, he'd announce it to everyone in the clubhouse before the game.

Today most professional baseball coaches or managers will not step on the chalk foul lines when going onto the field to talk to their pitcher. Detroit's manager Sparky Anderson jumps over the line. Others follow a different ritual. They intentionally step on the lines when they are going to take a pitcher out of a game.

How do these rituals and taboos get established in the first place? B. F. Skinner's early research with pigeons provides a clue. Like human beings, pigeons quickly learn to associate their behavior with rewards or punishment. By rewarding the birds at the appropriate time, Skinner taught them such elaborate games as table tennis, miniature bowling, or to play simple tunes on a toy piano.

On one occasion he decided to see what would happen if pigeons were rewarded with food pellets every fifteen seconds, regardless of what they did. He found the birds tended to associate the arrival of the food with a particular action—tucking the head under a wing, hopping from side to side, or turning in a clockwise direction. About ten seconds after the arrival of the last pellet, a bird would begin doing whatever it had associated with getting the food and keep it up until the next pellet arrived.

In the same way, baseball players tend to believe there is a causal connection between two events that are linked only temporally. If a superstitious player touches his crucifix and then gets a hit, he may decide the gesture was responsible for his good fortune and follow the same ritual the next time he comes to the plate. If he should get another hit, the chances are good that he will begin touching the crucifix each time he bats and that he will do so whether or not he hits safely each time.

The average batter hits safely approximately one quarter of the time. And if the behavior of Skinner's pigeons—or of gamblers at a Las Vegas slot machine—is any guide, that is more often than necessary to keep him believing in a ritual. Skinner found that once a pigeon associated one of its actions with the arrival of food or water, sporadic rewards would keep the connection going. One pigeon, apparently believing that hopping from side to side brought pellets into its feeding cup, hopped ten thousand times without a pellet before it gave up.

Since the batter associates his hits at least in some degree with his ritual touching of a crucifix, each hit he gets reinforces the strength of the ritual. Even if he falls into a batting slump and the hits temporarily stop, he will persist in touching the crucifix in the hope that this will change his luck.

Skinner's and Malinowski's explanations are not contradictory. Skinner focuses on how the individual comes to develop and maintain a particular ritual, taboo, or fetish. Malinowski focuses on why human beings turn to magic in precarious or uncertain situations. In their attempts to gain greater control over their performance, baseball players respond to chance and uncertainty in the same way as do people in simple societies. It is wrong to assume that magical practices are a waste of time for either group. The magic in baseball obviously does not make a pitch travel faster or more accurately, or a batted ball seek the gaps between fielders. Nor does the Trobriand brand of magic make the surrounding seas calmer and more abundant with fish. But both kinds of magic give their practitioners a sense of control—and an important element in any endeavor is confidence. —EFQ

An earlier version of this essay was originally published in *Human Nature* magazine. This version is printed with permission of the author.

Sociocultural Change: The Impact of the West

The origins of academic anthropology lie in the colonial and imperial ventures of the nineteenth and twentieth centuries. During these periods, many people of the world were brought into a relationship with Europe and the United States that was usually exploitative and often social and culturally disruptive. For almost a century, anthropologists have witnessed this process and the transformations that have taken place in those social and cultural systems brought under the umbrella of a world economic order. Early anthropological studies—even those widely regarded as pure research—directly or indirectly served colonial interests. Many anthropologists certainly believed that they were extending the benefits of Western technology and society while preserving the cultural rights of those people whom they studied. But representatives of poor nations challenge this view and are far less generous in describing the past role of the anthropologist. Most contemporary anthropologists, however, have a deep moral commitment to defending the legal, political, and economic rights of the people with whom they work.

When anthropologists discuss social change, they usually mean change brought about in preindustrial societies through long-standing interaction with the nation-states of the industrialized world. In early anthropology, contact between the West and the remainder of the world was characterized by the terms "acculturation" and "culture contact." These terms were used to describe the diffusion of cultural traits between the developed and less developed countries. Often this was analyzed as a one-way process in which cultures of the developing world

were seen, for better or worse, as receptacles for Western cultural traits. Nowadays, many anthropologists believe that the diffusion of cultural traits across social, political, and economic boundaries was emphasized at the expense of the real issues of dominance, subordinance, and dependence that characterized the colonial experience. Just as importantly, many anthropologists recognize that the present-day forms of cultural, economic, and political interaction between the developed and the so-called underdeveloped world are best characterized as neocolonial.

Most of the articles in this section take the perspective that anthropology should be critical as well as descriptive. They raise questions that are both interesting and troublesome about cultural contact and about the political economy of underdeveloped countries (see "Surviving the Revolution: Post Revolution Romania and Foreign Advisors").

In keeping with the notion that the negative impact of the West on traditional cultures began with colonial domination, this section opens with "Heart of Darkness, Heart of Light," "Why Can't People Feed Themselves?" and "Nomads at the Crossroads." These articles show that "progress" for the West has often meant poverty, hunger, and death for traditional peoples.

The following articles emphasize a different aspect of culture affected by the impact of the West: "Growing Up as a Fore" points to the problems of maintaining individual identity in a changing society. "Bicultural Conflict" describes the personal devastation inflicted upon people who are caught between two worlds, the traditional and

the modern. "Last Chance for First Peoples" helps us to understand that traditional peoples are not the only losers in the process of cultural destruction. All of humanity stands to suffer as a vast store of human knowledge, embodied in tribal subsistence practices, medicine, and folklore, is obliterated in a manner not unlike the burning of the library of Alexandria 1,600 years ago.

Finally, "Easter's End" delivers the sternest warning of all: If the downward spiral of human degradation is not broken soon, it will be too late.

Looking Ahead: Challenge Questions

What is a subsistence system?

What have been the effects of colonialism on formerly subsistence-oriented socioeconomic systems?

How do cash crops inevitably lead to class distinctions and poverty?

How can a nation with great ethnic diversity prevent a democracy from becoming a tyranny of the majority?

Is it possible for one nation to help another without being ethnocentric?

What was it about the Fore culture that made them so vulnerable to the harmful effects of the change from a subsistence economy to a cash-crop economy?

In what ways are traditional peoples struggling to maintain their cultures?

What ethical obligations do industrial societies have toward respecting the human rights and cultural diversity of traditional communities?

What ecological lessons should we be learning from the past?

Heart of Darkness, Heart of Light

The Saga of Alvar Núñez Cabeza de Vaca, the First American

Michael Ventura

Michael Ventura's most recent novel is "The Zoo Where You're Fed to God" (Simon & Schuster).

Alvar Núñez Cabeza de Vaca was and is a dangerous man. Not because he was violent (for he is perhaps the gentlest person of the American saga), but because he stands as a challenge to our reflexive beliefs and our tidy categories. Though he was the first European on record to spend significant time in North America, and the first to write a book about this land, even most well-educated people haven't heard of him because his story is too strange, too disturbing to be taught in schools. To encounter him is to encounter our own limits and possibilities. To tell his story is to challenge our taboos. To invoke his time is to reveal our own.

Cabeza de Vaca was born in 1490 and died in 1557. To Americans, whose sense of the past fades every year, he can't help but seem remote. The media constantly enshrine the cliché that our era has seen the greatest change in human history, but judge for yourself whether or not the changes in Cabeza de Vaca's lifetime were equally transformative:

Columbus discovered the Americas for Europe, beginning the greatest mass migration the world has ever seen (a migration that created no less than,

at present, 45 new nations and protectorates in the Americas alone); 800,000 Jews were expelled from Spain; Cortés conquered the Aztecs of Mexico and Pizarro the Incas of Peru, ending two civilizations; Michelangelo painted the ceiling of the Sistine Chapel; Leonardo da Vinci made the Mona Lisa; the painters Hieronymus Bosch, Dürer, Raphael, Titian and Bruegel were active; the first modern clock was built; the first pawnshop was opened; the first political cartoon was drawn; the German priest Martin Luther and the English King Henry VIII broke from the Church of Rome, ending 1,500 years of Roman domination; Machiavelli wrote "The Prince," initiating the modern view of politics; Copernicus developed the theory of the solar system—the first huge step in modern scientific development; the slave trade began, and with it the destruction of millennia of African traditions; the first insurance policies were written; Queen Elizabeth I was born; the first theory of germs was formulated; the first game of billiards was played; the Spanish Inquisition burned Protestants as heretics, and Nostradamus wrote his prophecies.

So Cabeza de Vaca lived as we live, in that his was a time when the certainties of many centuries suddenly dissolved. Like many of us, when he tried to fit into his time, he became something he never expected to become.

And like us, he lived in an era of gruesome, widespread violence, much

of which he saw firsthand. In 1512, at the age of 22, he was a soldier at the Battle of Ravenna, where 20,000 men were killed. He continued soldiering with distinction until, in 1527, at the advanced age of 37 (the average European life span was only about 40), he was respected enough to be appointed second-in-command to Pámfilo de Narváez for what was supposed to be the conquest of Florida.

Narváez was a vicious soul. Red-bearded and one-eyed, as governor of Cuba he had won the approval of his king (and the clout to mount this expedition) by such acts as ordering his men to slaughter 2,500 Indians who had come bringing them food. The fact that Cabeza de Vaca accepted a commission with such a killer tells us that he was quite willing to be your average murderous Spanish conquistador.

But he quickly revealed himself to be something more. The memoir he left us is called, in Spanish, "La Relación"; the most accessible American translation is titled "Cabeza de Vaca's Adventures in the Unknown Interior of America" (University of New Mexico Press). In it, he details an incident in Cuba in the summer of 1527: Narváez and he, with five ships and 460 men, were gathering provisions for the conquest of Florida. But a great storm came up.

"All the houses and churches went down," he wrote in the first published description of a West Indies hurricane. "We had to walk seven or eight together, locking arms to keep from being blown away. Walking in the woods gave us as much fear as the tumbling houses, for the trees were falling, too, and could have killed us. We wandered all night in this raging tempest. . . . Particularly from midnight on, we heard a great roaring and the sound of many voices, of little bells, also flutes, tambourines, and other instruments, most of which lasted till morning, when the storm ceased."

What was this music in the storm? A writer's touch? What literary critics call "magical realism"? From novelists like Gabriel García Márquez we expect flutes and voices on the winds, but Cabeza de Vaca was not a novelist; he was writing what he considered a factual account. He was aware that this and much else in his narrative would be hard to believe. "La Relación" is addressed to the King of Spain—Cabeza de Vaca's commander-in-chief, as we would say. He cautioned his king from the first page: "I have written very exactly. Novel or, for some persons, difficult to believe though the things narrated may be, I assure you they can be accepted without hesitation as strictly factual."

Most of us don't hear music in storms, and science would not only doubt but also scoff at the possibility. Let's say, then, that the music was in Cabeza de Vaca's head—which doesn't necessarily mean that he was crazy. His record of endurance and clear-headedness argues against that. Rather, his hurricane story shows that, in extreme situations, some strange inner sense opened in him. Catastrophes that caused others to go rigid with fear caused Cabeza de Vaca to experience a deepened, wild, even spiritual awareness. In the midst of a hurricane, and while fighting for his life, he could hear music.

This is the signature of the man. Even this early in his tale you can begin to see why he isn't taught much in classrooms. Few teachers want to deal with questions—from students or from contentious school boards—about guys who hear flutes in the wind.

The Narváez expedition finally reached the west coast of Florida in 1528. Drive that country now and all you see is a mall, a housing development, a mall, a mall, a development, a mall—on and on. Cabeza de Vaca, in his day, saw "immense trees and open woods," "three kinds of deer," "bears and lions [cougars]," a profusion of birds.

Florida was lush, but there wasn't much to conquer. Its small tribes were primitive, apprehensive and hostile. They possessed nothing that any European would want to steal. Yet they were no fools. Fearing the Spaniards and eager to see them leave, they told grand lies about rich tribes inland and to the north—lies that Pámfilo de Narváez was eager to believe. Here he made the disastrous decision to split his forces: The infantry and cavalry would explore inland while the ships headed up the coast, to rendezvous later. Cabeza de Vaca was furious. Even in known territory the tactic was foolish; in unknown territory, it was mad. The land force could be lost forever.

Narváez called Cabeza de Vaca a coward and ordered him to remain with the ships. He refused, writing later: "I would rather hazard the danger that lay ahead in the interior than give any occasion for questioning my honor by remaining safely aboard behind." This man who heard music in the wind cared more about his honor than his life.

If we allow the possibility that Cabeza de Vaca's music in the wind showed an aptitude for spirituality rather than, as they say now, "disassociative tendencies," then we're beginning to see a rare breed of the spiritual man: not a meditator, a recluse or a teacher; not a priest, an evangel or a mild or wild man; but a man of action, a decisive man with classical notions of honor who, if he heard music in the wind, simply said so. And if his comrades were going to their doom, he tried to dissuade them, but when he could not dissuade, he stood with them.

Native Americans have such models in their history, visionary warriors like Cochise, Geronimo and Crazy Horse. But it is hard to think of another European-American with these particular dimensions—as though we admire these qualities in others but are afraid to admit them in ourselves. Again we see why Cabeza de Vaca is a stranger to our textbooks. History is always taught as a reflection of the present, and he is more paradoxical than we want to believe we are.

It happened as Cabeza de Vaca feared it would. Narváez, with Cabeza de Vaca still second-in-command, got lost inland and couldn't find his ships. The terrain supplied little food, and the Spaniards could hardly hunt because they had to conserve their scarce ammunition for Indians who attacked guerrilla-style, killing many. Disease killed many more. Those who survived were exhausted and ill, and almost all (including Cabeza de Vaca) had been wounded. "You can imagine what it would be like," he wrote, "in a strange, remote land, destitute of means either to remain or to get out."

In a cove of what is now called Apalachicola Bay, on the west coast of Florida, they decided to build barges and try to make it around the coast toward the Río Grande, hoping to find the Spaniards in Mexico. Narváez picked the strongest men for his raft and said that it was every man for himself. His stronger men paddled swiftly away—and that's the last anyone ever saw of Narváez. Cabeza de Vaca was now in command.

They followed the coast as well as they could in bad weather, around the Florida Panhandle and to the waters of the Mississippi River near what is now New Orleans. They were the first Europeans to see the Mississippi, and Cabeza de Vaca was the first to write of it. They continued at the mercy of storms until they beached on what they called the Island of Doom, what is now Galveston, Tex. On the voyage, many died of hunger, thirst and disease. Remembering their state shortly before landfall, Cabeza de Vaca revealed his uncommon endurance when he wrote that "not five could stand. When night fell, only the navigator and I remained able to tend the barge."

When they landed on Galveston Island, they were "so emaciated we could easily count every bone and looked the very picture of death."

And now the story takes a turn. Indians came upon them. "Whatever their stature, they looked like giants to us in our fright. We could not hope to defend ourselves." What happened went against all expectations and stereotypes. "The Indians, understanding our full plight, sat down and lamented for half an hour so loudly they could have been heard a long way off. It was amazing to see these wild, untaught savages howling like brutes in compassion for us."

They had come to change the land, but the land changed them. This doesn't fit the prevailing heroic vision of Westerners.

By now, there were only about 80 survivors. The Indians cared for them. From this point on Cabeza de Vaca called his people "the Christians," to differentiate them from the pagan Indians. Here he recorded the first known cannibalism in North America: "Five Christians," cut off from the others on the coast, "came to the extremity of eating each other. . . . The Indians were so shocked at this cannibalism that, if they had seen it sometime earlier, they surely would have killed every one of us. In a very short while as it was, only 15 of the 80 who had come survived. . . . Then half the natives died from a disease of the bowels . . . and blamed us."

The Indians were probably right. The Spaniards had communicated the diseases they were dying of. We should pause for a moment. Imagine yourself one of those Indians, with half the people you've known all your life dead within days. Not surprisingly, the surviving Indians sought to kill the Spaniards. "When they came to kill us, the Indian who kept me interceded. He said: If we had so much power of sorcery we would not have let all but a few of our own perish."

It speaks of the stature of these Indians that, amid all this grief and

death, one person had the power to reason and others had the capacity to listen. The Spaniards were not only spared but also tended to. Cabeza de Vaca had come to conquer Indians. Now he owed his life to one. For the remainder of his eight years in North America, he would never kill, or even fight, another Indian. (A century later, Puritans, whom Indians saved from starvation on Thanksgiving Day would have no such compunctions.)

Time passed. The Spaniards, with no means to leave, lived among the Capoques and the Han tribes. Then things took another extraordinary turn. Cabeza de Vaca relates wryly that the Indians "wanted to make physicians of us without examination or a review of diplomas."

"Their method of cure," he relates, "is to blow on the sick, the breath and the laying-on of hands supposedly casting out the infirmity. They insisted we should do this too and be of some use to them. We scoffed at their cures and at the idea that we knew how to heal." The dialogue between Cabeza de Vaca (who could now speak the tribal language) and the Indians was apparently intense. "An Indian [probably a medicine man] told me I knew not whereof I spoke in saying their methods had no effect." The Indians denied them food until the Spaniards complied with their request. "Hunger forced us to obey, but disclaiming any responsibility for our failure or success."

They had come to subdue, and now they were commanded to heal. Not only was it a complete reversal of roles, it presented a sticky theological problem. According to their religion, if these Spanish Catholics practiced paganism, they would lose their souls; but according to the Indians, if they did nothing they'd lose their lives. And what if the attempt failed? Then, too, they might lose their lives. So they added Catholicism to the ceremony. "Our method . . . was to bless the sick, breathe upon them, recite a paternoster and Ave María and pray earnestly to God our Lord for their recovery."

No one was more surprised than Cabeza de Vaca when their method worked.

Here Cabeza de Vaca passes the point where history is prepared to accept him. He ceases to be a conquistador, ceases even to be an explorer, and enters what Joseph Conrad called "the heart of darkness"—by which Conrad meant a realm of the psyche in which civilized certitudes collapse. But Cabeza de Vaca, as we shall see, might have called the same realm "the heart of light."

More time passed, the Spanish healers became ill again. At this, the tribes lost faith in their healing and treated them harshly. "My life had become unbearable. . . . In addition to much other work, I had to grub roots in the water or from underground in the canebrakes. . . . The broken canes often slashed my flesh; I had to work amid them without benefit of clothes." This proud Spanish soldier, so devoted to his own honor, had become a naked slave. Yet note how he writes of this slavery with pain but no bitterness, no anger, no blame. You cannot find in this narrative one disrespectful word about his captors—without whom, after all, he would have long since died. Again, it's as though catastrophe somehow freed him. He accepted the blows of fate without succumbing to them.

More years passed, with many hardships, adventures and deaths. Some Spaniards were killed only because an Indian had bad dreams about them. (The Indians sometimes killed each other this way, too.) Finally, of the 80 who made it to Galveston Island, only four remained: Cabeza de Vaca, Alonso del Castillo, Andrés Dorantes and Dorantes' slave, the first black man to set foot in what is now the United States, a Moroccan Moor converted to Christianity named Estevánico. (Our African American history begins with this man, nearly a century before the Pilgrims.)

After much planning and many disappointments, in the autumn of 1534 they escaped the tribes that held them as slaves and made their way west. Now they were taken in by a tribe in the vicinity of Austin and San Antonio.

"They lodged Dorantes and the Negro in the house of one medicine man, and Castillo and me in that of another."

This is a significant sentence. They had become the province not of the chiefs or the tribe as a whole, but of the shamans. These Indians had "heard of us and the wonders [healings] our Lord worked by us." Note that this tribe threatened neither violence nor enslavement. We should also remember that by now these Christians didn't look like Europeans. They wore what Indians wore, could live off the land like the Indians and speak their languages.

They had come to change the land, but the land had changed them. This, too, doesn't fit the prevailing heroic vision of Westerners as people who molded the wilderness with their own desires. By this point in Cabeza de Vaca's journey, heroism consisted of something very different: the ability to survive on the land's own terms.

"The very evening of our arrival, some Indians came to Castillo begging him to cure them of terrible headaches." Castillo prayed over them, and they claimed to be healed. And here follows the most amazing passage of Cabeza de Vaca's narrative:

"Since the Indians all through the region talked only of the wonders which God our Lord worked through us, individuals sought us from many parts in hopes of healing. The evening of the second day after our arrival . . . some of the Susolas came to us and pressed Castillo to go treat their ailing kinsmen—one wounded, the others sick and, among them, a fellow very near his end. Castillo happened to be a timid practitioner—the more so, the more serious and dangerous the case—feeling that his sins would weigh and some day impede his performing cures. The Indians urged me to go heal them. . . . So I had to go with them. Dorantes brought Estevánico and accompanied me. As we drew near the huts of the afflicted, I saw that the man we hoped to save was dead: . . . I found his eyes rolled up, his pulse gone, and every appearance of death, as Dorantes agreed. Taking off the mat that covered him, I supplicated our Lord in his behalf and in behalf of the rest who ailed, as fervently as I could . . . blessing and breathing on him many times. . . .

"The natives then took me to treat many others, who had fallen into a stupor. . . . When [we] got back that evening, they brought the tidings that the 'dead' man I had treated had got up whole and walked . . . all I had ministered to had recovered and were glad. Throughout the land the effect was a profound wonder and fear. People talked of nothing else, and wherever the fame of it reached, people set out to find us so we should cure them and bless their children. . . .

"Up to now, Dorantes and his Negro had not attempted to practice; but under the soliciting pressure of these pilgrims from diverse places, we all became physicians, of whom I was the boldest and most venturous in trying to cure anything . . . If anyone did not actually recover, he still contended he would. What they who did recover related caused general rejoicing and dancing; so we got no sleep."

Before anyone gets too skeptical of these events, it should be noted that several years later, when Coronado's expedition passed through New Mexico, Indians told them of "four great doctors, one of them black, the other three white, who gave blessings [and] healed the sick." Historians and journalists call that "independent corroboration."

Were the healings real? Cabeza de Vaca himself admits that not all were healed. But the phenomenon, let us say, was real enough to be remembered by independent witnesses. There have been many witnessings, both ancient and modern, in every known culture, to healings very like these. It's a subject that discomforts scientists, because they've been able neither to prove nor disprove it conclusively, but there's too much documentation for the phenomenon to be dismissed. And if even only a few of these phenomena are genuine—if healings such as Cabeza de Vaca described are part of the human possibility—then the present civilized consensus, and its description of existence, is not only incomplete but also inaccurate.

Though they were the first to explore North America and leave a record, and though their reports inspired

the Coronado expedition, which resulted in the European settlement of the Southwest, still Cabeza de Vaca and his companions are lost to history because they challenge our consensus, our description, of reality. To teach of them at all is to at least consider the possibility that what they did was real.

Their healings can be contested, but what cannot be disputed is that the Indians of the Southeast adored them. Cabeza de Vaca, Dorantes, Castillo and Estevánico, hoping to run into Spaniards whom they thought might be exploring north from Mexico, proceeded into West Texas and New Mexico (some researchers think they got as far as Arizona). Thousands of Indians followed them. As Cabeza de Vaca writes, "we had been badly hampered by the hordes of Indians following us . . . they pursued so closely just to touch us. . . . Every Indian brought his portion to us to be breathed on and blessed before he would dare touch it. When you consider that we were frequently accompanied by 3,000 or 4,000 Indians and were obliged to sanctify the food and drink of each one, as well as grant permission for the many things they asked to do, you can appreciate our inconvenience."

Cabeza de Vaca attributed these wonders neither to himself nor to his friends. He gave all the credit to divine powers working through them. He was as much in awe of the events as the Indians themselves; therefore, though he found their adoration "inconvenient," he never looked down on the tribes. In fact, his verdict on the natives of this land was unique in his day and would be considered radical for the next several centuries: "They are a substantial people with a capacity for unlimited development."

That statement alone makes his story out of place in an education system that taught, until fairly recently, that tribal peoples were not the equals of Europeans. Cabeza de Vaca, writing to his king, added a note that would go against the future Indian policies of all governments, including the United States: "Clearly, to bring all these people to Christianity and subjection to Your Imperial Majesty, they must be won by kindness, the only certain way."

But when he finally came upon Spaniards, he found anything but kindness: "With heavy hearts we looked out over the lavishly watered and fertile, beautiful land, now abandoned and burned and the people thin and weak, scattering or hiding in fright. . . . [They] told us how the [Spaniards] had come through razing the towns and carrying off half the men and all the women and boys. . . . We told the natives we were going after those men to order them to stop killing, enslaving and dispossessing the Indians; which made our friends very glad."

As you can guess, they had no success with this project. When they found the Spaniards who had done those things, Cabeza de Vaca got into "a hot argument," for those Spaniards "meant to make slaves of the Indians in our train." The commander of those conquistadors, one Diego de Alcaraz, "bade his interpreter tell the Indians that we [Cabeza de Vaca and his friends] were members of his race who had been long lost; that his group were the lords of the land who must be obeyed and served, while we were inconsequential. The Indians paid no attention to this. Conferring among themselves, they replied that the Christians lied: We had come from the sunrise, they from the sunset; we healed the sick, they killed the sound; we came naked and barefoot, they clothed, horsed and lanced; we coveted nothing but gave whatever we were given, while they robbed whomever they found and bestowed nothing on anyone."

He added: "To the last I could not convince the Indians that we were of the same people as the Christian slavers."

Finally it was time for Cabeza de Vaca, Dorantes, Estevánico and Castillo to take their leave from the Indians—both those who had followed them for so long and those who had come to them for protection. Here Cabeza de Vaca added his most direct

and defiant note to his king: "When the Indians took their leave of us they said they would do as we commanded and rebuild their towns, if the Christians let them. And I solemnly swear that if they have not done so it is the fault of the Christians."

Cabeza de Vaca and his companions journeyed south, accompanied by Spanish soldiers, and met with the governor of Mexico, Nuño de Guzmán, in Compostela, where he made his report to Guzmán and to the now aging Cortés. "The Governor received us graciously and outfitted us from his wardrobe. I could not stand to wear any clothes for some time, or to sleep anywhere but on the bare floor."

I think of him in that interim—of how strange clothing felt to him after eight years of nakedness, and of how he could not bring himself to sleep on a civilized bed. If he ever used his healing powers again, he made no record of it. In 1540, Cabeza de Vaca was appointed governor of the South American provinces of the Río de la Plata, where he prohibited the slaving, raping and looting of Indians. This caused deep resentment among the soldiers in his command, and finally, in 1543, they imprisoned him and sent him back to Spain in chains. He remained in prison for about eight years (almost as long as he'd spent in North America), until his wife spent the better part of her fortune to free him. He died in 1557, at the age of 67 and, despite the writings he left, virtually disappeared from history because history could accept neither his actions nor his message.

Had he actually been given the gift of healing? In answer we have to ask ourselves: Why else would Indians have followed him by the thousands? It is certain that they did, for many Spaniards in Mexico witnessed it. Since this is the only incidence in the entire history of the meeting of Europeans and Native Americans when a white man had such an effect without military coercion, we must assume an extraordinary cause. That is what leads me to

believe Cabeza de Vaca's account credible.

But if he had such powers, why did they leave him when he was back among his own people? Perhaps because among his own kind his powers were neither wanted nor accepted; or perhaps because he had to wear again not only civilization's clothing but civilization's assumptions, and only when all trappings of civilization had been stripped away could the healing powers rise in him. Perhaps that is why he sought to return to the New World so soon. But as essentially a military governor in South America, he could not re-create the conditions that existed for him on his first journey.

Whatever the reason, it is clear that where others found, in the wilderness, Joseph Conrad's heart of darkness, Alvar Núñez Cabeza de Vaca experienced the heart of light. Is that heart of light still among us? Is it still reachable in this land that is no longer a wilderness—this land where society is in such turmoil, and where people feel so frightened, angry and insecure?

It may be because Cabeza de Vaca's journey raises this question that he has been, and is still, avoided in schools. Across the centuries he comes to suggest that being human may be a state of more possibilities that we have usually dared to dream. He tells us that only kindness, generosity and devotion are ultimately convincing—that they are "the only certain way" to reach across the barriers of our differences. He stands as a kindly, mysterious, courageous, yet disturbing figure, dangerous to our assumptions, challenging our limits.

He had begged that his story "be received as homage, since it is the most one could bring who returned thence naked." Instead we have ignored him. Yet it may be that, more than ever, we need him now—need to tell his story among ourselves and teach it to our children, meeting his challenge, giving consideration to his mysteries and living up to his example.

Why Can't People Feed Themselves?

Frances Moore Lappé and Joseph Collins

Frances Moore Lappé and Dr. Joseph Collins are founders and directors of the Institute for Food and Development Policy, located in San Francisco and New York.

Question: You have said that the hunger problem is not the result of overpopulation. But you have not yet answered the most basic and simple question of all: Why can't people feed themselves? As Senator Daniel P. Moynihan put it bluntly, when addressing himself to the Third World, "Food growing is the first thing you do when you come down out of the trees. The question is, how come the United States can grow food and you can't?"

Our Response: In the very first speech I, Frances, ever gave after writing *Diet for a Small Planet,* I tried to take my audience along the path that I had taken in attempting to understand why so many are hungry in this world. Here is the gist of that talk that was, in truth, a turning point in my life:

When I started I saw a world divided into two parts: a *minority* of nations that had "taken off" through their agricultural and industrial revolutions to reach a level of unparalleled material abundance and a *majority* that remained behind in a primitive, traditional, undeveloped state. This lagging behind of the majority of the world's peoples must be due, I thought, to some internal deficiency or even to several of them. It seemed obvious that the underdeveloped countries must be deficient in natural resources—particularly good land and climate—and in cultural development, including modern attitudes conducive to work and progress.

But when looking for the historical roots of the predicament, I learned that my picture of these two separate worlds was quite false. My "two separate worlds" were really just different sides of the same coin. One side was on top largely because the other side was on the bottom. Could this be true? How were these separate worlds related?

Colonialism appeared to me to be the link. Colonialism destroyed the cultural patterns of production and exchange by which traditional societies in "underdeveloped" countries previously had met the needs of the people. Many precolonial social structures, while dominated by exploitative elites, had evolved a system of mutual obligations among the classes that helped to ensure at least a minimal diet for all. A friend of mine once said: "Precolonial village existence in subsistence agriculture was a limited life indeed, but it's certainly not Calcutta." The misery of starvation in the streets of Calcutta can only be understood as the end-point of a long historical process—one that has destroyed a traditional social system.

"Underdeveloped," instead of being an adjective that evokes the picture of a static society, became for me a verb (to "underdevelop") meaning the *process* by which the minority of the world has transformed—indeed often robbed and degraded—the majority.

That was in 1972. I clearly recall my thoughts on my return home. I had stated publicly for the first time a world view that had taken me years of study to grasp. The sense of relief was tremendous. For me the breakthrough lay in realizing that today's "hunger crisis" could not be described in static, descriptive terms. Hunger and underdevelopment must always be thought of as a *process.*

To answer the question "why hunger?" it is counterproductive to simply *describe* the conditions in an underdeveloped country today. For these conditions, whether they be the degree of malnutrition, the levels of agricultural production, or even the country's ecological endowment, are not static factors—they are not "givens." They are rather the *results* of an ongoing historical process. As we dug ever deeper into that historical process for the preparation of this book, we began to discover the existence of scarcity-creating mechanisms that we had only vaguely intuited before.

We have gotten great satisfaction from probing into the past since we recognized it is the only way to approach a solution to hunger today. We have come to see that it is the *force* creating the condition, not the condition itself, that must be the target of change. Otherwise we might change the condition today, only to find tomorrow that it has been recreated—with a vengeance.

Asking the question "Why can't people feed themselves?" carries a sense of bewilderment that there are so many people in the world not able to feed themselves adequately. What astonished us, however, is that there are not *more* people in the world who are hungry—considering the weight of the centuries of effort by the few to undermine the capacity of the majority to feed themselves. No, we are not crying "conspiracy!" If these forces were entirely conspiratorial, they would be easier to detect and many more people would by now have risen up to resist. We are talking about something more subtle and insidious; a heritage of a colonial order in which people with the advantage of considerable power sought their own self-interest, often arrogantly believing they were acting in the interest of the people whose lives they were destroying.

7. SOCIOCULTURAL CHANGE: THE IMPACT OF THE WEST

THE COLONIAL MIND

The colonizer viewed agriculture in the subjugated lands as primitive and backward. Yet such a view contrasts sharply with documents from the colonial period now coming to light. For example, A. J. Voelker, a British agricultural scientist assigned to India during the 1890s, wrote:

Nowhere would one find better instances of keeping land scrupulously clean from weeds, of ingenuity in device of water-raising appliances, of knowledge of soils and their capabilities, as well as of the exact time to sow and reap, as one would find in Indian agriculture. It is wonderful, too, how much is known of rotation, the system of "mixed crops" and of fallowing. . . . I, at least, have never seen a more perfect picture of cultivation."[1]

None the less, viewing the agriculture of the vanquished as primitive and backward reinforced the colonizer's rationale for destroying it. To the colonizers of Africa, Asia, and Latin America, agriculture became merely a means to extract wealth—much as gold from a mine—on behalf of the colonizing power. Agriculture was no longer seen as a source of food for the local population, nor even as their livelihood. Indeed the English economist John Stuart Mill reasoned that colonies should not be thought of as civilizations or countries at all but as "agricultural establishments" whose sole purpose was to supply the "larger community to which they belong." The colonized society's agriculture was only a subdivision of the agricultural system of the metropolitan country. As Mill acknowledged, "Our West India colonies, for example, cannot be regarded as countries. . . . The West Indies are the place where England *finds it convenient* to carry on the production of sugar, coffee and a few other tropical commodities."[2]

Prior to European intervention, Africans practiced a diversified agriculture that included the introduction of new food plants of Asian or American origin. But colonial rule simplified this diversified production to single cash crops—often to the exclusion of staple foods—and in the process sowed the seeds of famine.[3] Rice farming once had been common

in Gambia. But with colonial rule so much of the best land was taken over by peanuts (grown for the European market) that rice had to be imported to counter the mounting prospect of famine. Northern Ghana, once famous for its yams and other food-stuffs, was forced to concentrate solely on cocoa. Most of the Gold Coast thus became dependent on cocoa. Liberia was turned into a virtual plantation subsidiary of Firestone Tire and Rubber. Food production in Dahomey and southeast Nigeria was all but abandoned in favor of palm oil; Tanganyika (now Tanzania) was forced to focus on sisal and Uganda on cotton.

The same happened in Indochina. About the time of the American Civil War the French decided that the Mekong Delta in Vietnam would be ideal for producing rice for export. Through a production system based on enriching the large landowners, Vietnam became the world's third largest exporter of rice by the 1930s; yet many landless Vietnamese went hungry.[4]

Rather than helping the peasants, colonialism's public works programs only reinforced export crop production. British irrigation works built in nineteenth-century India did help increase production, but the expansion was for spring export crops at the expense of millets and legumes grown in the fall as the basic local food crops.

Because people living on the land do not easily go against their natural and adaptive drive to grow food for themselves, colonial powers had to force the production of cash crops. The first strategy was to use physical or economic force to get the local population to grow cash crops instead of food on their own plots and then turn them over to the colonizer for export. The second strategy was the direct takeover of the land by large-scale plantations growing crops for export.

FORCED PEASANT PRODUCTION

As Walter Rodney recounts in *How Europe Underdeveloped Africa,* cash crops were often grown literally under threat of guns and whips.[5] One visitor

to the Sahel commented in 1928: "Cotton is an artificial crop and one the value of which is not entirely clear to the natives. . ." He wryly noted the "enforced enthusiasm with which the natives. . .have thrown themselves into. . .planting cotton."[6] The forced cultivation of cotton was a major grievance leading to the Maji Maji wars in Tanzania (then Tanganyika) and behind the nationalist revolt in Angola as late as 1960.[7]

Although raw force was used, taxation was the preferred colonial technique to force Africans to grow cash crops. The colonial administrations simply levied taxes on cattle, land, houses, and even the people themselves. Since the tax had to be paid in the coin of the realm, the peasants had either to grow crops to sell or to work on the plantations or in the mines of the Europeans.[8] Taxation was both an effective tool to "stimulate" cash cropping and a source of revenue that the colonial bureaucracy needed to enforce the system. To expand their production of export crops to pay the mounting taxes, peasant producers were forced to neglect the farming of food crops. In 1830, the Dutch administration in Java made the peasants an offer they could not refuse; if they would grow government-owned export crops on one fifth of their land, the Dutch would remit their land taxes.[9] If they refused and thus could not pay the taxes, they lost their land.

Marketing boards emerged in Africa in the 1930s as another technique for getting the profit from cash crop production by native producers into the hands of the colonial government and international firms. Purchases by the marketing boards were well below the world market price. Peanuts bought by the boards from peasant cultivators in West Africa were sold in Britain for more than *seven times* what the peasants received.[10]

The marketing board concept was born with the "cocoa hold-up" in the Gold Coast in 1937. Small cocoa farmers refused to sell to the large cocoa concerns like United Africa

Company (a subsidiary of the Anglo-Dutch firm, Unilever—which we know as Lever Brothers) and Cadbury until they got a higher price. When the British government stepped in and agreed to buy the cocoa directly in place of the big business concerns, the smallholders must have thought they had scored at least a minor victory. But had they really? The following year the British formally set up the West African Cocoa Control Board. Theoretically, its purpose was to pay the peasants a reasonable price for their crops. In practice, however, the board, as sole purchaser, was able to hold down the prices paid the peasants for their crops when the world prices were rising. Rodney sums up the real "victory":

None of the benefits went to Africans, but rather to the British government itself and to the private companies. . . Big companies like the United African Company and John Holt were given. . . quotas to fulfill on behalf of the boards. As agents of the government, they were no longer exposed to direct attack, and their profits were secure.[11]

These marketing boards, set up for most export crops, were actually controlled by the companies. The chairman of the Cocoa Board was none other than John Cadbury of Cadbury Brothers (ever had a Cadbury chocolate bar?) who was part of a buying pool exploiting West African cocoa farmers.

The marketing boards funneled part of the profits from the exploitation of peasant producers indirectly into the royal treasury. While the Cocoa Board sold to the British Food Ministry at low prices, the ministry upped the price for British manufacturers, thus netting a profit as high as 11 million pounds in some years.[12]

These marketing boards of Africa were only the institutionalized rendition of what is the essence of colonialism—the extraction of wealth. While profits continued to accrue to foreign interests and local elites, prices received by those actually growing the commodities remained low.

PLANTATIONS

A second approach was direct takeover of the land either by the colonizing government or by private foreign interests. Previously self-provisioning farmers were forced to cultivate the plantation fields through either enslavement or economic coercion.

After the conquest of the Kandyan Kingdom (in present day Sri Lanka), in 1815, the British designated all the vast central part of the island as crown land. When it was determined that coffee, a profitable export crop, could be grown there, the Kandyan lands were sold off to British investors and planters at a mere five shillings per acre, the government even defraying the cost of surveying and road building.[13]

Java is also a prime example of a colonial government seizing territory and then putting it into private foreign hands. In 1870, the Dutch declared all uncultivated land—called waste land—property of the state for lease to Dutch plantation enterprises. In addition, the Agrarian Land Law of 1870 authorized foreign companies to lease village-owned land. The peasants, in chronic need of ready cash for taxes and foreign consumer goods, were only too willing to lease their land to the foreign companies for very modest sums and under terms dictated by the firms. Where land was still held communally, the village headman was tempted by high cash commissions offered by plantation companies. He would lease the village land even more cheaply than would the individual peasant or, as was frequently the case, sell out the entire village to the company.[14]

The introduction of the plantation meant the divorce of agriculture from nourishment, as the notion of food value was lost to the overriding claim of "market value" in international trade. Crops such as sugar, tobacco, and coffee were selected, not on the basis of how well they feed people, but for their high price value relative to their weight and bulk so that profit margins could be maintained even after the costs of shipping to Europe.

SUPPRESSING PEASANT FARMING

The stagnation and impoverishment of the peasant food-producing sector was not the mere by-product of benign neglect, that is, the unintended consequence of an overemphasis on export production. Plantations—just like modern "agro-industrial complexes"—needed an abundant and readily available supply of low-wage agricultural workers. Colonial administrations thus devised a variety of tactics, all to undercut self-provisioning agriculture and thus make rural populations dependent on plantation wages. Government services and even the most minimal infrastructure (access to water, roads, seeds, credit, pest and disease control information, and so on) were systematically denied. Plantations usurped most of the good land, either making much of the rural population landless or pushing them onto marginal soils. (Yet the plantations have often held much of their land idle simply to prevent the peasants from using it—even to this day. Del Monte owns 57,000 acres of Guatemala but plants only 9000. The rest lies idle except for a few thousand head of grazing cattle.)[15]

In some cases a colonial administration would go even further to guarantee itself a labor supply. In at least twelve countries in the eastern and southern parts of Africa the exploitation of mineral wealth (gold, diamonds, and copper) and the establishment of cash-crop plantations demanded a continuous supply of low-cost labor. To assure this labor supply, colonial administrations simply expropriated the land of the African communities by violence and drove the people into small reserves.[16] With neither adequate land for their traditional slash-and-burn methods nor access to the means—tools, water, and fertilizer—to make continuous farming of such limited areas viable, the indigenous population could scarcely meet subsistence needs, much less produce surplus to sell in order to cover the colonial taxes. Hundreds of thousands of Africans were forced to become the cheap labor source so "needed" by the colonial plantations. Only by laboring on plantations and in the mines could they hope to pay the colonial taxes.

The tax scheme to produce reserves of cheap plantation and mining labor was particularly effective when the Great Depression hit and the bottom dropped out of cash crop economies. In 1929 the cotton market collapsed, leaving peasant cotton producers, such as those in Upper Volta, unable to pay their colonial taxes. More and more young people, in some years as many as 80,000, were thus forced to migrate to the Gold Coast to compete with each other for low-wage jobs on cocoa plantations.[17]

The forced migration of Africa's most able-bodied workers—stripping village food farming of needed hands—was a recurring feature of colonialism. As late as 1973 the Portuguese "exported" 400,000 Mozambican peasants to work in South Africa in exchange for gold deposited in the Lisbon treasury.

The many techniques of colonialism to undercut self-provisioning agriculture in order to ensure a cheap labor supply are no better illustrated than by the story of how, in the mid-nineteenth century, sugar plantation owners in British Guiana coped with the double blow of the emancipation of slaves and the crash in the world sugar market. The story is graphically recounted by Alan Adamson in *Sugar without Slaves*.[18]

Would the ex-slaves be allowed to take over the plantation land and grow the food they needed? The planters, many ruined by the sugar slump, were determined they would not. The planter-dominated government devised several schemes for thwarting food self-sufficiency. The price of crown land was kept artificially high, and the purchase of land in parcels smaller than 100 acres was outlawed—two measures guaranteeing that newly organized ex-slave cooperatives could not hope to gain access to much land. The government also prohibited cultivation on as much as 400,000 acres—on the grounds of "uncertain property titles." Moreover, although many planters held part of their land out of sugar production due to the depressed world price, they would not allow any alternative production on them. They feared that once the ex-slaves started growing food it would be difficult to return them to sugar production when world market prices began to recover. In addition, the government taxed peasant production, then turned around and used the funds to subsidize the immigration of laborers from India and Malaysia to replace the freed slaves, thereby making sugar production again profitable for the planters. Finally, the government neglected the infrastructure for subsistence agriculture and denied credit for small farmers.

Perhaps the most insidious tactic to "lure" the peasant away from food production—and the one with profound historical consequences—was a policy of keeping the price of imported food low through the removal of tariffs and subsidies. The policy was double-edged: first, peasants were told they need not grow food because they could always buy it cheaply with their plantation wages; second, cheap food imports destroyed the market for domestic food and thereby impoverished local food producers.

Adamson relates how both the Governor of British Guiana and the Secretary for the Colonies Earl Grey favored low duties on imports in order to erode local food production and thereby release labor for the plantations. In 1851 the governor rushed through a reduction of the duty on cereals in order to "divert" labor to the sugar estates. As Adamson comments, "Without realizing it, he [the governor] had put his finger on the most mordant feature of monoculture: . . . its convulsive need to destroy any other sector of the economy which might compete for 'its' labor."[19]

Many colonial governments succeeded in establishing dependence on imported foodstuffs. In 1647 an observer in the West Indies wrote to Governor Winthrop of Massachusetts: "Men are so intent upon planting sugar that they had rather buy foode at very deare rates than produce it by labour, so infinite is the profitt of sugar workes. . . ."[20] By 1770, the West Indies were importing most of the continental colonies' exports of dried fish, grain, beans, and vegetables. A dependence on imported food made the West Indian colonies vulnerable to any disruption in supply. This dependence on imported food stuffs spelled disaster when the thirteen continental colonies gained independence and food exports from the continent to the West Indies were interrupted. With no diversified food system to fall back on, 15,000 plantation workers died of famine between 1780 and 1787 in Jamaica alone.[21] The dependence of the West Indies on imported food persists to this day.

SUPPRESSING PEASANT COMPETITION

We have talked about the techniques by which indigenous populations were forced to cultivate cash crops. In some countries with large plantations, however, colonial governments found it necessary to *prevent* peasants from independently growing cash crops not out of concern for their welfare, but so that they would not compete with colonial interests growing the same crop. For peasant farmers, given a modicum of opportunity, proved themselves capable of outproducing the large plantations not only in terms of output per unit of land but, more important, in terms of capital cost per unit produced.

In the Dutch East Indies (Indonesia and Dutch New Guinea) colonial policy in the middle of the nineteenth century forbade the sugar refineries to buy sugar cane from indigenous growers and imposed a discriminatory tax on rubber produced by native smallholders.[22] A recent unpublished United Nations study of agricultural development in Africa concluded that large-scale agricultural operations owned and controlled by foreign commercial interests (such as the rubber plantations of Liberia, the sisal estates of Tanganyika [Tanzania], and the coffee estates of Angola) only survived the competition of peasant producers because "the authorities actively supported them by suppressing indigenous rural development."[23]

The suppression of indigenous agricultural development served the interests of the colonizing powers in two ways. Not only did it prevent direct competition from more efficient native producers of the same crops, but it also guaranteed a labor force to work on the foreign-owned estates. Planters and foreign investors were not unaware that peasants who could survive economically by their own production would be under less pressure to sell their labor cheaply to the large estates.

The answer to the question, then, "Why can't people feed themselves?" must begin with an understanding of how colonialism actively prevented people from doing just that.

Colonialism

- forced peasants to replace food crops with cash crops that were then expropriated at very low rates;
- took over the best agricultural land for export crop plantations and then forced the most able-bodied workers to leave the village fields to work as slaves or for very low wages on plantations;
- encouraged a dependence on imported food;
- blocked native peasant cash crop production from competing with cash crops produced by settlers or foreign firms.

These are concrete examples of the development of underdevelopment that we should have perceived as such even as we read our history schoolbooks. Why didn't we? Somehow our schoolbooks always seemed to make the flow of history appear to have its own logic—as if it could not have been any other way. I, Frances, recall, in particular, a grade-school, social studies pamphlet on the idyllic life of Pedro, a nine-year-old boy on a coffee plantation in South America. The drawings of lush vegetation and "exotic" huts made his life seem romantic indeed. Wasn't it natural and proper that South America should have plantations to supply my mother and father with coffee? Isn't that the way it was *meant* to be?

NOTES

[1]Radha Sinha, *Food and Poverty* (New York: Holmes and Meier, 1976), p. 26.

[2]John Stuart Mill, *Political Economy*, Book 3, Chapter 25 (emphasis added).

[3]Peter Feldman and David Lawrence, "Social and Economic Implications of the Large-Scale Introduction of New Varieties of Foodgrains," Africa Report, preliminary draft (Geneva: UNRISD, 1975), pp. 107–108.

[4]Edgar Owens, *The Right Side of History*, unpublished manuscript, 1976.

[5]Walter Rodney, *How Europe Underdeveloped Africa* (London: Bogle-L'Ouverture Publications, 1972), pp. 171–172.

[6]Ferdinand Ossendowski, *Slaves of the Sun* (New York: Dutton, 1928), p. 276.

[7]Rodney, *How Europe Underdeveloped Africa*, pp. 171–172.

[8]Ibid., p. 181.

[9]Clifford Geertz, *Agricultural Involution* (Berkeley and Los Angeles: University of California Press, 1963), pp. 52–53.

[10]Rodney, *How Europe Underdeveloped Africa*, p. 185.

[11]Ibid., p. 184.

[12]Ibid., p. 186.

[13]George L. Beckford, *Persistent Poverty: Underdevelopment in Plantation Economies of the Third World* (New York: Oxford University Press, 1972), p. 99.

[14]Ibid., p. 99, quoting from Erich Jacoby, *Agrarian Unrest in Southeast Asia* (New York: Asia Publishing House, 1961), p. 66.

[15]Pat Flynn and Roger Burbach, North American Congress on Latin America, Berkeley, California, recent investigation.

[16]Feldman and Lawrence, "Social and Economic Implications," p. 103.

[17]Special Sahelian Office Report, Food and Agriculture Organization, March 28, 1974, pp. 88–89.

[18]Alan Adamson, *Sugar Without Slaves: The Political Economy of British Guiana, 1838–1904* (New Haven and London: Yale University Press, 1972).

[19]Ibid., p. 41.

[20]Eric Williams, *Capitalism and Slavery* (New York: Putnam, 1966), p. 110.

[21]Ibid., p. 121.

[22]Gunnar Myrdal, *Asian Drama*, vol. 1 (New York: Pantheon, 1966), pp. 448–449.

[23]Feldman and Lawrence, "Social and Economic Implications," p. 189.

Nomads at the Crossroads

The conflict between settled societies and nomads is as old as Cain and Abel. But now it threatens to destroy nomadic societies. Wayne Ellwood explores the accelerating antagonism and suggests that we would do better to preserve our differences.

Wayne Ellwood

The Great Wall of China is one of history's boldest and clearest symbols of a frontier. Erected over 2,000 years ago this colossal piece of engineering snakes hundreds of miles across the undulating plains of China's Northwest. Gazing towards the horizon from the walkway on top of the wall the grassy steppes seem to stretch on forever, to the rugged mountains of Mongolia and beyond to the endless Siberian taiga. When it was built the Great Wall symbolized the outer edge of civilization, a clear demarcation between the nomadic bands of barbarians beyond and the first unified Chinese Empire.

One Chinese Imperial Secretary, fearful of invasion by the warlike Mongols, described the nomadic horsemen as wild animals: 'In their breasts beat the hearts of beasts,' he wrote. 'From the most ancient time they have never been regarded as part of humanity.'[1]

Today the Great Wall is a relic of history and an obligatory stop for foreign tourists on package tours. Buses disgorge swarms of visitors from New Jersey and Tokyo while industrious hawkers pitch postcards of Genghis Khan and bottles of Coca-Cola. The Mongol land north of the Wall (known as Inner Mongolia to distinguish it from the Republic of Mongolia) is now controlled by China. The nomads are still there, but they are a threat no longer.

The Chinese have discovered a way of keeping them in their place. Since 1949, when the Communists took control, millions of Han Chinese, with government encouragement, have flooded onto the steppes—with the result that Mongols are now a minority in their own country. There are 20 million Chinese in Inner Mongolia and barely four million Mongols. Thousands of acres of former pasture have been turned into irrigated farmland and leased to outsiders, disrupting centuries-old migration routes in the process.

Traditionally, Mongols are pastoral nomads: that means they move their animals in a predictable pattern according to the seasons and the availability of forage. In the summer they travel to high ground where rain is heavier and grasses more luxuriant; in the harsh winter, when temperatures may drop to minus 40 °C, they retreat to sheltered valleys.

This mobility is absolutely critical to Mongol culture—as it is to all nomads. But like governments the world over, the Chinese are suspicious of this central core of nomadism, this incomprehensible, alien urge to move. So they've set out to do something else about it. With the introduction of post-Maoist economic reforms herders no longer have customary rights to land. Instead they have to bid to win grazing rights to specific parcels, called *kulums* (enclosures). In return the Mongol owners are obliged to erect a house and dig a well. These ranches are big, often 20 or 30 square kilometres, but they are rarely vast enough to have both good summer and winter pastures.

What this means is that the Mongols have little choice but to plant crops to use as forage for their stock over the scarce winter months. Beijing has also demanded that the herders abandon their subsistence approach (essentially producing for themselves, selling animals when and if they need to) and enter the modern market economy—a shift which has led to much larger herds. With more animals the nomads now find themselves both cut off from their traditional migratory routes *and* increasingly hemmed in by expanding agriculture. The result? Serious overgrazing, soil compaction and, inevitably, advancing desertification.

Elsewhere this process of making nomads settle down (what is sometimes referred to as 'sedenterization') has been carried out with force. When Stalin imposed collectivization (making nomads into ranchers) on Kazakh herders in the 1930s, as many as half the population are estimated to have died fighting the change. Forty years later in Somalia forced settlement, influenced by the Soviet collectivist model, proved disastrous. After the drought of 1974 Somali planners attempted to move 120,000 camel herders from the north into four villages on the Indian

Ocean coast. The goal was to train them to be fishermen and small farmers, not an easy task in a region where pastoralism is considered nothing less than a divine calling and camels are fussed over and loved like children. No points for guessing the scheme was a flop.[2]

MODERN SERVICES

The desire to control nomads politically and to incorporate them into national (ie nonnomadic) culture has always been strong. By their very nature nomads rub nation states up the wrong way. They don't fit neatly into national boundaries and they tend to look and behave differently from majority populations. In post-colonial states run by bureaucrats wedded to the modernist vision of national progress, nomads are seen as distinctly 'unmodern'—an embarrassment, rather than productive members of society.

Whether we're talking about small bands of nomadic hunters in the Amazon Basin, Inuit hunters in the Canadian Arctic or nomadic pastoralists in East Africa, there is strong pressure from governments everywhere to make nomads stay put. The reasons are varied, sometimes benevolent, usually patronizing. They need to be brought together for their own good, government officials claim—so they can be educated, taxed and given proper health care, electricity and roads.

'We want, as a democratic government, to give all citizens the modern services that a state should give its citizens,' the Israeli advisor on Arab affairs said in 1978 in an effort to justify settlement of Bedouin nomads.[3] The same rationale was widely shared by African countries like the Sudan, home to nearly three million nomadic herders from various tribal groups. Efforts began to 'modernize' the livestock sector 30 years ago. One of the first goals of the (mainly Arab) Government in Khartoum was to settle the (mainly Black) nomads in the south. In the soothing words of a Government report of the time: 'sedenterization . . . is a means of improving the economic

and social conditions of those communities . . . to integrate them into the life of the nation and to enable them to contribute fully to national progress.'[4]

If not for their own good, then nomads must be settled for the good of the nation. State planners claim that wandering pastoralists are inefficient and that they are ignorant of modern animal husbandry. Their irrational tendency to increase herd numbers threatens to turn delicate rangeland into unproductive wasteland.

These assertions are bolstered by a theory known as the 'tragedy of the commons', a rationale which has shaped government and aid-agency attitudes to nomadic herders for the last three decades. Briefly the theory says this: lands held in common, rather than privately-owned, will inevitably suffer environmental degradation since it is in each nomad's interest to maximize returns by adding more animals to the family herd.

The logical solution following from this analysis is for common lands to be controlled by the state or put into the hands of private owners. And that is just what's happening in African countries like Kenya and Tanzania, where nomads are being dispossessed in their thousands.

PRIVATE OWNERSHIP

In Kenya the Maasai have lost more than 1,000 square miles of grazing land over the past century. And the process is accelerating. In the early 1970s the Government launched its 'Group Ranches' scheme to register large chunks of savannah to particular Maasai communities. This was to be the first step towards private ownership of all Maasai common lands. It was devastatingly effective. Before long more educated or influential Maasai used their guile to hive off huge portions of land within the group territory. As one nomad complained bitterly: 'We said all of us should be given equal pieces of land. But the chairman took a bigger portion than all the other people . . . My piece is small, only 60 hectares, while the chairman has 320 hectares.'[5]

This soon sparked a desperate free-for-all as ordinary herders saw they would be left with nothing if they did not claim land themselves. Eventually the ranches were subdivided with the majority of Maasai receiving plots too small to support their herds. Unable to make a living the nomads soon sold their small plots: today 40 per cent of some Group Ranches has been purchased by outsiders, mostly speculators.[6]

In addition, thousands of hectares of Maasai pasture have been creamed off by corrupt officials and local bigwigs. In his travels through Maasailand in 1992 British journalist George Monbiot found communities who had lost nearly all their land to outsiders. In some places, he wrote: 'The entire savannah had been divided among politicians and their friends. Some of the best land belonged to President Moi; the second best to George Saitoti, the Vice-President and the inferior places to their colleagues.'[7]

To the south, in Tanzania, a quarter of a million nomads have had lands snatched by sharp-eyed entrepreneurs and massive state-run farming projects. On the Hanang plains near Arusha the Barabaig people, semi-nomadic cattle herders, have lost more than 40,000 hectares to a mammoth wheat-growing project funded by Canadian Government aid dollars. In some cases the dispossession has been violent: pastoralists have been beaten and their homes torched by Government workers clearing the land in advance of the towering Canadian-supplied tractors. Evidence is already mounting that mechanized monocropping of wheat is eroding the land at a rapid rate.[8]

The view that common ownership causes nomads to abuse the land is rooted in ignorance. In fact countless examples show that pastoral peoples traditionally had sophisticated systems to manage common resources. And this makes sense. The land is all that nomads have—to degrade it or treat it foolishly would be tantamount to suicide. The Barabaig, for example, have complex layers of control involving the community, clans and individual households. Access to pasture and water is rigidly controlled to avoid over-grazing and serious sanctions are levied on those who abuse customary rules.

In Niger, FulBe pastoralists elect a traditional manager called a *Ruga* to regulate herders' use of natural resources. The Ruga decides which migration routes should be used according to local conditions and what animals should use which pastures. He also sets the times at which herds migrate and settles any conflicts which may arise between nomads and farmers along the way. If there are conflicts between nomads the Ruga alone decides on an appropriate punishment, including banishment from the community if necessary.[9] When nomadic herders 'own' the land in common they make the laws regulating its use—and they make sure that everyone obeys them for the good of the community. The real tragedy occurs when lands are enclosed and environmental stewardship is replaced by intensive use for short-term profit.

Nomadic hunters share this same approach: living in symbiosis with the natural world, taking no more than they need and respecting the limits of the land. For example, Cree hunters in northern Quebec consider the animals they kill *chashimikonow*—a 'gift' from God. They believe they must not kill too much and only what is given. As a way of showing their seamless connection to nature they burn a piece of meat after the hunt, so the smoke is dispersed in the wind as a sign of respect to the animal spirits.[10] As anthropologist Richard Lee notes: 'Nomadic hunting societies have used the land for millennia and even doing their worst they couldn't do much damage.'

VIOLENT CLASHES

Now, as age-old cultures are deprived of their lands, their mobility is rapidly changing. The damage is emerging everywhere. A classic example is the national park system in Africa. Under the guise of 'conservation' both hunter-gatherers and pastoralists are excluded—often by force—from forests

and grasslands they have used for thousands of years. As local communities no longer 'own' the land they have little incentive to 'manage' it in a traditional, sustainable manner. The result is increased poaching and violent clashes between conservationists and nomads. In Waza National Park in Cameroon villagers were moved outside the park fence and can be jailed or fined if found on their former territory. With no stake of their own in the wildlife local people now act as guides for Nigerian poachers with high-powered rifles who slaughter any animal that happens to wander into range.[11]

The attitudes and practices of nomadic peoples toward the environment differ profoundly from the values of modern industrial society. It is by now a cliché (but no less compelling) to suggest that tribal peoples feel a mysterious spiritual link to the natural world—a fundamental bond which the rest of us, chained to our houses and property, have lost.

This may go some way towards explaining the deep-rooted ambivalence that settled cultures everywhere seem to feel for nomads. We admire them for their perceived independence as we resent them for an imagined freedom which has always escaped our grasp. In their disdain for national borders and distrust of centralized authority nomads exhibit a healthy scepticism of power—a scepticism we would do well to heed. Nomadic peoples tend to be politically egalitarian: their mobility gives them a safety valve. Like the Maku hunters of the Northwest Amazon most nomads bristle at the abuse of power by tribal leaders. If one Maku gets too bossy the others will simply pack up and leave.[12]

In his meditation on Australian Aborigines, *The Songlines*, Bruce Chatwin wrote that 'psychiatrists, politicians, tyrants are forever assuring us that the wandering life is an aberrant form of behaviour; a neurosis; a form of unfulfilled sexual longing; a sickness which, in the interests of civilization, must be suppressed.'

Part of this suspicion is lodged deep in our cultural memory: the warlike, rapacious Huns; the marauding Mon-

gol hordes; the shifty Native Americans who hunt buffalo and refuse to till the soil. This fear, now groundless, is still felt. In Europe, Gypsies have been reviled as vagrants and thieves for generations. A quarter of a million perished in Nazi concentration camps during the Second World War. And the hate continues—in February this year a Gypsy community in eastern Austria was attacked and four men were killed. The Gypsies were warned to 'go back to India'. They've lived in the area for more than 600 years.

It is their 'wandering life' that makes nomads unique. Whether hunters or herders they display an uncanny resourcefulness and flexibility in their ability to survive on some of the most marginal lands on earth. Their elusive mobility enables them to adapt, and sometimes to prosper, in harsh and unpredictable environments. Reason enough for us to support their struggle to maintain their distinct way of life—on their own terms. But if we are really to accept our common links with nomads—and challenge our deep-seated prejudices—we're going to have to confront a more basic and perhaps more primal fear. Our stubborn refusal to look in the mirror and recognize ourselves.

NOTES

1. *What Am I Doing Here?*, Bruce Chatwin, Penguin 1990.

2. 'Resettlement Schemes for Nomads: The Case of Somalia', Jorg Janzen, *Atlas of World Development*, Wiley, Chichester 1994.

3. *The Bedouin of the Negev*, Minority Rights Group, London 1990.

4. *Project of Community Development for Settlement of Nomads in the Sudan*, Government of Sudan 1962.

5., 6. 'Social and Economic Factors in the Privatization, Sub-Division and Sale of Maasai Ranches', John Galaty, *Nomadic Peoples* 30:1992.

7. *No Man's Land*, George Monbiot, Macmillan, London 1994.

8. 'The Barabaig/NAFCO Conflict in Tanzania', Charles Lane, *Forests, Trees and People Newsletter No. 20*.

9. *Baobab 14*, ALIN, Dakar, July 1994.

10. 'The Enduring Pursuit', Harvey A Feit, *Key Issues in Hunter-Gatherer Research*, Berg, Oxford 1994.

11. *Whose Eden?* IIED, London 1994.

12. 'Forest Rovers of the Amazon', John Reid, *UNESCO Courier*, November 1994.

Surviving the Revolution: Post Revolution Romania and Foreign Advisors[1]

Arthur W. Helweg

Western Michigan University

INTRODUCTION

Since the 1989 Revolution, Romania, like many other nations in Europe, is going through the process of nation building. The process involves the development of political and economic institutions to insure national security and social stability.[2] However Edmund Burke[3] pointed out over two hundred years ago the dangers of a revolution. He argued that a revolution tears down a social structure, destroys agreed upon norms, causes chaos and creates confusion. To make matters worse, there are very high expectations after a revolution, and as a result may not meet the expectations of the citizens supporting the overthrow. To bring about order, an authoritarian regime is often implemented. Thus Burke felt that the ultimate end was not worth the price.

Edmund Burke argued against revolution partly on the above grounds. He saw the social costs to be so great that he felt that an exploiting monarchy was better than the social, political and economic costs of a revolution. History has generally showed Burke to be correct; but, whether the costs of a revolution are too great depends on the individual situation of the community involved. Only they can determine

whether the detriments outweigh the benefits.

Since the writings of Burke, however, a new phenomenon has cast its influence on the process of post-revolution nation building; external influence through economic and political advisors. The nature of the recent process stems from the successful Marshall Plan that was instrumental in rebuilding Western Europe after the Second World War and developed during the Cold War between East and West. The phenomenon is supported by the ideology that there are universally ethical, economic, political and social systems that should be employed by all nations. It is a belief aided by the Cold War and takes the form of a religious fervor, known as "civil religion."[4] It is an ethnocentric view where the justification takes a form reminiscent of the crusades. The ideology is not religious, it is civil: such as democracy versus communism and free market versus state ownership. The relevance of this process of "converting" others to civil religious beliefs is ultimately tied to the advice and structures placed on Eastern European countries as well as many other societies today.

THE POST REVOLUTIONARY PROCESS TODAY

Since the collapse of the Soviet Union, many Eastern European and Asian regions have looked to the West

for political advice and economic assistance. However, aid and advice is not always in the best interest of the recipient country. Although foreign advisors and donors may believe that they are giving the best counsel, the recommendations may not be objective, rational or free. In fact, the country may not even have a choice as to whether they want to use it or not. To illustrate: Romania has just gone through a revolution and has instituted a government of majority rule. For many, the term majority rule still needs to be defined. Is it a majority of the population or just those who vote? Should those boycotting an election out of protest be considered? The Romanian Constitution, as ratified, defines these issues, but that does not mean it is the accepted political ideology of the people. Besides, in a system where matters are determined by the majority, minorities are always subject to the will of the majority. In any election, minorities will lose. To put it in emotional terms, it is a tyranny of the majority. The only time minorities are assured of any rights is either by force, succession, or the consent of the majority.

In the case of Romania, they are pressured by the United States and some Western European countries to have majority rule; yet, they are also chastised for not having adequate minority rights. The two concepts are opposed to each other. This does not mean they cannot be worked out, but it takes time. In the case of the United

States, they have been working on the problem for 200 years. However, they withhold granting Romania Most Favored Nation (MFN) Trade Status due to their human rights violations. Yet, the denial of MFN is not imposed on China, a country of vicious human rights violations. The problem for Romania, like those of many countries that have recently achieved their freedom, is that they are expected to solve burning social and political issues quickly, often a feat which was not accomplished by the country imposing the restrictions. This does not mean that Romania and other countries should not have minority and human rights, but, careful consideration should be made on the part of others who dictate terms. In other words, powerful donor countries are imposing criteria on Romania that they have not achieved themselves. The donor countries often perceive of themselves as having achieved the criteria imposed, such as human rights, but in actuality, this may not be the case.[5]

Societies perceive of themselves in terms of "ideal culture": that is, they see themselves in terms of their ideal of themselves, not what actually may be the case, or "real culture."[6] Thus, many western countries perceive of themselves as leaders in human rights and feel that since they are fair to all people, they can require the same behavior from others. This may or may not be reality, but people act on perceptions, interpretations and beliefs, not facts.

The concepts of civil religion, ideal culture and real culture influence the biggest problem facing many countries today; namely, economic development. The situation in Eastern Europe and the former Soviet Union developed so suddenly and is changing so fast that no one knows if the current thinking on economic development is applicable. Advisors may not know what to recommend; but, they are doing so anyway; and, their ideas are supported by monetary policies of the World Bank and other countries. One such position is that set forth by Jeffery Sachs, a Harvard University Economics Professor who advocates economic devel-

opment in Eastern Europe by what he terms "shock therapy".[7] His argument is as follows. He contends that public and private sectors cannot coexist. He argues using the analogy that it is like a country trying to shift from a right hand drive traffic system to a left hand drive traffic system. It has to be done suddenly. You cannot have trucks change one day and cars the next.

The principle of going to a free market, Sachs argues, is the same, the change must be sudden. If it is not done this way, the public sector will eventually destroy the private sector. He goes on to argue that nowhere in the world is there a successful economy where there are both private and public sectors operating side by side. The corollary to this proposition is that those countries that are capable should obtain loans to develop their economies.

In theory, Sachs seems very logical; but, does it really work? Human behavior is not always as logical as broad economic theories assume. The first question to ask is, "Has Sachs's view been tested?" The answer is "yes", in Brazil. According to Francis Moore Lappé,[8] a Development Economist, Brazil did everything right. They followed the economic school of Milton Friedman of the University of Chicago, the same basic economic philosophy advocated by Sachs. They borrowed heavily, developed industrially and had excellent economic indicators. Yet, in spite of having some of the highest paid executives in the world today, their tuberculosis rate, poverty level and rate of sickness is among the worst in the world. Brazil's international debit is among the highest in the world and the economy is on the verge of collapse. It was an absolute failure. Brazil is not the only example, an examination will reveal many cases similar to Brazil, although differences may exist in degree.

Is Sachs correct in saying that private and public ownership cannot exist side by side? The answer is "No". The United States is a case in point. When companies like the Chrysler Corporation were about to go bankrupt, the United States Government awarded them massive loans. Public companies

like the Tennessee Valley Authority exist. And, many institutions, like the American farmer, although private enterprises, are heavily subsidized and regulated by the United States government.

In fact, one should look at the United States to determine what did happen when a totally free market was instituted. During the turn of the century, when there was little or no regulation of enterprise, the rich got richer and poor got poorer. Once an individual or company got an advantage, they could use their power to exploit others almost on the level of feudalism. A good example was Standard Oil. Because the company was the first major oil producer, it was able to become so big and powerful that any business starting to compete could be immediately crushed. Standard Oil could sell gas next to the small competitor at a loss, as other parts of the corporation countered the loss by their profits. Thus, the small competitor could be quickly crushed and Standard Oil could raise the prices to recover the loss. Companies like General Motors became so powerful that they could buy out or crush their competition and maintain a monopoly on the market. In some cases they pressured the United States Congress to pass laws to limit public transportation, so people would have to buy their automobiles.

As economic conditions worsened, and social injustices were seen, the United States Congress passed laws to regulate the market so that competition would be fair. Companies like Standard Oil had to sell their holdings so that they did not have a monopoly. Even now it is not perfect, but it is better than the abject exploitation of some companies over others. The point is that laws had to be implemented to regulate the market so all could benefit. Next, an infrastructure[9] had to be instituted to enforce the regulations. The United States Interstate Commerce Commission (ICC) is a case in point. It is an administrative body charged to enforce the federal laws regulating trade and communications between states within the country. It does not take but a cursory knowledge of American history at the beginning of the Twentieth Century to realize that the free market system did not work in the United States until sufficient regulations and an adequate infrastructure were in place to insure that the market worked for the benefit of the society as a whole.

Today, Eastern European, former Soviet countries and Asia are being forced to implement "shock therapy" on the populace without adequate controls or infrastructures. Can you have a good free market if the roads are not adequate to transport goods? Can one compete with another when the phones work for some and not others? Infrastructures regulate and support. If sufficient regulations and infrastructures are not in place when the "shock therapy" is instituted, the result will be shortages.[10] There cannot be a free market if the roads are not adequate to transport goods, or customs officials will not let supplies enter the country without bribes. If shortages are of necessities, such as heat and food, it is disastrous. A person without food cannot afford to wait for the free market to develop naturally without governmental help. He will starve or revolt.

Part of the problem lies with the fact that advisors do not fully understand the local situation. I was talking with a western advisor soon after I arrived in Romania and he said, "The Romanian people are going to have to sacrifice to get their economy stabilized."[11]

I was living in an apartment with no heat, hot water and water was intermittent, and there were shortages in food. I was told by another foreign advisor that Romania wanted to keep isolated, this was bad and the country should borrow money. Yet, I just came from the States where countries like Brazil were consistently criticized for the fact that they borrow too much money.

Countries like Poland and Hungary are held up as models to follow, yet, a massive Polish debt was canceled by the United States, while Romania, a county that has been financially responsible in paying off her international debt and war reparations, has difficulty getting loans. Hungary has been open to the West since 1965 and

has had almost thirty years of experience in dealing with western economic and political systems. Yet, countries like Romania are expected to have these abilities immediately.

Advisors and authorities are applying their ideology to the situation of Romania and other countries without thinking through the complexity of the issues involved.

ANALYSIS

The above is only a brief essay to illustrate a question. Is the advice of foreigners applicable to the situation in Romania and other countries of Eastern Europe and Asia? The answer is not easy. Issues have to be looked at with their complexity, not in terms of ideology or civil religion. One reason for this is that the conflict between East and West had taken the form of a clash of ideologies, or put another way, the competition between civil religions. With the collapse of the Soviet Union, the West saw their ideology, or civil religion, as victorious and thus interpreted this to mean that their ideology was correct. Thus, they are forcing the implementation of this ideology, or civil religion, on others. However, like many religious people, they are forcing others to adopt an ideal form rather than what is actually practiced in their own society.

The issue is not capitalism versus communism or centralization versus privatization. Both systems implemented in their ideal forms may cause disaster. The issue is what kind of communism or what kind of democracy should be used. Each philosophy and practice must be modified to suit the particular situation. Just because a policy works in France does not mean it will work in Hungary, Romania or Poland. The process may work, it may work if modified, or it may not work at all. Each culture provides a unique context. What works in one may not work the same way in another or it may not even work at all. What is accepted, what is rejected and what is modified must be scrutinised carefully.

The record of foreign aid and advisors is abysmal. Frances Moore Lappé[12] argues that aid is one of the causes of world hunger. John Bodley[13] records numerous cases where modernization and foreign advice caused the destruction of a people. Unfortunately, foreign aid is never free. Joint ventures have a price. The aid may be tied to the particular ideology of the donor. The joint venture may result in a company taking excessive profits out of the country. In each situation, Romania must decide if the costs outweigh the benefits. Will the conditions cause social discontent and disorder? Having a stable economy is not a viable goal if it causes social upheaval in the society.[14]

Choosing whether to accept aid or advice is not easy. Current assumptions and advice must be thought through very carefully before the advice or dictates of outsiders is followed. It is good to receive ideas from the outside. It must be realized, however, that outsiders have their cultural biases, cultural base and self interests. If foreign advice and influence is not scrutinized, the results may be what Burke predicted, the revolution will be a failure.

NOTES

1. Reprinted from *Revue Des Études Sud-Est Européennes*, XXXI, 1-2, pp. 99-104, Bucharest, 1993.

2. Although national security and social stability are general goals, what these mean and the addition of other criteria vary from country to country.

3. Burke was a political philosopher arguing against revolution. For a good treatment of his ideas within the ideological origins of the American Revolution, see B. Ballyn, *The Ideological Origins of the American Revolution*, Cambridge, MA, USA, 1967.

4. The term "Civil Religion" stems from the phenomenon of political and economic ideology taking the fervor of a religious crusade; people, communities and nations work too convert or win others to their particular belief. Often proponents expound an ideal rather than a real application of their point of view. It is ethnocentrism in its most extreme form.

5. The issue of MFN for Romania is complicated because the United States, as pointed out, is not consistent in its application of criteria. However, it sees itself as a leader for promoting the rights of all people. When there is too much

to be lost by forcing compliance, as would be the case in alienating China, the criteria is not strictly enforced. Even if Romania refuses compliance, the national and economic interests of the United States will not be harmed. When there is a cost, sometimes the compromise of ideology is made and later rationalized.

6. "Ideal culture" is a term which refers to how people perceive of themselves. "Real culture" indicates how people actually behave. Generally, members of a community see themselves in ideal terms and others in real terms. To illustrate, a Christian business person may view himself as a charitable individual, while a person patronizing his store may see a vicious competitive person who charges excessive costs for inferior service.

7. One place where his views were set forth was on the Public Broadcasting (PBS) program in the United States titled *World Net*, aired on September 25, 1990.

8. *The Politics of Food*, a television program produced by Public Broadcasting Corporation (PBS) in the United States.

9. "Infrastructure" refers to the supporting mechanisms needed for a program to succeed. Making televisions available is of little value if people are not trained to repair them and spare parts are not accessible. The training of repair people and making spare parts available is part of "infrastructure". "Infrastructure" can be both a regulatory and a supporting mechanism. Having the means to prevent a company from exploiting workers is a regulatory function.

Having schools to train repair technicians is a support system. Both are considered "infrastructure".

10. This may be a cause of the massive food shortages in Russia today.

11. What he also did not realize was that the Romanian people have been sacrificing for the last 40 years and losing their patience.

12. Frances Moore Lappé and Joseph Collins, *World Hunger: Twelve Myths*, New York, 1986.

13. John H. Bodley, *Victims of Progress*, Mountain View, CA, USA, 1990.

14. It is possible that the current unrest in Russia is partly due to the tight monetary policies imposed by the World Bank and other donor agencies.

Bicultural Conflict

Chinese cultural traits conflict with those encountered in America, posing dilemmas for immigrant children

Betty Lee Sung

Betty Lee Sung, professor of Asian studies at City College of New York, is the author of many books and articles on Chinese immigrants in the United States.

The moment a child is born, he begins to absorb the culture of his primary group; these ways are so ingrained they become a second nature to him. Imagine for a moment how wrenching it must be for an immigrant child who finds his cumulative life experiences completely invalidated, and who must learn a whole new set of speech patterns and behaviors when he settles in a new country. The severity of this culture shock is underlined by Teper's definition of culture:

Culture is called a habit system in which "truths" that have been perpetuated by a group over centuries have permeated the unconscious. This basic belief system, from which "rational" conclusions spring, may be so deeply ingrained that it becomes indistinguishable from human perception—the way one sees, feels, believes, knows. It is the continuity of cultural assumptions and patterns that gives order to one's world, reduces an infinite variety of options to a manageable stream of beliefs, gives a person a firm footing in time and space, and binds the lone individual to the communality of a group.

The language barrier was the problem most commonly mentioned by the immigrant Chinese among whom I have conducted field research. Language looms largest because it is the conduit through which people interact with other people. It is the means by which

we think, learn, and express ourselves. Less obvious is the basis upon which we speak or act or think. If there are bicultural conflicts, these may engender problems and psychological difficulties, which may not be immediately apparent but may nevertheless impact on the development of immigrant children.

This article will address some of the cultural conflicts that commonly confront the Chinese child in the home and, particularly, in the schools. Oftentimes, teachers and parents are not aware of these conflicts and ascribe other meanings or other motives to the child's behavior, frequently in a disapproving fashion. Such censure confuses the child and quite often forces him to choose between what he is taught at home and what is commonly accepted by American society. In his desire to be accepted and to be liked, he may want to throw off that which is second nature to him; this may cause anguish and pain not only to himself but also to his parents and family. Teachers and parents should be aware of these differences and try to help the children resolve their conflicts, instead of exacerbating them.

AGGRESSIVENESS AND SEXUALITY

In Chinese culture, the soldier, or the man who resorts to violence, is at the bottom of the social ladder. The sage or gentleman uses his wits, not his fists. The American father will take his son out to the backyard and give him a

few lessons in self-defense at the age of puberty. He teaches his son that the ability to fight is a sign of manhood. The Chinese parent teaches his son the exact opposite: Stay out of fights. Yet, when the Chinese child goes to the school playground, he becomes the victim of bullies who pick on him and call him a sissy. New York's teenagers can be pretty tough and cruel. If the child goes home with bruises and a black eye, his parents will yell at him and chastise him. What is he to do? The unresolved conflict about aggressive behavior is a major problem for Chinese-American males. They feel that their masculinity has been affected by their childhood upbringing.

What do the teachers or monitors do? In most instances, they are derisive of the Chinese boys. "Why don't the Chinese fight back?" they exclaim. "Why do they stand there and just take it?" This derision only shames the Chinese boys, who feel that their courage is questioned. This bicultural conflict may be reflected in the self-hatred of some Asian-American male activists who condemn the passivity of our forefathers in response to the discrimination and oppression they endured. Ignorant about their cultural heritage, the activists want to disassociate themselves from such "weakness," and they search for historical instances in which Asians put up a brave but costly and oftentimes futile fight to prove their manhood. The outbreak of gang violence may be another manifestation of the Chinese male's efforts to prove that he is "macho" also. He may be

From *The World & I*, August 1989, pp. 670-679. Originally from the *Journal of Comparative Family Studies*, 1985. © 1985 by the *Journal of Comparative Family Studes*, University of Calgary, Department of Sociology, Calgary, Alberta T2N 1N4, Canada. Reprinted by permission.

overcompensating for the derision that he has suffered.

In American schools, sexuality is a very strong and pervasive force. Boys and girls start noticing each other in the junior highs; at the high school level, sexual awareness is very pronounced. School is as much a place for male/female socialization as it is an institution for learning. Not so for the Chinese. Education is highly valued, and it is a serious business. To give their children an opportunity for a better education may be the primary reason why the parents push their children to study, study, study. Interest in the opposite sex is highly distracting and, according to some old-fashioned parents, improper. Dating is an unfamiliar concept and sexual attractiveness is underplayed, not flaunted as it is according to American ways.

This difference in attitudes and customs poses another dilemma for both the Chinese boys and girls. In school, the white, black, or Hispanic girls like to talk about clothes, makeup, and the dates they had over the weekend. They talk about brassiere sizes and tampons. The popular girl is the sexy one who dates the most. She is the envy of the other girls.

For the Chinese girl, the openness with which other girls discuss boys and sex is extremely embarrassing. Chinese girls used to bind their breasts, not show them off in tight sweaters. Their attitude toward the opposite sex is quite ambivalent. They feel that they are missing something very exciting when other girls talk about phone calls from their boyfriends or about their dates over the weekends, yet they will shy away and feel very uncomfortable if a boy shows an interest in them.

Most Chinese parents have had no dating experience. Their marriages were usually arranged by their own parents or through matchmakers. Good girls simply did not go out with boys alone, so the parents are very suspicious and apprehensive about their daughters dating, and they watch them very carefully. Most Chinese girls are not permitted to date,

and for the daring girl who tries to go out against her parents' wishes, there will be a price to pay.

It is no easier for Chinese boys. The pressure to succeed in school is even greater than for girls, and parental opposition to dating is even more intense. Naturally, the parents want their children to adhere to the old ways. Some children do not agree with their parents and have to carry on their high school romances on the sly. These children are bombarded by television, advertisements, stories, magazines, and real-life examples of boy-girl attraction. The teenager is undergoing puberty and experiencing the instinctive urges surging within him or her. In this society they are titillated, whereas in China they are kept under wraps until they are married.

The problem is exacerbated when teachers make fun of Chinese customs and the parents. I saw an instance of this at one of the Chinatown schools. A young Chinese girl had been forbidden by her parents to walk to school with a

Many Chinese immigrant parents walk their children to and from school, even as late as the junior high level. Some mothers come to the schools to feed their children lunch.

young Puerto Rican boy who was in the habit of accompanying her every day. To make sure that the parents were being obeyed, the grandmother would walk behind the girl to see that she did not walk with the boy. Grandma even hung around until her granddaughter went into class, and then she would peer through the window to make sure all was proper before she went home.

Naturally, this was embarrassing for the girl, and it must have been noticed by the homeroom teacher. He exploded in anger at the little old lady and made some rather uncomplimentary remarks about this being the United States and that Chinese customs should have been left behind in China. To my mind, this teacher's attitude and remarks could only push the daughter farther away from her parents. What he could have done was explain to the girl, or even to the entire class, the cultural values and traditions of her parents, so that she would understand how they thought and why they behaved in such a fashion. Putting down the parents and their customs is the worst thing he could have done.

SPORTS

The Chinese attitude toward sports is illustrated by an oft-told joke about two Englishmen who were considered somewhat mad. The two lived in Shanghai where they had gone to do business. In the afternoons, they would each take a racquet, go out in the hot sun, and bat a fuzzy ball across the net. As they ran back and forth across the court, sweat would pour from their faces, and they would be exhausted at the end of the game. To the Chinese onlookers standing on the side, this was sheer lunacy. They would shake their heads in disbelief and ask: "Why do these crazy Englishmen work so hard? They can afford to hire coolies to run around and hit the ball for them." The Chinese attitude toward sports has changed considerably, but it still does not assume the importance that it enjoys in American life.

Turn on any news program on radio or television, and you will find one-third of the air time devoted to sports. Who are the school heros? The football quarterback, the track star, the baseball pitcher. What are the big events in school? The games. What is used to rally school spirits? The games.

Yet in the traditional Chinese way of thinking, development of the mental faculties was more important than development of the physique. The image of a scholar was one with a sallow face and long fingernails, indicating that he spent long hours with his books and had not had to do physical labor. Games that required brute strength, such as football and boxing, were not even played in China. Kung fu or other disciplines of the martial arts did not call for physical strength as much as concentration, skill, and agility. In the minds of many Chinese, sports are viewed as frivolous play and a waste of time and energy. Add to this the generally smaller physique of the Chinese immigrant student in comparison to his classmates, and we do not find many of them on any of the school teams.

What does this mean to the Chinese immigrant students, especially the boys? On the one hand, they may think that the heavy emphasis upon sports is a displaced value. They may want to participate, but they are either too small in stature or unable to devote the time necessary for practice to make the school teams. If the "letter men" are the big wheels, the Chinese student will feel that his kind are just the little guys. But most important of all, an entire dimension of American school life is lost to the Chinese immigrant children.

Chinese-American students enjoy a break on the playground at Sun Yat Sen Intermediate School in New York City's Chinatown.

TATTLING

Should one report a wrongdoing? Should one tell the teacher that a schoolmate is cheating on his exam? Should one report to the school authorities that a fellow student is trying to extort money from him? The American values on this score are ambiguous and confusing. For example, in the West Point scandal a few years ago, most of the cadets involved were not cheaters themselves but they knew about the cheating and did not report it to the authorities. Their honor code required that they tell, but the unwritten code among their fellow cadets said that they should not tattle or "fink." If they had reported the cheating of their fellow cadets, they would have been socially ostracized. There is a dilemma for the American here as well.

This bicultural conflict was noted by Denise Kandel and Gerald S. Lesser in the book, *Youth in Two Worlds*, in which their reference groups were

Participation in sports—so heavily emphasized in America—frequently becomes a dilemma for Chinese immigrant students, who experience sharp contrasts in cultures when they come into contact with children from other ethnic groups in public schools.

Danish and American children. The Danish children, like the Chinese, feel duty bound to report wrongdoing. There is no dichotomy of consequences here. Authorities and peers are consistent in their attitude in this respect, and this consistency helps to maintain social control. The teacher cannot be expected to have four pairs of eyes and see everything. The parents cannot be everywhere at once to know what their child is doing during the day. If the siblings or schoolmates will help by reporting wrongdoing, the task of teaching the child is shared and made easier for the adults. But when social ostracism stands in the way of enforcing ethical values, an intense conflict ensues and contributes to the breakdown of social control.

DEMONSTRATION OF AFFECTION

A commonly voiced concern among Chinese children is, "My parents do not love me. They are so cold, distant, and remote." The children long for human warmth and affection because they see it on the movie and television screens, and they read about it in books and magazines. Because their experiences with mother and father and the other members of the family as well are so formal and distant, they come to the conclusion that love is lacking. In China, where such behavior is the norm, children do not question it. But in this country, where expressions of affection are outwardly effusive and commonly exhibited, they feel deprived.

This lack of demonstrative affection extends also to the spouse and friends. To the Chinese, physical intimacy and love are private matters never exhibited in public. Even in handshaking, the traditional Chinese way was to clasp one's own hands in greeting. Kissing and hugging a friend would be most inappropriate, and to kiss one's spouse in public would be considered shameless and ill-mannered.

Nevertheless, Chinese children in this country are attracted to the physical expressions of love and affection. While they crave it for themselves,

they are often unable to reciprocate or be demonstrative in their relations with their own spouses, children, or friends because of their detached emotional upbringing.

In the schools, this contrast in culture is made all the sharper because of the large numbers of Hispanics. In general, the Hispanics are very outgoing and are not the least bit inhibited about embracing, holding hands, or kissing even a casual acquaintance. The Chinese children may interpret these gestures of friendliness as overstepping the bounds of propriety, but more often than not they wish they could shed their reserve and reach out to others in a more informal manner.

On the other hand, the aloofness of the Chinese students is often wrongly interpreted as unfriendliness, standoffishness, as a desire to keep apart. If all the students in the schools were made aware of these cultural differences, they would not misread the intentions and behavior of one another.

EDUCATION

That education is a highly prized cultural value among the Chinese is commonly known, and the fact that Chinese children generally do well scholastically may be due to the hard push parents exert in this direction. None of this means, however, that these children do not experience a bicultural conflict regarding education when they see that the bright student is not the one who is respected and looked up to in American schools. Labels such as "bookworm," "egghead," and "teacher's pet" are applied to the intelligent students, and these terms are not laudatory, but derisive. When parents urge their children to study hard and get good grades, the children know that the payoff will not be social acceptance by their schoolmates. The rewards are not consistent with values taught at home.

Nevertheless, the Chinese immigrant high school students indicated in their survey questionnaire that they prized the opportunity to get an education. In fact, they identified the opportunity to get a free education as one of the most important reasons why they are satisfied with their schoolwork. Of 143 students who said that they were satisfied with their schoolwork, 135 mentioned this one factor. Education is not easily available to everyone in China, Hong Kong, or Taiwan. It is attained at great personal sacrifice on the part of the parents. It is costly and it is earned by diligence and industry on the part of the student. In this country, school is free through high school. Everyone has to go to school until sixteen years of age in New York, for example. It is not a matter of students trying to gain admittance by passing rigorous entrance exams, but a matter of the authorities trying to keep the dropout rates low that characterizes the educational system here.

This is ground also for conflict, however, since what is free and easy to get is often taken lightly. New York State's academic standards are lower than those in Hong Kong or Taiwan, and the schoolwork is easier to keep up with. As a result, there is less distinction attached to being able to stay in school or graduate. What the Chinese immigrant students prize highly has less value in the larger society, and again the newcomers to this country start to have doubts about the goals that they are striving for.

THRIFT

Twelve, perhaps thirteen, banks can be found within the small core area of New York's Chinatown. When the Manhattan Savings Bank opened a new branch in October 1977 it attracted to its coffers $3 million within a few months' time. Most of the large banks are aware that Chinatown is fertile ground for the accumulation of capital because the Chinese tend to save more of what they earn than other ethnic groups in America, in spite of the fact that their earnings are small.

Two major factors encourage the growth of savings among Chinese immigrants. One is the sense of insecurity common to all immigrants, who need a cushion for the uncertainties that they feel acutely. The other is the esteem with which thrift is regarded by the

Chinese. A person who is frugal is thought of more highly than is one who can sport material symbols of success.

I was once sent on an assignment to cover the story of a very wealthy Chinese man from Bangkok who was reputed to own shipping lines, rice mills, and many other industries. He was a special guest of the United States Department of State, and that evening he was to be honored at the Waldorf-Astoria. I found this gentleman in a very modestly-priced midtown hotel. When he extended his hand to shake mine, I saw that his suit sleeves were frayed.

The value placed upon thrift poses acute bicultural conflict for Chinese immigrant children who see all about them evidence of an economic system that encourages the accumulation and conspicuous consumption of material possessions. A very important segment of the consumer market is now the teenage population. The urge to have stylish clothes, a stereo, a camera, a hi-fi radio, sports equipment, and even a car creates a painful conflict in the child who is enticed by television and other advertising media, but whose parents reserve a large percentage of their meager earnings for stashing away in the banks.

In school, the girl who gets money to spend on fashionable dresses and the latest rock record feels more poised and confident about herself than do her less materially fortunate classmates. She is also admired, complimented, and envied. In the Chinese community, on the other hand, a Chinese girl who spent a lot of money on clothes and frivolities would soon be the object of grapevine gossip, stigmatized as a less-than-desirable prospective wife or daughter-in-law, whereas praises would be sung for the more modestly dressed girl who saved her money.

From my students I hear a commonly voiced complaint about their parents as "money-hungry." They give their children very little spending money. They do not buy fashionable clothing; rather, they buy only serviceable garments in which the children are ashamed to be seen. The Chinese home is generally not furnished for comfort

or aesthetics, so when Chinese children visit the homes of their non-Chinese friends and compare them with their own living quarters, they feel deprived and ashamed of their parents and their family. They certainly do not want to bring their friends home to play, and the teenagers may themselves stay away from home as much as possible, feeling more comfortable with their peers in clubhouses or on the streets.

The contrast in spending attitudes between the underdeveloped economy from which many Chinese immigrants have come and the American economy, which emphasizes mass and even wasteful consumption, is very sharp, and it creates many an unresolved conflict in the children, who do not realize that cultural differences lie behind it. They think that their parents value money more than they care for their children, and exhibit this by denying material possessions that give them pleasure and status in the eyes of their peers.

Credit is another concept foreign to immigrants from the Far East. If one does not have the money, one should not be tempted to buy. Credit is borrowing money, and borrowing should be resorted to only in extreme emergencies. The buy now, pay later idea goes against the Chinese grain. So the Chinese families postpone buying until they have saved up enough to cover the entire purchase price. This attitude is fairly common even when it comes to the purchase of a home. The family will scrimp and economize, putting aside a large portion of its income for this goal, denying itself small pleasures along the way for many, many years until the large sum is accumulated. To the Chinese way of thinking, this singleness of purpose shows character, but to the more hedonistic American mind, this habit of thrift may appear asinine and unnecessary.

DEPENDENCY

In her study, "Socialization Patterns among the Chinese in Hawaii," Nancy F. Young noted the prolonged period of dependency of the children commonly

221

found in the child-rearing practices of the Chinese in Hawaii. She wrote:

Observations of Chinese families in Hawaii indicate that both immigrant and local parents utilize child-rearing techniques that result in parent-oriented, as opposed to peer-oriented, behavior. . . . Chinese parents maximize their control over their children by limiting their experiences with models exhibiting nonsanctioned behavior.

Analyzing and comparing the results of the Chance Independence Training Questionnaire that she administered to six ethnic groups and local (American-born) Chinese as well as immigrant Chinese, she found the mean age of independence training for American-born Chinese to be the lowest (6.78 years), while that for immigrant Chinese to be the highest (8.85 years). Among other ethnic groups in Young's study, the mean age of independence training ranged as follows: Jewish, 6.83; Protestant, 6.87 years; Negro, 7.23 years; Greek, 7.67 years; French-Canadian, 7.99 years; and Italian, 8.03 years.

Immigrant mothers exercise constant and strict supervision over their children. They take the children wherever they go, and babysitters are unheard of. They prefer their children to stay home rather than go out to play with their friends. Friends are carefully screened by the mother, and the child is not expected to do things for himself until about two years beyond the mean age that a Jewish mother would expect her child to do for himself.

On the other hand, American-born Chinese parents expect their children to cut the apron strings sooner than any of the other ethnic groups surveyed. Young did not elaborate and explain why, but it seems that Chinese parents who are American-born have assimilated the American values of independence at an early age and may even have gone overboard in rearing their own children. There are areas of dependence and independence in which Young found divergence. The immigrant Chinese child is expected to be able to take care of himself at an earlier age, but he is discouraged from socializing with people outside the family until a much later age.

The extremes exhibited between the American-born and immigrant Chinese may be indicative of the bicultural conflict that the Chinese in this country feel. As children, they may have felt that their parents were overprotective; this was frequently mentioned by the teachers to whom we talked. We saw evidence of this in the elementary schools—the previously mentioned practice of mothers coming to the school from the garment factories during their own lunch hours to feed their children lunch. Many walked their children to and from school, even as late as the junior high level, but it was not clear to us whether the parents were justifiably afraid for their children's safety from the gangs or whether they were being overprotective. The teachers thought the mothers were smothering the children and restricting their freedom of action. By adolescence, the children must have felt the same. They were chafing against parental control over what they presumed to be their own business, while the parents thought they were merely doing their parental duty.

Teachers and parents do not agree on this score, with the result that parental authority is often undermined by a teacher's scoffing attitude. A personal experience of my own reveals how damaging this can be to a parent's ability to maintain some kind of control over the growing teenager.

My seventeen-year-old son was

Many adolescents in Chinese immigrant families chafe under parental control, considering their parents overprotective. Stylish dress and dating are two issues indicative of the bicultural conflict Chinese immigrant families experience.

Chinese immigrant mothers exercise constant and strict supervision over their children and do not expect a child to do things for himself until he is nearly nine years old—the highest mean age for independence training among all ethnic groups in America.

coming home late at night, and I found it hard to fall asleep until he was home. I did not feel that he should be up so late, nor did I wish my sleep to be disturbed. My son objected strenuously to a curfew of midnight during the week and 1 A.M. on the weekends. His objection was based on the fact that no other teenagers he knew had such restrictions, that most get-togethers did not get going until 11 P.M., and that he would be the "wet blanket" if he left early. I understood his concerns and tried to get the parents of his friends to agree to a uniform time when the group should break up and go home to bed. I felt that if everybody had to go, my son would not mind leaving.

To my utter surprise, not one of the parents felt that boys or girls of seventeen years of age should have a curfew. They felt that I was being too strict and overprotective and that it was time for me to cut the apron strings. The worst part of it was that my conversation with the parents got back to my son, who immediately and gleefully confronted me with, "See, none of the other parents agree with you. You are the only old-fashioned, strict one." This lack of understanding on the part of the other parents in telling my son about our conversation undermined my authority. From that day, I was unable to set hours for him anymore.

The Chinese value of respect for one's elders and for authority is common knowledge and needs no further elaboration here. We have already mentioned that the Chinese immigrant children encountering the disrespect accorded teachers and school authorities for the first time in American classrooms find themselves extremely upset and dismayed. In our interviews with the students, this concern was voiced frequently.

Challenging established authority has been a notable feature of youth culture over the past two decades. The parents, the teachers, the police, the government, the church—all authority figures in the past—have been knocked down and even reviled. Violence against teachers is the leading problem in schools across the nation. If students do not have respect for the teacher, neither will they have respect for the knowledge that the teacher tries to impart. The issue is a disturbing one, not only for the immigrant children but for the entire American society as well.

HEROES, HEROINES, AND INDIVIDUALISM

Who are the people who are praised, admired, looked up to, and revered? The idols of different cultures are themselves different types of people, and the values of a society may be deduced from the type of people who are respected and emulated in that culture. In the United States, the most popular figures are movie, television, and stage stars, sports figures, politicians, successful authors, inventors, and scientists; probably in that order. Who are the heroes and heroines of China? If we use literature as a guide, they are the filial sons or daughters, the sacrificing mother, the loyal minister, the patriot or war hero who saves his country, and revolutionaries who overthrow despotic rulers and set up their own dynasties. Even in modern China, the persons honored and emulated are the self-sacrificing workers who put nation above self.

Priests, ministers, and rabbis once commanded prestige in this country, but the status of these men of God has declined. In China, monks or priests have always occupied lowly positions. In contrast to the United States, in China actors were riffraff. Women did not act in the theater, so men had to play the female roles. Western influence has brought about changes in the pseudo-Chinese cultures of Hong Kong and Singapore and stage performers and movie stars are now popular and emulated, but this was not always so.

As a rule, Chinese heroes and heroines were people of high moral virtues, and they set the standards of conduct for others. In this country, the more sensational the exposé of the private lives of our national leaders or entertainment figures, the more our curiosity is aroused. How movie stars retain their popularity in spite of the relentless campaigns to strip them naked is very difficult for someone not brought up in the United States to comprehend. An old adage says, "No man is a hero to his valet." Yet, the very fact that American heroes and heroines survive and thrive on notoriety and self-confession can only mean that the American people admire such behavior. One might say, Chinese heroes are saints; American heroes are sinners.

Noted anthropologist Francis L. K. Hsu has written extensively about individualism as a prominent characteristic of American life. According to Hsu, the basic ingredient of rugged individualism is self-reliance. The individual constantly tells himself and others that he controls his own destiny and that he does not need help from others. The individual-centered person enjoins himself to find means of fulfilling his own desires and ambitions.

Individualism is the driving force behind the competitiveness and creativity that has pushed this nation forward. Loose family ties, superficial human relationships, little community control, and weak traditions have given the individual leeway to strike out on his own without being hindered by sentimentality, convention, and tradition. Self-interest has been a powerful incentive.

In contrast, Dr. Hsu contends, the Chinese are situation-centered. Their way of life encourages the individual to find a satisfactory adjustment with the external environment of men and things. The Chinese individual sees the world in relativistic terms. He is dependent upon others and others are dependent upon him. Like bricks in a wall, one lends support to the other and they all hold up the society as a whole. If even one brick becomes loose, the wall is considerably weakened; interlocked, the wall is strong. The wall is the network of human relations. The individual subordinates his own wishes and ambitions for the common good.

Dr. Kenneth Abbott, in his book *Harmony and Individualism*, also points out that the Western ideas of creativity and individualism are not accented in Chinese and must be held within accepted norms. One of the reasons for this is the importance ascribed to maintenance of harmony. Harmony is the key concept in all relationships between god(s) and man and between man and man. It is the highest good.

To the Chinese, the sense of duty and obligation takes precedence over self-gratification. It is not uncommon to find Chinese teenagers handing over their entire paychecks to their parents for family use or for young Chinese males to pursue a course of study chosen for them by their parents rather than one of their own choosing. Responsibility toward distant kin is more keenly felt by the Chinese than by other Americans. Honor and glory accrue not only to the individual but to all those who helped him climb the ladder. This sense of being part of something greater than oneself gives the Chinese a feeling of belonging and security in the knowledge that they do not stand alone. On the other hand, individual freedom of action is very much restricted.

Some of the better known problems that confront a Chinese immigrant to these shores, such as respect for elders, modesty and humility, and male superiority, were omitted here because they have been dealt with at length elsewhere. The foregoing examples—aggressiveness, sexuality, sports, tattling, demonstration of affection, education, thrift, independence training, respect for authority, heros and heroines, and individualism—represent other important areas of bicultural conflict that confront Chinese newcomers to these shores.

ADDITIONAL READING

Francis L. K. Hsu, "Rugged Individualism Reconsidered," *The Colorado Quarterly*, vol. 9, no. 2, Autumn 1960.

_____ *Americans and Chinese: Reflections on Two Cultures and Their People*, American Museum of Science Books, New York, 1972.

_____ "Culture Change and the Persistence of the Chinese Personality," in George DeVos, ed., *In Response to Change*, D. Van Nostrand, New York, 1976.

Denise Kandel and Gerald S. Lesser, *Youth in Two Worlds*, Jossey-Bass, Inc., San Francisco, 1972.

Richard Sollenger, "Chinese-American Child Rearing Practices and Juvenile Delinquency," *Journal of Social Psychology*, vol. 74, 1968.

Shirley Teper, "Ethnicity, Race and Human Development," N.Y. Institute on Pluralism and Group Identity of the American Jewish Committee, 1977.

Nancy F. Young, "Socialization Patterns among the Chinese in Hawaii," in *Amerasia Journal*, vol. 1, no. 4, February 1972.

Growing up as a Fore

E. Richard Sorenson

Dr. Sorenson, director of the Smithsonian's National Anthropological Film Center, wrote The Edge of the Forest *on his Fore studies.*

Untouched by the outside world, they had lived for thousands of years in isolated mountains and valleys deep in the interior of Papua New Guinea. They had no cloth, no metal, no money, no idea that their homeland was an island—or that what surrounded it was salt water. Yet the Fore (for'ay) people had developed remarkable and sophisticated approaches to human relations, and their child-rearing practices gave their young unusual freedom to explore. Successful as hunter-gatherers and as subsistence gardeners, they also had great adaptability, which brought rapid accommodation with the outside world after their lands were opened up.

It was alone that I first visited the Fore in 1963—a day's walk from a recently built airstrip. I stayed six months. Perplexed and fascinated, I returned six times in the next ten years, eventually spending a year and a half living with them in their hamlets.

Theirs was a way of life different from anything I had seen or heard about before. There were no chiefs, patriarchs, priests, medicine men or the like. A striking personal freedom was enjoyed even by the very young, who could move about at will and be where or with whom they liked. Infants rarely cried, and they played

Exploring, two youngsters walk confidently past men's house in hamlet. Smaller women's house is at right.

confidently with knives, axes, and fire. Conflict between old and young did not arise; there was no "generation gap."

Older children enjoyed deferring to the interests and desires of the younger, and sibling rivalry was virtually undetectable. A responsive sixth sense seemed to attune the Fore hamlet mates to each other's interests and needs. They did not have to directly ask, inveigle, bargain or speak out for what they needed or wanted. Subtle, even fleeting expressions of interest, desire, and discomfort were quickly read and helpfully acted on by one's associates. This spontaneous urge to share food, affection, work, trust, tools and pleasure was the social cement that held the Fore hamlets together. It was a pleasant way of life, for one could

always be with those with whom one got along well.

Ranging and planting, sharing and living, the Fore diverged and expanded through high virgin lands in a pioneer region. They hunted out their gardens, tilled them while they lasted, then hunted again. Moving ever away from lands peopled and used they had a self-contained life with its own special ways.

The underlying ecological conditions were like those that must have encompassed the world before agriculture set its imprint so broadly. Abutting the Fore was virtually unlimited virgin land, and they had food plants they could introduce into it. Like hunter-gatherers they sought their sources of sustenance first in one locale and then another, across an extended range, following opportunities provided by a providential nature. But like agriculturalists they concentrated their effort and attention more narrowly on selected sites of production, on their gardens. They were both seekers and producers. A pioneer people in a pioneer land, they ranged freely into a vast territory, but they planted to live.

Cooperative groups formed hamlets and gardened together. When the fertility of a garden declined, they abandoned it. Grass sprung up to cover these abandoned sites of earlier cultivation, and, as the Fore moved on to other parts of the forest, they left uninhabited grasslands to mark their passage.

The traditional hamlets were small, with a rather fluid system of social relations. A single large men's house provided shelter for 10 to 20 men and boys and their visiting friends. The several smaller women's houses each normally sheltered two married women, their unmarried daughters and their sons up to about six years of age. Formal kinship bonds were less important than friendship was. Fraternal "gangs" of youths formed the hamlets; their "clubhouses" were the men's houses.

Learning to be a toddler, a Fore baby takes its first experimental steps. No one urges him on.

In infancy, Fore children begin experimental play with knives and other lethal objects. Sorenson never saw a child warned away or injured by them.

During the day the gardens became the center of life. Hamlets were virtually deserted as friends, relatives and children went to one or more garden plots to mingle their social, economic and erotic pursuits in a pleasant and emotionally filled Gestalt of garden life. The boys and unmarried youths preferred to explore and hunt in the outlying lands, but they also passed through and tarried in the gardens.

Daily activities were not scheduled. No one made demands, and the land was bountiful. Not surprisingly the line between work and play was never clear. The transmission of the Fore behavioral pattern to the young began in early infancy during a period of unceasing human physical contact. The effect of being constantly "in touch" with hamlet mates and their daily life seemed to start a process which proceeded by degrees: close rapport, involvement in regular activity, ability to handle seemingly dangerous implements safely, and responsible freedom to pursue individual interests at will without danger.

While very young, infants remained in almost continuous bodily contact with their mother, her house mates or her gardening associates. At first, mothers' laps were the center of activity, and infants occupied themselves there by nursing, sleeping and playing with their own bodies or those of their caretakers. They were not put aside for the sake of other activities, as when food was being prepared or heavy loads were being carried. Remaining in close, uninterrupted physical contact with those around them, their basic needs such as rest, nourishment, stimulation and security were continuously satisfied without obstacle.

By being physically in touch from their earliest days, Fore youngsters learned to communicate needs, desires and feelings through a body language of touch and response that

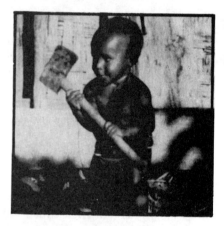

Babies have free access to the breast and later, like this toddler being helped to kernels of corn by an older girl, can help themselves to whatever food is around—indulged by children and grown-ups.

developed before speech. This opened the door to a much closer rapport with those around them than otherwise would have been possible, and led ultimately to the Fore brand of social cement and the sixth sense that bound groups together through spontaneous, responsive sharing.

As the infant's awareness increased, his interests broadened to the things his mother and other caretakers did and to the objects and materials they used. Then these youngsters began crawling out to explore things that attracted their attention. By the time they were toddling, their interests continually took them on short sorties to nearby objects and persons. As soon as they could walk well, the excursions ex-

tended to the entire hamlet and its gardens, and then beyond with other children. Developing without interference or supervision, this personal exploratory learning quest freely touched on whatever was around, even axes, knives, machetes, fire, and the like. When I first went to the Fore, I was aghast.

Eventually I discovered that this capability emerged naturally from Fore infant-handling practices in their milieu of close human physical proximity and tactile interaction. Because touch and bodily contact lend themselves naturally to satisfying the basic needs of young children, an early kind of communicative experience fostered cooperative interaction between infants and their caretakers,

also kinesthetic contact with the activities at hand. This made it easy for them to learn the appropriate handling of the tools of life.

The early pattern of exploratory activity included frequent return to one of the "mothers." Serving as home base, the bastion of security, a woman might occasionally give the youngster a nod of encouragement, if he glanced in her direction with uncertainty. Yet rarely did the women attempt to control or direct, nor did they participate in the child's quests or jaunts.

As a result Fore children did not have to adjust to rule and schedule in order to find their place in life. They could pursue their interests and whims wherever they might lead and

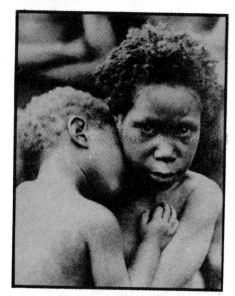

Close, constant body contact, as between this baby and older girl, creates security in Fore children.

still be part of a richly responsive world of human touch which constantly provided sustenance, comfort, diversion and security.

Learning proceeded during the course of pursuing interests and exploring. Constantly "in touch" with people who were busy with daily activities, the Fore young quickly learned the skills of life from example. Muscle tone, movement and mood were components of this learning process; formal lessons and commands were not. Kinesthetic skills developed so quickly that infants were able to casually handle knives and similar objects before they could walk.

Even after several visits I continued to be surprised that the unsupervised Fore toddlers did not recklessly thrust themselves into unappreciated dangers, the way our own children tend to do. But then, why should they? From their earliest days, they enjoyed a benevolent sanctuary from which the world could be confidently viewed, tested and appreciated. This sanctuary remained ever available, but did not demand, restrain or impose. One could go and come at will.

In close harmony with their source of life, the Fore young were able confidently, not furtively, to extend their inquiry. They could widen their understanding as they chose. There

On the way to hunt birds, cuscus (a marsupial) or rats, Fore boys stride through a sweet-potato garden.

was no need to play tricks or deceive in order to pursue life.

Emerging from this early childhood was a freely ranging young child rather in tune with his older and younger hamlet mates, disinclined to act out impulsively, and with a capable appreciation of the properties of potentially dangerous objects. Such children could be permitted to move out on their own, unsupervised and unrestricted. They were safe.

Such a pattern could persist indefinitely, re-creating itself in each new generation. However, hidden within the receptive character it produced was an Achilles heel; it also permitted adoption of new practices, including child-handling practices, which did *not* act to perpetuate the pattern. In only one generation after Western contact, the cycle of Fore life was broken.

Attuned as they were to individual pursuit of economic and social good, it did not take the Fore long to recognize the value of the new materials, practices and ideas that began to flow in. Indeed, change began almost immediately with efforts to obtain steel axes, salt, medicine and cloth. The Fore were quick to shed indigenous practices in favor of Western example. They rapidly altered their ways to adapt to Western law, government, religion, materials and trade.

Sometimes change was so rapid that many people seemed to be afflicted by a kind of cultural shock. An anomie, even cultural amnesia, seemed to pervade some hamlets for a time. There were individuals who appeared temporarily to have lost memory of recent past events. Some Fore even forgot what type and style of traditional garments they had worn only a few years earlier, or that they had used stone axes and had eaten their dead close relatives.

Remarkably open-minded, the Fore so readily accepted reformulation of identity and practice that suggestion or example by the new government officers, missionaries and scientists could alter tribal affiliation, place names, conduct and hamlet style. When the first Australian patrol officer began to map the region in 1957, an error in communication led him to refer to these people as the "Fore." Actually they had had no name for themselves and the word, Fore, was their name for a quite different group, the Awa, who spoke another language and lived in another valley. They did not correct the patrol officer but adopted his usage. They all now refer to themselves as the Fore. Regional and even personal names changed just as readily.

More than anything else, it was the completion of a steep, rough, always muddy Jeep road into the Fore lands that undermined the traditional life. Almost overnight their isolated region was opened. Hamlets began to move down from their ridgetop sites in order to be nearer the road, consolidating with others.

The power of the road is hard to overestimate. It was a great artery where only restricted capillaries had existed before. And down this artery came a flood of new goods, new ideas and new people. This new road, often impassable even with four-wheel-drive vehicles, was perhaps the single most dramatic stroke wrought by the government. It was to the Fore an opening to a new world. As they began to use the road, they started to shed traditions evolved in the protective insularity of their mountain fastness, to adopt in their stead an emerging market culture.

THE COMING OF THE COFFEE ECONOMY

"Walkabout," nonexistent as an institution before contact, quickly became an accepted way of life. Fore boys began to roam hundreds of miles from their homeland in the quest for new experience, trade goods, jobs and money. Like the classic practice of the Australian aborigine, this "walkabout" took one away from his home for periods of varying length. But unlike the Australian practice, it usually took the boys to jobs and schools rather than to a solitary life in traditional lands. Obviously it sprang from the earlier pattern of individual freedom to pursue personal interests and opportunity wherever it might lead. It was a new expression of the old Fore exploratory pattern.

Some boys did not roam far, whereas others found ways to go to distant cities. The roaming boys often sought places where they might be welcomed as visitors, workers or students for a while. Mission stations and schools, plantation work camps, and the servants' quarters of the European population became way-stations in the lives of the modernizing Fore boys.

Some took jobs on coffee plantations. Impressed by the care and attention lavished on coffee by European planters and by the money they saw paid to coffee growers, these young Fore workers returned home with coffee beans to plant.

Coffee grew well on the Fore hillsides, and in the mid-1960s, when the first sizable crop matured, Fore who previously had felt lucky to earn a few dollars found themselves able to earn a few hundred dollars. A rush to coffee ensued, and when the new gardens became productive a few years later, the Fore income from coffee jumped to a quarter of a million dollars a year. The coffee revolution was established.

At first the coffee was carried on the backs of its growers (sometimes for several days) over steep, rough mountain trails to a place where it could be sold to a buyer with a jeep. However, as more and more coffee was produced, the villagers began to turn with efforts to planning and constructing roads in association with neighboring villages. The newly built roads, in turn, stimulated further economic development and the opening of new trade stores throughout the region.

Following European example, the segregated collective men's and women's houses were abandoned. Family houses were adopted. This changed the social and territorial arena for all the young children, who hitherto had been accustomed to living equally with many members of their hamlet. It gave them a narrower place to belong, and it made them more distinctly someone's children. Uncomfortable in the family houses, boys who had grown up in a freer territory began to gather in "boys' houses," away from the adult men who were now beginning to live in family houses with their wives. Mothers began to wear blouses, altering the early freer access to the breast. Episodes of infant and child frustration, not seen in traditional Fore hamlets, began to take place along with repeated incidents of anger, withdrawal, aggressiveness and stinginess.

So Western technology worked its magic on the Fore, its powerful materials and practices quickly shattering their isolated autonomy and lifestyle. It took only a few years from the time Western intruders built their first grass-thatched patrol station before the Fore way of life they found was gone.

Fortunately, enough of the Fore traditional ways were systematically documented on film to reveal how unique a flower of human creation they were. Like nothing else, film made it possible to see the behavioral patterns of this way of life. The visual record, once made, captured data which was unnoticed and unanticipated at the time of filming and which was simply impossible to study without such records. Difficult-to-spot subtle patterns and fleeting nuances of manner, mood and human relations emerged by use of repeated reexamination of related incidents, sometimes by slow motion and stopped frame. Eventually the characteristic behavioral patterns of Fore life became clear, and an important aspect of human adaptive creation was revealed.

The Fore way of life was only one of the many natural experiments in living that have come into being through thousands of years of independent development in the world. The Fore way is now gone; those which remain are threatened. Under the impact of modern technology and commerce, the entire world is now rapidly becoming one system. By the year 2000 all the independent natural experiments that have come into being during the world's history will be merging into a single world system.

One of the great tragedies of our modern time may be that most of these independent experiments in living are disappearing before we can discover the implication of their special expressions of human possibility. Ironically, the same technology responsible for the worldwide cultural convergence has also provided the means by which we may capture detailed visual records of the yet remaining independent cultures. The question is whether we will be able to seize this never-to-be repeated opportunity. Soon it will be too late. Yet, obviously, increasing our understanding of the behavioral repertoire of humankind would strengthen our ability to improve life in the world.

Last Chance for First Peoples

Can gene banks preserve the past?

Stephen Mills

Levi Yanomami squatted beneath the grassy fringe of the *moloca* (great thatched lodge), where an assembly of the world's tribal leaders sat patiently. The setting was the Kari-Oca Indian village an hour outside Rio de Janeiro, at the first-ever World Conference of Indigenous Peoples, where native peoples hoped to encourage world leaders to save the natural world from environmental disaster.

Levi was about to perform a little voodoo and answer tribal prayers, if only the chieftains would listen—and heed their own call for help in the face of cultural extinction. Clad only in red running shorts (for decorum's sake), flip-flops, and an arm band of shocking pink parrot feathers, Levi cut a discordant figure. But the best was yet to come—verging on the miraculous.

Levi entered the hut and began to sing in guttural chants, stretching his stocky frame to appear gaunt as he paced up and down in stilted egret-like steps while beating his chest. His chants changed to choking fits and bodily contortions. Abruptly he left the circle to consult his companion, Davi Kopenawa Yanomami, a soothsayer who would interpret Levi's spiritual visions, tell him not to be afraid, and to continue the ritual. For more than half an hour, Levi wailed, stomped, and writhed, occasionally returning to Davi for comfort and advice.

Levi's physical incantations reached near hysteria, then subsided suddenly. As he wandered off mumbling, the entire hut and its occupants rose slowly as if on a cushion of air and hovered two feet off the ground—for this observer, anyway.

"We can speak for the earth because we have treated it well."

No kidding. Oh yeah, you say, what was I on? Air, it seemed. Eerie, uncanny, and downright spooky. This had to be some trick of the mind, but I could have sworn. . . . Stumbling as I tried to step two feet down onto the ground only confounded my disbelief.

Tribal leaders emerged, exchanging knowing looks while Western observers appeared dazed and confused, still in a trance. Some remained in denial, unable to accept their own metaphysical encounter. But many others wanted to believe, and everyone's story was different. "It was as if I turned into an exotic bird and flew off into the forest," remarked one colleague, while others spoke of leaving their bodies, as in astral travel. The general consensus was that this was definitely a "happening."

But what exactly *had* happened, and just what was the message to the rest of the world? In essence, the tribal leaders' message was simply that only spiritual reverence for the earth would save it—and to fail would be fatal. As Kari-Oca organizer Marcus Terena remarked,

"We can speak for the earth because we have treated it well."

Several thousand miles away north of the equator, an American university professor sat and also contemplated the collective fate of indigenous peoples threatened with cultural extinction. Luigi Cavalli-Sforza, a professor of genetics at Stanford University, is well aware that native peoples will be the first domino to fall in efforts to exploit the world's last remaining natural resources. "I am one of a group of scientists," he explains, "who have elected, on the initial suggestion of a smaller group of scientists, including myself, to collect a sample of the world population for a coordinated genetic study with modern means of analysis." Cavalli-Sforza is also chair of the international executive committee of the Human Genome Diversity project, which plans to study genetic samples from around the world including samples from indigenous peoples.

But scientific research is not enough. Professor David Maybury-Lewis, founder and president of Cultural Survival which fights for indigenous rights worldwide, expresses his concern that some scientists may overlook the need for more strident measures in regards to protecting indigenous peoples than the cataloging of their DNA. "If you're fearful of their dying out, you would have some kind of responsibility to do something for them as well. Just doing science and saying this is what I do, and what happens to them is none of my business, is quite unacceptable," he says.

Professor Cavalli-Sforza defends the value of his research, while acknowledging the obvious problem that genetic research cannot resolve what is essentially an economic problem. "I don't believe that a particular indigenous people could be damaged by our studies. There are examples where some people have been studied genetically, and it has been very good for them." But he says, "There are many other ethnic groups, indigenous or not, that need economic support or at least protection from abuse."

The struggle for cultural survival begs many questions: Who are indigenous peoples, what are their problems, who are the players in their survival or demise, and what are the viable alternatives to their extinction?

The answers may come from many places, including political, economic, and scientific quarters which heretofore have been thought to be inimical to indigenous interests. In politics, changing attitudes in the United Nations, and positive signs from the Clinton administration have raised hopes for new support on indigenous issues. Science and technology, traditionally feared by indigenous groups because it identified and exploited their resources at their expense, have found new ways to preserve and harness rainforests' resources which may be the key to the forests' and their people's future survival. And indigenous peoples themselves have seized the initiative and begun to fight back through legal channels and protests which have attracted international attention and support.

The world's approximately 500 million indigenous people, sometimes called "first peoples," are found throughout the world, from Australian Aborigines and African tribesmen to Native American and Amazon Indians. Conversely, and perversely, they are also described as the "Fourth World," firmly lodged at the bottom of the global socio-economic pecking order.

Summing up their plight, veteran campaigner for indigenous peoples' rights, Jason Clay, remarked: "What we're talking about here is a quiver of arrows between them and cultural extinction—they have nothing else with

From Huti tribesmen in Africa to Asmat tribes in Brazil, indigenous peoples are fighting to save their cultural identity, while scientists hope to preserve genetic evidence that will help uncover the history of migration.

which to deal with the problem." Similarly, Julian Burger, a U.N. coordinator responsible for indigenous peoples, explains that "indigenous cultures are threatened by forms of contemporary development when they are removed from their lands. However," he points out, "they are not victims. They are organizing in order to defend their interests."

Despite this bleak assessment, there are signs of significant change. In the political arena, the United Nations, heretofore intractable on the issue of sovereign rights for indigenous peoples, designated 1993 as the U.N. Year of the World's Indigenous People. It has been a critical window of opportunity for the cause, providing a world platform for debate, raising money for community projects, and drawing up a universal Declaration of Indigenous Rights. Rigoberta Menchú, the Guatemalan Quiché Indian and 1993 Nobel Peace Prize winner for her crusade against the brutal repression of her people, was named goodwill ambassador for the U.N. indigenous year, and has successfully launched a Decade of Indigenous People, which began in 1994, to extend and expand the program.

Considerable hope has also been generated by President Clinton's pledge to address the needs of impoverished Native American Indians, with speculation that he will support the indigenous cause internationally.

Indigenous peoples themselves have now also actively joined the fight to defend their rights and resources through protests and the courts, aided by media campaigns by private organizations like Cultural Survival and the Body Shop. Both of these organizations also help them economically by creating markets for sustainable products they harvest from their wild homelands.

Meanwhile, back in the lab, the tribal gene bank will allow scientists to study the origins of vanishing tribes long after they are gone. It is part of a much larger international project by the London-based Human Genome Organization (HUGO) to map all the human genes. When all the information is in, the tribal gene bank will be used to help draw up mankind's entire family tree, revealing how humanity colonized the planet over the past 100,000 years.

The project has already identified as many as 600 groups of interest. This number will probably be reduced to about 100 distinct or pure ethnic groups including the Marsh Arabs in southern Iraq, believed to be descended from the ancient Sumerians and currently threatened by Saddam Hussein's plan to eliminate his Shi'ite political foes; Stone Age Amazonian Yanomamo Indians and highland Papua New Guineans, both threatened by invasion of their lands; and African pygmies and bushmen and the Ainu peoples of Japan, all threatened by assimilation.

In his genetic study of tribes to plot the migration of man across the planet over millennia, Cavalli-Sforza has already had considerable success as a pioneer of "gene geography" since he first began gene mapping 40 years ago. His earlier research supports archaeological evidence that mankind first emerged from Africa 100,000 years ago and demonstrates that intensive farming practices which began in the Fertile Crescent led to a population and cultural explosion that triggered migration across Europe. The establishment of communities and cities effectively froze genetic drift, making it possible to track movement through genetic similarities. For example, the timing of the diffusion of farming showed that the spread was slow and regular, taking some 4,000 years to cover the approximately 4,000 kilometers from the Fertile Crescent to the remotest area north of Britain a rate of 1 kilometer a year.

Perhaps the most compelling and widely cited argument for safeguarding indigenous environments (and hence their human inhabitants) is the environments' unequalled abundance and diversity of medicinal plants. The case has again been made by various researchers who say that many indigenous lands, especially rainforests, may hold the key to treating pernicious ailments like AIDS, cancer, and heart disease. Genetic scientists argue that preserving precious indigenous knowledge to unlock the secrets of potential

plant species is an essential element in the equation.

Although 1.4 million plant species have been cataloged, there may be as many as 100 million different species, of which up to 80 percent are found in rainforests. One estimate further claims that about 80 percent of the world's population rely on plant-derived medicines for health products.

Recent discoveries of cancer-fighting extracts from plants as diverse as broccoli and the yew tree have sparked a scramble to find other miracle cures. As a result, chemical prospecting, biodiversity, and ethnobotany are among the new mantras in pharmaceutical boardrooms in the race to capitalize on biotech products. In the United States alone, 25 percent of all prescription drugs are plant-derived, and the biotech industry, currently worth $2 billion a year, is expected to soar to $50 billion by the year 2000. Businesses are beginning to realize that preserving the rainforest is an investment in that future.

Scientists have recently discovered that rainforests are actually more profitable left standing for their medicinal uses than cut down for lumber, farming, ranching, or new settlements. For instance, in a recent study, Dr. Michael Balick, director of the Institute of Economic Botany at the New York Botanical Garden, studied small plots of native forest which yielded herbal remedies worth $1,346 per acre, based on sustainable yields. In contrast, clearing rainforests for agriculture is worth only $137 per acre in Brazil and $117 per acre in Guatemala.

According to Dr. Balick, "It seems clear now that the decision whether to cut a forest or preserve it revolves around the question of how much money a farmer can make, how effectively he or she can feed the family. One of our jobs is to find economically viable alternatives to deforestation."

Scientists have also demonstrated the flaw in the argument that old growth forests can simply be replanted. Studies clearly show that understory flowering plants of replanted secondary forests are only one-third as abundant and only one-half as diverse as in original

old-growth forests, and may take as long as 1,000 years to fully recover.

Through his work for the National Cancer Institute, Dr. Balick is involved in a $1.2 million, five-year partnership with colleagues from many countries, including Belize, working directly with traditional healers to evaluate, promote, and preserve natural medicines. If any successful medicines are developed, royalties will be paid to the indigenous communities. A similar effort to preserve and prospect for medicinal plants in the forests of Costa Rica has been sponsored by Merck & Company, the world's largest drug maker, which has invested $1 million in the project and also promised royalties for any successful drugs developed.

Dr. Balick also points out that the value of plants is intrinsically tied to indigenous peoples' knowledge of which plants are useful and how to prepare them. But he warned that much of that precious knowledge is being lost forever as forest-dwellers increasingly come into contact with the outside world.

"I work with the Maya, for example, in Central America," Balick said, "who were thought to have crossed the Bering Strait 25,000 years ago. By my calculations, that's given them at least 200 generations of trial and error experimentation to become familiar their environment. And most of this is being lost in this generation.

"The great tragedy," he continues, "is that we are on the cusp of identifying hundreds if not thousands of useful plants for medicine, food, and fiber, and the forest is being converted at unprecedented rates. It's a false economic analysis that leads to the conclusion that land is more valuable cut than forest left standing. It's terribly sad to see 300-year-old trees being cut down, and then the fires that follow. You see devastation of both plant and animal life, and you know that devastation to humans is not far behind."

The level of suffering for native peoples was all too apparent at the Kari-Oca indigenous conference in Brazil. Between colorful spectacles— of Xingú Indians daubed in bright body paint and blowing bamboo pipes, Karaja Indians donning exquisite feather

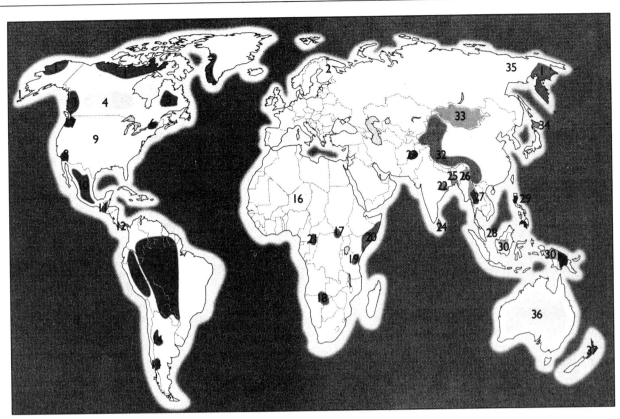

MAP OF INDIGENOUS PEOPLES

1. Arctic: Inuit (Eskimo) in Alaska, Canada, Greenland, and the former USSR; Aleut in Alaska
2. Europe: Saami in Norway, Sweden, Finland, and the former USSR
3. Pacific Coast: Haida, Tlingit, Kwakiutl, Bella Coola, Tsimshian, Nootka
4. Central Canada: Cree, Meti, Chipewyan, Blackfoot, Dene
5. Eastern Canada: Innu, Cree, including James Bay Cree
6. Canada/United States border: Micmac; the Six Nation Confederacy, or Haudenosaunee, comprising Mohawk, Oneida, Onondaga, Cayuga, Seneca, Tuscarora
7. Northwestern United States: Nez Perce
8. Southwestern United States: Navajo, Uti, Dine, Pueblo, including Hopi, Keres, Zuni
9. Plains States: Crow, Cheyenne, Arapaho, Pawnee, Comanche, Oglala Sioux, Shoshone
10. Mexico: Mayan descendants—Lacandon, Yucatec; Aztec descendants—Huichol, Tarahumara, Nahua, Zapotec; also refugees
11. Guatemala, Belize: Maya, including Chol, Chuj, Kekchi, Quiche; Nicaragua: Miskito, Sumu, Rama; El Salvador, Honduras: Lenca, Pipile
12. Panama: Kuna, Guaymi
13. Highland Peru, Bolivia, Ecuador, Colombian Highlands: Quechua, Aymara
14. Argentina, Chile: Mapuche
15. Amazon Basin—Brazil: Tukano, Xavante, Yanomami, Parakana, Kreen-Akrore, Nambikwara, Kayapo, Makuxi, Waimiri-Atroari; Amazon Basin—Ecuador, Bolivia, Peru, Colombia, Venezuela: Amarakaeri, Amuesha, Aguaruna, Matsigenka, Yagua, Shipibo, Tukano, Panare, Sanema, Secoya, Shuar, Quichua, Guajiro, Yanesha, Waorani, Ufaina; Paraguay: Ache, Ayoreo, Guarani, Toba-Maskoy; Guyana, French Guiana, Surinam: Arawak, Lakono, Kalinja, Wayana, Akawaio
16. Sahara, Sahel: Tuareg, Fulani
17. Southern Sudan: Dinka, Nuer, Shilluk
18. Angola, Botswana, Namibia: San (Bushmen)
19. Kenya, Tanzania: Maasai
20. Ethiopia: Oromo, Somali, Tigrayan, Eritrean
21. Zaire, Cameroon, Central African Republic, Congo: Mbuti, Efe, Lese
22. India: Naga, Santal, Gond, Kameng, Lohit, Dandami
23. Afghanistan, Pakistan: Pathan
24. Sri Lanka: Vedda
25. Bangladesh: Chittagong Hill Tract Peoples, including Chakma, Marma, Tripura
26. Myanmar (Burma): Karen, Kachin, Shan, Chin
27. Thailand: Karen, Hmong, Lisu
28. Malaysia: Penan, Kayan, Iban
29. Philippines: Kalinga, Ifugao, Hanunoo, Bontoc, Bangsa Moro
30. Indonesia—Kalimantan: Dayak; Lembata: Kedang; West Papua (Irian Jaya): West Papuan, including Asmat, Dani
31. Papua New Guinea: Mae-Enga, Dani, Tsembaga
32. China: Tibetan, Uighur
33. Mongolia: Mongolian
34. Japan: Ainu
35. The former USSR: Yuit, Kazakh, Saami, Chukchi, Nemet Oceania
36. Australia: Aborigines
37. New Zealand: Maoris
Pacific Islands: Kanak, Hawaiian, Tahitian, Chamorro

head-dresses for photo sessions, and plaintive song rituals by Japanese Ainu and Norwegian Sammi peoples—native spokesmen sat grouped in circles and testified about the systematic destruction of their people and their environment.

Mimmie Degawan spoke of the "Total War Policy" by the Philippine government to eliminate resistance to hydroelectric and logging projects on ancestral lands. "If the government takes away our land, we will starve and cease to exist as a people," she said. "So we have to resist—to resist is to exist. They not only walk through the land and kill people, but also drop bombs on entire communities."

Sinjbout Jackman recounted how the new civilian government in Bangladesh has pursued a policy of genocide against the Juma hill people. In one recent massacre, soldiers herded 1,200 villagers into their homes and burned them alive. Murder, torture, and rape remain daily terrors for the Juma. Jackman said, "My people have been compelled to leave their own villages and forced to live in cluster villages like in Vietnam and Peru. They are effectively enslaved, working for the military camps and the forest service. The government doesn't want us, they want our land."

Charles Uwiragiye of the African Batwa pygmy tribe in Rwanda, the world's fastest growing country, related how population explosion had triggered an invasion of his tribal lands. "We are the first people, the indigenous people, but two other tribes came in and took everything," he said. "We have problems of being removed from our lands, and other people replacing us. My people were thrown away, just like you throw away rubbish."

The desperation was summed up by Kanhok Kayapo of the northern Brazilian Kayapo tribe. "We need help to stop the white man from cutting down our forest and killing our people. The white man says Indians don't work, don't plant, and sends his machines to plant for himself. But the Indian does work, with the plow, and plants many things. He asks why the Indian wants to live in the forest, but he doesn't

want to live in the forest. He just wants to take it away from us." His brother, Tutopombo Kayapo added, "Who is going to help us? Will any government help us? I don't think so. I have asked before, and nothing happened, so I'm asking again. You say you don't want the forest to be burned away. So send us money to help my people, to buy medicine so they don't die. We will use it to keep the woods safe."

Threaded through these countless stories of invasion, slaughter, and displacement is the stark realization that the laws of nations were never designed to protect their rights. Worse still, many governments do not even recognize the existence of these tribes as a legitimate group of peoples.

Closer to home, in the United States, there is considerable concern about the fate of Native American Indians. The Oglala Sioux Indians in South Dakota, descendants of those who suffered the horrific defeat at Wounded Knee, are among the poorest citizens in America. According to the government's own Census Bureau statistics, 63.8 percent live below the poverty line, compared with the national average of 15.1 percent; and death rates from suicide, alcoholism, infant mortality, diabetes, and homicide are some of the highest in the country. Among Native Americans' many concerns are disputes over sovereign rights, land rights, gambling casinos on reservations, and efforts to entice reservations to accept toxic and nuclear waste.

Robert Leavitt, the former education and public policy director at Cultural Survival, a Boston-based organization supporting indigenous rights worldwide, is nonetheless optimistic about changes to come. "Clinton made some effort during his election campaign to reach out to Native American Indians," Leavitt noted. "He has since followed through in terms of further consultation with Native American leaders and in terms of making several appointments. Al Gore is at least knowledgeable and understanding of native affairs, and when they organized the Oregon Forest Summit, they asked Native Americans to participate. Hillary Clinton has talked about the deplorable

state of health care on reservations. Ada Deer, the incoming head of the Bureau of Indian Affairs, is very well-respected and is a Native American Indian, which is not usually the case. Carol Browner, the head of the Environmental Protection Agency, is concerned about the government and companies targeting reservations for toxic and nuclear-waste dumping. Bruce Babbitt, Secretary of the Interior, has worked with Native Americans in Arizona. So on the Native American Indian side, we're more optimistic, and there should be some steps forward."

The current education and public policy director at Cultural Survival, Marchell Weshaw, is similarly encouraged. "I'm indigenous myself, so I see the whole indigenous rights issue on a personal level as well as a professional one. I do see conditions improving. The indigenous peoples—as communities and as nations—are coming together to make a stand. The positive aspect is that they're doing it for themselves. I also think that public awareness has grown steadily within the last five years, riding piggyback on the environmental movement."

On the other hand, Leavitt notes that there had been much less support from the Clinton administration for global indigenous rights, and a signal lack of financial commitment. "There's a real unwillingness to accept the idea of group rights on an international level— that groups, peoples, collectively have sovereign rights over land, natural resources, and governance," he says.

The United States has rejected an appeal to fund the U.N. Year of the World's Indigenous People. A State Department official said the United States was in substantial arrears to the United Nations already and owed millions more for peacekeeping activities, adding, "That's not to say the year isn't important. It's a matter of having to make choices. We have obligations that we legally need to meet before we can go about making grants that are purely voluntary."

Despite the lack of U.S. support, the U.N. program on indigenous issues, coupled with private projects, remains the best hope of future gains for native peoples. A U.N. voluntary fund has already raised over $300,000 with donations from other developed nations.

Six community projects recommended for approval include two democracy and indigenous-rights programs in Bolivia and the Philippines; a chicken and rabbit farm for Mapuche Indian women in Chile; a reforestation project in Guatemala; a community bakery in Ecuador; and a community center in Belize. The news of the grant for the community center in Belize provoked Garifuna peoples' representative, Felix Miranda, to observe, "This is good news. The community center will allow us to open a museum of artifacts together with books and displays about our history, and provide a cultural focus for the community."

Similar projects worldwide by private groups have also provided economic alternatives to environmental destruction for indigenous peoples. Among the best-known proponents of this philosophy is the London-based Body Shop. Through its Fair Trade project, the Body Shop has several co-op agreements with native peoples who produce sustainable products like nut oil in Brazil, Nepalese paper, New Mexico's organic blue-corn oil, Mexican cactus body scrubs, Bangladeshi baskets, and Siberian birchwood combs. Body Shop spokesman Mark Johnston said the company seeks to "make consumerism a moral act. I remember going back to Nepal and being flabbergasted at how well the project had helped the community put all its kids through school and buy smokeless ovens, because smoke-related respiratory ailments are a problem in that part of Asia. It was the same with the Nanhu women in Mexico, who in the absence of their men—forced to find work elsewhere—were able to feed, clothe, and house their children. It's as basic as that, and very rewarding."

Cultural Survival Enterprises trades in sustainable products like Brazil nuts for Rainforest Crunch, Zambian organic honey and beeswax, Minnesotan wild rice, and Amazon rainforest cookies, with plans for many new product lines. Since its 1989 launch, product sales have totaled $2.5 million, and a 5 percent price premium has yielded another $250,000 which is plowed back into participating communities. The program has attracted another $600,000 from foundations, governments, and businesses to start new projects. Former program director, Jason Clay, said, "People have to take responsibility for their consumption, and ultimately they can force corporations to market sustainable products they want to buy."

As executive director of Rights and Resources, a private Washington, DC, agency which defines and defends native resources, Clay plans to develop an early-warning database system to identify and prevent potential disasters for indigenous peoples before they happen. "I think we need to start looking at root causes," Clay said. "Humanitarian assistance after the fact, when people are in real jeopardy, is fundamentally wrong. We need to be able to see more accurately what forces contribute to persecution, ethnocide, and genocide, so that when those indicators appear, we can target attention on those areas to actually prevent those killings from occurring."

For those involved in the struggle, the strategy for the future is clear: Consolidate the United Nations' lead to defend indigenous rights at both the grassroots and international levels; harness science and technology to identify, protect, and safely utilize indigenous resources; economically empower native peoples to finance legal campaigns for their sovereign and resource rights; encourage alternative land use through consumer demand for sustainable products; and build public support for indigenous issues through education and media campaigns.

Many problems remain, from ethnic cleansing in the Balkans which threatens to discredit indigenous calls for autonomy, to the Asian block's refusal to address serious human-rights abuses against native peoples, to the resource plunder of Siberia in Russia's desperate search for foreign investment.

Despite many hopeful signs, Clay conceded, "It's still going to be a thousand points of fight—not light. For those of us who have been doing this work for the last 20 years, the work in 1995 will be just as hard as the work in 1994, but the work has to go on."

"If over the next 10 years, we as a world don't do something, it will be too late for many cultures," Robert Leavitt said. "But we do have a wonderful opportunity to build a much stronger movement for indigenous peoples. What we have to do is institutionalize the gains. The real challenge for Cultural Survival—and other organizations involved—and indigenous peoples themselves, is to cement our gains, strengthen indigenous participation in the United Nations and Native American participation n the U.S. government, and take advantage of popular culture and concern, so that the movement goes from being flavor of the month to flavor of the decade, and beyond."

Easter's End

In just a few centuries, the people of Easter Island wiped out their forest, drove their plants and animals to extinction, and saw their complex society spiral into chaos and cannibalism. Are we about to follow their lead?

Jared Diamond

Jared Diamond is a contributing editor of Discover, *a professor of physiology at the UCLA School of Medicine, and a recipient of a MacArthur genius award. Expanded versions of many of his* Discover *articles appear in his book* The Third Chimpanzee: The Evolution and Future of the Human Animal, *which won Britain's 1992* copus *prize for best science book and the* Los Angeles Times *science book prize.*

Among the most riveting mysteries of human history are those posed by vanished civilizations. Everyone who has seen the abandoned buildings of the Khmer, the Maya, or the Anasazi is immediately moved to ask the same question: Why did the societies that erected those structures disappear?

Their vanishing touches us as the disappearance of other animals, even the dinosaurs, never can. No matter how exotic those lost civilizations seem, their framers were humans like us. Who is to say we won't succumb to the same fate? Perhaps someday New York's skyscrapers will stand derelict and overgrown with vegetation, like the temples at Angkor Wat and Tikal.

Among all such vanished civilizations, that of the former Polynesian society on Easter Island remains unsurpassed in mystery and isolation. The mystery stems especially from the island's gigantic stone statues and its

impoverished landscape, but it is enhanced by our associations with the specific people involved: Polynesians represent for us the ultimate in exotic romance, the background for many a child's, and an adult's, vision of paradise. My own interest in Easter was kindled over 30 years ago when I read Thor Heyerdahl's fabulous accounts of his *Kon-Tiki* voyage.

But my interest has been revived recently by a much more exciting account, one not of heroic voyages but of painstaking research and analysis. My friend David Steadman, a paleontologist, has been working with a number of other researchers who are carrying out the first systematic excavations on Easter intended to identify the animals and plants that once lived there. Their work is contributing to a new interpretation of the island's history that makes it a tale not only of wonder but of warning as well.

Easter Island, with an area of only 64 square miles, is the world's most isolated scrap of habitable land. It lies in the Pacific Ocean more than 2,000 miles west of the nearest continent (South America), 1,400 miles from even the nearest habitable island (Pitcairn). Its subtropical location and latitude—at 27 degrees south, it is approximately as far below the equator as Houston is north of it—help give it a rather mild climate, while its volcanic origins make its soil fertile. In theory, this combination of blessings should have made Eas-

ter a miniature paradise, remote from problems that beset the rest of the world.

The island derives its name from its "discovery" by the Dutch explorer Jacob Roggeveen, on Easter (April 5) in 1722. Roggeveen's first impression was not of a paradise but of a wasteland: "We originally, from a further distance, have considered the said Easter Island as sandy; the reason for that is this, that we counted as sand the withered grass, hay, or other scorched and burnt vegetation, because its wasted appearance could give no other impression than of a singular poverty and barrenness."

When Europeans arrived, the native animals included nothing larger than insects— not a single species of bat, land snail, or lizard.

The island Roggeveen saw was a grassland without a single tree or bush over ten feet high. Modern botanists have identified only 47 species of higher plants native to Easter, most of them grasses, sedges, and ferns. The list includes just two species of small trees and two of woody shrubs. With such flora, the islanders Roggeveen encountered had no source of real firewood to warm themselves during Easter's cool, wet, windy winters. Their native animals included nothing larger than insects, not even a single species of native bat, land bird, land snail, or lizard. For domestic animals, they had only chickens.

European visitors throughout the eighteenth and early nineteenth centuries estimated Easter's human population at about 2,000, a modest number considering the island's fertility. As Captain James Cook recognized during his brief visit in 1774, the islanders were Polynesians (a Tahitian man accompanying Cook was able to converse with them). Yet despite the Polynesians' well-deserved fame as a great seafaring people, the Easter Islanders who came out to Roggeveen's and Cook's ships did so by swimming or paddling canoes that Roggeveen described as "bad and frail." Their craft, he wrote, were "put together with manifold small planks and light inner timbers, which they cleverly stitched together with very fine twisted threads. . . . But as they lack the knowledge and particularly the materials for caulking and making tight the great number of seams of the canoes, these are accordingly very leaky, for which reason they are compelled to spend half the time in bailing." The canoes, only ten feet long, held at most two people, and only three or four canoes were observed on the entire island.

With such flimsy craft, Polynesians could never have colonized Easter from even the nearest island, nor could they have traveled far offshore to fish. The islanders Roggeveen met were totally isolated unaware that other people existed. Investigators in all the years since his visit have discovered no trace of the islanders' having any outside contacts: not a single Easter Island rock or product has turned up elsewhere, nor has anything been found on the island that could have been brought by anyone other than the original settlers or the Europeans. Yet the people living on Easter claimed memories of visiting the uninhabited Sala y Gomez reef 260 miles away, far beyond the range of the leaky canoes seen by Roggeveen. How did the islanders' ancestors reach that reef from Easter, or reach Easter from anywhere else?

Easter Island's most famous feature is its huge stone statues, more than 200 of which once stood on massive stone platforms lining the coast. At least 700 more, in all stages of completion, were abandoned in quarries or on ancient roads between the quarries and the coast, as if the carvers and moving crews had thrown down their tools and walked off the job. Most of the erected statues were carved in a single quarry and then somehow transported as far as six miles—despite heights as great as 33 feet and weights up to 82 tons. The abandoned statues, meanwhile, were as much as 65 feet tall and weighed up to 270 tons. The stone platforms were equally gigantic: up to 500 feet long and 10 feet high, with facing slabs weighing up to 10 tons.

Roggeveen himself quickly recognized the problem the statues posed: "The stone images at first caused us to be struck with astonishment," he wrote, "because we could not comprehend how it was possible that these people, who are devoid of heavy thick timber for making any machines, as well as strong ropes, nevertheless had been able to erect such images." Roggeveen might have added that the islanders had no wheels, no draft animals, and no source of power except their own muscles. How did they transport the giant statues for miles, even before erecting them? To deepen the mystery, the statues were still standing in 1770, but by 1864 all of them had been pulled down, by the islanders themselves. Why then did they carve them in the first place? And why did they stop?

The statues imply a society very different from the one Roggeveen saw in 1722. Their sheer number and size suggest a population much larger than 2,000 people. What became of everyone? Furthermore, that society must have been highly organized. Easter's resources were scattered across the island: the best stone for the statues was quarried at Rano Raraku near Easter's northeast end; red stone, used for large crowns adorning some of the statues, was quarried at Puna Pau, inland in the southwest; stone carving tools came mostly from Aroi in the northwest. Meanwhile, the best farm-

land lay in the south and east, and the best fishing grounds on the north and west coasts. Extracting and redistributing all those goods required complex political organization. What happened to that organization, and how could it ever have arisen in such a barren landscape?

Easter Island's mysteries have spawned volumes of speculation for more than two and a half centuries. Many Europeans were incredulous that Polynesians—commonly characterized as "mere savages"—could have created the statues or the beautifully constructed stone platforms. In the 1950s, Heyerdahl argued that Polynesia must have been settled by advanced societies of American Indians, who in turn must have received civilization across the Atlantic from more advanced societies of the Old World. Heyerdahl's raft voyages aimed to prove the feasibility of such prehistoric transoceanic contacts. In the 1960s the Swiss writer Erich von Däniken, an ardent believer in Earth visits by extraterrestrial astronauts, went further, claiming that Easter's statues were the work of intelligent beings who owned ultramodern tools, became stranded on Easter, and were finally rescued.

Heyerdahl and Von Däniken both brushed aside overwhelming evidence that the Easter Islanders were typical Polynesians derived from Asia rather than from the Americas and that their culture (including their statues) grew out of Polynesian culture. Their language was Polynesian, as Cook had already concluded. Specifically, they spoke an eastern Polynesian dialect related to Hawaiian and Marquesan, a dialect isolated since about A.D. 400, as estimated from slight differences in vocabulary. Their fishhooks and stone adzes resembled early Marquesan models. Last year DNA extracted from 12 Easter Island skeletons was also shown to be Polynesian. The islanders grew bananas, taro, sweet potatoes, sugarcane, and paper mulberry—typical Polynesian crops, mostly of Southeast Asian origin. Their sole domestic animal, the chicken, was also typically Polynesian and ultimately Asian, as were the rats that arrived as stowaways in the canoes of the first settlers.

What happened to those settlers? The fanciful theories of the past must give way to evidence gathered by hardworking practitioners in three fields: archeology, pollen analysis, and paleontology.

Modern archeological excavations on Easter have continued since Heyerdahl's 1955 expedition. The earliest radiocarbon dates associated with human activities are around A.D. 400 to 700, in reasonable agreement with the approximate settlement date of 400 estimated by linguists. The period of statue construction peaked around 1200 to 1500, with few if any statues erected thereafter. Densities of archeological sites suggest a large population; an estimate of 7,000 people is widely quoted by archeologists, but other estimates range up to 20,000, which does not seem implausible for an island of Easter's area and fertility.

Cannibalism replaced only part of Easter's lost foods. Statuettes with sunken cheeks and visible ribs suggest people were starving.

Archeologists have also enlisted surviving islanders in experiments aimed at figuring out how the statues might have been carved and erected. Twenty people, using only stone chisels, could have carved even the largest completed statue within a year. Given enough timber and fiber for making ropes, teams of at most a few hundred people could have loaded the statues onto wooden sleds, dragged them over lubricated wooden tracks or rollers, and used logs as levers to maneuver them into a standing position. Rope could have been made from the fiber of a small native tree, related to the linden, called the hauhau. However, that tree is now extremely scarce on Easter, and hauling one statue would have required hundreds of yards of rope. Did Easter's now barren landscape once support the necessary trees?

That question can be answered by the technique of pollen analysis, which involves boring out a column of sediment from a swamp or pond, with the most recent deposits at the top and relatively more ancient deposits at the bottom. The absolute age of each layer can be dated by radiocarbon methods. Then begins the hard work: examining tens of thousands of pollen grains under a microscope, counting them, and identifying the plant species that produced each one by comparing the grains with modern pollen from known plant species. For Easter Island, the bleary-eyed scientists who performed that task were John Flenley, now at Massey University in New Zealand, and Sarah King of the University of Hull in England.

Flenley and King's heroic efforts were rewarded by the striking new picture that emerged of Easter's prehistoric landscape. For at least 30,000 years before human arrival and during the early years of Polynesian settlement, Easter was not a wasteland at all. Instead, a subtropical forest of trees and woody bushes towered over a ground layer of shrubs, herbs, ferns, and grasses. In the forest grew tree daisies, the rope-yielding hauhau tree, and the toromiro tree, which furnishes a dense, mesquite-like firewood. The most common tree in the forest was a species of palm now absent on Easter but formerly so abundant that the bottom strata of the sediment column were packed with its pollen. The Easter Island palm was closely related to the still-surviving Chilean wine palm, which grows up to 82 feet tall and 6 feet in diameter. The tall, unbranched trunks of the Easter Island palm would have been ideal for transporting and erecting statues and constructing large canoes. The palm would also have been a valuable food source, since its Chilean relative yields edible nuts as well as sap from which Chileans make sugar, syrup, honey, and wine.

What did the first settlers of Easter Island eat when they were not glutting themselves on the local equivalent of maple syrup? Recent excavations by David Steadman, of the New York State Museum at Albany, have yielded a picture of Easter's original animal world as surprising as Flenley and King's picture of its plant world. Steadman's expectations for Easter were conditioned by his experiences elsewhere in Polynesia, where fish are overwhelmingly the main food at archeological sites, typically accounting for more than 90 percent of the bones in ancient Polynesian garbage heaps. Easter, though, is too cool for the coral reefs beloved by fish, and its cliff-girded coastline permits shallow-water fishing in only a few places. Less than a quarter of the bones in its early garbage heaps (from the period 900 to 1300) belonged to fish; instead, nearly one-third of all bones came from porpoises.

Nowhere else in Polynesia do porpoises account for even 1 percent of discarded food bones. But most other Polynesian islands offered animal food in the form of birds and mammals, such as New Zealand's now extinct giant moas and Hawaii's now extinct flightless geese. Most other islanders also had domestic pigs and dogs. On Easter, porpoises would have been the largest animal available—other than humans. The porpoise species identified at Easter, the common dolphin, weighs up to 165 pounds. It generally lives out at sea, so it could not have been hunted by line fishing or spearfishing from shore. Instead, it must have been harpooned far offshore, in big seaworthy canoes built from the extinct palm tree.

In addition to porpoise meat, Steadman found, the early Polynesian settlers were feasting on seabirds. For those birds, Easter's remoteness and lack of predators made it an ideal haven as a breeding site, at least until humans arrived. Among the prodigious numbers of seabirds that bred on Easter were albatross, boobies, frigate birds, fulmars, petrels, prions, shearwaters, storm petrels, terns, and tropic birds. With at least 25 nesting species, Easter was the richest seabird breeding site in Polynesia and probably in the whole Pacific.

Land birds as well went into early Easter Island cooking pots. Steadman identified bones of at least six species, including barn owls, herons, parrots, and rail. Bird stew would have been seasoned with meat from large numbers of rats, which the Polynesian colonists inadvertently brought with them; Easter Island is the sole known Polynesian island where rat bones out-number fish bones at archeological sites. (In case you're squeamish and consider rats inedible, I still recall recipes for creamed laboratory rat that my British biologist friends used to supplement their diet during their years of wartime food rationing.)

Porpoises, seabirds, land birds, and rats did not complete the list of meat sources formerly available on Easter. A few bones hint at the possibility of breeding seal colonies as well. All these delicacies were cooked in ovens fired by wood from the island's forests.

Such evidence lets us imagine the island onto which Easter's first Polynesian colonists stepped ashore some 1,600 years ago, after a long canoe voyage from eastern Polynesia. They found themselves in a pristine paradise. What then happened to it? The pollen grains and the bones yield a grim answer.

Pollen records show that destruction of Easter's forests was well under way by the year 800, just a few centuries after the start of human settlement. Then charcoal from wood fires came to fill the sediment cores, while pollen of palms and other trees and woody shrubs decreased or disappeared, and pollen of the grasses that replaced the forest became more abundant. Not long after 1400 the palm finally became extinct, not only as a result of being chopped down but also because the now ubiquitous rats prevented its regeneration: of the dozens of preserved palm nuts discovered in caves on Easter, all had been chewed by rats and could no longer germinate. While the hauhau tree did not become extinct in Polynesian times, its numbers declined drastically until there weren't enough left to make ropes from. By the time Heyerdahl visited Easter, only a single, nearly dead toromiro tree remained on the island, and even that lone survivor has now disappeared.

(Fortunately, the toromiro still grows in botanical gardens elsewhere.)

Earth's inhabitants have no emigration valve. We can no more escape into space than the Easter Islanders could flee into the ocean.

The fifteenth century marked the end not only for Easter's palm but for the forest itself. Its doom had been approaching as people cleared land to plant gardens; as they felled trees to build canoes, to transport and erect statues, and to burn; as rats devoured seeds; and probably as the native birds died out that had pollinated the trees' flowers and dispersed their fruit. The overall picture is among the most extreme examples of forest destruction anywhere in the world: the whole forest gone, and most of its tree species extinct.

The destruction of the island's animals was as extreme as that of the forest: without exception, every species of native land bird became extinct. Even shellfish were overexploited, until people had to settle for small sea snails instead of larger cowries. Porpoise bones disappeared abruptly from garbage heaps around 1500; no one could harpoon porpoises anymore, since the trees used for constructing the big seagoing canoes no longer existed. The colonies of more than half of the seabird species breeding on Easter or on its offshore islets were wiped out.

In place of these meat supplies, the Easter Islanders intensified their production of chickens, which had been only an occasional food item. They also turned to the largest remaining meat source available: humans, whose bones became common in late Easter Island garbage heaps. Oral traditions of the islanders are rife with cannibalism; the most inflammatory taunt that could be snarled at an enemy was "The flesh of your mother sticks between my teeth." With no wood avail-

able to cook these new goodies, the islanders resorted to sugarcane scraps, grass, and sedges to fuel their fires.

All these strands of evidence can be wound into a coherent narrative of a society's decline and fall. The first Polynesian colonists found themselves on an island with fertile soil, abundant food, bountiful building materials, ample lebensraum, and all the prerequisites for comfortable living. They prospered and multiplied.

After a few centuries, they began erecting stone statues on platforms, like the ones their Polynesian forebears had carved. With passing years, the statues and platforms became larger and larger, and the statues began sporting ten-ton red crowns—probably in an escalating spiral of one-upmanship, as rival clans tried to surpass each other with shows of wealth and power. (In the same way, successive Egyptian pharaohs built ever-larger pyramids. Today Hollywood movie moguls near my home in Los Angeles are displaying their wealth and power by building ever more ostentatious mansions. Tycoon Marvin Davis topped previous moguls with plans for a 50,000-square-foot house, so now Aaron Spelling has topped Davis with a 56,000-square-foot house. All that those buildings lack to make the message explicit are ten-ton red crowns.) On Easter, as in modern America, society was held together by a complex political system to redistribute locally available resources and to integrate the economies of different areas.

Eventually Easter's growing population was cutting the forest more rapidly than the forest was regenerating. The people used the land for gardens and the wood for fuel, canoes, and houses—and of course, for lugging statues. As forest disappeared, the islanders ran out of timber and rope to transport and erect their statues. Life became more uncomfortable—springs and streams dried up, and wood was no longer available for fires.

People also found it harder to fill their stomachs, as land birds, large sea snails, and many seabirds disappeared. Because timber for building seagoing canoes vanished, fish catches declined and porpoises disappeared from the table. Crop yields also declined, since deforestation allowed the soil to be eroded by rain and wind, dried by the sun, and its nutrients to be leeched from it. Intensified chicken production and cannibalism replaced only part of all those lost foods. Preserved statuettes with sunken cheeks and visible ribs suggest that people were starving.

With the disappearance of food surpluses, Easter Island could no longer feed the chiefs, bureaucrats, and priests who had kept a complex society running. Surviving islanders described to early European visitors how local chaos replaced centralized government and a warrior class took over from the hereditary chiefs. The stone points of spears and daggers, made by the warriors during their heyday in the 1600s and 1700s, still litter the ground of Easter today. By around 1700, the population began to crash toward between one-quarter and one-tenth of its former number. People took to living in caves for protection against their enemies. Around 1770 rival clans started to topple each other's statues, breaking the heads off. By 1864 the last statue had been thrown down and desecrated.

As we try to imagine the decline of Easter's civilization, we ask ourselves, "Why didn't they look around, realize what they were doing, and stop before it was too late? What were they thinking when they cut down the last palm tree?"

I suspect, though, that the disaster happened not with a bang but with a whimper. After all, there are those hundreds of abandoned statues to consider. The forest the islanders depended on for rollers and rope didn't simply disappear one day—it vanished slowly, over decades. Perhaps war interrupted the moving teams; perhaps by the time the carvers had finished their work, the last rope snapped. In the meantime, any islander who tried to warn about the dangers of progressive deforestation would have been overridden by vested interests of carvers, bureaucrats, and chiefs, whose jobs depended on continued deforestation. Our Pacific Northwest loggers are only the latest in a long line of loggers to cry, "Jobs over trees!" The changes in forest cover from year to year would have been hard to detect: yes, this year we cleared those woods over there, but trees are starting to grow back again on this abandoned garden site here. Only older people, recollecting their childhoods decades earlier, could have recognized a difference. Their children could no more have comprehended their parents' tales than my eight-year-old sons today can comprehend my wife's and my tales of what Los Angeles was like 30 years ago.

Gradually trees became fewer, smaller, and less important. By the time the last fruit-bearing adult palm tree was cut, palms had long since ceased to be of economic significance. That left only smaller and smaller palm saplings to clear each year, along with other bushes and treelets. No one would have noticed the felling of the last small palm.

By now the meaning of Easter Island for us should be chillingly obvious. Easter Island is Earth writ small. Today, again, a rising population confronts shrinking resources. We too have no emigration valve, because all human societies are linked by international transport, and we can no more escape into space than the Easter Islanders could flee into the ocean. If we continue to follow our present course, we shall have exhausted the world's major fisheries, tropical rain forests, fossil fuels, and much of our soil by the time my sons reach my current age.

Every day newspapers report details of famished countries—Afghanistan, Liberia, Rwanda, Sierra Leone, Somalia, the former Yugoslavia, Zaire—where soldiers have appropriated the wealth or where central government is yielding to local gangs of thugs. With the risk of nuclear war receding, the threat of our ending with a bang no longer has a chance of galvanizing us to halt our course. Our risk now is of winding down, slowly, in a whimper. Corrective action is blocked by vested interests, by well-intentioned political and business leaders, and by their electorates, all of whom are perfectly correct in not noticing big changes from year to year. Instead, each year there are just somewhat more people, and somewhat fewer resources, on Earth.

It would be easy to close our eyes or to give up in despair. If mere thousands of Easter Islanders with only stone tools and their own muscle power sufficed to destroy their society, how can billions of people with metal tools and machine power fail to do worse? But there is one crucial difference. The Easter Islanders had no books and no histories of other doomed societies. Unlike the Easter Islanders, we have histories of the past—information that can save us. My main hope for my sons' generation is that we may now choose to learn from the fates of societies like Easter's.

Credits/ Acknowledgments

Cover design by Charles Vitelli

1. Anthropological Perspectives
Facing overview—United Nations photo by Doranne Jacobson.

2. Culture and Communication
Facing overview—United Nations photo.

3. The Organization of Society and Culture
Facing overview—United Nations photo by S. Jackson. 70-72—Photos by Kenneth Good. 78—Photos by Jason Laure.

4. Other Families, Other Ways
Facing overview—United Nations photo. 115—Photo by Enid Schildkrout. 124—United Nations photo by Ian Steele.

5. Gender and Status
Facing overview—United Nations photo by Oddbjorn Monsen.

6. Religion, Belief, and Ritual
Facing overview—United Nations photo by S. Stokes.

7. Sociocultural Change
Facing overview—Woodfin Camp & Associates photo by Robert Azzi. 218-220, 222—*The World & I* photos by Paolo Galli. 225-228—Photos by E. Richard Sorenson. 231—*Omni* photos by Malcolm Kirk. 233—*Omni* map by Steven Stankiewicz.

ANNUAL EDITIONS ARTICLE REVIEW FORM

■ NAME: _____ DATE: _____

■ TITLE AND NUMBER OF ARTICLE: _____

■ BRIEFLY STATE THE MAIN IDEA OF THIS ARTICLE: _____

_____

■ LIST THREE IMPORTANT FACTS THAT THE AUTHOR USES TO SUPPORT THE MAIN IDEA:

_____

_____

_____

_____

_____

■ WHAT INFORMATION OR IDEAS DISCUSSED IN THIS ARTICLE ARE ALSO DISCUSSED IN YOUR TEXTBOOK OR OTHER READING YOU HAVE DONE? LIST THE TEXTBOOK CHAPTERS AND PAGE NUMBERS:

_____

_____

_____

_____

_____

_____

■ LIST ANY EXAMPLES OF BIAS OR FAULTY REASONING THAT YOU FOUND IN THE ARTICLE:

_____

_____

_____

_____

■ LIST ANY NEW TERMS/CONCEPTS THAT WERE DISCUSSED IN THE ARTICLE AND WRITE A SHORT DEFINITION:

_____

_____

_____

_____

_____

ANNUAL EDITIONS: ANTHROPOLOGY 96/97
Article Rating Form

Here is an opportunity for you to have direct input into the next revision of this volume. We would like you to rate each of the 46 articles listed below, using the following scale:

1. **Excellent: should definitely be retained**
2. **Above average: should probably be retained**
3. **Below average: should probably be deleted**
4. **Poor: should definitely be deleted**

Your ratings will play a vital part in the next revision. So please mail this prepaid form to us just as soon as you complete it.
Thanks for your help!

Annual Editions revisions depend on two major opinion sources: one is our Advisory Board, listed in the front of this volume, which works with us in scanning the thousands of articles published in the public press each year; the other is you—the person actually using the book. Please help us and the users of the next edition by completing the prepaid article rating form on this page and returning it to us. Thank you.

Rating	Article
	1. Doing Fieldwork among the Yąnomamö
	2. Doctor, Lawyer, Indian Chief
	3. Eating Christmas in the Kalahari
	4. A Cross-Cultural Experience: A Chinese Anthropologist in the United States
	5. Cultural Relativism and Universal Rights
	6. Language, Appearance, and Reality: Doublespeak in 1984
	7. Why Don't You Say What You Mean?
	8. Navigating Nigerian Bureaucracies; or "Why Can't You Beg?" She Demanded
	9. The Gift of Tongues
	10. Shakespeare in the Bush
	11. Understanding Eskimo Science
	12. The Blood in Their Veins
	13. The Yanomami Keep on Trekking
	14. Mystique of the Masai
	15. Camels in the Land of Kings
	16. Too Many Bananas, Not Enough Pineapples, and No Watermelon at All: Three Object Lessons in Living with Reciprocity
	17. From Shells to Money
	18. Life without Chiefs
	19. Memories of a !Kung Girlhood
	20. When Brothers Share a Wife
	21. Young Traders of Northern Nigeria
	22. Death without Weeping
	23. Arranging a Marriage in India

Rating	Article
	24. Society and Sex Roles
	25. Yellow Woman and a Beauty of the Spirit
	26. Status, Property, and the Value on Virginity
	27. Female Circumcision
	28. The War against Women
	29. The Initiation of a Maasai Warrior
	30. The Little Emperors
	31. Psychotherapy in Africa
	32. The Mbuti Pygmies: Change and Adaptation
	33. No Pain, No Game
	34. Cargo Cults
	35. The Secrets of Haiti's Living Dead
	36. Rituals of Death
	37. Body Ritual among the Nacirema
	38. Superstition and Ritual in American Baseball
	39. Heart of Darkness, Heart of Light
	40. Why Can't People Feed Themselves?
	41. Nomads at the Crossroads
	42. Surviving the Revolution: Post Revolution Romania and Foreign Advisors
	43. Bicultural Conflict
	44. Growing Up as a Fore
	45. Last Chance for First Peoples
	46. Easter's End

(Continued on next page)

ABOUT YOU

Name _____ Date _____
Are you a teacher? ❏ Or student? ❏
Your School Name _____
Department _____
Address _____
City _____ State _____ Zip _____
School Telephone # _____

YOUR COMMENTS ARE IMPORTANT TO US!

Please fill in the following information:

For which course did you use this book? _____
Did you use a text with this Annual Edition? ❏ yes ❏ no
The title of the text? _____
What are your general reactions to the Annual Editions concept?

Have you read any particular articles recently that you think should be included in the next edition?

Are there any articles you feel should be replaced in the next edition? Why?

Are there other areas that you feel would utilize an Annual Edition?

May we contact you for editorial input?

May we quote you from above?

ANNUAL EDITIONS: ANTHROPOLOGY 96/97

BUSINESS REPLY MAIL

First Class   Permit No. 84   Guilford, CT

Postage will be paid by addressee

Dushkin Publishing Group/
Brown & Benchmark Publishers
Sluice Dock
Guilford, Connecticut 06437